The Northern Counties to AD 1000

A Regional History of England

General Editors: Barry Cunliffe and David Hey
For full details of the series, see pp. xiv–xv.

The Northern Counties
to AD 1000

Nick Higham

Longman
London and New York

Longman Group Limited
Longman House, Burnt Mill, Harlow
Essex CM20 2JE, England
Associated companies throughout the world

Published in the United States of America
by Longman Inc., New York

First published 1986

British Library Cataloguing in Publication Data

Higham, N. J.
  The Northern Counties to AD 1000 – (Regional
  history of England)
  1. Northumberland – History   2. Cumbria –
  History
  I. Title.   II. Series.
  942.8′8   DA670.N8

ISBN 0-582-49275-0 csd
ISBN 0-582-49276-9 ppr

Library of Congress Cataloging in Publication Data

Higham, N. J.
  The northern counties to AD 1000
  (Regional history of England)
  Bibliography: p.
  Includes index.
  1. Great Britain – History – To 1066.   2. England,
Northern – History.   3. Man, Prehistoric – Great Britain.
I. Title.   II. Series.
DA135.H47   1986   941.01   85–4292
ISBN 0–582–49275–0
ISBN 0–582–49276–9 (pbk.)

Set in Linotron 202 10/12pt Sabon Roman
Produced by Longman Singapore Publishers (Pte) Ltd.
Printed in Singapore.

Contents

List of plates

List of figures

Acknowledgements

Most of this work is based on primary research by scholars who have come before me. It is perhaps unfair to single out individuals, but it is only right that the unique contribution of Prof. George Jobey should be recognized. Within the Anglo-Saxon period, Prof. Rosemary Cramp and Dr Richard Bailey are indirectly responsible for much of the material incorporated here.

For their patient correspondence or advice, I would like to thank Colin Burgess, Roger Miket, Adrian Oliver, Terry Cane, Paul Selden, Chris Smith, Paul Holder, Barri Jones, David Hill, John Peter Wild, David Coombs, Steve Dickinson, Dennis Coggins, John Dore, Vin Davis and my very close friend, guide and mentor, John Smith.

I am grateful to the following for their permission to reproduce the Plates which appear in the text: *Archaeologia Aeliana* (Plates 3.9, 3.14 & 5.2); the Bowes Museum (Plates 3.1 & 3.6); Cleveland County, Archaeology Section (Plate 6.2); R. Cramp (Plate 7.1); W. S. Hanson (Plate 4.1); G. D. B. Jones (Plates 3.4, 3.7, 3.11, 4.2 & 4.4); R. Miket (Plates 2.2, 2.4 & 6.1); the Museum of Antiquities, University and Society of Antiquaries of Newcastle-Upon-Tyne (Plates 3.3 & 5.1); A. Oliver (Plate 4.6); SEARCH Kentmere Archaeological Project/1983 (Plate 7.3); C. Smith (Plate 3.10); and the University of Durham (Plates 7.2 & 7.4).

To my own research in the North, many have contributed, among whom I would like to thank the Dargue family of Smardale Hall, Ian and Bob Bewley, Brian Berry and the many friends and colleagues who have helped in field exercises and excavations over the last ten years.

The massive burden of typing this text was undertaken by my wife Anne and father-in-law Keith Claridge. In addition an early draft of Chapter 2 was typed by Mrs V. Seth, who also typed the Index, and Mrs P. Burns typed the notes. Much of the writing of this volume was achieved during a sabbatical term conferred by the Victoria University of Manchester. Denise Kenyon took upon herself the massive task of indexing the text, and has in addition suggested numerous corrections.

To all go my grateful thanks. While I believe that this work owes far more than can ever be paid, all errors within it are the sole responsibility of the author.

General preface

England cannot be divided satisfactorily into recognizable regions based on former kingdoms or principalities in the manner of France, Germany or Italy. Few of the Anglo-Saxon tribal divisions had much meaning in later times and from the eleventh century onwards England was a united country. English regional identities are imprecise and no firm boundaries can be drawn. In planning this series we have recognized that any attempt to define a region must be somewhat arbitrary, particularly in the Midlands, and that boundaries must be flexible. Even the South-West, which is surrounded on three sides by the sea, has no agreed border on the remaining side and in many ways, historically and culturally, the River Tamar divides the area into two. Likewise, the Pennines present a formidable barrier between the eastern and western counties on the Northern Borders; contrasts as much as similarities need to be emphasized here.

The concept of a region does not imply that the inhabitants had a similar experience of life, nor that they were all inward-looking. A Hull merchant might have more in common with his Dutch trading partner than with his fellow Yorkshireman who farmed a Pennine smallholding: a Roman soldier stationed for years on Hadrian's Wall probably had very different ethnic origins from a native farmer living on the Durham boulder clay. To differing degrees, everyone moved in an international climate of belief and opinion with common working practices and standards of living.

Yet regional differences were nonetheless real; even today a Yorkshireman may be readily distinguished from someone from the South East. Life in Lancashire and Cheshire has always been different from life in the Thames Valley. Even the East Midlands has a character that is subtly different from that of the West Midlands. People still feel that they belong to a particular region within England as a whole.

In writing these histories we have become aware how much regional identities may vary over time; moreover how a farming region, say, may not coincide with a region defined by its building styles or its dialect. We have dwelt upon the diversity that can be found within a region as well as upon common characteristics in order to illustrate the local peculiarites of provincial life. Yet, despite all these problems of definition, we feel that the time is ripe to attempt an ambitious scheme outlining the history of England's regions in 21 volumes. London has not been included – except for demonstrating the many ways in which it has influenced the provinces – for its history has been very different from that of the towns and rural parishes that are our principal concern.

In recent years an enormous amount of local research both historical and archaeological has deepened our understanding of the former concerns of ordinary men and women and has altered our perception of everyday life in the past in many significant ways, yet the results of this work are not widely known even within the regions themselves.

This series offers a synthesis of this new work from authors who have themselves been actively involved in local research and who are present or former residents of the regions they describe.

Each region will be covered in two linked but independent volumes, the first covering the period up to AD 1000 and necessarily relying heavily on archaeological data, and the second bringing the story up to the present day. Only by taking a wide time-span and by studying continuity and change over many centuries do distinctive regional characteristics become clear.

This series portrays life as it was experienced by the great majority of the people of Southern Britain or England as it was to become. The 21 volumes will – it is hoped – substantially enrich our understanding of English history.

Barry Cunliffe
David Hey

A Regional History of England

General Editors: Barry Cunliffe (to AD 1000) and David Hey (from AD 1000)

The regionalization used in this series is illustrated on the map opposite.

*The Northern Counties to AD 1000 *Nick Higham*
 The Northern Counties from AD 1000 *Norman McCord & Richard Thompson*

 The Lancashire/Cheshire Region to AD 1000 *G. D. B. Jones with Denise Kenyon & Nick Higham*
 The Lancashire/Cheshire Region from AD 1500 *John Smith*

 Yorkshire to AD 1000 *T. G. Manby*
 Yorkshire from AD 1000 *David Hey*

 The Severn Valley and West Midlands to AD 1000 *R. T. Rowley*
 The West Midlands from AD 1000 *Marie B. Rowlands*
 The Welsh Borders from AD 1000 *R. T. Rowley*

 The East Midlands to AD 1000 *Jeffrey May*
 The East Midlands from AD 1000 *J. V. Beckett*

 The South Midlands and Upper Thames to AD 1000 *David Miles*
 The South Midlands and Upper Thames from AD 1000 *John Broad*

 The Eastern Counties to AD 1000 *W. J. Rodwell*
 The Eastern Counties from AD 1000 *B. A. Holderness*

 The South West to AD 1000 *Malcolm Todd*
 The South West from AD 1000 *Bruce Coleman & R. A. Higham*

 Wessex to AD 1000 *Barry Cunliffe*
*Wessex from AD 1000 *J. H. Bettey*

 The South East to AD 1000 *Peter Drewett*
 The South East from AD 1000 *Peter Brandon & Brian Short*

*already published

1. The Northern Counties
2. The Lancashire/Cheshire Region
3. Yorkshire
4. The Severn Valley and West Midlands
5. The East Midlands
6. The South Midlands and the Upper Thames
7. The Eastern Counties
8. The South West
9. Wessex
10. The South East

To Jennifer

Introduction

This volume of the regional archaeology series will cover the four northern counties of England – Cumbria, Northumberland, Tyne and Wear, Durham – and northern Cleveland. Prior to the recent redrawing of county boundaries, this area comprised the whole of Cumberland and Westmorland, that part of Lancashire north of Morecambe Bay, the whole of Northumberland and all Durham.

In comparatively modern times the area displays some measure of historical homogeneity, largely due to the presence of the Anglo-Scottish frontier forming the northern boundary. Since the fourteenth century AD it has been possible to talk of 'Border Society' as a unifying concept equally applicable west and east of the Pennine ridge. However, in a wider context the political frontier is a comparatively modern phenomenon, the result of a series of historical accidents and strategies predominantly in the period AD 1100–1330. Certainly, before the Norman Conquest no such frontier line existed, and the further back we look, the more irrelevant this line becomes. The Northumbrian kingdom, for example, extended well to the north on both sides of the Pennines. The kingdom of Strathclyde exercised control well to the south in the tenth century, Rheged probably straddled the frontier and Hadrian's Wall and the Antonine Wall offered very different limits to the Roman province. Nor is the modern political boundary relevant to what is known of the tribal territories of late pre-Roman Britain. In the first millennium AD it is arguable that the major elements of physical structure, with a basic north–south alignment, were more important as determinants of economic, social and cultural activity, than any factors for east–west homogeneity. Therefore, it must be borne in mind that we are dealing with an area that falls into two contrasting zones of human activity, neither of which is wholly within the area which is the subject of this book, and while detailed discussion will be limited to that area, it would be improper to ignore, for example, the history of settlement in Dumfriesshire when dealing with north Cumberland, or of Lothian when speaking of Northumberland.

It is best at this stage to resolve one major problem before proceeding

1

further. For an absolute dating system, particularly for the prehistoric period, we have become dependent on carbon-14 dating, derived from the measure of the decay of the element carbon-14 from palaeobotanical cores and archaeological contexts. Research in the 1960s demonstrated, via comparison of carbon-14 years with dendrochronological determinates, that substantial errors existed in the carbon-14 chronology, particularly in the Stone Age and early metal-using periods. As a result, several scientists put forward corrected tables of dates. However, since there is not yet uniformity in these correction factors, and because of the intrinsic inexactness of carbon-14 dating, I have chosen here to follow Piggott (1981) in offering dates in carbon years, appending bc or bp in lower case, to signify whether the date is given as before Christ or before the present (i.e. 1950). Where absolute or corrected years are used, I append BC or BP in small capitals.

An awareness of the archaeological heritage in the northern counties emerged initially via an interest in the relics of classical civilization, which attracted antiquarians and topographers such as Camden (1586) and Stukeley (1776), and stray observations in works as eclectic as Defoe's (1724), with its passing references to Roman roads and the 'Pictish Wall'. Study of the Roman Wall was established on a scientific basis by John Horsley (1732); his detailed measuring and structural analysis laid the foundations of all modern research, even if it may have become less popular than the romantic interpretation of the wall enshrined in works of fiction in Kipling's generation. Among relics of prehistoric communities, only barrows or cairns consistently attracted the nineteenth-century antiquarian; of those which were robbed, less than a tithe were published in any meaningful form and many hitherto extant prehistoric landscapes were destroyed as upland reclamation proceeded in the nineteenth century. However, increasing local interest on both sides of the Pennines led to the organization first of the Society of Antiquaries of Newcastle upon Tyne and secondly of the Cumberland and Westmorland Antiquarian and Archaeological Society. As initially conceived, the societies acted as information exchanges, and organized resources to pursue survey and excavation, while at the same time formulating the type of historical synthesis that quickly came to be associated in Cumbria with the work of Richard Ferguson, and in the North-east with the emergence of the Northumberland County History project.

The growing need for disciplined field research was apparent to men like W. G. Collingwood and F. Haverfield. Within the learned societies, excavation committees were organized, operating an annual season of excavation which emerged in subsequent years as reports in the society *Transactions*. The task of monitoring widespread physical remains attracted specialists with surveying skills, undertaking specific projects of the kind organized by Cowper (1893) and Dymond (1893) in the southern Lakes, from which emerged plans the equal of any produced since. The mantle was taken up by R. G. Collingwood (1933b) whose survey of the ancient settlements of Crosby Ravensworth complemented his father's excavation of Ewe Close, and contributed substantially to the eventual completion of a Royal Commission Survey of Westmorland in 1936.

The process of amassing evidence was pursued hand in hand with attempts to organize that knowledge; among the latter there stands out the exceptional achievement of W. G. Collingwood in the compilation of his major *opus* on the pre-Norman crosses of the North. Most Roman forts were at least trial excavated before 1950, under the leadership of Simpson, Richmond and E. Birley, but the growing realization that major problems could not be solved by trial trenching led to the long-term concentration of resources on Corbridge and a handful of other fort sites.

During the early post-war era, the archaeology of the North was suffering an imbalance of major proportions, with a concentration of resources on Roman military sites, and a resultant lethargy in the pursuit of other areas of research. Exceptions exist, of course, and the academic career of Miss Fell and her furtherance of Cumbrian prehistory is one important case in point, from which eventually was to emerge (1950b) the basis for an evaluation of local tool manufacturing in the northern neolithic.

The mantle of the Collingwoods was taken up not initially in Cumbria, but in Northumberland where George Jobey undertook the identification of 'native' archaeology, the cataloguing of the characteristics of those sites he had located, and the excavation of examples within each category. The result was a series of major contributions, both as type sites and in synthesis, that stretch in unbroken sequence to the present day. Yet it was Northumberland almost alone that benefited: the one-line dismissal of the prehistory of Co. Durham that occurs in Hawkes's *Prehistoric Britain* in 1947 could as easily have been written a generation later. Roman archaeology continued to attract the lion's share of expertise and resources, with the inception of the Vindolanda project, and extensive work at Housesteads and ultimately at Wallsend, eventually to be mirrored in excavations, admittedly of a lesser scale, in the 1970s at Piercebridge, Watercrook and Ravenglass. A growing awareness of the significance of the *vici* permeates much of this research and has dominated work at Vindolanda. One result has been the excavation of major Roman cemeteries at Brougham, Brough and Corbridge.

The enormous concentration of limited resources on Roman sites has allowed significant advances in our understanding of the frontier, but has tended to diminish access to more difficult 'native' activity whether prehistoric, 'Roman' or later. The only major exception lay in the impetus given to Anglo-Saxon archaeology by the series of monastic excavations undertaken by Prof. Rosemary Cramp in the 1960s.

While not wishing to slight the work of Lowndes, or other fieldworkers in the 1960s, it was only the adoption of aerial photography on a broad basis in the North in the late 1960s, and during the 1970s that allowed the potential of the local archaeological heritage to emerge. Not surprisingly, the University of

Newcastle with the expertise of Prof. Norman McCord led the field, but at Durham Dennis Harding and at Manchester both Barri Jones and the author followed this lead. The result was an explosion of information from which has derived many of the most successful of subsequent research projects, from the examination of the Milfield henges or Yeavering Palace to the attack on Romano-British rural settlement and land-use in Cumbria and Durham.

The reliance of post-Roman archaeology on the Northumbrian monasteries could now be challenged; key excavations at Thirlings and in Kentdale now await publication, and the imminent publication of a regional catalogue of sculpted stone will release fresh resources and expertise. A more formal response has been the funding of archaeological posts in the North, with centrally supported units and officers operating from the Universities of Durham, Newcastle and Lancaster, and from within the counties, from whom should emerge fundamental alterations in the way we regard the past in the North. Until such time, the analysis that has been achieved to date has been overshadowed by the historic regional, financial imbalance, and in many fields accomplishment remains in the hands not of the affluent but of the dedicated, among whom it is obligatory to recall the work not just of Prof. Jobey, but of his colleague Colin Burgess, of Roger Miket, Anthony Harding, Prof. Barri Jones, and a host of others.

Note: full details of journals abbreviated in parentheses in the text can be found in the *List of Abbreviations* on pp. 340–1.

Chapter 1

The Formation of the Landscape

Solid Geology [1]

Rock types play a dominant role in determining the general physical character of the border counties, where there is a larger proportion of high ground and mountainous terrain than anywhere else in England. These uplands are composed of rocks laid down over a long period (from 500 to 280 million years ago) and have since been subjected to a complex process of movement, uplift and erosion.

The oldest rocks stretch in a discontinuous band south-west–north-east, from the outlying eminence of the Isle of Man in the Irish Sea, through the Lake District to the Cheviots (King 1976: 8). On the mainland, sediments laid down in marine conditions, from particles derived from a continent to the south, form the Skiddaw slates of the Northern Lake District. A second phase of marine deposition produced the Coniston limestone, and the Silurian mudstones, shales, flags and gritstones of the southern Lakes and Howgill Fells. Intermediate both chronologically and geographically is the Borrowdale series of the central lakes, the result of volcanoes producing new land in the marine environment of the Ordovician period. A later volcanic episode (345–410 million years ago) produced the roughly circular outcrop of igneous rocks that form the Cheviots, centred on a granite intrusion that has replaced the volcanic core, and surrounded by coarse ashes, agglomerates and lavas that are responsible for the steep but rounded contours of the Cheviot Hills. A Devonian granite batholith underlies almost the whole area and is also exposed at Weardale, Shap, Skiddaw and Eskdale (Fig. 1.1).

While these are the oldest and highest mountain blocks, the bulk of the uplands that form the Pennine chain are composed of younger rocks, laid down in deltaic and marine conditions in the Carboniferous period (280–345 million years ago), after a series of episodes that resulted in severe folding and great erosion of the older rocks. The dominant early deposits were the limestones that were originally laid down over the whole area, and then covered successively by Upper Carboniferous deposits – Millstone Grit, and

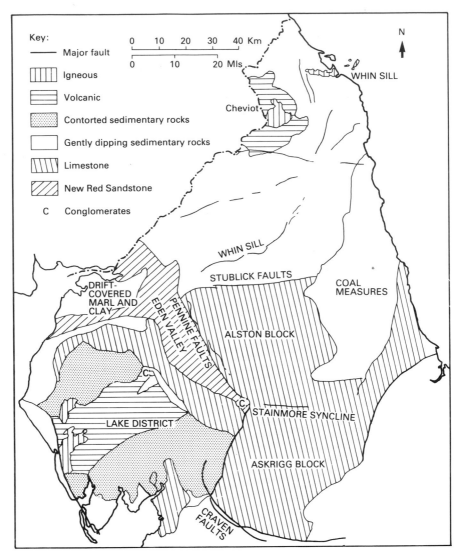

Figure 1.1 The solid geology: one determinant of the physical characteristics of the northern counties.

successively by the lower, middle and upper Coal Measures. Carboniferous Limestone crops out most obviously along the western Pennine scarp and through the Tyne gap into coastal Northumberland, but a rim is also present fringing the Lake District, providing good examples of karst scenery in the Lune and Furness Fells, and in a band from Kirkby Stephen round to the north of the Ordovician deposits and into the valley of the river Ellen. The narrowness of the Carboniferous deposits fringing the Lake District derives from erosion during and after the Tertiary uplift of the area to form an elongated dome.

The Pennines are formed of comparatively horizontal strata, sloping gently to the east, therefore providing far wider belts of all types of Carboniferous rock, from Alston to the sea, with a significant widening of these strata south of the Tyne where they are separated from the sea by younger rocks, including a ridge of Magnesian Limestone laid down in the Permian. The rocks of Carboniferous Limestone age north of the Tyne consist largely of sandstone and shale, (i.e. similar to the Calciferous Sandstone of Scotland) and volcanics near the Tweed. This fell sandstone of Northumberland forms a series of bold scarps arranged in arcuate form around the Cheviots and Bewcastle Fells, again the result of uplift and erosion.

The Pennines have been affected by igneous activity, for example by the intrusion of the Whin Sill, a Carboniferous dolerite, which outcrops along the Eden fault, but is at its most spectacular in the Tyne gap, where it is followed by Hadrian's Wall, and on the coast at Bamburgh and the Farne Islands. It is probably also igneous activity that caused block-faulting in the Pennines and uplift both here and in Lakeland. Granite batholiths have been proved underlying the Alston and Askrigg blocks.

The Armorican and Alpine earth movements brought major faulting to northern England, producing the sigma-shaped fault system which is most obvious at the steep western scarp of the Pennines above the Eden, but which also skirts the Tyne valley to the north of the Alston block (the Stublick faults), governs the Stainmore syncline, and fringes the Askrigg block (the Dent and Craven faults). Displacement measures over 2,000 m and is still continuing.

The lowlying, negative nature of the Solway drainage area, the west and south Cumbrian coast and south-east Durham was already established in the Permian age, and continued to attract deposition in the marine conditions of the Jurassic (136–195 million years ago). In Durham the deposition of Magnesian Limestone was succeeded by Upper Permian and Triassic sandstones and mudstones, which form the most recent sedimentary strata east of the Pennines, dipping to the east. The basal Permian sandstones of the Eden valley are called brockram around Appleby and Kirkby Stephen; these are derived from particles eroded from the Pennine limestones. North of Penrith and west of the Eden a well-marked north–south scarp is formed of Permian, Penrith sandstone, laid down by wind deposition in arid conditions. Between the Eden and the Pennines, and from St Bees southwards along the coast of Cumbria, stretch further deposits of Triassic sandstone. In the Solway plain sandstones and mudstones are overlain by thick glacial till.

By the end of the Tertiary period (2–65 million years ago), the dominant uplands that govern the topography of the northern counties were well developed with the Cheviots and Pennines acting as a central spine with steep slopes into Cumbria but gently tilting towards the North Sea, and the central Lakeland mountain range occupying much of the west. These ranges of high upland divide the lowland of the North into three unequal parts. By far the largest is the eastern coastal plain continuing north into Scotland and discontinuously into Yorkshire. Smaller but more dramatic coastal plains occur on the west of the Pennines, the larger on the Solway, divided by Lakeland and Howgill Fells from the Furness and Lonsdale lowlands which historically, as well as morphologically, have tended to be associated with the Lancashire lowlands.

The structural relationship of these zones has been the major factor in determining their climatic characteristics, and, to a great extent, their value as a habitat, to flora as well as man. For example, the substantial mountain block of the Lake District attracts a substantial percolation, at its heaviest on the western slopes. This has led to environmental degradation of the uplands, and climatic limitations on vegetation at a far lower altitude than on the eastern slopes of the Pennines. The Eden valley enjoys something of a rain-shadow status, and the North Sea littoral has this characteristic to a far greater extent. Structure is responsible for substantial local distortion of climate, with oceanity dominant on the west side and weakening on the east, and this pattern can be seen reflected in the palaeobotanical record in a number of ways.

Pleistocene History and Vegetation Succession

The present drainage pattern reflects the broad structural features of the upland zones. The bulk of the Pennine spine drains eastwards to the North Sea. The Cheviots provide a good example of a radial drainage system, while the Lake District has a less well-defined radial structure with a discernible east–west watershed. Except for the Eden and Lune, the longest rivers are those flowing down the dominant tilt of the Pennines eastwards. The Eden flows along the down-faulted trough west of the Pennine faults, and the Lune runs south, after drawing off most of the runoff from the Howgill Fells as a result of river capture. The other western rivers flowing into the Irish Sea are comparatively short and steep.

Glacial modification, particularly the effects of the last Ice Age, have obscured the drainage development that accompanied the general uplift of the area in the Tertiary period, when the removal of much of the Mesozoic rock coverage took place. The presence of these, now denuded, rocks on the surface of the uplands may have had considerable importance in the formation of surface drainage, but they had probably been removed by mid-Tertiary times, by which stage the landscape would have been one of comparatively low relief. New uplifts have since been responsible for the essential relief of the area, and for modifying existing drainage patterns. For example, one should expect the

Tertiary drainage pattern of the Alston uplands to have flowed west–east from the Pennine faults (Trotter 1929a). One such stream is still traceable in relics that have since been captured to form sections of rival drainage patterns consisting of part of the north Tyne, the upper river Pont and the Seaton Burn. Much of the east-flowing south Tyne and the main river Tyne probably represent a second consequent river. These rivers must have become disrupted during the formation of the peneplain by north–south running drainage along the softer bedrocks exposed by erosion. This process, for example, caused the

Figure 1.2 The drainage quality of soils in the north (based loosely on the *Soil Survey of England and Wales* sheet 1. 1:250,000).

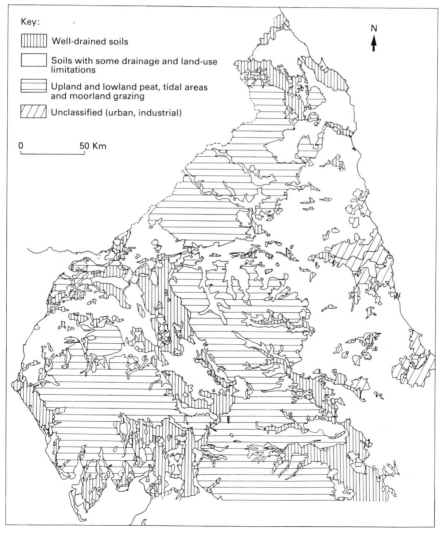

Wear to flow into the Tyne via the Team, and capture a series of east-flowing rivers in passing.

The fault systems were also major factors in determining drainage, with the Eden and Tyne both occupying faulted synclines, and the Stainmore depression drained by the tributaries of the river Tees. The northern Howgill Fells originally drained to the north, but this pattern was disrupted by an eastward-flowing subsequent working westwards along the weaker beds of Ashfell sandstone, forming the valley now occupied by Sunbiggin Tarn but still flowing into the Eden. The entire system was diverted southwards by the Lune breaking through the fells at Tebay and capturing the headwaters of the Eden as far east as the Scandal Beck – since returned to the Eden by glacial activity.

On the west side of the Eden valley a further striking example of river capture is that of the Lowther, working its way along the base of the Carboniferous scarp and capturing a series of dip streams that originally flowed into the Eden via independent channels (Hollingworth 1929). These provide good examples of the greater erosive power of the steeper and faster-flowing rivers, which pushed their headwaters considerable distances and through substantial watersheds (e.g. the Lune gorge at Tebay).

The long process of uplift and erosion in the Tertiary resulted in a denuded landscape lacking striking topographical variation, and balanced by substantial marine deposition. Since that time, uplift has tended to obscure the homogeneity of the northern landscape by affecting the several districts differentially, forming the major uplands of the Lake District and Cheviots and the faulted and tilted Pennines. The combination of these comparatively late movements with the successive glaciations of the Pleistocene period has been responsible for a reshaping of the landscape of the area.

Over a long period, ending approximately in 10,000 BP, there occurred a series of glacial episodes, interspersed with interglacials when temperate and even subtropical conditions were experienced. During the 'Ice Ages' northern England was covered by ice-sheets. Each successive ice-sheet removed or seriously distorted the evidence of earlier events, including most traces of vegetation and fauna, including man. During the later, or upper, Pleistocene the Wolstonian glacial period was succeeded by a warm period – termed the Ipswichian – and this was replaced successively by renewed ice advance in the Devensian, the most recent and best understood glacial episode. During the last glacial maximum, ice-sheets covered the whole of northern Britain, and the uplands of Wales. Ice from Scandinavia invaded the basin of the North Sea, and may have reached the coast of Durham, although it is thought that the narrow deposit of boulder clay on the coast of Durham that derives from Scandinavian ice was laid down in the earlier Wolstonian glaciation. Scottish ice invaded the Irish Sea basin and crossed the Solway, but both ice-flows were diverted from northern England by local ice centres, of which the Lake District with its heavy snowfall proved by far the most active (Hollingworth 1931;

King 1976). Lake District ice flowed south as far as the north-west Midlands. It diverted Scottish ice on the Solway into the Irish Sea, and a combined flow moved through the Tyne gap and on to the eastern plains. The Eden valley experienced substantial ice movement, northwards and westwards, with an 'ice shed' near Carlisle, and another in the Upper Eden (Appleby) from which a secondary flow passed over the Stainmore. Less active centres on the Pennines, based on Cross Fell, and the Howgill Fells, also deposited their debris on the eastern plains, but from these sources ice was relatively slow-moving, suffering from the competition of Lake District and Scottish ice, and, therefore, building up to a considerable thickness. It is still a matter of controversy whether any high ground escaped the ice cover of the glacial maximum, but even if it did, permanent snow would have obscured it. Active and erosive ice seems at least to have been present as high as 300 m against the Cheviots on both the Solway and Tweed sides.

During the height of the Devensian glacial episode it is possible that even the southernmost areas of Britain were evacuated by the Upper Palaeolithic hunting groups (18,000–15,000 BP). Certainly there is no likelihood of human activity present or detectable in the glaciated areas in the North. However, as might be expected, the glacial maximum came comparatively late in the last 'Ice Age', owing to the cumulative nature of the ice-sheets, and the inbuilt inertia of their response to temperate climatic change. Consequently, the ensuing ice retreat stage was comparatively fast, though intermittent. The melting of the ice-sheets, during the retreat stages and before, resulted in the deposition of substantial quantities of debris across the northern landscape, derived from upland areas, whether local or distant.

The glacial episodes were characterized by considerable direct erosion of the upland areas, particularly in the Lake District. The major watercourses received the most obvious attention, with significant over-deepening, and many have as a result an irregular longitudinal profile, in places since flooded to produce lakes. Elsewhere, considerable but less spectacular erosion occurred, in particular of the less resistant strata of the shales (Lake District and Pennines) and New Red Sandstone (Cheviots) from which striated boulders were deposited across the bulk of the northern lowlands, within a matrix of fine clay. This combination laid down by the glacial sheets provides the typical subsoil of the lowlands both east and west of the Pennines, often 6 m or more thick and covering broad belts of Durham, Northumberland, the Solway and the Cumbrian coast. Interspersed with them are deposits of glacial sands and gravels, the result of meltwater deposition. Some deposits were laid down as drumlins underneath the ice and mirror the ice-flow pattern. Drumlins are common in the Eden valley and provide the only 'dry' terrain on the Solway plain around Holme Abbey. They also occur widely around Kendal. As the Devensian ice retreated westwards through the Tyne gap it deposited a substantial esker of sand and gravel from Hexham to Haltwhistle, the watershed. As it retreated further westwards downhill, a meltwater lake developed, normally called Lake Eden, trapped between the high ground of central England and the Scottish and Lake District ice still closing off the Solway (Trotter 1929b). A col near Haltwhistle acted as the overflow at 143 m above Ordnance datum (OD), which was then lowered sufficiently by the erosive force of the meltwaters to allow the south Tyne to escape eastwards. Lakes like Lake Eden left stratified deposits of sands and gravels with deltaic features. A similar ice-dammed lake developed at Milfield, Northumberland, formed by local meltwater trapped by 'foreign' ice retreating downhill from the Cheviots, and another example lies in the Upper Eden valley, where meltwaters were trapped behind Ash Fell, escaped via the Scandal Beck and cut a steep gorge through the Orton ridge limestone. Fluvio-glacial deposits are widespread in Northumberland north of the Breamish river, particularly between the Cheviots and the Tweed.

Elsewhere, the erosive effect of meltwaters has been considerable. For example, the Old Red Sandstone hills in the vicinity of Wooler were cut by meltwater channels often flowing across watersheds, suggesting that the meltwater initially adopted its channel when flowing over ice.

The glacial episodes had a substantial and locally divergent impact on the landscape. The area east of the Pennines was characterized by the degree to which it received glacial debris flowing generally eastwards close to the Pennines, and southwards along the coast. This resulted in the deposition of boulder clay in a blanket that is characterized by lower profiles and relief than most areas west of the Pennines. In some areas these deposits overlie kettle moraines (the middle sands), the result of melt from withdrawing Pennine glaciers and the later withdrawal of the northern ice that succeeded the local product. One of the results of this deposition was the infilling of deep, old river valleys with clay, particularly along the coast. For example, Whitburn and Whitley Bay in Northumberland are old valleys, blocked by drift, and the substantial till cliffs along some sections of the coast betray the depth and consistency of this deposition, which has diverted several of the major west–east rivers from their pre-glacial beds. On the west side, glacial till has totally infilled the Solway basin (except where drumlins stand clear), and is responsible for the raising of the Solway plain above OD. The wide Eden/Petteril valley below Penrith is likewise largely covered by thick red clay deposits. Deposits of clay and fluvio-glacial sands and gravels encircle the Lake District, and till also dominates the Furness and Lonsdale lowlands to the south.

Authorities vary in their assessment of the speed and chronology of the ice withdrawal from the north, but by about 12,400 bp (Hollingworth 1951) or by 11,000 BP (Morrison 1980) at the latest it is reasonable to assume that the ice-sheets had withdrawn into Scotland, with the possible exception of minor glacial centres in the Lake District. Excluding deposits from earlier interglacial episodes, the earliest organic deposits from northern England are from Blelham Bog, a kettlehole near Windermere (dated 12380 ± 230 bc).

These provide a picture of a pioneer vegetation becoming established in the late glacial period and is typical of a tundra or Alpine zone, with lichens, grasses and dwarf shrubs (Hollingworth 1951). These early colonizers were probably gaining a hold, in periglacial conditions typified by permafrost, heavy and long-lying snow and primitive mineral soils, attractive to a typical tundra fauna, and principally, among the large ungulates, to reindeer.

It may have been the hunting of these animals that attracted the presence of at least one human group, which made temporary use of Kirkhead Cave, Lower Allithwaite (Wood, Ashmead and Mellars 1970), and abandoned there a limited range of flint tools. It is no accident that Kirkhead Cave lies in the extreme south of the northern counties, close to sea-level and overlooking the wide expanses of lowland hunting ranges that incorporated at that time not only the Lancashire plain, but also much of the Irish Sea as far west as the Isle of Man. There is no evidence of late Upper Palaeolithic hunters moving further into the upland zone north of Victoria Cave, Settle. Nor would there seem to be much incentive for them, bearing in mind the effect high altitudes must have had on local climatic conditions, and it is still an open question whether the presence of man at Kirkhead should be seen in this context, or after the significant amelioration of the period around 10000 bc. The remarkably late carbon-14 dates from Derbyshire's Cresswellian deposits at Anston Cave imply an Upper Palaeolithic hunting economy surviving in the southern Pennines into the beginning of the eighth millennium bc (Mellars 1969).

During the Devensian ice advance, as presumably during earlier glacial episodes, the extension of the polar ice-caps locked up a great deal of water and brought about a general lowering of sea-level globally, sufficient to produce land in the Irish Sea and North Sea basins. The progressive retreat of the ice produced a rapid rise in sea-level, termed a eustatic rise, but this was offset in northern latitudes by the isostatic uplift of areas that had been compressed by ice-sheets, and this initially ensured the survival of the enlarged coastal territories between Cumbria and the Isle of Man, and in a narrow strip along the north-east coast, as well as the major land corridor between England south of the Humber and the European continent, south from Denmark (Synge 1977; Tooley 1978b). These coastal plains provided a lowlying, climatically favourable habitat that was probably attractive to the small population of humans in Britain in the later stages of the Devensian. Isostatic uplift in Britain affected only those areas covered by the Devensian ice. Earlier episodes have occurred, for example, resulting in the raised beach at Easington, Durham dated from shells to more than 38,000 bp, presumably created during an interglacial period (King 1976). By far the greatest uplift has occurred in Scotland, particularly in the western Highlands, and the effects are decreasingly apparent on the periphery. In northern England, isostatic uplift has been responsible for raised beaches and cliffs, but rarely more than 8 m above OD, and eustatic rises in sea-level have had a proportionally greater impact (Donner 1970).

The beginning of a recognizable, general plant succession in northern

England came in the tenth millennium bc, when the organically barren sediments of the ice moraines deposited in the deep lakes of Cumbria were succeeded by deposits exhibiting a developing organic content, and the pollen of juniper and then birch. At Windermere, where the earliest organic deposits have been dated by carbon-14 to 9920 ± 120 bc (Pennington 1970), this opens a lengthy period in which there can be traced an uninterrupted vegetational succession on soils that were becoming more stable, the direct result of a rise in the mean and average temperature probably starting late in the eleventh

Figure 1.3 Sites from which pollen cores mentioned in the text have been collected.

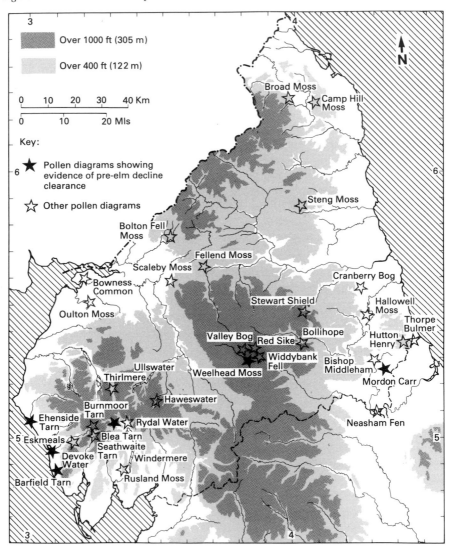

millennium bc. Despite some signs of oscillations in the early stages, for example at Blea Tarn where there was evidence that tundra vegetation followed an initial rise in juniper pollen, the Alleröd climatic improvement had begun, which eventually brought with it the first phase of post-glacial afforestation (Fig. 1.3).

Our evidence for the vegetational succession of the early post-glacial period comes overwhelmingly from the Lake District, where, by 1970, Pennington could draw on over sixty pollen diagrams from a habitat range that took in the lowlands of the Solway (Walker 1966), Morecambe Bay (Oldfield 1960) and the central Lakes, and included then the best regional range of dated diagrams in Britain [2]. What has become increasingly clear is the vulnerability of vegetation to local conditions, whether produced by particular local mineral rocks, topography, or by climatic conditions. There are major differences visible in the vegetational succession in upland and lowland, and between the areas of lowland, both in the dispersal of specific plants, and in the chronology of the generally valid succession (Smith 1965; Taylor 1975).

Therefore, we should not assume that vegetational succession boundaries dated in one area of Cumbria are applicable east of the Pennines, or to a lesser extent, even in the next valley. Unfortunately, although some eastern pollen work has been undertaken the results are still incomparably inferior in detail and chronological precision to those available from the Lake District [3]. Therefore, while recognizing the basic regionality of the evidence, we have to draw upon a geographically biased sample that provides a picture at its weakest on the coastal plain of Durham.

The improving climate of the Alleröd interstadial produced an explosion of birch forest in the northern counties and the introduction of the thermophilous birch *Pendula* to the sheltered environment of the south Lakes. Even so, in the highlands, this expansion of tree pollen was less marked, and even non-existent at Seathwaite Tarn, on the north-facing slopes of the Old Man of Coniston, where Alpine conditions prevailed. The Pennines and Cheviots probably fared little better, but it is reasonable to assume a northward extension of birch forest along the north-east coast as far as Lothian. The improving vegetation attracted in its wake a fauna better suited to a less open environment. The remains of an elk were dated *c.* 11,561–10,851 bp at Neasham, Co. Durham (Blackburn 1952) and another example associated with barbed points, was excavated at Poulton-le-Fylde, Lancashire (Hallam *et al.* 1973) and provides positive evidence for the hunting of these large animals about 10000 bc in the lowlands bordering the northern counties (see also Noe-Hygaard 1975). Examples of the horse have come from Flixton, North Yorkshire, and the Irish elk (*Megaloceros giganticus*) and reindeer were probably present but have not been dated (Grigson 1978).

The Alleröd interstadial was brought to a close by worsening climatic conditions late in the tenth millennium bc. Temperature dropped to a mean annual temperature just below 0 °C, and this was accompanied by a tilt in the balance between rainfall and evaporation that produced a greater surface runoff and led to an increase in the leaching of minerals from the immature soils. This resulted in the creation of increasingly humic soils, and podzolization, first on the 'fragile' base soils on the uplands and eventually widespread, forcing the retreat of the tree-line and the spread of heath vegetation and an open habitat in which plants associated with broken ground (plantago, etc.) re-emerged. At Scaleby Moss (Godwin, Walker and Willis 1957; Pennington 1970) the established plant communities had broken down by the second century of the ninth millennium bc. On the uplands the presence in the drainage basins of solifluction silts deficient in organic material is suggestive of severe winters accompanied by periglacial erosion. By about 8800 bc *Artemisia* (a species of mugwort) had attained a dominance in uplands and lowlands, and tree pollen had begun a steep decline, remaining buoyant only in the protected environment of Morecambe Bay.

This cold episode, often termed the post-Alleröd Glaciation, the Younger Dryas, or pollen zone III (Godwin 1956), was accompanied by a re-advance of ice-sheets in the north-west of Scotland – the Loch Lomond Re-advance, and by local glaciation in the Lake District, developing from high corries and generating sufficient ice to introduce glaciers into the higher valleys. End moraines provide evidence of their melting, for example, in the Coniston valley at Nibthwaite 140–150 m above OD and at a similar altitude in Wastdale and Borrowdale. Other less sheltered valleys were never so badly affected, with glacial melting at lowest in Ennerdale at 270 m and in Eskdale at 350 m (Manley 1959).

An improving climate brought this last glacial episode to a close about 8300 bc, and created conditions suitable for the recolonization of first the lowland zone and eventually the uplands by shrub species, initially juniper. The juniper was supplanted as the dominant species in the lowlands before the eighth millennium bc by tree birch which formed a more or less blanket cover, and then in turn by deciduous woodland, dominated successively by hazel and pine, oak and elm and, more particularly in the West, alder, which formed a closed deciduous forest. The forest cover was successful in competing with other species, to the extent that non-tree pollen declined to less than 10 per cent of the total (Pennington 1970), and shade-intolerant plants were confined to a habitat above the tree-line or along the coast. An upland pollen diagram from 518 m shows relatively late survival of the pre-boreal herbaceous flora, showing that the last glacial episode did not only retreat laterally towards the north, but also altitudinally. In Upper Teesdale peat formation in bogs was already occurring by 8000 bc, incarcerating the remains of a flora dominated by typical late glacial vegetation – grasses, sedges, *plantago*, etc. The spread of true forest failed to reach this upland area until about 6800 bc, when hazel, birch and pine forest made an appearance, and then achieved dominance by about 6000 bc. Even so, this dominance was clearly very variable, dependent on microsystems in climatic and other environmental factors, with pine dominant on the better-drained soils forming thin woodland cover with a rich variety of herbs, and hazel and birch common elsewhere up to 760 m above OD (Turner 1978). In general terms, pine was a more important constituent of the northern forests in Co. Durham than elsewhere, while oak made a greater impact west of the Pennines.

Under deciduous forest conditions, soils reached a state of maturity, to an extent protected from excess water action by the foliage cover, and bound together by the root complex. In these conditions streams were at their lowest, most predictable level, without rush floods and unable to carry out much erosion or carrying activity, and the major rivers were comparatively sluggish. The tree roots may have played a significant role in replacing minerals in the upper levels of the soil and thereby counteracting the leaching effects of rainfall and the increased acidity of water dropping from leaves (Ball 1975). The high incidence of earthworms, etc. and the low disturbance rate of the surface normal in a closed deciduous forest are equally factors in a forest soil resisting podzolization, which may have played a part in the stability of the brown soils which dominated even the uplands during the 'climatic optimum'.

In the northern counties, the tree cover was not absolutely uniform. While there is a great deal of debate as to the height of the tree-line above sea-level there is little doubt that there was one, even though Pennington has placed it as high as 762 m (see also Simmons, Dimbleby and Grigson 1981). It is probably also reasonable to suppose that the natural tree-line was rising from about 8000 bc to at least 5000 bc and probably later on climatic determinants alone. It is possible to distinguish some further regional variations in the North. Pine was not ubiquitously present in Cumbria, and may have had a range dependent more on soil and drainage than on climate, and *Tilia* (lime) only appears comparatively late (end of pollen zone VI) and only in the limestone areas fringing Morecambe Bay.

The considerable and maintained climatic improvement of the eighth millennium bc brought with it a substantial rise in sea-level, as retreating ice-sheets close to the Poles released water into the sea. The earliest major inroads came in the Irish Sea basin, where the marine transgression reached Morecambe Bay by about 7200 bc. The absence of much of the forest fauna from Ireland (elk, roe deer, etc.) reinforces the early date for the flooding of the area west of the Isle of Man, but the loss of the coastal plains between south Lakeland and the north coast of Wales underlines the diminishing lowland territory available to British fauna from the eighth millennium onwards. At the same time, temperatures rose from a yearly mean below 0 °C at 8000 bc until soon after 6000 bc they were sustained at an average somewhat higher than at present. The northern counties had hitherto been largely outside the range of post-glacial man. At this stage they fell more certainly within.

Increasingly wet climatic conditions in the sixth millennium were probably associated with the greater oceanity of Britain, as rapidly rising sea-levels eroded the land-link with the Continent in the North Sea basin in the seventh and early sixth millennia bc. The island status of Britain was probably established at the very latest by about 5800 bc, and marine transgressions were occurring along the modern coastline, with maxima early in the fifth millennium, about 4300 bc, 3800 bc and 3000 bc (Tooley 1978a), with major consequences for lowlying coastal areas, like the Solway, and for river estuaries. So-called raised beaches formed in the sixth millennium are present on both the Cumbrian and North Sea coastlines, as the rising sea-level outstripped the isostatic rise of the land mass of northern England. Detailed examination of the estuarine and coastal deposits on both the North Sea coast, and more particularly the Irish Sea coast, has demonstrated the complicated and local aspects of these phases of marine transgression and deposition (Godwin 1943; Trechmann 1936; Tooley 1978a; 1978b).

The increasing rainfall also had effects upon vegetation in what is often called the Atlantic phase or pollen zone VIIa, beginning about 5000 bc, which saw a ubiquitous increase in alder, replacing willow-birch in the drainage basins of the uplands, and a retreat of the pine, to be replaced by deciduous woodland south of the Lakes and in the East. East of the Pennines in the rain-shadow deciduous woodland remained dominant, but now included a large proportion of alder. With a rising water-table, the oak and elm lost ground except on the better-drained lowland and deeper upland soils. Generally the increasing percolation appears to have brought about an increase in the leaching of minerals through the topsoil (Mackereth 1966), but there is less sign of increasing surface-water erosion until near to 3000 bc. The leaching may have resulted in significant soil changes, with increasing acidity and humic content and the development of podzols. If this is the case, it would have affected first those habitats where woodland was already marginal – on the altitudinal limits and on the more mineral-deficient soils, but there is little sign of a natural disafforestation as a result. Even so, it is arguable, but not proven that by about 3500 bc much of the forest cover of the northern counties was in a fragile condition except where it enjoyed peculiar advantages such as a limestone substrate, and that there was present serious soil degradation, leading in many areas to gleying and podzolization.

In several comparable areas it has been shown that peat formation was already occurring under the stimulus of climatic and soil changes on poorly drained uplands by 5000 bc. This receives some support also in the lowlands, with the coastal peat beds of south Durham producing mesolithic artifacts and snails from below the peat typical of an alder marsh (Trechmann 1936). These formed before marine inundation. Certainly on the west side of the Lake District, where we should expect the earliest and most obvious affects of increasing wetness to appear, *sphagnum* made an appearance before the beginning of the Atlantic phase at Brant Rake Moss near Devoke water. However, the local nature of these environmental conditions is emphasized by the virtual non-appearance of sphagnum at Burnmoor Tarn close by, until at or around 3000 bc (Pennington 1970). While it is clear that the Atlantic phase in particular was characterized by local peat formation, particularly in inflow drainage hollows (e.g. Solway mosses) and on poorly draining upland plateaux (e.g. Pennine gritstones), this appears to have been restricted in its impact, until about 5,000 bp, when peat accumulation, for example in Upper Teesdale, appears to have speeded up, and taken over the high plateau areas and lower-lying hollows (Turner 1978).

The forest of the boreal and Atlantic periods (broadly 8000–3500 bc) carried a substantial and predictable fauna. Several species seem to have adapted from tundra conditions to woodland dwelling, including the wolf, to join the species derived from the subarctic forest and temperate forest conditions before the European land-bridge was severed. The latter included the elk, red deer, roe deer and aurochs (*Bos primigenius*), as well as the bulk of the lesser mammalia that still constitute the natural fauna of Britain (Simmons and Tooley 1981). The survival of the horse as a native into forest conditions is very doubtful, but a wide range of ungulates and lesser mammals, birds and fish were available as a resource for man. It seems unlikely that the Irish elk (*Megaloceros giganticus*) successfully adapted itself to dense woodland conditions, although its remains have been found in the peat beds of West Hartlepool (Trechmann 1936).

Subsistence Strategies

As has already been noted, the northern counties were outside the range of man for most of that part of Pleistocene history for which we have evidence – that is, from the Devensian glacial maximum onwards. Ameliorating climatic conditions and an improving habitat attracted only marginal hunting activity, probably centred on the extensive coastal lowlands now under the Irish Sea as well as on the Fylde about 10000 years bc (see above, p. 15). It is unlikely that human communities were present in the area in the renewed glacial episode of the ninth millennium. Therefore, subsistence strategies are only detectable in northern England during the mesolithic period, or middle Stone Age, and the evidence for this activity weighs heavily towards the latter end (5000–3500 bc approximately).

The identification of flint artifacts of distinctive mesolithic cultures began in all seriousness in the 1920s with the work of Frances Buckley (Buckley 1922). The artefacts that Buckley and his successors examined were predominantly small stone implements or the waste products of implement manufacture. The vast majority of implements are struck flakes, normally termed 'microliths'. These are flakes struck from a core, and either not further developed or alternatively retouched to form distinctive shapes, presumably for specific tasks, such as awls, burins or scrapers. A small minority of implements derive from cores, and these are mostly axes or adzes in style. These assemblages were compared to well-researched continental forms, and on stylistic grounds have been divided broadly into two distinctive cultures, labelled from the European parallels 'Maglemosian' and 'Tardenoisian'. Wary of using continental-type sites, other fieldworkers have insisted on using only a morphological or stylistic distinction between the two styles, labelling the former 'broad-blade' and the latter 'narrow-blade'. Since 1950 carbon-14 dating has established the general chronological primacy of the broad-blade industry, dating in the North largely within the eighth millennium bc (Jacobi 1975; 1976), but there is no clear separation of the two, and mixed assemblages are not uncommon.

The broad-blade or earlier forms, where these can be distinguished, are characterized by a lack of geometric shapes among the microliths, with the exception of one or two large and elongated isosceles triangles, and large trapezes. The predominant and diagnostic microlith type is the obliquely blunted point which appears in several forms, the result of intentional secondary breakage at the point by sideways pressure. Assemblages are normally characterized by a balanced nature, with a comparatively constant ratio of microlith forms to scrapers and core axes (Jacobi 1976).

The narrow-blade or later forms are generally smaller, and characterized by the dominance of geometric forms, such as scalene triangles, rods and crescents. Assemblages are often unbalanced in nature, with the proportion of microliths to scrapers, etc. being highly variable. It has been suggested that this variable balance between the various types of artefact may be a factor which can provide evidence of the function of a particular site (Mellars 1976a). This type of analysis is only possible where finds are concentrated in large numbers in a comparatively limited area, and significant differences have to date only been noted in sites in the narrow-blade later tradition. Although not totally unrepresented in the northern counties, broad-blade industries are rare, and to date no substantial manufacturing or usage site has been scientifically examined to a standard that allows any comments to be made. The standard of site publication is also a problem when dealing with the narrow-blade industries in the North since many sites have only been published in very limited accounts, and the majority were found and described early this century before the introduction of many of the current methods of assessing the function of the site.

The earliest narrow-blade culture known in Britain is that of Filpoke Beacon in south-east Durham, dated to 6810 bc (Jacobi 1976), and it is probably no coincidence that this lies at the end of the land 'corridor' which was probably finally cut late on in the seventh millennium. The substantial increase in evidence for human subsistence activity in the seventh and subsequent millennia may well be associated with the drowning of the preferred habitat of the North Sea basin, and the consequent forced migration of human communities to areas above OD.

The strategies adopted by mesolithic man in order to exist in the North are not obviously different from the early to the later mesolithic, although significant changes in the environment must imply at least a shift of emphasis. It is thought that the equipment that provides most of our direct evidence of human activity was largely designed for hunting or 'domestic' activities associated with a hunting regime, although a far greater flexibility in usage cannot be ruled out. Unfortunately, in the northern counties, the vast majority of sites are only known from scatters of surface finds. Scientific excavation has only been applied to a small minority of sites, for example, in the last decade at Eskmeals in south-west Cumberland (Bonsall 1981) and earlier at Beacon Edge, Durham. Only from excavated sites can we expect a substantial array of organic equipment or rubbish, and Eskmeals has so far conspicuously failed to provide such evidence. On excavations carried out before the war, organic remains were normally only inadequately sampled. In general terms, the stone industries of the northern counties are poor, with a scarcity of axes or adzes and a significant proportion of poor chert used in the industries, probably from the Magnesian Limestone strata of Durham. Late mesolithic coastal assemblages contain also a small proportion of artefacts of volcanic tuff. The early assemblages are dominated by comparatively large and simple forms that probably made up the tips and barbs of wooden arrows, as at Sheddon's Hill, Gateshead (Coupland 1925) and a few axes have also been found (e.g. one from Monkwearmouth). From the evidence provided by the eighth millennium site of Star Carr in Yorkshire, spears were normally equipped with barbed points derived from antler (Clark 1954, 1972). Only one such point has been found in the North, from the east coast at Whitburn, Co. Durham, but this more properly belongs with the similar harpoon weapons typically found in the west of Scotland at Oban and these are representative of a late mesolithic coastal economy (Mellars 1970). The later assemblages are dominated by microliths, – flakes that were probably used to barb a wooden spearhead and used in hunting, – which replaced the earlier use of antler barbs. With them occur scrapers and burins, probably used in hide preparation (Clark 1932).

There is little evidence to support or to reject Clarke's suggestion that microliths could equally well have been utilized in reaping (Clarke 1976). Hammer-stones were probably used in tool manufacture, among other things (Clark 1932). Axes and adzes were probably used to cut down trees and shape timber, but their general scarcity suggests little direct felling was underway. The poverty of the northern industries was due at least in part to the poor sources of workable stone – largely from small beach pebbles and from drift deposits. At Eskmeals the bipolar striking of the cores may have been intended to make the most of a barely adequate flint source (Bonsall 1931) (Fig. 4). The northern assemblages in general are poor in variety, and lack implements of any size.

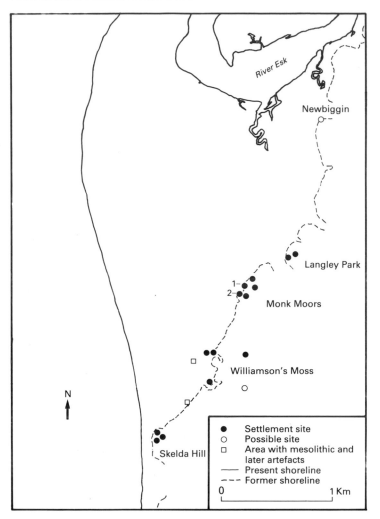

Figure 1.4 The late mesolithic occupation of the Eskmeals raised shore line (after Bonsall, 1978).

Mesolithic sites are concentrated in the northern counties on the coasts, particularly along the North Sea, but to a lesser extent also in south-west Cumbria. No inland sites have been located west of the Pennines, but there are a small number of inland sites in Durham along the Cumbrian Pennine fringe and, to a lesser extent, in Tyne and Wear and Northumberland. Of the inland sites most are in the major river valleys. If we break them down statistically, of the 140 or so sites or small groups of sites so far located, 80 (or 57%) are coastal or estuarine locations, while a further 36 (or 26%) are within 2 km of a major river and below 244 m. This coastal concentration is underlined when we recall that the coastline of the early mesolithic (and later episodes of marine withdrawal) is now under the sea and so is removed from our calculations. However, a site distribution in which only 17 per cent of located sites are upland sites is at variance with evidence from comparable upland habitats near by. The North York Moors, for example, and the central and southern Pennines have provided a great deal of evidence of hunting activity (Jacobi 1978). It is probable that north Pennine sites are under-represented, particularly since so much of the evidence has come from the dedicated work of a few local amateurs. For example, Hildyard's survey of flint sites in Weardale has produced thousands of flints from most periods from over forty sites, although most of these are from valley ploughing (Fell and Hildyard 1953, 1955b). This is also true on the coast, particularly in Cumbria where the bulk of the sites have been located since 1960 [4]. It is unavoidable that our distribution maps at this stage are as much a record of where fieldwork has been carried out, as a true record of where mesolithic communities were sited. Because most of the sites have been detected only as a surface scatter, it is difficult to assess their size. Certainly, many sites are only a very few square metres in extent, such as the scatter of flints from the rock shelter at Goatscrag in north Northumberland (Burgess 1972), which should be classed as an upland site, or the 'small workshop site' at Spindleston (Buckley 1922). Another upland flint-working site is that at Sheddon's Hill, near the Black Fell, Gateshead (Coupland 1925). Within a very limited area of the hilltop were found over 400 flint fragments the majority of which were used small blades or flakes (microliths) or waste pieces. Two hammer-stones were evidence of manufacture, and thirty-nine fragments showed signs of burning. It seems likely that this was a favoured spot used by hunters over a long period, but like many others in the North it lies no distance into the uplands. Sites like Goatscrag and Sheddon's Hill have been diagnosed as typical of small, mobile hunting groups active in the summer months (Mellars 1976a), and on the southern and central Pennines are typified by a high proportion of microliths, presumably reflecting their use as barbs for hunting spears. The available evidence does not allow us to assume such sites were present in the northern Pennines in any quantity.

Far more typical of the northern settlements seem to be those sites from which a balanced tool kit of microliths, scrapers and points have come, with or without the microburins and cores that signify manufacture on the site. The Cumbrian coastal sites certainly fit into this category as do Filpoke Beacon in Durham and Spindleston, and Lyne Hill in Northumberland (Raistrick 1933). Although the records do not allow a statistical approach it seems likely that several of the Weardale sites and those at Ross, Budle Crags and Chester Craggs, Basalt Crags and Caster, all in Northumberland (Buckley 1919–22; 1922) betray the same balanced tool assemblages.

Some of these sites are comparatively large (larger than Star Carr). As defined by the scatter of artefacts, the Eskmeals site at Monks Moor I is 35×15 m in a total area scatter of 250×150 m, and at Williamson's Moss

22×21 m (Bonsall 1981: 455). Elsewhere, the disturbed nature of newly located sites, and the poverty of old records should warn us against attempts at estimating the size of a site from recorded artefact distribution.

What does stand out is the degree to which sites congregate in particular areas; for example, sites are grouped in a narrow strip of shoreline at Eskmeals and a second definite group is present at, and south of, St Bees Head (Cherry and Cherry 1973). Obvious preferred locations also exist in the Upper and Middle Wear valley, on the coast of Durham and Tyne and Wear between Blackhall and the mouth of the Wear at Tynemouth and around Bamburgh, in Northumberland. If this is not entirely due to the differential input of fieldwork, the density of sites in these areas suggest a preference for certain types of location, and imply repeated occupation over a long period.

Traces of a structure have been found only on three sites (at Eskmeals), but this points more to the poverty of modern research than to their absence (Fig. 1.4). Bonsall reported at Monks Moor I an oval arrangement of hearths and stake-holes 7×2.4 m in extent with the highest concentration of artefacts centred here and aligned so as to minimize wind resistance (Bonsall 1981: 456). This is consistent with other sites from the upland zone, where evidence has been forthcoming for flimsy living or sleeping quarters for example, at Deepcar, Yorkshire (Radley and Mellars 1964) and Morton, Fife (Coles 1971). It seems likely that new research will greatly increase our knowledge of these settlements with their flimsy shelters, hearths and scatters of implements and rubbish.

The seasonality of mesolithic subsistence strategies has attracted a great deal of attention, particularly in recent analysis of activity in the southern Pennines and North Yorkshire (Simmons 1975a). The Star Carr model as propounded by Clark supposes that a lowland site would normally be occupied during the winter months, when the deer congregate in coastal or valley areas and consequently a balanced tool kit would be produced as the inhabitants took advantage of a relatively sedentary period to carry out seasonal 'domestic' activities such as working on antler and hides (Clark 1954, 1972). The habitual seasonal movement of deer, in particular, and possibly other ungulates like the aurochs (Evans 1975) – is from a wide and dispersed summer range in the uplands to a reduced, more sheltered, lowland habitat in the autumn (Chaplin 1975). This congregation would certainly make them easier to hunt and thereby increase the chances of the human community exploiting this food resource in winter. The Star Carr model assumed a removal of herds and human population into the uplands during the summer months, and plentiful traces of this activity have been forthcoming, for example, in the North York Moors (Simmons 1975a).

Evidence that might be consistent with a comparable but later trans-humance economy comes from Cleveland, on the other side of the North York Moors. The concentration of sites in the protected coastal area may represent seasonal winter activity associated with the increased population of deer during the winter months in the Tees basin where they have congregated from their summer pastures in the Pennines, or on the North York Moors. However, the bulk of the sites are not situated so as easily to exploit the Tees valley, but are located further north on the coastal lowlands (for example, Coupland 1923, 1925). Nor is there a concentration of sites in that part of the Tees basin which lies south of the Tees. The comparative scarcity of upland sites on the Durham Pennines likewise argues against a widespread or successful subsistence strategy founded on the summer movement of deer herds into the uplands to exploit the tree-line area and high open herbage. Although it is probable that some upland hunting did occur, particularly late in the mesolithic, giving rise to a scatter of moorland flint sites, this appears not to have attained great significance. No upland sites have been found in Lakeland, and very few in Northumberland. Recent excavations on upland complexes centring on later prehistoric monuments have produced some evidence of mesolithic activity in the shape of widespread scatters of flints which include types supposedly diagnostic, such as tiny blades and microliths. Jobey records such finds from inland Northumberland, on Rosebrough Moor and Hepburn Moor, some 10–15 km from the North Sea, and these probably represent some degree of seasonal hunting activity (Jobey 1981a). At the same time, these finds imply that the scarcity of upland sites in the north of England may be due as much to the poverty of fieldwork as to any real absence of such occupation, and recent research leaves open the possibility of mesolithic interference with the mid-Flandrian forests of the northern Pennines (Turner and Hodgson 1983).

A different type of subsistence strategy was practised in the late mesolithic on the Scottish coasts, a strategy that can best be illustrated at Gronsay in the Inner Hebrides (Bishop 1913–14; Mellars and Payne 1971; Mellars and Wilkinson 1980). In a group of sites that had little direct contact with even the normal winter habitat of the red deer, organic remains point to a subsistence strategy that concentrated upon sea-fish (saithe in particular), shellfish, crabs and lobsters, sea-birds, seals and dolphins, and land mammals (including deer), listed in descending order of importance. Carbon-14 dating demonstrated occupation in the second half of the fourth millennium bc at Cnoc Coig – as late as is possible within the normal chronological parameters of the mesolithic. Perhaps of more direct comparative importance are the sites of south-west Scotland and the east coast. At Barnsalloch, Wigtownshire, a mesolithic occupation dating to about 4000 bc was poorly placed to exploit land-mammal resources (Cormack 1970). At Morton in Fife, excavations on a site where the dominant occupation phase was during the fifth millennium bc produced evidence for a food economy in which marine molluscs, crabs and sea-fish were important but which also featured deer, wild cattle, pigs, sea-birds and a variety of plant resources (Coles 1971).

What we are probably witnessing in the northern counties of England are a series of local compromises between the two extremes of subsistence strategy represented by Star Carr to the south, and the much later shell midden sites of Oronsay and the Scottish seashores to the north. Along the Cumbrian coast this has already been argued convincingly by Bonsall, who puts forward the thesis that the Eskmeals communities were likely to have remained close to the coast throughout the year, although they probably did not occupy a permanent site. From this location they could have access to comparatively predictable coastal resources, the shellfish, seaweed, crustaceans and sea-fish, and to the estuary resources, the wildfowl and plants. For the seasonal salmon runs, they might have been obliged to move upstream beyond the tidal reaches. Winter exploitation of local ungulate populations would be quite feasible. Bonsall also argues for an early- to mid-fifth-millennium occupation when local estuarine conditions were at an optimum as regards resource availability.

It is probable that the local subsistence strategy utilized vegetable resources, but these have left no trace. Edible seaweed is still locally available, and certain plants of the estuary and salt-marshes may have provided useful vitamin and base mineral sources. From the deciduous forest of the coastal lowland, hazel-nuts provide the most important vegetable protein source, and this is the only vegetable product that has come from a northern site (Filpoke Beacon), where it occurred in sufficient quantity to suggest intentional storage as a winter food source. However, despite the range of berries, roots and fungi available in the woodlands (Clarke 1976), it is unlikely that vegetable resources provided a significant protein or calorie intake, particularly in this northerly area of the cool temperate zone, and with the exception of the hazel-nut, their significance should not be overemphasized. At Morton, in Fife, hazel-nuts were represented among the organic remains, along with seeds of plants normally associated with waste or cultivated ground, such as corn, spurrey or chickweed, and these were presumably collected for food (Coles 1971), but it is impossible to say how important a contribution such foods made to mesolithic man's diet. What we can be reasonably sure of is that these communities were omnivorous, and made a pragmatic series of choices concerning resource use, in both hunting and gathering, and that both these basic methods of obtaining food were essential to the well-being and continued existence of the group. For this reason, it is arguable that each community required a territory from which to obtain its needs that offered a diversity of resources which could be exploited in turn as each became available. A group territory in the northern counties seems to have had as its primary resource access to the sea and shore, but other needs could only be satisfied from estuaries and rivers and possibly also river banks, marshes and woodland areas.

It is difficult to see obvious advantages in the location of the communities sited on the Cumbrian coast between St Bees Head and the mouth of the Ellen. While the sites south of St Bees were well placed to exploit the resources provided by a coastal location, access to the shore cannot have been so simple for the sites on St Bees Head where the cliffs are substantial. However, the total absence of recorded sites in the hinterland mitigates against the strategy that depended heavily on ungulate populations in the summer months. The equipment is consistent with the exploitation of shoreline resources. We should picture these communities, like those at Barnsalloch in Wigtownshire on the north coast of the Solway, utilizing gathering techniques that relied more upon the wicker fish-trap than on the stabbing spear (Nickson and McDonald 1956; Cherry 1969; Cormack 1970).

On the east side of the Pennines, a similar subsistence strategy seems to have attracted communities to the Bamburgh area. The area offered all the normal resources associated with the coast, with some quite distinct local advantages, which in this case include reasonably simple access to the sea. The presence of Holy Island gave protection to a wide area of shallow coastal waters, and Budle Bay itself provided an extensive inland salt-water resource from which late mesolithic man might expect to extract a supply of water-fowl, plants, fish and crustaceans. In addition, the offshore resource of the Farne Islands probably then as now provided a sanctuary for thousands of nesting sea-birds and a seal community, both of which may have been culled in season by man. We should be in no doubt that these coastal communities were able to cross at least inshore waters, and may, like the Indians of north-west America have been equipped for short sea voyages. At Morton in Fife, the bones of three- or four-year-old codfish were discovered in quantities that suggest that these formed a regularly exploited food resource, and this must have necessitated fishing activities off shore. Although none of those so far discovered have been dated to this period, it is not unlikely that dug-out canoes were utilized by mesolithic man, for offshore gathering activities and fishing. Alternatively, boats of skin or leather on a wickerwork frame might have been used.

A less dramatic, but still perennial series of resources was probably available along the coast of south Northumberland and Durham, with most communities normally resident on the coastal littoral for most of the year (cf. the situation in Ulster; Woodman 1973–74). The communities that exploited the Newbiggin-by-the-Sea area in Northumberland could count on the normal perennial resources of the coast, and were well placed to exploit seasonal salmon runs into the Wansbeck and the lesser streams to the north. A single site close to Hartburn in the Wansbeck valley may represent a second seasonal location of the same group, located so as to maximize the potential resource of the shallow river closer to the spawning grounds, and similar sites exist on the rivers Till and Coquet, possibly the summer camps of groups normally based close to Bamburgh. The greater density of sites along the coast of Durham may represent the perennial exploitation of coastal resources, but the significant number of sites in the middle reaches of the river Wear and to a lesser extent the Tyne and the Upper Tees, may represent regular seasonal migrations from winter quarters on the shore to summer valley sites, where groups could rely upon the regularity of the spawning grounds as a food source, as well as exploit a wide variety of woodland and river-bank resources, both animal and vegetable, that would have been less easy to obtain on the coast, where resources may have been exhausted by seasonal occupation. A comparable, coast-oriented survival strategy appears typical of the Isle of Man (Woodman 1978).

The northern counties do appear to offer a contrast with the transhumance hunting strategies adopted in Yorkshire. The presence of mesolithic sites in the inland valleys suggests comparatively regular sorties to intercept the annual run of salmon and trout to their spawning grounds, but only the small scatter of sites well above 305 m recorded in Upper Weardale implies a summer hunting strategy centred on the upland grazing territories of deer and aurochs. These upland activities appear to dwindle both west and east of Co. Durham, with a handful of sites representing either river-valley or upland exploitation in Northumberland and none at all in Lakeland where parallels with western Scotland appear more apt. Admittedly, any direct comparison with the south of Scotland suggests that numerically mesolithic sites are badly under-represented in the northern counties (e.g. Mulholland 1970), but even there, true upland sites are scarce.

There is little evidence that man had a direct impact upon his environment in the northern counties before about 3500 bc. In contrast, on the North York Moors and southern Pennines recent intensive research has revealed a direct association between fire, mesolithic implements and temporary or permanent disafforestation (Dimbleby 1962; Smith 1970; Simmons 1975a, b; Jacobi, Tallis and Mellars 1976). In Upper Teesdale, Turner noted major environmental changes as the increasing oceanity and wetness took effect from about 5000 bc, leading to podzolization, the spread of alder and a stimulus to the development of peat. Within this picture of a deteriorating environment, there appeared to be no evidence that man had significantly affected the process (Turner 1978). In the Lake District, there is evidence in some of the numerous pollen diagrams for significant if short-lived disafforestation possibly associated with human activity in the middle of the fourth millennium, while in the Solway plain, the first evidence for a decline in elm occurred at 3390 bc (Pennington 1970). These episodes will be elaborated in Chapter 2.

If these land-management strategies were in use on the North York Moors, then it is inconceivable that the late mesolithic population of south Durham, at least, were unaware of them. If they were not applied in Upper Teesdale, then we are tempted to look to other factors to explain this rather surprising contrast. The most obvious reason would be a lower human population density in the northern counties than in Yorkshire, and the presence of communities which had adopted subsistence strategies in which exploitation of the high uplands above and close to the tree-line was unimportant. One of the resources which has often been quoted as one that is made more abundant by occasional burning is the supply of hazel-nuts. Certainly the remains of hazel-nuts have come from a site in Durham (Filpoke Beacon) and one in Fife (Morton), Scotland. In neither case is it likely that the source of these deposits lay near the upland tree-line. In general, the absence of upland sites implies that upland exploitation of vegetable or animal resources were not a regular part of the annual cycle of the mesolithic communities of northern England. Only further research can establish the real extent of upland activity.

Along the coast, there is little evidence for disafforestation. Axes were present, particularly in the early mesolithic, but they are scarce in comparison to the tranchet axe distribution of southern Britain (Wymer 1977), and there is no demonstrable connection between the axe from the Durham coastal forest beds, for example, and the peat that developed above it (Trechmann 1947– 49). Local use of fire is suggested at Spindleston (Buckley 1922) by the number of flints apparently subjected to burning and the presence of abundant char- coal, but this is reliable evidence at the present stage only for the 'domestic' use of fire. At Eskmeals, excavations in 1983 located quantities of timber thought to derive from quite substantial structures of the fourth millennium, probably constructed on platforms, but detailed dating is awaited (*C & W Newsletter*, 2, 1984). Such timber work at least implies an interest in forestry and a capacity for carpentry, but it may be that this belongs in a slightly later context.

Relying on the information currently available, there seems little reason to assume any great environmental impact by human activity in the mesolithic. While subtle changes may have resulted from the indiscriminate culling of preferred or vulnerable species, the archaeological record is still inadequate to detect changes at this level.

Hunting and gathering communities did exploit a selection of the re- sources of the northern counties in the mesolithic, but their activity was only significant after the North and Irish Sea basins had flooded, and their presence may even have been due to their displacement from those preferred lowlands. They appear to have adopted a pragmatic range of survival strategies, specifi- cally relating to the available resource pattern. The early deer-hunting style of economy found in Yorkshire may have spread into Durham, but it is likely that most of the activity so far located was associated with a settlement and resource utilization that concentrated upon coastal and estuarine locations. These provided a range of resources which were comparatively predictable, and able to support small human communities throughout the year, though probably not at any one specific site. The choice of location suggests a reliance on shellfish and sea-fish, with the addition of water-fowl and sea-birds, and off the east coast in particular, water-mammals.

In winter, the likely pattern of seasonal migrations of deer and aurochs probably resulted in the congregation of substantial stocks of ungulates in the coastal plains and major valleys, and this may have provided the coastal populations with an important winter resource. The microlithic content of tool assemblages may in part reflect this seasonal activity, but upland sites which might imply the summer hunting of these herds are scarce in Durham, more scarce in Northumberland and almost totally unrepresented in Cumbria and the Isle of Man (Woodman 1978). More common are sites in the eastern river valleys, and these may imply summer fishing activities.

29

On the whole the northern counties and south-east Scotland appear to have been a transitional area, over which the intensive exploitation of the ungulate populations, which seems to have been typical of Yorkshire, gave way to the coastal economics typical of western Scotland. This transitional area was probably typified by a population level lower than that of the southern Pennines and associated lowlands, probably due to the poorer climatic (and therefore habitative) conditions of the North, and to a general inaccessibility that seems particularly apparent west of the Pennines. This smaller population may have had a wider range of choices of subsistence strategies available, particularly in the summer, than their southern neighbours, and the exercise of this option enabled most communities to spend the bulk of their time in the relatively resource-rich coastal areas, leaving the bulk of the more strenuous activities associated with the hunting of upland summer ungulate populations to their natural competitor, the wolf.

Notes

1. Taylor *et al.* (1971) provides the basis for this summary. King (1976) is a useful guide. My thanks to Paul Selden, who read an early draft of this section.

2. Any survey of this area must rely on the guidance of Pennington (1970, 1975), particularly in the interpretation of the major pollen diagrams dated by comparative rather than by absolute criteria. See also Godwin, Walker and Willis (1957), and in general Godwin (1975).

3. Pearson (1960). More detailed work with carbon-14 dating is now available: Turner and Kershaw (1973); Bartley, Chambers and Hart-Jones (1976), but these are dependent on peat development and consequently are largely post-mesolithic in inception.

4. For St Bees Head and Eskmeals see Cherry (1963, 1967, 1969), and Bonsall (1981). For Walney Island see Barnes and Hobbs (1950). Microliths were found in Furness but it was suggested these derived from the use of seaweed fertilizer from Walney; Barnes and Hobbs (1951). Recent fieldwork by Jim Cherry has identified microliths on the limestone fells of the Kirkby Stephen area. My thanks to Terry Cane who read an early draft of this section.

Chapter 2

The Food-Producing Economies 4000–2000 bc

Ecological Change [1]

By 4000 bc Britain's climate had reached the warmest levels yet attained during the current interglacial, with mean air temperatures as much as 4 °C higher than modern times. The temperature then dropped gradually during the fourth millennium to about + 2°C at the end, but by this stage the downward curve was steepening, and by the mid third millennium temperatures were no higher than at present. At that level they probably remained relatively constant into the second millennium, despite minor, periodic oscillations. Associated with this comparatively warm phase was a high level of precipitation. Rainfall had been rising steadily through the sixth and fifth millennia, and probably peaked about 4000 bc, subsequently falling until by the last quarter of the third millennium rainfall was no higher than today. At its greatest, the level was in the order of 5–10 per cent higher than at present.

This general climatic picture would have been intensified in the northern counties, particularly in the Lake District and on the Pennines. The dominant west winds must have increased the oceanity of particularly the Cumbrian seaboard, and the high ground must have attracted a weather pattern markedly cloudier, wetter and windier than the north-eastern lowlands.

These climatic conditions suited deciduous forest. No discernible human manipulation of the ecological balance had occurred in the fifth millennium, so that a 'natural' development of forest cover had occurred, reaching a 'vegetational optimum' within the 1,000 years centred on 4000 bc. The forest cover was not static, in that the tree-line continued to climb throughout the fourth millennium and there were changes in the distribution of species within the forest. However, deciduous tree cover was stable, and occupied and protected the brown earths. The pollen evidence suggests that oak, alder and elm dominated the lowlands, valleys and mountain slopes up to 760 m in Lakeland, but rather less on the Pennines. The increasing drainage flooded many bogs in the fourth millennium. Elm may have retreated to the base-rich better-drained slopes of the foothills, and there are signs that the soil that had

31

been protected by deciduous tree cover from excessive leaching, etc. was in some areas at least becoming less resilient to the erosive and podzolic properties of the increased rainfall. The upper forest close to the tree-line was occupied predominantly by colonizer species. In Lakeland the forest fringe seems to have been dominated by pine and birch, but excessive wetness on the Pennines seems to have led to a lower tree-line, and the failure of pine even on the limestone areas of the Upper Tees valley, where forest cover was very open and tree pollen comprised only 30–50 per cent of the total (Turner *et al.* 1973).

Above the tree-line, species typical of tundra vegetation retained a precarious existence in an open shrub-, herb- and grass-dominated landscape, but increasing rainfall was already converting extensive poorly drained areas to peat bog.

Blanket, mixed deciduous forest was the hallmark of a high proportion of the area in the fourth millennium. Locally, geological differences, topography and exposure favoured the dominance of specific species, but oak was probably the most important component, followed by alder, with elm and particularly lime occupying more specialist niches. Large tracts of open land occurred only at a high altitude. In the lowlands, open areas might temporarily be created by the fall of a forest tree, and in these circumstances primary colonizers, hazel, *Rumex*, birch, etc. were able to establish a short-lived presence. Otherwise, lowland open space was restricted to specialist environments, such as dune complexes, raised beaches and other coastal, riverine or estuarine locations.

There are signs that the conditions that had enabled deciduous forest to attain a dominant position were worsening. The flooding of peat bogs in Upper Teasdale and at Beamish (Turner and Kershaw 1973) is indicative of a progressive failure of the forest to regulate drainage successfully. The water-table rose, and surface erosion and podzolization probably began for the first time to have a serious impact on the brown soils and mars of the forest. Increasingly virulent surface runoff began to deposit growing quantities of organic and inorganic material in the lake sediments. By late in the fourth millennium, the erosive process had reached the stage whereby forest regeneration in vulnerable areas may have been jeopardized (Pennington 1975: 75).

During the fourth millennium occurred the first anthropogenic disturbances in the forest cover. By far the greatest evidence for clearance comes in the last two centuries of the millennium, and is synchronous or near-synchronous with the 'elm decline'. However, earlier less substantial clearance episodes occurred, so far traced exclusively on the west of the Pennines, and particularly in south-west Cumbria. At Blea Tarn there was recorded a short-lived decline in the pollen of birch, pine and elm during the second quarter of the millennium (Pennington 1975: 76). At Ehenside Tarn a series of forest clearance episodes affected the oak and elm well before the elm decline, and at Williamson's Moss, Eskmeals, there were fluctuations in the pollen of oak and elm against birch –

the primary colonizer – in the middle of the millennium. At Barfield Tarn similar minor clearance episodes were recorded, dated well before the elm decline, beginning as early as *c.* 3700 bc.

These episodes are characterized by their temporary and small-scale nature. There is no marked increase in grass or herb pollen, and in no case was there found any charcoal in association, as might have been expected if fire was the means of clearance. Despite a superficial resemblance, there are important differences between these clearances and the type of short-lived clearances of upland, marginal forest by hunter–gatherer communities that was common in North Yorkshire and on the southern Pennines (see p. 28). We should, therefore, question the assumption of the palaeobotanists that local mesolithic communities were responsible for these clearances.

The elm decline can be documented in all areas of the northern counties between *c.* 3200 and 2900 bc, largely clustering around *c.* 3100 bc. In some, but not all, locations, this phenomenon was accompanied by evidence of a significant increase in clearance activity. The cause of the permanent decline in elm pollen (which is both proportional and absolute) is still not fully resolved, even though the event occurs so widely within such a short space of time that it is used as diagnostic of the end of pollen zone VIIa and the beginning of VIIb. When it was first detected, it was assumed that natural causes were responsible, and current experience would lead us to disease as an obvious possibility. However, the common accompaniment of anthropogenic forest disturbance has encouraged the hypothesis that the elm decline was also due to human activity (see discussion in Simmons and Tooley 1981: 152). The suggestion was made that the collection of the branches and leaves of the elm for use as animal fodder brought about a substantial loss, initially of the flowering parts of the tree, but eventually of the species. The finding of bundles of elm twigs and leaves in the Swiss lake villages has tended to support this attractive possibility, and anthropogenic causation has now received some general support. However, it is only one factor in a complicated balance of human and climatic determinants (Smith 1970: 90). It is possible that a short cold spell initiated a decline in the vulnerable elm population which then failed to respond to improved climatic conditions because of human disturbance of vulnerable soil resources. If the elm was intermingled with other forest trees, then clearance cannot have been the cause of this selective decline, except where there is a comparable decline in other forest species. In the northern counties it is unsafe to assume that anthropogenic factors lay behind the late fourth millennium decline in elm pollen. Only where there are other signs of human activity in the pollen spectrum does it seem likely that there was a real connection.

If we are to isolate the elm decline from other signs of human clearance, then there is currently less evidence for such activity east of the Pennines before the second millennium bc. For example, at Fellend Moss in the south-west of Northumberland, the elm decline was present, but no evidence of clearance was detected until a millennium and a half later (Davies and Turner 1979). In Durham there were only infrequent and small-scale clearance episodes close to the elm decline (Bartley, Chambers and Hart-Jones 1976), and this was concentrated on the limestone areas, although early clearance occurred at Morden Carr as early as *c.* 3355 bc, and at Wheelhead Moss *c.* 3270 bc. At the same time a decline in *Tilia* (lime) occurred, suggesting the cause might be selective clearance of base-rich soils, and species associated with disturbance occurred in small and temporary episodes in the lowlands. Over much of the eastern counties, however, there are few signs of forest disturbance in the late fourth or early third millennia.

By contrast, the evidence for clearance in coastal Cumbria is widespread and unmistakable. To some extent this may be due to the far greater research effort that has given Cumbria the best-understood vegetational history in the British Isles, but there are signs that the contrast is more real than imagined. Diagrams from the coastal plain demonstrate a significant upturn in clearance activity synchronous with, or marginally post-dating the elm decline. The decline in elm pollen was accompanied, or immediately followed, by an absolute decline in the pollen of oak. A synchronous event was the first major rise in the pollen of species of grass and heliophilous herbs. For the first time the pollen of species associated with broken ground like *Plantago lanceolata* occurred in diagrams over a wide area, and in a few diagrams, pollen of domesticated grain crops was detected. Charcoal has commonly been found in sediments at this level, and there is widespread evidence for a rapid increase in the speed of sediment deposition and accumulation in the coastal lakes and tarns. This accumulation rate increased within a few centuries to ten or twenty times its level before the elm decline, and was almost certainly the result of increased runoff and erosion due to deforestation. Where cultivation occurred this situation can only have been aggravated. At the same time, significant changes occurred that suggest alterations in the material being deposited. The rise in the proportion of inorganic material represents the growing gap that developed between the creation of organic soil and the increasing erosive force of the less well-regulated rainfall (Mackereth 1966).

The lowland clearances occurred in areas of oak and elm forest, and were predominantly in favour of herbaceous grazing. Over a period of time, the grazing appears to have suffered as inedible ferns and unpalatable weeds invaded, and this led to abandonment in many cases, allowing forest to regenerate, unless new activity or fundamental changes in the environment intervened. Clearances seem to have been maintained for variable periods, with some being retained with very little evidence of abandonment throughout the period (e.g. Ehenside Tarn) and others allowed to fall into disuse after two or more centuries (e.g. Bowness Common). The general pattern was for the most substantial and long-lived clearance to occur on the coastal borders of southern and south-western Cumbria, and lesser, later clearances in the north and east, particularly away from the coast.

Clearance is not thought to have occurred in the Lake District valleys at this early date and the elm decline seems to have been isolated in many areas from more conclusive evidence of human activity. Even so, there are some signs that anthropogenic factors were present. The diagram from the old north basin of Thirlmere (Pennington 1970: 75) shows a proportionate decline in oak synchronous with the elm decline and a consequent rise in birch, and temporary oscillations of these species recurred in the third millennium. The first occurrence of *Plantago lanceolata* was at the elm decline, and there was a rise in the proportion of grass pollen.

In only one area of the uplands is there significant evidence for clearance activity before 2000 bc. This is in the Langdale Fells of southern central lakeland. Here there occurred an absolute decrease in the pollen of birch and pine, and for the first time the widespread deposition of charcoal in tarn sediments suggests the use of fire in clearance. Weeds of clearance occurred and there was a substantial extension of the upland grasslands. By the end of the third millennium the total deforestation of these uplands was imminent, and the consequent environmental changes radically exacerbated any natural deterioration of the soils that had already occurred. The degenerative changes were permanent, and created circumstances in which reforestation could not occur, and peat bogs eventually developed on high ground (e.g. Blea Tarn; Pennington 1975: 78–79). As Pennington (1975: 85) has said, 'in this way began man's attack on the accumulated reserves of fertility present in the soils of the primary forest of the Highland Zone in Northern Britain.' These reserves proved alarmingly frail. The Langdale Fells have an exceptional vegetational history. Elsewhere, even in south-west Cumbria the uplands seem to have survived relatively unscathed the beginnings of pastoral and agricultural activity in the lowland zone.

Although signs of human activity persisted throughout the third millennium at most sites in the lowlands of Cumbria, there do appear to have been quantitative fluctuations. For example, the clearance activity at Barfield Tarn can be traced from *c.* 3390 bc, and incorporated evidence of cereal cultivation, which probably caused the rapid deposition of clay in the tarn. In the mid third millennium, activity slackened, but reforestation was never complete, and an even more vigorous clearance episode began late in the millennium which eventually led to permanent deforestation. At Ehenside Tarn a similar pattern emerges. Occupation seems to have been unbroken although the environmental impact lessened in the middle of the millennium. Again, renewed, vigorous clearance occurred about 2000 bc. At Blea Tarn, in the Langdales, on the other hand, clearance peaked in the mid millennium. Further impetus at the end was associated with evidence of fire, and eventually resulted in the precocious expansion of peat. An identical episode was dated at Red Tarn Moss to *c.* 1940 bc, and on the Solway lowlands there is further evidence for a rapid deforestation about 2000 bc on an unprecedented scale (Walker 1966).

The Food Producers

Origins

Human communities were resident in northern England in the fourth and third millennia bc and developed a range of strategies which enabled them to tap the resources available to them in novel ways and to a novel extent. The management techniques and equipment that evolved enabled them to make a far greater impact on the natural environment than their predecessors had achieved. Various aspects of this impact were unintentional, but this in no way detracts from the achievement.

The characteristic economic strategies of the period were the adoption of pastoralism and somewhat later, agriculture, both of which have left an impact on the palaeobotanical record. These strategies supplanted hunting and gathering as the major means of obtaining sufficient food to support the community, and had important repercussions for the social and economic structure of the population, at which we can often do little more than guess. At the same time, a novel range of artefacts developed in association with the new strategies.

So distinct have seemed these novel 'neolithic' cultures from the mesolithic communities of the fifth millennium, that it has long been assumed that their appearance in Britain was the result of the import of a full-grown material and ideological culture, and, therefore, of substantial immigration. The continental source of such immigrants has been sought from Scandinavia to the Iberian peninsula, but most commentators are prepared to accept the Rhineland and the Low Countries as the source (Piggott 1954; Whittle 1977). In general terms, immigration as an explanation of culture change is currently unpopular, and is no longer accepted as the principal cause of phenomena such as the beaker 'culture' of the early second millennium (Clark 1966). It has, however, been retained as an explanation of the 'neolithic revolution' in Britain, because of the totality of the cultural changes and the absence of any archaeological evidence for communities in transition. Even so, it is now accepted that acculturation may have been a significant factor in the spread of neolithic culture in continental Europe (de Laet 1976), and some of the assumptions are now being challenged for Britain (Ashbee 1982). It is possible that we are about to see a major shift away from some of the thinking on this subject (e.g. Case 1969).

In the northern counties of England, immigration is a less than satisfactory explanation of neolithic activity. If, as Case argued, small leather boats were used, crossing the North Sea seems an unlikely route for migration, when the coastline of south-east England could be seen from adjacent areas of the Continent. The absence of any pre-elm decline clearance episodes along the north-east coast safely rules out this possibility. The migration theory is dependent, therefore, on a diffusion model, with primary colonization occurring in southern coastal England, and subsequent expansion via coastal movements into the remainder of Britain. Piggott assumed a comparatively late arrival of neolithic people in the North and West, where he envisaged they may have been strongly reinforced by indigenous mesolithic populations, and he referred to these as 'secondary neolithic' and treated them as derivatives of the well-defined southern culture for which the type-site lay on Windmill Hill. The increasing availability of carbon-14 dates in the 1950s and 1960s has led to a reappraisal of these assumptions.

The earliest carbon date for an unequivocally neolithic occupation site comes from Ballynagilly, Co. Tyrone in Ireland (3795 ± 90 bc). Although there are dates in lowland England in the second half of the fourth millennium, the type-site of Windmill Hill has been dated no earlier than the mid third millennium bc. Other important areas facing the Continent, such as East Anglia, lack dates any earlier than this. In the current state of knowledge immigration is an unsatisfactory explanation of the neolithic activity in lowland Cumbria in the fourth millennium bc, although it cannot be ruled out and it is quite conceivable that future research will vindicate this long-established hypothesis. At present, however, a more coherent and less contrived case can be made for acculturation than for substantial immigration.

Late hunter–gatherer communities have only been detected in Cumbria along the coast from St Bees Head to Walney Island. This distribution is exactly shared by those pollen diagrams which record pre-elm decline manipulation of the vegetation, with the one exception of Blea Tarn in the Langdales, discussed below. At Ehenside Tarn, at Storrs Moss, at Eskmeals and at Barfield Tarn there is evidence for synchronous oscillations in the deposition of oak and elm pollen which were small in scale and temporary. The impact upon the two species suggests that anthropogenic clearance was the cause. The absence of charcoal implies the use of axes in the physical labour involved, and the evidence is consistent with the creation of small open spaces to provide pasture for domesticated livestock. It is possible that clearances of this type could have been made by hunter–gatherer communities in order to encourage and manipulate stocks of wild ungulates, but several factors mitigate against this. Upland, not lowland, clearance is the hallmark of mesolithic communities on the Pennines, and the preferred method seems to have been by fire. Clearances of this type in the lowlands would be of dubious value to a hunting strategy, since the summer herbage would have coincided with the absence of most ungulates in the upland pastures. The use of axes is unproven, but is at least a possibility, and tree-felling on this scale is inconsistent with established strategies in the British mesolithic without the use of fire. The balance of the evidence leans towards a neolithic interpretation, if only in the sense of communities practising limited pastoralism.

The exceptional case is that of Blea Tarn, at well above the 305 m

Plate 2.1   The scree at Pike of Stickle, Langdale (Cumb.). At this site Neolithic communities chose suitable fragments and shaped them roughly, using hammer-stones, on the massive anvil blocks that still stand amid the scree.

contour, immediately south of the Langdales, which has provided evidence of human interference with the vegetation in the second quarter of the fourth millennium (Pennington 1975: 76). A temporary drop occurred in the deposition of the pollen of birch, pine and elm, and responsibility has been placed on the mesolithic community. However, although hunter–gatherer activity could easily explain the burning of the upland forest margins, it is unlikely to have been responsible for a series of small-scale clearance episodes which appear to have been entirely disassociated from burning, and which affected the elm, which, although it was probably present in the upper valleys, cannot be described as a species typical of the upland forest margins. Again, pastoralists are more likely to have had this impact upon the vegetation than hunting communities, and the selective drop in elm may have been due to its use as a fodder crop.

The clearance episodes in the Langdale area are unlikely to be the product of perennial occupation by human communities, otherwise we would expect to find evidence for occupation elsewhere in the uplands. Langdale is exceptional, and the likeliest origin of these vegetational changes lies in the early development of a transhumance strategy by which communities exploited a territory containing a variety of ecozones from the coast to the uplands. A summer removal of cattle from the lowlands to the uplands only maintained the migratory habits of wild ungulate populations, and drew heavily upon the experience of mesolithic communities on the Pennines and the adjacent low ground. In fact, a hunter–gatherer community that adopted a pastoralist strategy may well have retained the transhumance migratory pattern normal to that animal without even considering possible alternatives.

There is, however, one more resource at Langdale that must have attracted any community engaged in coastal forest clearance, and that is the volcanic tuffs which provided the raw material for tree-felling equipment. The coincidence of early- and mid-fourth-millennium clearance from the coastal plain and from Langdale, exclusive of any other upland area, implies an early recourse to this raw material in order to extend the available range of lithic equipment to encompass the new importance of tree-felling (see p. 54). Beach pebbles are unlikely to have provided an adequate range and number of suitable artefacts, and it is difficult to accept the possibility of lowland clearance before the exploitation of the axe 'factories' had begun. While recognizing this implies an earlier starting date than has hitherto been argued, the suggestion is at least consistent with other evidence of early activity in the area which is otherwise difficult to explain.

At present it is impossible to say with any certainty whether the pastoralists of the fourth millennium were derived from immigrant communities, or from indigenous mesolithic groups. While admitting the very real possibility of the former, it is at least instructive to construct a hypothetical model for the latter, if only to allow later criticism to destroy it.

The mesolithic communities present in the Eskmeals area and elsewhere in the first half of the fifth millennium were exploiting a complex habitat that was rich in resources (Bonsall 1981). These resources were eroded by changes in sea-level which began *c.* 4400–4300 bc and which may have diminished the supply of a variety of estuarine food sources. A synchronous increase in rainfall led to a rise in the water-table with maximum effect along the Cumbrian west coast, and led to a substantial increase in wetlands and the spread of alder. One response of such a community in these circumstances may have been the domestication of locally available species of ungulate (probably the aurochs) in order to ensure the predictability of the food supply. The intellectual stimulus might have come from contact with pastoralists elsewhere, perhaps in Ireland, during the type of fishing trips after cod which were clearly customary in the North Sea (Coles 1971). Such cross-cultural contact, by accident or design, is more likely than episodes involving immigration with all the implications that these entail, and could easily have provided indigenous communities with domesticated strains of livestock and seed grain for the eventual development of cereal cultivation. It is at least arguable that coastal mesolithic communities had far greater need for expertise in boat construction and use than agriculturalists exploiting inland resources and operating within a culture which had been developed in continental Europe, and, therefore, it is more likely that seafarers among mesolithic communities than among neolithic groups brought agricultural strategies to northern England.

Recent experiments in the domestication of wild ungulates have proved surprisingly successful and easy, and have opened a series of doubts concerning existing models for neolithic immigration. Small-scale clearance of better-drained lowland woodland would have been an optimum strategy in this respect, designed to provide rich grazing and so localize ungulate populations and accustom them to contact with human communities. If domesticated ungulates were allowed to maintain a seasonal transhumance pattern, the presence of herders in the uplands is by far the easiest explanation of the discovery and initial use of the Langdale volcanic tuffs as a tool resource, and recognition of this resource would explain local clearance in the Langdales as herders encouraged their charges to concentrate in areas in which another important resource was available. The early discovery of Langdale tuffs and of their potential as a raw material is more likely to have been due to indigenous mesolithic activity than to immigrant coastal communities. It was the mesolithic communities who had recognized the value of volcanic tuffs for the manufacture of tools in the fifth millennium, probably using beach pebbles as the raw material (Bonsall 1981). The technological leap to the manufacture of axes is less than has been suggested.

If the local mesolithic population adopted one of the survival strategies which is a hallmark of neolithic communities, various otherwise inconsistent factors fall into place. For example, it is difficult otherwise to justify the extent of continuity in the distribution of mesolithic communities and early clearance episodes. It is difficult to see that south-west Cumbria enjoyed advantages such as would have attracted early immigrant communities in the fourth millennium – in fact, rather the reverse. It is the increasing disadvantages of the habitat which are likely to have lain behind changes in strategies. The incidence of reuse of specific sites by successive mesolithic and neolithic cultural groups is suspiciously high in the northern counties. At most the nature of the evidence is such that the chronological relationship between artefacts is unknown, but artefacts diagnostic of both cultures have come from sites in Weardale, from Riding Mill in the Lower Tyne valley, and from Walney Island and other coastal locations in south-west Cumbria. The possibility must exist that these sites were occupied by communities in a transitional phase of development.

Furthermore, this model is a highly adaptable one, which can accommodate the possibility, for example, that successive abandonment of pastoralism as a strategy may have occurred without total abandonments of the area. It can also accommodate the non-synchronous appearance of such a strategy around the coast, with dates as early as *c.* 3700 bc at Barfield Tarn, but elsewhere rather later. The absence of early clearance activity on the north-east coast is acceptable, since the effects of increasing rainfall were here far less, and the sea transgression that was at its greatest in the Irish Sea was, in Hartlepool Bay, for example, less, and of shorter duration. Any consequent experimentation with pastoralism would naturally have been less vigorously pursued and harder to detect.

Lastly, acculturation has advantages over the immigration model in that the translation and adoption of particular strategies or elements from one culture to another are comprehensible. If immigrant communities indirectly derived from continental Europe were responsible for the small-scale clearance activity on the Cumbrian coast we should expect to find other traces of a new cultural group. There are none. No cultivation of cereals seems to predate the elm decline. There are no novel artefacts with imported antecedents, no new structural traditions whether sepulchral or occupational, no pottery. If immigrants were mainly responsible, they were remarkably conservative in their choice of site location and crept like ghosts into this new land. We should not be tied by old theories where the balance of evidence seems to open new possibilities of gradual development via a process of acculturation and local adaptability to a changing environment.

The Developing Community

Whatever the origins of the small-scale pastoralism of the early mid fourth millennium, there occurred a significant change in pace synchronous with the elm decline. East of the Pennines evidence of clearance activity is at its slightest and enjoys only a narrow distribution, presently detected only on the base-rich Magnesian Limestone of north-east Durham and the neighbouring portion of Tyne and Wear, where pastoralism without cultivation was present. In upland Durham no evidence of clearance was associated with the elm decline which may, therefore, have resulted from natural soil pauperization. Few of the Northumberland bogs so far examined have provided evidence for even temporary clearance before the second millennium bc, although other factors do point to some activity in the third millennium, and future pollen analysis is likely to date earlier episodes in specific areas. Only in Cumbria is there widespread evidence for human activity which begins characteristically at, or immediately after, the elm decline. Absolute diagrams have demonstrated a real drop in the quantity of tree pollen, associated with an influx of primary colonizers, grass and herbs. At only a minority of sites does cereal pollen begin to be present as early as the elm decline, but these are concentrated along the south-west coast. At Barfield Tarn the deposition of pink clay was probably caused by soil erosion resulting from cultivation of the boulder clays around the tarn and was stratigraphically associated with the primary elm decline (*c.* 3070 bc), and the second appearance of *Plantago lanceolata*, *Rumex*, grasses, cereals and *Pteridium* (Pennington 1970). At the same time a relative increase in oak pollen was beginning, in inverse proportions to changes in the percentage of birch pollen. At Ehenside Tarn, the high forest trees were felled or defoliated, hazel and birch enjoyed a temporary resurgence before being replaced by grasses and herbs in the beginning of a lengthy period of human activity which maintained clearance in the area for over 700 years (Walker 1966). Comparable activity has been demonstrated on the Solway mosses and elsewhere along the coastal plain.

The nature and distribution of the evidence leaves little doubt that the major vegetational changes were derived from human activity, and this received confirmation when a decline in oak woodland immediately after the elm decline was recorded at Williamson's Moss, Eskmeals, in direct association with a rough-out axe (Pennington 1975: 84). The new wave of activity is characterized by the use of fire at some stage in the clearance process in both lowland and upland locations, and by the extension of the open area available for pasture. Cereal cultivation is attested, but remained small in scale and only intermittently detectable throughout the third millennium in a minority of pollen diagrams, and it is unlikely that cultivation was a serious rival to pastoralism as a food source in this traditionally pastoral area. Where cultivation did take place, it is possible that a system of shifting agriculture was in use, but this is not proven. Such a system would have enabled communities to benefit from the high but short-lived fertility of newly cleared forest in which the firing of the underbrush had raised the level of nutrients artificially (see discussion, Simmons and Tooley 1981: 155). Such episodes have been characterized by the term *landnam* and may have been widespread after the elm decline [2]. Around the head of Morecambe Bay a primary elm decline was distinguished from the *landnam* phase which followed it, when the decline in elm pollen steepened and was associated with weeds typical of clearance activity, and some local forest regeneration (Oldfield 1963). Further episodes followed, the first probably for pasture but the second betraying evidence of cereal cultivation, possibly about 2000 bc. However, there are considerable problems involved in dating these changes, and most *landnam*-type clearances seem to have lasted not for decades but for centuries.

It is becoming increasingly clear that the amount of agricultural activity in the third millennium has been under-represented. Evidence is only available under exceptional circumstances, but traces beneath long barrows in Yorkshire and elsewhere implies plough cultivation, and, in all instances, the erection of monuments occurred in cleared areas (e.g. Manby 1976; Piggott 1972).

Although it seems likely that most clearance was associated with pastoral activity, there is no direct evidence in the North for the species of livestock involved. With the exception of the elk, the wild ungulates of the mesolithic period survived the neolithic, presumably occupying the remaining, immense tracts of untouched forest. It is quite possible that experiments in the domestication of various species were made, but certainly by the mid third millennium domesticated livestock derived from imported stock seem to have reached a dominant position, at least in southern England. These included the relatively small domesticated breed of cattle, distinguished from aurochs on the criteria of size, and the non-indigenous sheep and goats that form a minority of faunal remains. In the South and in Yorkshire, pigs were an important resource, although they are unlikely to have been associated with intentional clearance (Simmons and Tooley 1981: 197).

The human population that was involved in this activity was still a very small one, but there are signs that a significant increase was taking place *c.* 3200–2800 bc. However, this population has left such limited archaeological evidence for its presence that any assessment of the material and intellectual culture can only be of an interim nature. An unrepresentative range of equipment has survived, and a scatter of sepulchral remains, but occupation sites are few and poorly defined.

Where occupation sites have been located, they generally lie in a narrow range of habitats, on the coast, or on or close to the shores of inland water and rivers. There is a marked similarity between the sites chosen by neolithic and mesolithic communities, and the incidence of use of the same localities or even the same sites is remarkable. The best-known settlements are those at Ehenside Tarn. The tarn was drained for agricultural purposes in 1869, and much of the associated import of topsoil had already occurred when the discovery of 'celts' stimulated an unusually detailed but brief, professional investigation. Three to six hearths were located on the edges of the old tarn, in some case associated with artefacts. Within the tarn a 'forest bed' was identified, made of leaves, branches and small trunks of oak and beech, and about 1 m thick, resting on a mass of vegetable matter of comparable thickness which overlay the sphagnum bog. The forest bed may have been a lakeside platform on the Swiss analogy, and may have had an occupation function. There are also close parallels between this and the nearby platforms of a supposed late mesolithic date found at Eskmeals in 1983. Charred wood from one of the hearths was dated to *c*. 3014 bc, but a stake from the 'platform' gave a date of *c*. 2175–2102 bc. Axes of Langdale tuff were found, some of which were finished but others still unpolished, and sandstone and gritstone rubbers found in the forest bed were probably used in the finishing process. A thick oval flag of New Red Sandstone with a greenstone rubber has been interpreted as a saucer-quern and may have been used in the preparation of cereals. Pottery from the shore was of the wide rounded-bottom type, with parallels in the Lyles Hill and Peterborough wares (Piggott 1954).

The evidence for occupation on the lakesides and possibly on a platform seems well established, but the specific nature of the site is obscure, and there is no evidence of structures. The presence of axe-heads apparently undergoing finishing and polishing implies occupation at least for some part of the six months between September and March, and the palaeobotanical evidence suggests significant local clearance for pasture, with cereal cultivation developing late in the neolothic period, by which time perennial occupation may have been present. The picture of neolithic man cooking his evening meal on the lakeside and then paddling off to the relative security of lake platforms for the night is unlikely to be an accurate representation, particularly given that the carbon-14 dates for these two episodes lie almost a millennium apart. The 'platform' might have been a base for occupation, but it might equally well have been associated with some economic strategy, such as fishing, and this is supported by the range of wooden artefacts discovered. These make up a unique collection of organic equipment from a neolithic context, paralleled only in the Somerset Levels and in stray finds from elsewhere. Caution is called for, since a carbon-14 date from the wood of one of these implements gave a result in the mid second millennium bc, so that it is quite possible that the finds represent at least three separate occupation episodes in prehistory [3]. Even so, the presence of two axe-hafts (one with the axe *in situ*) implies that a part at least of this equipment belonged within an extended 'neolithic' context. One was a socketed section of beech-root, and the other a length of oakwood split, and then presumably tied, and there were additional fragments of two other hafts or clubs (see Fig. 2.2). Three clubs were also found, the most complete being of tapered beechwood 47 cm long, and another fragment was decorated with a finely executed lattice-work pattern incised upon it. Further implements included a fragment of a wooden bowl, and two strange objects with broken but apparently lengthy handles, equipped with prongs up to 25.5 cm long, which have been interpreted as fishing-spears, and a paddle with a 30.5 cm blade. There may have been a dug-out canoe found close by. If there was a dug-out canoe (and even if there was not, the paddle suggests a craft of some sort) this implies lake surface activity consistent with fishing and the collection of shellfish, etc. from the tarn. The 'fishing-spears' may have been a type of rake rather than a spear as such. A further example of a similarly hafted stone axe was dug from deep in peat on Solway Moss near Longtown in the nineteenth century (Evans 1897: 152).

On Walney Island a limited area of coastal sand has provided evidence for use (and probably occupation) in every millennium from the fifth to the first [4]. Rough-outs and waste fragments of Langdale tuff suggest the finishing of stone axes on the beach.

There are signs that extensive flint-chipping also took place, presumably utilizing local beach pebbles, but possibly also Irish flint. Pebble flint provided hollow scrapers, perhaps designed for smoothing arrowshafts, and lozenge-shaped, single-barbed and leaf-shaped arrowheads have all been found and at least one flake of Irish porcellanite. Hearths suggest occupation, and meat bones of ox and sheep (and possibly a dog skeleton) imply consumption, but it is impossible to be sure which episode these should be associated with. The balance of evidence so far discovered suggests an occupation date at earliest at the end of the third millennium, and quite possibly several centuries into the second, since 'beaker'-type pottery seems to have been associated with most of these finds. So far no trace of buildings has been found, and the nature and location of the site implies the exploitation of coastal resources, combined with limited contact with other communities in the Irish Sea basin, and artefact manufacture. The close parallel with the use of coastal resources in the late mesolithic hardly needs stating. It is, however, unclear whether this occupation was perennial or merely one part of an annual cycle of activity which involved a presence in the summer on the Langdale Fells.

At Storrs Moss, inland from Silverdale in what was until reorganization, north Lancashire, a comparable site on low ground was investigated in the 1960s, and produced evidence of relatively sophisticated timber joinery, possibly a split-plank constructional style (of Ballinagilly). Clearance had occurred, associated with an enigmatic lithic industry that predated the elm decline, and which Powell believed lay in an early-fourth-millennium context. However, the excavations appear to have narrowly missed the habitation site, which he concluded was on marginally higher and drier ground on the moss edge [5].

Elsewhere in lowland Cumbria, concentrations of finds of axe-heads imply clearance activity local to settlements [6]. Predictably these occur on the coastal plain, widely in Furness, but also in the vicinity of Drigg and Seascale, and around Allerby and Kirkbride north of Maryport (Fig. 2.1). The Dalston area is similarly well endowed with axes as is the central Eden basin, around Clifton and Hunsonby on the opposite side of the river. Less predictable is the concentration of axe finds in the Keswick area, several of which are of unfinished examples, and similarly around Bewaldeth at the north end of

Bassenthwaite lake. In these localities, no firm occupation sites have been located with the exception of Drigg where flint chippings on the coast were associated with environmental changes probably within the third millennium bc (Cherry 1965). However, the presence of microliths and flint arrowheads of styles characteristically neolithic and Bronze Age within a very limited area implies at the minimum repeated reuse of a resource-rich locality by a succession of communities.

On the east of the Pennines evidence for occupation is even more limited, and the scatter of stone axes is far thinner in density, although it is characteristically riverine and lowland in distribution, below approx. 120–150 m above OD. Occupation in the third millennium was so slight or so localized as to leave practically no evidence in the pollen record outside the Milfield basin, although it should be added that the examination of deposits has so far been less extensive than in Cumbria. However, there are some ephemeral traces of occupation. For example, in central Weardale the finding of stray axe-heads was accompanied by a sickle blade as well as arrowheads, implying activity more concentrated than occasional hunting forays at least between the Rookhope Burn and Bollihope Burn (Fell and Hildyard 1953; 1956). An extensive flint-chipping site was discovered at Low Shilford, Riding Mill, in the Tyne valley, extending over two fields and into a third, where over 1,000 flints were recovered, that ranged from neat geometric microliths (characteristic of late 'mesolithic' assemblages) to leaf-shaped arrowheads, a knife and other tools normally thought of as neolithic in date, and including a sharpening flake from an axe (Weyman 1980). A possible coastal occupation on Ross peninsula, between Budle Bay and Holy Island (Northumberland) may parallel the beach exploitation in southern Cumbria, and Greenwell recorded the finding of a hammer-stone and sandstone which appeared to have been used for grinding of axes at Bamburgh (Greenwell 1877: CXCIII). However, by far the most concentrated evidence for occupation in the North-east comes from the valley of the river Till in the far north of Northumberland. While this reflects the considerable recent archaeological interest in the area, there are cogent reasons for seeing the Milfield basin as the heartland of neolithic occupation in the North-east.

The river Till drains an area of *c*. 3,000 ha of lowlying terrain of gravels and sand deposited by a late-glacial lake (p. 12). It is bounded on the south and west by the Cheviots and on the north and east by fell sandstone. A series of important sites – Yeavering, Thirlings, forts, the Devil's Causeway – all point to the extraordinary importance of this area in Northumberland's prehistory and protohistory, and it is not surprising that traces of third-millennium occupation are present [7]. The deforestation of the area is not securely dated but has been recorded in local pollen diagrams, and was associated with a rise in grass pollen, *Plantago*, *Artemisia* and the presence of charcoal, so that man's responsibility is not in doubt. Of the neolithic pottery of the north-eastern counties, 95 per cent has come from this area, including examples of

Grimston/Lyles Hill ware – round-based carinated bowls with concave necks and slightly everted rims. Examples have come from pits and post-pits at Yeavering, where excavations were designed to examine the Anglian palace complex, and at Thirlings where a pit produced fragments of a minimum of twelve vessels with a probable carbon-14 date of *c.* 3280 bc. It has been suggested that some barrows may also have been constructed over the top of occupation rubbish, presumably from local sites. For example, the barrow at Broomridge, Ford (Northumb.), excavated by Greenwell in the nineteenth century covered an old land surface that contained numerous sherds of pottery closely comparable to those from Thirlings and Yeavering, a leaf-shaped arrowhead and the butt-end of a flint axe-head. Elsewhere a similar situation may be present at the round barrow reported by Trechmann near Warden Law (Co. Durham) where the mound covered not only the remains of two individuals but also a small hoard of flint implements, a fragment of undecorated pottery, and flakes and a fragment of a 'greenstone' (probably Langdale) axe-head, on the original ground surface (Trechmann, 1914).

The presence of small pits is characteristic of British neolithic occupation sites, and often provides the bulk of the evidence, containing sherds of pottery and lithic equipment, often associated with burnt material that implies the deliberate burial of site detritus [8]. Some may have been used as grain storage pits, and the presence of lining, either of crushed pottery or wicker-work tends to support this. Examples of the former came from the defended promontory site at Peebles, in south-east Scotland, dated to the second half of the third millennium bc, and among the contents were burnt hazel-nuts in 'considerable quantities' suggesting that some storage facility was present on the site (Burgess 1976b). Most domestic pits in the North-east are small, rarely more than 1 m across and 0.25 m deep and bowl-shaped or steep-sided, although it is likely that in most cases ploughing has removed an unquantifiable depth. The Peebles site, although strictly outside the northern counties of England, is within a cultural context that is inextricable from that of the Milfield basin, and it is worth noting the great size (20 ha) of the site and the large timbers used in the construction of the 500 m long palisade which was erected in the later third millennium bc. Despite the absence of much convincing evidence of occupation on the promontory, a substantial local population is implied by the scale of the structure, which may have served the same sort of function as the southern English causewayed camps. The possibility that causewayed camps will eventually be identified in the North-east is also well worth further consideration.

The Peebles promontory site is unique, both in its size and in its defensive nature. Elsewhere, sites are characterized by hearths, pits, gullies and artefact scatters, rather than by structures, although it seems likely that future research may well locate further structural remains. The sites so far located on the west of the Pennines occupy a specialist environment close to water and may be only representative of one type of occupation associated with a limited range of economic strategies, which have more in common with the economy of hunter–gatherer communities than with the type of agricultural strategy adopted for example, in southern Britain on the chalklands. There is nothing to suggest that the population had adopted a wholly settled life-style, but rather the contrary.

Evidence for human subsistence strategies in the third millennium is poor, but there are pointers to a range of activities that may have fallen into a recognizable seasonal pattern of resource utilization. The pasturing of livestock appears to have been the most significant novel strategy, apparently beginning in a small and localized context in the early to mid fourth millennium, but of growing significance, and requiring much-increased areas of improved herbage by *c.* 3000 bc. The feeding of elm, etc. as a fodder crop is not proven but may have occurred, but a more significant environmental impact stemmed from widespread overgrazing, tree-felling and clearance by axe and fire. There are signs that a seasonal transhumance occurred, involving at least a portion of the community in upland exploitation in the summer months, with a particular marked impact on the environment around the volcanic tuff sources of the Langdale area (see Fig. 2.2), and it seems at the least possible that this transhumance movement enabled communities based primarily on the coast to exploit the tuff in order to make tools for use in the lowlands. It is not clear whether the domesticated stock was of British origin or from immigrant strains, but cattle probably made up the bulk of the livestock, and this receives some support from the sepulchral remains (p. 69).

The cultivation of cereal crops was practised, but has only been detected as yet at a small number of sites. The scale of this activity was probably small. It may have been organized in a 'slash and burn' system, with frequent abandonment of exhausted soils. On such a small scale, agriculture is unlikely to have made a significant regional contribution to the pollen spectrum, and so its detection is likely to be random within the range over which it was practised. Even so, it is worth noting that early occupation does appear to have utilized well-drained, base-rich soils, including, in particular, areas of limestone, and avoided badly drained lowland soils.

No bulk finds of cereals have occurred. Where grains have left an indentation on pottery, six-row barley appears to have been responsible, and this is consistent with evidence from the remainder of the country. However, information is very thinly scattered and generally from the late neolithic, and the storage facility in pits present on a few sites may not have been intended for grain storage. At Yeavering henge, a small pit contained burnt domestic material which yielded a carbon-14 date of *c.* 2940 bc, and the upper layers incorporated carbonized nut remains (Harding 1981).

Other strategies have failed to make a substantial impact on the palaeobotanical record, but may have been of considerable importance. The coastal exploitation that characterized late mesolithic communities appears to have continued, and there are some signs of lakeside occupation that suggest a range of activities that probably included fishing, wildfowling, the collection of shellfish and the trapping of animals along the shore.

The occasional finds of flint arrowheads suggest that hunting activity played a part in the strategies of neolithic communities, and also provide evidence for a new lithic tradition. The use of microliths and composite, barbed spears seems to have been abandoned in favour of arrows equipped with heads formed from a single flint, in a leaf-shape or single-barbed form. Such arrowheads must have been labour and skill intensive in manufacturing, and were probably not intended for use on only a single occasion. Scrapers and flint knives or daggers are not common, but do form a part of the equipment. Antler continued to be used for tool manufacture, as occasional finds demonstrate. A perforated antler mace-head was found at Newsham, Blyth (Northumb.), that was probably of late neolithic manufacture, and the occurrence of antlers or tines from antlers at stone circles and under barrows is not exceptional. In Britain, few sites have provided statistically valid deposits of third-millennium bc food bones, but where they are available, the skeletal remains of wild animals has represented less than 10 per cent of the total. However, hunting and food collection may have been more important in the North than on the southern chalklands where most counts have been possible. Hunting and collecting activities may have made a very substantial contribution to neolithic food resources, but are rarely evidenced. In Lakeland, at least, it is hard to believe that the resource-rich lakes were not areas of importance, and few communities appear to have occupied territories that did not include either coastal or lakeside habitats.

It is probable that communities were peripatetic each within its own territory during the third millennium, and it is possible to suggest that a radial pattern of resource territories radiated from the universally exploited 'factory' sites around Langdale, each incorporating a variety of resources that included upland (summer) pasturage, lowland (winter) pastures, lakeside or coastal fishing grounds and river or estuarine habitats. It is not likely that any one site was perennially occupied, so perhaps it is unsurprising that the evidence for settlement is so poor. Least consistent with a peripatetic life-style is the evidence for storage pits and the growth of cereals or other crops. These traces of a more sedentary occupation are concentrated on the best-drained lowland areas, and are probably of late date, suggesting that within the third millennium there was a gradual increase in agricultural activity and a consequent restriction in the degree of mobility of the group. Even so, there is no evidence for fields or enclosure systems, or any other sign that agricultural techniques had progressed beyond the *landnam* phase much before the end of the millennium. In the Milfield Basin, several pit alignments have been detected which may be relevant in this context, but their function is obscure (Plate 2.4).

The Tool-Makers

As a necessary part of the pursuit of a complex of economic strategies, neolithic communities developed and utilized a tool kit, drawing upon the raw materials of stone, clay, wood or vegetable and animal products. Because of the variable durability of these materials, the relics of this tool kit which are still identifiable are highly unrepresentative. Bone and antler are under-represented, as are wooden artefacts. Less durable vegetable matter and animal hides, etc. are totally absent, and with these raw materials have gone a range of equipment not otherwise represented. These materials also played a role in the manufacture and maintenance of complex equipment, which is now represented only by the components made from more durable materials. The unique collection of wooden artefacts from Ehenside Tarn has already been mentioned. These display a wide range of uses for wood, from the propulsion of a boat, to hafting, and the manufacture of entire artefacts – clubs and 'fishing-spears'. The manufacturing techniques were relatively sophisticated. The hafting of axes required the perforation of a hardwood handle to make a controlled and symmetrical socket. The axe-haft of beech-root had been finished at the head by grinding, and tool marks ran spirally around the shaft, implying some crude lathe work. The clubs display a comparable command of cutting and grinding techniques, and one fragment was elegantly decorated with an incised lattice pattern (Piggott 1954: 296–8). The fragments of wooden bowls from Ehenside Tarn and Storrs Moss suggest that wooden vessels were a normal part of the domestic equipment, and these again demonstrate a mastery of chiselling and gouging techniques. The tenoned timber and possible split planks found at Storrs Moss may represent a relic of techniques of building construction comparable to those found in Ireland at Ballynagilly, and these suggest that communities had already mastered basic techniques in structural carpentry by the mid fourth millennium (Powell, Oldfield and Corcoran 1971) using a tool kit based on wood, bone and stone (Fig. 2.1).

The use of bone is badly under-represented, although it is possible that bones were among the range of equipment used in pottery decoration, along with cord and sticks. An antler mace-head was found at Newsham near Blyth (Northumb.), which on comparative evidence should probably date to the late neolithic. A haft-hole had been cut or gouged out, and the edges have retained a highly polished and slightly resinous finish which suggested a wooden haft had been inserted (Allason-Jones 1980). Antler, whether shed or from butchered animals, probably provided an important source of workable material, and may have been used unaltered as a digging tool. Examples have been found, admittedly in an unreliable chronological context, in or close to several monuments constructed in the third millennium, including the

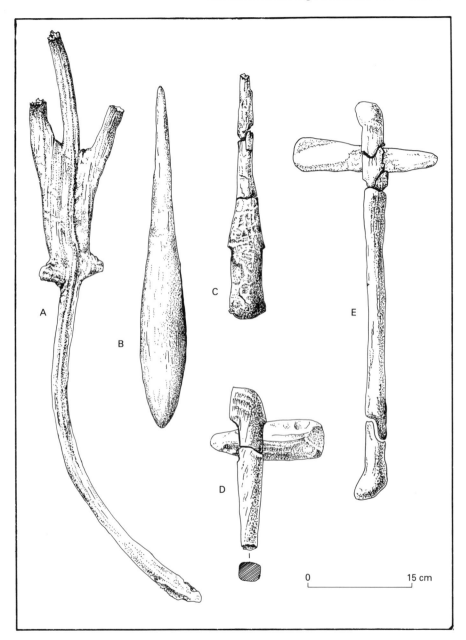

Figure 2.1   Neolithic equipment from Ehenside Tarn (after Darbishire, 1874) and Solway Moss (after Evans, 1897). Ehenside Tarn: A. 'spear' or 'rake'; B. and C. clubs; D. shafted stone axe, Solway Moss; E. shafted stone axe (scale approx.).

stone circle of Brats Hill.

By far the most common surviving equipment of the neolithic is the wide range of stone, flint or chert artefacts, and these also provide the most common indicators of settlement and clearance activity. Although the local sources of flint or chert were poor both qualitatively and quantitatively, there is evidence that they continued to be utilized. West of the Pennines, particularly, beach pebbles provided the main source of flint and chert. In the east, some poor-quality chert may have come from the limestone. These sources were exploited in the production of an industry with few distinctive features beyond its poverty. At Storrs Moss, for example, very poor-grade flint had been brought on to the site and waste flakes implied some industrial activity, although no finished artefacts were found. Equipment designed for hunting and the preparation of organic material may have commonly been manufactured, including points and scrapers. However, a high proportion of artefacts are not diagnostic of neolithic as opposed to Bronze Age communities, and there is certainly no break in the lithic traditions between third- and second-millennia industries. The few flint tool types which are thought to be specifically neolithic are uncommon in the North, and some were made from flint of uncharacteristically high quality, which suggests that they are exotic imports. Novel types of arrowheads, for example, shaped like the leaf of the alder or lime, or provided with one or two barbs (late neolithic–Bronze Age), are present in the North but not in large numbers. Another late neolithic artefact is the flint knife, a single long blade, occasionally found as a grave good, and this type of high-quality flint product is likely to derive from East Yorkshire, or further afield, and not be representative of local, domestic manufacture, unless the raw material was imported from a distance. Leaf-shaped and tanged and barbed arrowheads were made at the chipping site at Drigg, and it was probably the availability there of local beach flint which encouraged the long use of the area, from the mesolithic to the Bronze Age, for tool manufacture. A similar pattern of activity was present on Walney Island, where a series of chipping sites utilizing local and imported material produced a range of artefacts which include arrowheads of a diagnostic style as well as a range of less easily dated equipment with more in common with mesolithic equipment. The newly discovered site at Riding Mill in the Tyne valley provides a close parallel in the East (Weyman 1980).

The axe-makers

By far the most characteristic artefact of the neolithic was the stone axe. Axes of flint are not unknown in a late mesolithic context but they are characteristically scarce. In as much as the clearance of lowland forest was a novel strategy of the neolithic, so was the proliferation of a tool kit designed to perform a variety of tasks in the clearance activity. Owing to its relatively large size and easily recognizable form as well as its indestructibility, the axe-head has attained the status of a characteristic of neolithic material culture.

The last century and a half has seen the development of stone artefact typology until it has attained the status of a science [9]. In the northern counties, the collection and recording of 'celts' was haphazardly undertaken by a few amateur antiquarians in the last century, and a part only of their finds have reached public collections. For many finds we have no provenance at all, for others the provenance is as inexact as a parish or group of parishes. Most examples have come to light by accident, in the course of land improvement, drainage, reclamation or building activity. It is therefore not possible to record accurately the find-spot of many axe-heads in the northern counties. Even so, certain factors in their distribution do stand out. Axe-heads are more common on the west than they are on the east of the Pennines, and are particularly common in lowland Furness. In the whole area the distribution is heavily biased in favour of the lowlands, with scatters from all parts of the coastal plains and from the major river valleys, with a tiny minority of finds above the 305 m contour. This distribution is understandable, and faithfully mirrors the likely distribution of clearance activity in the lowland deciduous forest. The distribution of stray axes is likely to be representative of the distribution of the more intensive types of land-use practised during this period, but not all types of land-use, some of which, such as hunting, may not have involved the use of this equipment. Concentrations of axes in particular areas like Weardale (Harding 1970) or Furness represent nodal areas, within resource territories that may have extended far beyond.

In southern England and Yorkshire, flint was present in nodules sufficiently large to enable the manufacture of axes, and there is every reason to think that flint axes finished by flaking and polishing were the most effective felling equipment until the advent of metals. The mining of flint for artefact manufacture had already begun in Sussex by the end of the fourth millennium, which may suggest a growing scarcity of suitable raw material on the surface. In the northern counties hunter–gatherers had utilized the beach pebbles as a source of poor-quality flint, but this source could not provide nodules of sufficient quantity, size and quality for axe manufacture. Mesolithic communities had already discovered that volcanic tuff could be used as an alternative to flint, although the resultant industry was never a large one and probably only utilized beach pebbles as a raw material (Bonsall 1981: 457). The need for a new range of equipment in the fourth millennium led to the exploitation of the volcanic tuffs which outcrop in the Langdale area (Fig. 2.2). That they recognized the properties of the Langdale tuff is in some ways surprising, and is arguably more likely in a community already experienced in working with the same material even if from a different source. It does say much for the ingenuity and adaptability of those who developed the resource.

53

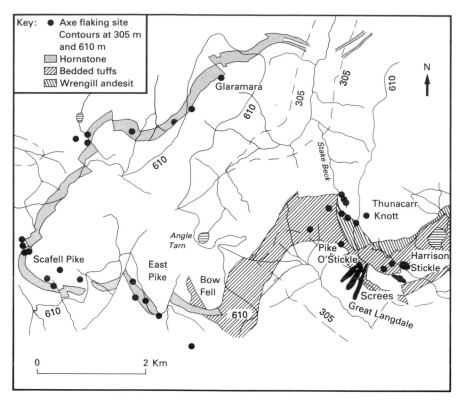

Figure 2.2 The Langdale 'axe factory' sites (after Houlder, 1979, with additions).

The raw material of the Langdale axes has been described as 'an epidotized tuff of intermediate or basic composition' which contains small fragments or microlites of feldspar, crypto-crystalline silica and possibly quartz (Keiller, Piggott and Wallis 1941). Since the first report of the subcommittee of the South-Western Group of Museums and Art Galleries on the petrological identification of stone axes (1941), it has been recognized that a large and widespread group of axes were made from this material and these have been designated as Group VI to distinguish them from artefacts from other sources.

The axes made from this material display a general homogeneity of form, there being only a single basic common shape, with considerable variations in size. The finished and unused Cumbrian axe has a broad-butted, tapered form with a cross-section approximate to a parallelogram. In length they range up to 380 mm, but are commonly around 250 mm in length. There are also found a significant number which are much shorter (less than 150 mm), which may be the result of reworking of broken blades after use (e.g. Manby 1979: 65). The finished axe invariably has been 'polished' all over, with sides that have been faceted, or less commonly rounded. Some display evidence of 'waisting' – a thinning of the blade in the centre to give it a slight hour-glass profile – and this was presumably to assist in stabilizing the blade within the haft (Fell 1950b).

Although the vast majority of the Langdale products so far discovered have been axe-heads, these were not the exclusive finished product. Narrower blades which are described as knives or chisels have been found, and in the late neolithic attempts were made to produce perforated artefacts, with little success. However, the axe-head should be seen as the characteristic product, even though it is probably simplistic to think of them solely in a clearance context [10]. A series of other functions for the equipment can be envisaged, including basic carpentry. It is conceivable that large blades may have been used as digging implements, although this suggestion has received no support from the study of wear patterns. The use of the material for blades and scrapers is unusual, and since these functions were better served by flint equipment, the attempt to use tuff reflects the poor quality and general unavailability of flint in the northern counties and other parts of Britain.

When the initial identification of the Group VI tuff was made, the exact location of the rock source was unknown, although it was generally supposed that central southern Lakeland was the likely area. At that stage only a single chipping site had been discovered, close to the Stake Pass to the north of Langdale, but it was recognized that the large numbers of axes by then identified could not have come from this site alone, which, in any case, has since proved difficult to reidentify. In the 1940s, the major chipping sites and the source of the material were eventually identified (Bunch and Fell 1949). The evidence comprised chippings, flakes and rejected rough-outs on the screes below Pike of Stickle and adjacent rock outcrops, which demonstrated that it was very largely material from these screes that was being utilized. Since then, a major working site has been located below Scafell Pike, and many small chipping floors have been added, which show that exploitation of the raw material has occurred widely along and below the outcrop bedded tuffs and hornstone that is present in a broken and faulted arc from Gt Langdale to Scafell Pike and to a lesser extent, northwards to Glaramara. It is quite clear that axe-heads were roughed-out wherever suitable and convenient strata had been eroded to form a screen, and the discovery of more small working sites is highly likely in the future, particularly since as yet unpublished research by Vin Davis has identified petrologically indistinguishable outcrops of rock at a distance from the Gt Langdale area [11]. Furthermore, it is likely that some at least of the unclassified tuffs which have been petrologically identified will eventually prove to have derived from related volcanic material in the same area, and this would extend the spatial range of workings still further. Indeed, rocks matching descriptions of Groups VIII, XI and XX have been identified in the North-west, and are represented in artefacts found locally.

By far the greatest concentration of working debris has come from the very substantial screes below Pike of Stickle, Thorn Crag and Harrison Stickle.

Despite the activity of modern walkers, it is still not difficult to find rejected rough-outs on these sites. There is a small cave above the scree at the base of Pike of Stickle which may be man-made. However, the preferred strata for axe production do not occur at this point, so that this is not the result of mining activity. There is no evidence here or anywhere else in northern England of quarrying, nor was there any need; the screes contain a large amount of suitable material already broken into fragments of convenient size. Although some artefacts may have resulted from the splitting of boulders, the raw material for most was probably picked up from the scree.

The manufacture of an axe-head began at the 'factory' site, located on the source of the raw material, in a spot the choice of which may have been influenced by environmental factors. A suitable fragment was chosen, and was then roughly shaped by striking off flakes with a large hammer-stone, detaching flakes from alternate sides, and longitudinal thinning flakes. The crudely shaped blade was then trimmed by resolved flaking on an 'anvil' stone or boulder, of which numerous examples are present on the screes. For finer flaking small hammer-stones were used. Large hammer-stones are commonly of granite, and the smaller are sandstone, both necessarily imported into the Langdales from deposits on the fringes of Lakeland, for example, Shap granite or Ennerdale or Penrith sandstone. The vast majority of axe-heads found at the factory sites were rejected at some stage during these processes, thrown away because of a failure to satisfy the expectations of the artificer, or because of some mistake on his part. Those that were considered satisfactory were removed as 'rough-outs', that is, crudely shaped by flaking, to be finished on another site at a later date.

The finishing processes probably involved a minimum of flaking, but rather time-consuming grinding and polishing of the blade against sandstone, or some other abrasive substance, to produce the characteristic shape with faceted sides, in some cases a waisted form, and a broad cutting edge. The blade was then hafted, probably using one of the two methods for which we have evidence at Ehenside Tarn (p. 50), although there may have been variations upon these methods.

The duality of the manufacturing process provides a crucial insight to the territorial habits and resource utilization of neolithic man. The location of the factory sites – in the inhospitable, inland and mountainous Langdales – is one side of this pattern of resource utilization. The preference for roughing-out axes on the spot implies a lack of confidence in the artificer in any one product begun, and a high failure rate during the early stages of manufacture. Once the flaking was finished, confidence seems to have risen, and the rough-out could be removed for finishing with a low risk of failure, and, therefore, little fear that a large amount of the material being carried would be wasted. The dispersal of the axes during the process of production has meant that finishing sites are far more difficult to identify than 'factory' sites at the raw material source.

Where finishing sites have been identified, it has been through the presence of rough-outs and grinding or polishing stones. Sharpening flakes alone are not a reliable guide to finishing, since sharpening, and considerable reworking would be normal during the useful life of the axe. Rough-outs and grinding stones have come from the periphery of Lakeland on all sides. Sites have been identified on Walney Island and by Ehenside Tarn where the finishing process can be associated with traces of other occupational activity. Elsewhere, rough-outs have been found at Williamson's Moss (Eskmeals), in the coastal area around Allonby and between Dalston and Carlisle in the Solway plain. Inland, concentrations lie around the south of Bassenthwaite lake and Keswick, northern Windermere and in the central Eden basin (Manby 1965). These finds imply that the communities involved in the exploitation of the Langdale tuffs incorporated surrounding lowland and coastal or riverine habitats within their resource territories, and a radial resource utilization is discernible. It is hard to take seriously any possibility of the exploitation of the factory sites in the Langdales during the winter, since weather conditions would have rendered the area extremely uncomfortable, impoverished and at times dangerous. A pattern of summer upland utilization seems most likely, involving transhumance pastoralism and quite possibly a variety of hunting and gathering activities as well as the roughing-out of axe-heads. The finishing sites were most probably occupied during the autumn to spring period, and betray a very different pattern of economic use.

Rough-outs are scarce outside Cumbria. Seven have been identified in Yorkshire, scattered widely from the Dales to the Wolds. No hoards have been found. These finds suggest that other communities from outside the Lake District fringes may have had at least occasional direct access to the Langdale 'factory' sites (Manby 1979), and this can only have occurred in the summer months. However, by far the majority of rough-outs have been found in Cumbria, and it seems likely that the bulk of the finishing was carried out there.

The nature of most axe finds is such that the chronology of manufacturing is imprecise. Carbon-14 dates are available from only one finishing site – Ehenside Tarn – and here there is a wide range of dates from *c.* 3014 bc to *c.* 1500 bc. At Williamson's Moss a rough-out was probably associated with activity early in the third millennium, but other dates are possible (Pennington 1975: 84). The rough-outs found on Walney Island seem to have been associated with beaker pottery, and so probably date from the first half of the second millennium bc. A 'factory' site at Thunacarr Knott, immediately north of the Langdale Pikes, was contemporary with charcoal that provided carbon-14 dates within the second quarter of the third millennium, and pollen analysis supported this date and demonstrated that a long phase of activity had led to the establishment of herbaceous grassland. This gave way to heather moorland and peat developed above the chipping floor and woodland soils (Clough 1973). The excavator argued that this period was the *floruit* of the Langdale 'industry'. Dates from further afield do offer some support, although the vast majority of finds are from an undated context. Group VI axes from Windmill Hill and Henge 'A' Llandegai came from deposits with similar dates. Those from Abingdon and Fengate may be associated with late-fourth-millennium deposits, but in both cases alternative, mid-third-millennium dates are equally plausible (Smith 1979: 18). There is no reason to suppose that these dates are necessarily even typical, and they are unlikely to embrace the entire chronological span during which production took place.

It has already been argued that the Langdale tuffs were already utilized by Cumbrian communities for the manufacture of forestry equipment by the mid fourth millennium bc, although at present no conclusive proof is available. However, it seems likely that the local utilization of Langdale axes began before their arrival as exotic imports on sites in Wessex or Wales, and it is arguable that this gap of time may have been of several centuries' duration. The process of manufacturing seems to have been already standardized before 'export' of significant quantities began, and this must imply a long local use and lends credence to the hypothesis that exploitation of the Langdale 'factories' preceded the elm decline. The development of the 'industry' in the third millennium involved the 'export' of large numbers of axe-heads in all directions, and this period certainly required the greatest production activity. By early in the next millennium, production was probably declining and few examples are associated with beaker material outside Cumbria. However, the Walney Island associations support the continued manufacture and use of Langdale products by local communities well into the early centuries of the second millennium, producing a small number of cushion mace-heads, until the unsuitability of the Langdale tuffs for perforation defeated them.

Industry, Trade and Communications

Through thin-section microscopy, great advances have been made in the last forty-five years in determining the source of stone implements [12]. Sufficient work has been published to allow the build-up of a picture for all England from Yorkshire southwards, but the programme for Scotland and the border counties has not yet reached publication. We are, therefore, in the difficult position of being able to trace the distribution of Group VI axes in some areas distant from the source, but not close to it (Fig. 2.3).

In lowland England, Group VI axes are by far the most common group in the Midlands on both sides of the country (Shotton 1959; Moore 1979). In East Anglia, eighty-three examples had been identified by 1972, and again the Langdale tuffs were the most common source material, with a majority west of the Icknield Way, along the fen edges (Clough and Green 1972). In southern England, Langdale material loses its dominance to Cornish sources, but even in

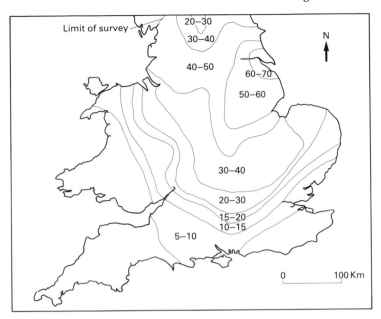

Figure 2.3 The distribution of Group VI axes (and other artefacts from the same source) in southern Britain by relative frequency (after Cummins, 1979).

the South-west, Group VI axes are widespread, and the most common, after Cornish sources (Evens, Smith and Wallis 1972: Fig. 3). Put simply, Group VI axes are dominant in northern and central England, and common in most other areas. It is not possible to be so precise when dealing with Scotland and Ireland, but Langdale axes are present in relatively large numbers in both areas, with particular concentrations in south-west and coastal, eastern Scotland and Northern Ireland, and examples have also been found in the Isle of Man. In the northern counties of England, Group VI artefacts are present and are almost exclusive of other non-perforated axe sources, with significant concentrations in southern lowland Cumbria, and a scatter with occasional concentrations throughout the lowlands on both sides of the Pennines, with many of the Durham examples found in the river valleys.

The vast majority of the axes found away from Cumbria were finished products, the exceptions being a small number from Yorkshire and one rough-out from Mull of Kintyre. The implication must be that the traffic in axes outside the Lake District was very largely in finished products, and this is reinforced by the degree of standardization noted in their size and shape, for example, among finds from the east Midlands. Stray axe finds in the Pennine valleys were largely of unused specimens, suggestive of accidental loss during transit, and these support the suggestion that the 'import' of rough-outs into Yorkshire was unusual. In that county 287 Group VI axes have been identified, of which only 7 are rough-outs (only approx. 2.5%). This is an unreasonably low rate of loss or discard if the normal practice was to 'import' unfinished Group VI axes to the area. It seems likely that most, if not all, of the Group VI axes identified in Yorkshire and the east Midlands reached there as finished products, from finishing sites in Cumbria and adjacent areas.

When it became possible to adopt an overview of axe distribution in lowland England, it was clear that, for most major lithic groups, the mean frequency of finds per unit area is inversely proportional to the distance from the source (Cummins 1979, 1980). Despite the inadequacy of this analysis in the northern counties, one certain and one probable exception exists to this rule. Group I axes with a Cornish source have a distribution density centred in south-east England. In the case of Group VI axes, the apparent density centres on the Yorkshire and Lincolnshire Wolds. This anomaly implies a substantial population of axe users in this area – an impression which receives support from other indicators. It may be that this population was sufficiently close to the source and so comparatively numerous as to distort the normal 'factory'-based distribution pattern. Twenty-seven per cent of the Langdale axes identified in lowland Britain south of Yorkshire were located in east Lincolnshire. However, it is dangerous to bring to a neolithic exchange system concepts derived from modern trade. There is no evidence that the inhabitants of the Wolds acted as 'middlemen' in any sense in which the term would be understood today. Nor should we think of 'commercial enterprise' as being present in north-west England in the third millennium (Cummins 1979). It seems unlikely that communities in Yorkshire were actively involved in the Langdale 'factories' or in the finishing of the bulk of the production, although such enterprises cannot be totally ruled out [13].

The dissemination of Langdale axes probably occurred without the existence of a trader class, and could have involved the movement of individuals over only modest distances (Clark 1965). Communities, enjoying until recently a comparable technology in Australasia, exchanged equipment and livestock between ecozones without any commercial class developing, and in some cases receiver communities seem to have been ignorant of the source of the stone tools (Phillips 1979). The process of exchange or acquisition might be via a variety of social or economic contacts, including the ostentatious provision of gifts by marriage, or barter. Given these analogies we should avoid the trap of assuming that a system of 'trade' existed in third-millennium Britain, while recognizing the presence of social contact between communities sufficient to spread a product like the Group VI axes over a wide area by land and sea.

It is worth remembering that the total of Group VI axes so far identified in England south of Lonsdale is only about 700. If we suppose that finds yet to be petrologically examined in the remainder of Britain are sufficiently numerous to raise this total to 1,000, this still only represents the 'export' from Langdale to all communities (including those of the artificers) of a single axe per year in the third millennium, and it is likely that axe manufacture occurred both earlier and later than this. Of course, the axes so far discovered represent only a small proportion of those actually made and 'exported', but even so an average annual output numbered in tens, rather than in hundreds, seems most consistent with the evidence. There is every reason to suppose that an exchange system operating on the Australasian model could have achieved the eventual widespread distribution of axes.

On grounds of expediency, we should probably look to communities whose territory included coastal or estuarine resources as the source of the finished products found around the Irish Sea, in Ireland, western Scotland and the Isle of Man. North Wales and Lancashire may also have been easiest approached by water, perhaps from Furness and the Morecambe Bay area. Sites in eastern Cumbria, in Lonsdale and the Eden valley were probably the sources of most of the axes found east of the Pennines. It is generally supposed that the major river valleys provided the routes the products took, crossing the Pennines via the Aire gap, Wensleydale, Weardale and the Tyne gap, but such movements need not reflect the movement of individuals over the whole distance. In Lakeland, axes were probably a minor part by weight of the upland resources carried down in the autumn to lowland sites. Some routes through the northern Lakes were clearly practicable, to enable communities around Keswick and on the Solway plain to participate in axe manufacture in all its stages. However, by far the easiest routes from the Langdales are to the south-west and south, and may explain the concentration of indicators in Furness and neighbouring areas (e.g. Powell *et al.* 1963), where small hoards have been discovered.

One further possibility has been explored: that the distribution of axes is based on the distribution of glacial erratics, and that axe manufacture was far more localized than has been thought (Stephen Briggs 1976). There are several objections to this. It may be possible to find Langdale erratics among the enormous quantities of Lake District material which successive glaciations have scattered over northern England on both sides of the Pennines and parts of the Midlands, but the forest cover of the fourth and third millennia would have hidden most of them and rendered them a most unreliable resource. The large numbers of Group VI axes in Scotland and Ireland are far beyond the reasonable limits of glacial deposition, and the scale of 'trade' which their presence implies is by far the simplest explanation for the entire distribution. The scale of the 'factory' sites is consistent with this explanation, and incongruous if a pattern of local production was prevalent. No working sites (as opposed to resharpening activity) or finishing sites have been identified outside Cumbria. The balance of evidence is such that there can be no reasonable doubt that the vast bulk of the Group VI axes derive from the 'factory' sites of southern Cumbria, and this generalization applies no less to the large numbers found in Britain than to the occasional find in Europe as far east as Germany and Gdansk in Poland. Even so, it is becoming clear that small glacial erratics originally from southern Cumbria are a possible source of a significant part of the raw material for mesolithic tool manufacture in lowland Lancashire and Cheshire.

Pottery

If the axe-heads of Langdale are the most durable relics of 'exchange' from the neolithic in the northern counties, others may be represented. We have already mentioned the possibility that some flint artefacts were 'imported' to the area. Neolithic pottery is scarce in the North, but has been found on both sides of the Pennines. There is no evidence that pottery was in use before the last few centuries of the fourth millennium. In fact, up to about 3000 bc the communities may have been largely aceramic, using other materials including wood and animal products as substitutes. The appearance of pottery is contemporary with the development of the exchange system that carried axe-heads to southern England, and it may derive from the same exchange process. It has been shown by petrological analysis that some neolithic pottery manufactured on the Lizard (Cornwall) was disseminated throughout south-west England to sites where it formed a small proportion of the pottery in use, but made a contribution of high quality (Peacock 1969). It is quite possible that some pottery was imported to the northern counties from neighbouring communities in Ireland and Yorkshire.

The earliest dated deposit is that from Thirlings (Northumb.) where a minimum of twelve vessels came from a pit with a probable carbon-14 date of *c.* 3280 bc (Miket 1976). Comparable material in some quantity has come from Yeavering (Harding 1981: 122). These were largely sherds of Grimston/Lyles Hill ware. This is the commonest early neolithic pottery style found in the British Isles, and appears to have been modelled not on continental prototypes but on leather or wooden vessels. The characteristic shape is a shallow bowl, somewhat baggy and with a rounded base, presumably designed to be placed on, or in, soft ground or the ashes of a fire. These bowls were commonly carinated, and made of a highly fired, hard, reddish fabric. Complete pots are very rare, and many of our examples derive from the deposition of already broken vessels under sepulchral monuments. In the North they are generally associated with cremations, and a second, less common ware of heavy, simple, rimmed bowl or cup (sometimes termed Towthorpe ware) has been found at Houghton-le-Spring (Tyne and Wear) and Crosby Garrett (Cumbria) associated with inhumations on a paved floor (Manby 1970: 17). Pottery directly from a domestic context is scarce. To add to Thirlings, there are only the sherds from pits and surface scatter at Yeavering, and the near-complete, lost, vessels from Ehenside Tarn. At Thirlings, there has been an attempt to distinguish between pottery with local

Plate 2.2   Reconstructed Neolithic pottery from excavations at Thirlings; this material demonstrates beyond doubt the presence of an early prehistoric occupation of the site, although most of the timber structures belong in a post-Roman context.

grits and the bulk of the vessels in which close parallels in the fabric, etc. with Yorkshire wares may imply importation of these vessels as well perhaps as the other large deposit of over 200 fragments from closely comparable vessels found under the barrow at Brommridge, Ford in the Milfield basin (Greenwell 1877).

Only one location has yielded pottery of unmistakably 'foreign' extraction, and this came from a coastal midden between West Hartlepool and Seaton Carew (Co. Durham). The site was discovered in the 1880s and yielded several sherds of Danish origin, but these may be of the early-second rather than third-millennium date (Childe 1932: 84), although in the light of carbon-14 dating since this publication, the date should probably be revised backwards.

The styles of domestic pottery in the north of the British Isles seems to have become established and relatively uniform by the end of the fourth millennium, and shows remarkable stability of form and decoration until at least the middle of the third millennium, within which it is possible to identify certain regional characteristics that imply local manufacture on both sides of the Pennines. The evidence suggests a stable community exercising a constant set of requirements of its ceramic traditions. The use to which it was put is not entirely clear, but food storage and cooking are obvious possibilities. There seems to have been no special wares associated with human burial (e.g. Newbiggin 1935).

The second half of the millennium saw the introduction of new styles of pottery derived from the earlier, plain, round-based vessels of the Grimston/Lyles Hill series. A variety of decorative techniques developed, and the pottery industry may have altered in its organizational structure. Peterborough ware, a decorated, fine fabric vessel, occurs at Brougham, Warton and on St Bees Head (Cumbria) and at Kyloe Crags and Ford Castle (Northumb.). Northumberland, in particular, shares a Scottish tradition of manufacture in the later neolithic, and the cultural links of the Milfield basin may have been strongest to the north. Pottery sporting impressed decoration of a type with Scottish parallels came from Ford (McInnes 1969b). Another style of pottery, grooved ware, also appears in small quantities in the North, but the largest concentrations lie in the south and east of England. This pottery is distinguished from the Peterborough wares by its lack of cord ornamentation or of pit-comb techniques (Piggott 1954: 322). Examples have come from the Milfield basin and from Walney Island.

Most of these styles are represented by only a handful of vessels and the total number of find-spots is very small (between twenty and thirty). There are some signs of a local pottery industry, but the wide cultural parallels of the vessels found are consistent with importation of at least prototypes to the area. Pottery sherds of the Peterborough tradition from Brougham contained temper probably matched in Lake District rocks, suggesting wares had travelled a minimum of 8–16 km (Fell 1972a). Recent finds suggest that pottery may have been a more important element in domestic equipment than the numbers of find-spots suggest, and if so pottery may have been both an important product and a significant element in exchange systems. Even so, the number of vessels known is wretchedly small.

Social, Ritual and Territorial Behaviour

The early neolithic population seems to have been organized in small, relatively independent communities, probably based on some sort of family unit operating within an environment so large that contact with other human groups was rare, perhaps even to the point where inbreeding may have been a problem. However, there seems to be some evidence for increasing population at least from the elm decline onwards, and this may have led to a greater degree of social stress between these segmentary social groups. This is at least one suggestion to explain the development of a variety of monuments constructed in the late fourth and throughout the first half of the third millennium to act as places of burial, and perhaps as nodal points in a group resource territory otherwise unmarked. In the North such nodal points, if such they are, are particularly poorly researched, and some types are uncommon. Within the context of the third millennium there are sepulchral mounds, stone circles and perhaps henges, but the chronology of their development is poorly supported by carbon-14 dating, except in the Milfield basin or by analogy with sites elsewhere in Britin.

The barrow-builders

Perhaps the most characteristic of the sepulchral remains of the neolithic period is the long mound, barrow, or trapezoidal mound, common particularly in Wessex and in east Yorkshire. In the northern counties, they occur in south-west Cumbria on the coastal plain, near to Wastwater and Devoke Water and the river Calder, on St Bees Head, at Seathwaite and in Low Furness (see Fig. 2.1). East of the Pennines, two lie in Upper Redesdale, and possible examples have been located by aerial photography, west of Milfield and at Ewart (Miket 1976). Elsewhere, two examples exist in the central Eden basin and two more in the Upper Eden area at Crosby Garrett and Crosby Ravensworth. Although these do not exactly share the distribution of other artefacts of the 'neolithic' communities, their distribution provides general support for significant populations in three areas – south-west Cumbria, the central Eden valley and the Milfield basin – and this bears out the other indicators of activity and occupation. The major anomalies in this distribution are the existence of trapezoidal mounds in Upper Redesdale and the valley of the Upper Eden and these imply communities utilizing the well-drained sandstone uplands of Upper Redesdale, and the limestone fells of the Orton ridge (Fig. 2.4).

The chronology of construction of the trapezoidal sepulchral mound in Britain lies well within the neolithic period, but it is clear that these monuments were not a product of the first neolithic communities. The earliest carbon-14 dates for their construction congregate in the last two centuries of the fourth millennium bc, and an early example at Lochhill, New Abbey (3120 ± 150 bc) lies only just outside the northern counties (in Dumfries and Galloway). In other words, their initial appearance is roughly contemporary with the elm decline, and the significant increase in clearing activities synchronous with or closely following that episode. Perhaps earlier, pioneer, neolithic communities lacked the resources or the need to erect such substantial edifices. It is unreasonable to interpret the long mound, or any other mid- or late-neolithic cultural artefact, as a component in the culture of an immigrant group which

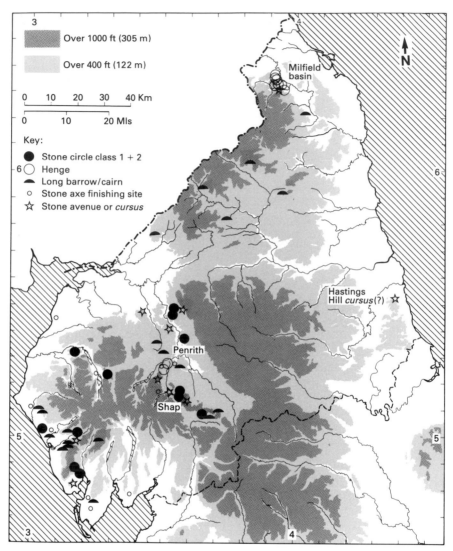

Figure 2.4 The architecture of ritual: long barrows, great stone circles, henges, stone alignments and *cursi* in the North.

then lay dormant for several centuries before it was required. The degree of local variation in sepulchral monuments of this period implies the regional interpretation of the needs and resources of the community which may then have resulted in the construction of a monument with characteristics noticeably dissimilar to those of other regions. The movement of 'trade' goods such as axes implies the existence of the means of communication by which the basic idea of monument construction was disseminated from a source that could have been either British or continental. The widespread adoption of variants upon the basic theme demonstrates the almost universal relevance to societies in the third millennium of the functions they were designed to perform. What those functions were is still very unclear, although most, but not all, appear to have served as a burial site.

Excavations at Fussell's Lodge (Hants) and elsewhere have demonstrated that long mounds or cairns were rather more sophisticated structures than had been supposed previously (Ashbee 1966; Manby 1970). In the North, only four examples have been even partially excavated, those at Crosby Garrett and Crosby Ravensworth by Greenwell (Greenwell 1877), that at Bellshiel Law by Newbiggin (Newbiggin 1936) and that of Skelmore Head, a diminutive example, by Powell (Powell *et al.* 1963). The mounds vary enormously in size and in alignment. The largest of the northern examples, at Lowther is 274 m long. Bellshiel Law is more normal at 114 m, and the smallest is Skelmore Heads, only approx. 18.3×10.7 m. Most are aligned approximately east–west, with the higher and wider end towards the east, but this is no more than a general comment.

That at Bellshiel Law was only partially examined, but was shown to be based on an edging kerb of well-laid stones with a rubble infill, covering a single rock-cut grave inside the kerb of the east end where a burnt flint and part of a 'pot-boiler' were discovered. The cairn was apparently constructed in a cleared environment, but could not be dated. The excavator considered it 'a monster of degeneracy', because of its crudeness and unsophisticated structure.

The stone and earth mound of Raiset Pike, Crosby Garrett (Greenwell 1877: CCXXVIII) is, perhaps, the most informative of the excavated examples, and was described in some detail by Greenwell. The mound was trapezoidal – approx. 55 m long and with ends approx. 19 m (east–south) and 11 m (north–west) across, covering a series of deposits lain on the natural surface but with the turf removed, under a structure about 1–1.25 m wide of stones and wood. Ashbee's reconsideration of the site suggests that features originally interpreted as cremation flues might have been structural, and that a mortuary house or building preceded the barrow on the site. A trench with evidence of burning transverse to the barrow implied a façade bedding trench and pit combined, on the parallel of the Willerby Wold example (Manby 1963). The skeletons of six or possibly seven adults were located between a 'hollow' and a large standing stone, most in a disarticulated condition, some on the ground and some on flat stones, encased in charcoal and in a mass of calcined limestone. Beyond the standing stone many further bones were discovered in what Greenwell considered a 'secondary' episode. All were burnt and disarticulated and he considered them to be principally from the skeletons of children. No dateable finds were located, and no carbon-14 dating has been possible.

The Raiset Pike monument raises several issues. The site appears to have been selected as a crematorium for sections, at least, of the community significantly before the erection of the mound. In most cases, when a barrow was constructed, clearance of the site had already taken place, and this may have occurred at a substantially earlier date. The Raiset Pike mound reinforces this view if only because of the need to gather surface material in large quantities, probably from several acres, which implies a cleared area. As deaths occurred, the bodies were deposited elsewhere, whether above or below ground is unclear. They were then gathered together in a 'clean' condition, by which time many of the lesser bones may have gone missing or decayed, and were redeposited on the barrow site perhaps in some type of timber structure. The Lochhill example was a rectangular structure approx. 7.5 m × 1.4 m with slabs forming a porch. If the area between the standing stone and the 'hollow' at Raiset Pike was covered, a mortuary house approx. 4 × 1 m might be envisaged, possibly with a tent-like shape, on the Fussell's Lodge example. This mortuary may have stood inside a demarcated enclosure, as the Bellshiel Law 'kerb' seems to suggest.

The construction of the mound (in this case largely of surface stones) was begun and it was only after construction of at least the east end that the skeletal remains and timber that had been piled over them was fired via a cremation tunnel. This fire reached a sufficient temperature to convert the limestone piled upon it into lime. The construction may have been equipped with a timber 'façade' at the south-east end. It seems likely that the mound was constructed from the south-east, and that further disarticulated, cremated skeletons were incorporated before the construction of the west end, whether according to the original design or to caprice is impossible to know. Alternatively, these might represent later additions to the mound after its completion.

The construction of a mound like Raiset Pike implies the ability to plan over several years, and required resources in manpower available for use in a non-subsistence strategy. It is a cultural artefact of a substantial and comparatively settled community with a strong territorial identity. The nature of the religious or philosophical/astrological imperatives that may have lain behind the development of the monumental form is lost, but some type of ancestor veneration may be implied by the communal burial or reburial of some (but probably not all) members of the community. It is unclear whether the trapezoidal shape has any spiritual significance or whether it represents a memory if nothing more of the longhouse tradition of the neolithic communities of previous centuries on the Continent.

The mound probably performed some role as a 'central place within the local polity' (Tainter 1975) but even this is not certain, although current fieldwork on the limestone around Raiset Pike is yielding widespread evidence of pottery and flint which may be contemporary (information from J. Cherry).

Several traits of the long barrow on Raiset Pike are typical of the region, while others are more unusual. For example, while cremation is not universal in the North, it is almost entirely absent south of Yorkshire where most comparable examples are located. Raiset Pike has been isolated as unusual as incorporating in the primary deposit adult males only, implying that in this case the privilege of burial was reserved for an unusually specific group within the community (the national ratio is forty-five males to thirty-seven females). Other aspects of the burial practice is shared by other types of burial in the North, such as round barrows or cairns, and even an apparently unmarked grave for a single uncontracted inhumation in a rectangular stone setting at Hartburn. The presence of traces there of a mortuary structure without a covering barrow poses the possibility that the construction of the barrow may have been a less essential episode in the complicated procedure of redeposition than has been supposed. Furthermore, the existence of structures under the protecting material of mounds implies that were it not for the destructive agencies of post-neolithic land-use, far more evidence of neolithic structures serving a wide variety of functions might have survived. What seems certain is that a variety of burial practices were in use within the third millennium in the northern counties, and these may reflect a medley of local or even displaced traditions derived from the late fourth millennium. The problems of the chronology of the cemetery traditions in the neolithic are driven home by the confusing diversity of styles present on the Manx sites, where long cairns are present, in several cases containing segmented chambers as at King Orry's grave and Cashtal yn Ard. These are peripheral to the major concentrations of chambered tombs in Ireland and Scotland, but embody parallels typical of both areas. Other examples of Manx long barrows or cairns contained no chamber, and are closer to the northern English and Yorkshire examples, but examples of passage graves, as at The Kew, are paralleled most closely in Ireland, Scilly and Galloway (Henshall 1978).

A second sepulchral monument at Crosby Garrett makes this point forcibly (Greenwell 1877: CCXXIII). A round barrow covered a well-paved central mortuary floor upon which lay the disarticulated skeletons of about six persons from which the smaller bones were noticeably missing. The presence of 'numerous' bones of the ox, and others from kids or lambs implies the inclusion of domestic rubbish by accident or as an offering or a dedication associated with the act of inhumation. Sherds of pottery of the Towthorpe ware variety (named after the type-site Towthorpe Barrow 18) were also present, reinforcing the 'domestic' nature of the deposit. While the round barrow may generally be later than the trapezoidal barrow, an example from Pitnacree, Perthshire, that contained traces of a mortuary building and grouped cremations, had been erected on a ground surface that provided a carbon-14 date *c.* 2860 bc. A substantial and closely comparable example was excavated at Copt Hill, near Houghton-le-Spring, Tyne and Wear (Trechmann 1914). A round barrow approx. 20 m in diameter covered a 'primary' deposit 10.7 × 1.8 m comprising several disarticulated skeletons laid on the ground, in a cremation deposit with affinities with that at Crosby Garrett, and producing sherds of similar pottery. Interments of the second millennium bc and later had been added. This site on the Magnesian Limestone may have served as an early focal point of the communities responsible for the clearance episodes noted on that terrain in the third millennium.

Another example was excavated by Greenwell at Broomhill, Ford (Greenwell 1877: CLXXXVIII), where he found on the ground surface a layer of burnt earth and bones containing large numbers of sherds from 'a very large number of vessels ... of plain, hard baked pottery, quite unlike that of which the sepulchral vases are made and had the appearance of domestic vessels'. The burial deposit was of a jumble of bones from several people that the excavator could only describe as 'very peculiar'. Here, 204 sherds were extracted, most from wide bowls about 25–26 cm across at the mouth, and 112 were from vessels identifiably plain, with a convex shape and round bottom.

The practice of mass burial and reburial in barrows has a long history in the northern counties, whatever its origin. Some of the early sites were reused at a later date. Other examples were raised over cemeteries of the Bronze Age, and some of these also contain burials that were added as late as the second half of the first millennium AD. In few cases is there an inexplicable absence of burial remains. Even so, only a small minority of the neolithic population can be accounted for under the known burial mounds, and other forms of disposal were presumably practised, perhaps including the use of long mortuary enclosures as provisionally identified in the Milfield basin (Miket 1976).

Burial mounds did require a degree of co-operation within a community, and their construction may point to the growth of a hierarchical social system, with responsibility for ritual, and for the economic structure that supported it, vested in segments of the community who may have exercised selective control over the right of burial within a monument [14]. If they served a nodal, territorial function it is arguable that they are generally not located on or even very close to likely winter occupation sites. They normally overlook valleys, and are characteristically situated on shelves and fell edges between 153 and 305 m.

However, the trapezoidal mound was only one element in a complex tradition of burial rites, and may not have been the most important. Round barrows fulfilled a function in all senses apparently identical. Under some monuments were found only single deposits, and this opens the door to a reinterpretation of the many monuments excavated before the availability of carbon-14 dating, in which grave-goods were absent. It seems likely that at least a proportion of these dates to the end of the third millennium, and, if that is the case, then burial in cists, may predate the beaker culture of the early second millennium by several centuries. At Chatton Sandyford (Northumb.) burial of a (probable) single individual in a subrectangular pit under a small cairn, associated with traces of a fire, occurred *c.* 2890 bc. The cairn later became subsumed into a substantial cairnfield, constructed partly for sepulchral and probably in part for clearance purposes (Jobey 1968a: Cairn E). It is possible to see in this and similar monuments the prototypes for the diverse network of burial traditions which seem to have taken over from the long mound when that petered out in the middle of the millennium. It will probably not now be possible to distinguish between early and late burials in old excavation reports where grave-goods are absent or undiagnostic. What can be made of the barrow on Hastings Hill near Offerton (Tyne and Wear) where of the 14 or 15 burials discovered, 9 were associated with pottery of the second millennium, but others were unaccompanied cremations or inhumations (Trechmann 1915)? Similar doubts must surround the cremation under a round barrow near Murton Moor, where charcoal, a flint knife and calcined scraper accompanied the deposit, and at Low Hills near Easington, where a rough cist held a cremation accompanied by a flint knife and oak charcoal. If some of these sepulchral monuments represent a neolithic phase of activity, the evidence for occupation of north-east Durham and adjacent areas of Tyne and Wear is increased severalfold.

The greater stone circles

The development of communal cemetery sites probably represents evidence for population increase, and growth in both the territoriality and social cohesiveness of communities or groups of communities *c.* 3200–2000 bc. The greater stone circles of Cumbria reinforce this picture, and provide a strongly regional flavour to its expression. Unlike long mounds, etc. which are

Plate 2.3 The stone circle at Swinside, south-west Cumbria, looking south-east. This is one of the great stone circles of late Neolithic/early Bronze Age construction which occur throughout western and central Cumbria. The circle has a well-defined 'threshold' on the east side.

distributed throughout much of Britain, only a few widely separated areas (e.g. Cornwall, Scottish isles) have greater stone circles. It is possible that these supply the same range of social/ritual needs as the causewayed camps of southern central England. If so, they may have been coming into existence in the second half of the fourth millennium bc. Unfortunately, none have provided datable evidence, and by their nature they are unlikely to do so. Even so, it is likely that we have here evidence for a precocious and distinctive expression of group needs and activity, and few would argue with construction of some examples in the late third millennium.

The greater circles are located in the lowlands that skirt the Lake District fells, regularly but not invariably placed in areas of good agricultural land, close to obvious lines of communication and about 15–30 km apart. The possibility of their association with the axe 'trade' has been proposed, and at the least it is reasonable to assert that the axe 'factories' must have been exploited by the same communities who constructed and utilized the stone circles. The greater circles are characterized by having large numbers of stones set relatively close together enclosing a flattish area, roughly circular, of 27–110 m diameter, usually with a recognizable, single entrance, or break in the circle, which in some cases is picked out by portal stones or by an outlying stone. The largest by far is Long Meg and her daughters, situated on the edge of a wide sandstone terrace above the east bank of the Eden, forming a slightly flattened circle 109.4×93.0 m, with a single outlier, Long Meg measuring 3.4×2.1×1.5 m (Burl 1976: 89). The outlier lies immediately outside the circle, opposite the entrance and may have acted as a marker, since it is visible significantly further away than the lower stones of the circle. Long Meg alone is a Red Sandstone block, presumably from the banks of the Eden, 3 km away, and is crudely decorated with circular marks and a cup-and-ring (see p. 114).

Other examples are lesser in scale, but perhaps more crucially located. For example, Swinside lies at the end of a natural route from Langdale down the Duddon valley to the Irish Sea littoral, and it is possible to find close structural parallels on the Irish coast. Carles occupies a key position in Borrowdale, near Keswick, and Elva Plain lies close to Derwentwater. All are central, or, at the very least, marginal to major concentrations of axes, and other signs of clearance activity and occupation.

We do not know what function the early circles performed. Although some bear traces of sepulchral monuments, these appear to have been later in date, and added to an extant monument. Various astronomical possibilities have been suggested, and it is likely that at least some alignments based on equinox or solstice risings and settings of the sun have been incorporated. There is the possibility that lunar observations were also made. However, the lack of any uniformity in the alignments or dimensions of the circles, makes it unlikely that the circles were designed principally for such purposes. A wide range of ritual activities could have occurred within them which would have left little trace; alternatively the concept of a regular meeting-place for

Plate 2.4 A Neolithic pit alignment at Ewart Park in the Milfield Basin (Northumb.), under excavation in 1980. Such divisions of the landscape were a novel feature of the third millennium bc, although their function is far from clear.

scattered communities for the purpose of various social, economic and genetic interchanges is one which is difficult to fault. The circles at least seem to occupy positions close to the natural foci of activity in several areas of preferred occupation, and their location close to routeways might be associated with the annual migrations of portions, or the whole, of communities between various sectors in a large resource territory.

Circles have been used as a guide to crude population estimates (Burl 1976: 74). Long Meg was considered to be the product of a community of 250–400 persons, and Swinside and Carles of about 140 persons, of whom half would have had to be available and fit to assist in the construction. With figures of this sort of range in mind, it seems quite possible that the population of Cumbria by the later third millennium may have reached several thousand. It is unlikely that the areas east of the Pennines would have been comparable numerically, but even there significant pockets of occupation had developed in the Milfield basin of Northumberland, and possibly also in north-east Durham and Tyne and Wear, where on Hastings Hill, a possible *cursus* has been identified by aerial photography, closely associated with a possible interrupted ditch system, which may be a northerly example of the causewayed camps typical of southern England (Harding 1979: Plate 3, IV).

The Later Neolithic

A natural break occurs in the neolithic period between the initial phases of colonization and establishment, before and after the elm decline, which seem to peter out before the middle of the third millennium, and the next wave of activity which may have gathered its initial momentum in the late third, but is essentially an early-second-millennium phenomenon. That is not to say that immigration is likely to have been responsible for this renewed momentum, although some immigration seems possible. However, relatively small proportional changes in the balance between births and deaths within the indigenous community are likely to have been the major factors in long-term alterations in population density. Climatic factors are likely to have played a part, allied to soil exhaustion in over-exploited areas. The partial regeneration of forest in the middle of the third millennium implies human populations may have declined; if not, there certainly seems to have been little increase. Over wide areas, particularly on, and to the east of, the Pennines the human population had little or no identifiable impact on the lowland vegetation during the middle centuries of the millennium, although it has been suggested that deterioration of conditions in the nodal settlement areas may have led to a wide but thin dissemination of parts of the population into adjacent areas.

The level of activity within the preferred lowland territories dropped but did not disappear, and it was this population that, reorganized probably under a new hierarchy, was able to maintain and further develop the culture that had originated in the centuries around 3000 bc, of which so many traits can be seen in the second millennium. The population may have fallen from its peak in the early second millennium, but it was still sufficient to retain a presence in all the nodal areas, and some new areas may have been colonized as is suggested by the dramatic fall in forest cover around Burnswark (Dumfries and Galloway) in the latter part of the millennium (Jobey 1977–78: 102). The strategies of food production had been successively combined with those of acquisition, even though pastoralism seems to have heavily outweighed cultivation as a source of food, and it is unlikely that any real dietary revolution in favour of grain plants had occurred in the North. Communities had established and maintained forest clearances in the lowlands, and utilized local lithic resources to equip themselves with crucial equipment that made the new range of strategies feasible. The subsequent increase in population was among the stimulants which resulted in an increased awareness of territoriality and the construction of a variety of social, ritual and sepulchral monuments. Some of the initial range of monuments were abandoned in the mid millennium, only to be replaced by new designs at the end. It was a successful cultural 'package' that the neolithic communities bequeathed to subsequent generations, who drew upon it extensively in the centuries to come. Under conditions of renewed population growth, the 'package' was developed in new areas with a consequent extensive impact on the landscape, by communities of whom most reasonably it can be claimed that they first peopled England.

Notes

1. In general, see Godwin (1975); discussed in detail by Pennington in two key articles (1970–1975). Also for Cumbria see Walker (1966) particularly p. 196 but a degree of chronological imprecision results from the limited availability of objectively dated horizons. For Northumberland see Davies and Turner (1979); for Durham see Turner and Kershaw (1973), Bartley, Chambers and Hart-Jones (1976), Turner (1978, 1983); for changes in lake sediments see Mackereth (1966); for distribution of key pollen diagrams see Fig. 1.3.

2. The terminology used to denote this type of clearance actively reflects the genesis of pollen analysis as a tool for historical research in Denmark.

3. Archaeological investigation was cursory, and postdated agricultural redevelopment. The wooden equipment subsequently suffered from severe distortion. See Darbishire (1874: 273–92; Fair (1932); Piggott (1954: 295–99).

4. See successive publications of Cross, Barnes and Hobbs.

5. The examination of this site was never concluded, and the project was abandoned after the untimely death of Professor Powell. See Powell, Oldfield and Corcoran (1971); Powell (1972).

6. For the use of axes see Iverson (1956); Harding and Young (1979); Coles (1979).

7. My thanks to Colin Burgess and Roger Miket for their help in this section.

8. Recent excavation at Tatton (Cheshire) has revealed one such pit dated to the mid third millennium bc carefully dug to bury charcoal, carbonized grain and bone.

9. Keiller, Piggott and Wallis (1941); Shotton (1959); Evens *et al.* (1962); Clark (1965); Evens, Smith and Wallis (1972); Clough and Cummins (1979); Cummins (1980).

10. The practical value of a Langdale axe for felling deciduous forest is debatable. See note 6.

11. My thanks to Vin Davis for his comments, and for access to his conclusions prior to publication.

12. See note 9, and Cummins (1979).

13. Both Manley (1959) and Cummins (1979, 1980) have made a case for either direct exploitation of Langdale by Yorkshire-based communities, or for a complex trade relationship involving specialists in exchange.

14. See Renfrew, 1976; 208–11, where such a hypothesis was tested against cairn distribution on Ronsay and Arran.

Chapter 3

The Metal-Users: 2000–0 bc

The last two millennia before Christ witnessed the introduction of a range of new technologies which were adopted in conjunction with changes in the structure and distribution of human communities in the northern counties. Most noticeably the period saw the novel appearance of metal-work which appears hesitantly in the archaeological record soon after 2000 bc, and there occurred also the development of new ceramic traditions particularly as used in burial rites. Traditional interpretations of these phenomena as migrations or invasions continue to retain some credence, and such hypotheses underlie the structure of several major works published as late as the early 1980s [1]. These interpretations have been derived largely from the increasingly detailed process of artefact typology, based on ceramic and metal-working traditions, and rely on the assumption that even small stylistic changes must be the result of culture contact [2]. The advent of carbon-14 dating, and the subsequent establishment of an independent chronology for later prehistory has removed our previous reliance on typologies, and has at the same time seriously undermined the veracity of the existing structure of knowledge (e.g. Burgess 1980: 297). It is suggested here that environmental factors may have been of greater significance in regional development, and much of the social and technological history of this period stems not from migration but from the changing balance between the human population, its perceived needs, and variations in the resources available to it. The environmental deterioration of *c.* 1200–800 bc serves as a major watershed, and divides two periods with important and distinctive cultural traits.

An Age of Expansion: 2000–800 bc

Ecological change

The gradual and spasmodic deterioration of climate which had already typified the fourth and third millennia (see Lamb 1972–77) continued to be a factor, but an inconsistent one, in the later prehistoric period. A climatic plateau of comparative warmth and at least seasonal dryness stretched across most of the second millennium (the Sub-Boreal) which probably enjoyed better climatic conditions than the previous Boreal or the present. This plateau began to disintegrate during the last quarter of the millennium, and this deterioration was probably substantial, with mean temperatures dropping below those of the present, coupled with increasing oceanity. The result was a period of unusual coldness and wetness in the first half of the last millennium bc, which was not reversed until the moderate recovery in the last few hundred years of prehistory, and during the Roman period. In the northern counties, the widespread uplands were particularly vulnerable to dropping temperatures, and possibly even more so to increased rainfall. These factors were critical during later prehistory, with substantial tracts of upland crossing the thin dividing line from marginal or even not-so-marginal resource territories to 'waste' land. There is some evidence to suggest that the impact of worsening climate spread across England from the West, where the threshold of peat accumulation was reached earlier than in the East, and in types of habitat which elsewhere were not affected. It seems likely that only marginal changes in the precipitation/evaporation ratio were necessary on the Irish Sea coasts to bring about dramatic deterioration. The areas where this threshold was crossed correspond closely with those areas subject to high rainfall in the modern era, and it seems likely that rainfall, rather than temperature, was the crucial factor in the development of upland peat, and denuded moorland soils. Increasing oceanity was probably a factor in the decline in alder pollen in the period *c.* 1200–500 bc at the western and upland site of Burnmoor Tarn, and the alder woodland was subsequently replaced by high-level peat bogs (Pennington 1970: 72). In southern Cumbria and north Lancashire, the lowland raised bogs have recurrence levels which indicate periods during which the peat failed to accumulate. These could be due to local causes, but most likely represent periods of climatic change, when flooding made peat accumulation impossible. Increased flooding seems to have occurred at Kate's Pad, Pilling (Lancs.), which prompted a split-log trackway to be laid across the peat, dated *c.* 810 bc (*Radiocarbon* 1960: 69). A further, undated, example of this type of timber trackway made from birch and ash, perhaps associated with a bronze spearhead, was found in Stakes Moss on the west side of the Kent estuary (Barnes 1904), and a wooden palisade covered by peat was found on Bowness Common about the same time. These represent northern examples of a communication and enclosure strategy well known elsewhere in western England, particularly in the Somerset Levels.

On the Pennines there is evidence that a worsening climate began to affect upland vegetation. A recurrence surface was dated at Red Sike Moss to *c.* 1440 bc. Subsequently, new peat mosses began to form, and peat expanded at the expense of woodland wherever the soil had become waterlogged (Turner *et al.* 1973). It has been calculated that in Upper Teesdale most of the present-day spread of peat was already present by the mid first millennium bc, and on much of the high Pennines blanket peat was already established a millennium earlier (e.g. Johnson and Dunham 1962).

East of the Pennines, the lowlands and lower hills of north-east England reveal very little evidence for climatically induced, vegetational change. Peat generation has not generally occurred and woodland probably remained the natural, dominant vegetation, protected even at relatively high altitudes in the rain shadow of the Lake District and the Pennines. Even so, the soils of the sandstone uplands of central Northumberland were probably seriously denuded and consequently became increasingly inhospitable to man.

There is some evidence for renewed marine transgressions during the period, apparently linked to the increasing oceanity of the climate. Tooley (1978a) recorded an episode in Lancashire which occurred throughout the central 500 years of the second millennium, and widespread lowland flooding occurred in the period 800–500 bc, although this was due to fresh as much as salt water.

While climatic change has been held responsible for a minority of specific phenomena in pollen diagrams, the impact of man has far outweighed environmental factors, and has been responsible for most changes, particularly in the balance between arboreal and non-arboreal pollen. Following the comparative retrenchment of the later third millennium, clearance phases have been detected throughout the northern counties early in the second millennium, which were characteristically widespread, and indicative of a greater degree of deforestation than had previously occurred. In many areas, particularly to the east of the Pennines, it is these clearance episodes which provide the first evidence of human impact upon the environment. In contrast to the evidence for third-millennium clearance activity, the renewed phase of clearance in the second millennium was at least as strong, and in some respects was more dramatic, in the eastern counties than in the west.

For the first time, areas of lowland Durham experienced widespread small-scale deforestation, that was at least semi-permanent in its impact. On and around the Magnesian Limestone, between Durham and Hartlepool, a sharp drop was recorded in the pollen of *Tilia* (lime) and all other trees except birch, accompanied by steep rises in grasses and herbs typical of grassland, dated to the first half of the second millennium. In the second half, the record was enriched by the addition of pollen of cereal types and of *Cannabis* at Hutton Henry. At greatest the extent of the woodland clearance seems to have been very considerable indeed. Tree pollen as a proportion of the total declined to a mere 10 per cent, and this was accompanied by an increase in one of the typical grassland weeds, *Plantago lanceolata* to 41 per cent (Bartley, Chambers and Hart-Jones 1976: 462).

Nowhere else in lowland Durham was the decline in tree cover so dramatic. Clearance may have only been this intensive and permanent on the better-drained soils. Elsewhere, where soils were naturally less well drained, clearance episodes were of a smaller scale, or more widely scattered, and less permanent. At Neasham Fen on the lower Tees, and at Mordon Carr on glacial drift, tree pollen never fell below 50–60 per cent of the total during the second millennium, and the pollen record is best interpreted as providing evidence for successive short-lived clearance episodes primarily intended for pastoral use. Even so, cereal pollen was recorded from both sites, at Mordon Carr at a precocious late-third-millennium date, and at both sites clearance in the area was substantial and long-lived.

In Northumberland and Tyne and Wear, there is little published evidence currently available of this type of semi-permanent clearance during the second millennium, although it seems certain that such must have occurred in the valley of the river Till. Even so, all the sites examined (Davies and Turner 1979) produced evidence of some small-scale clearance episodes during the second millennium. The earliest recorded came from the Tyne valley, where a clearance episode centred on *c*. 1738 bc. At Steng Moss, approximately in the centre of the county, there occurred a succession of episodes centred on dates in the seventeenth, eleventh and seventh centuries bc. A diagram from Camp Hill Moss near Bamburgh, showed a small-scale, but long-lived, clearance episode beginning at *c*. 1560 bc and lasting about 400 years. There is little or no evidence of cultivation, and these sporadic fluctuations in the pollen diagrams are easiest explained as clearance associated predominantly with pastoralism, and present in each area on average for about two centuries. Each of these episodes may have incorporated a series of short-lived clearances of a few hundred square metres in a single vicinity, such as were isolated at Tregaron Bog, Dyfed and Bloak Moss, Ayrshire (Turner 1965, 1970), where each individual clearing was reforested within fifty years, but other interpretations are equally possible.

On the basis of this evidence, there seems to have been a marked dissimilarity in the degree, extent and longevity of deforestation in the limestone areas of Durham, and the less hospitable terrains of the north-eastern lowlands. Both these extremes are also present in Cumbria, where the better-drained, lowland soils betray evidence of widespread human activity in the second millennium. In parts of the south-west, some areas had remained in use throughout the late third millennium, and provided a nucleus from which a fresh attack on the lowland forests was then launched. For example, the Ehenside Tarn area was subjected to renewed clearance activity *c*. 1600 bc, with unusually high cereal pollen counts which can only be interpreted as evidence of mixed agriculture. Elsewhere in the lowlands, a new impetus to clearance began about 2000 bc, which extended old, and created new, areas of open landscape (Walker 1966: 199).

North of the Lake District, at Bowness Common, grass pollen replaced that of forest species and shrubs during a long-lived clearance episode that was maintained throughout the millennium, and which, from *c*. 1700 bc also incorporated the pollen of cereals and weeds of cultivation. At Oulton Moss, the first evidence of clearance occurred *c.* 2000 bc in favour of grassland, although a temporary and partial reforestation occurred *c.* 1500 bc. Renewed clearance in the second half of the millennium was associated with the first appearance of cereal pollen and charcoal. A comparable impetus to deforestation occurred in the poorly drained Scaleby area *c.* 1400 bc. The general picture of the north Cumbrian lowlands is an unusually clear one although little carbon-14 dating is available. Clearance activity spread initially across the better-drained soils *c.* 2000 bc, and impetus was renewed about the middle of the millennium when cereal pollen is first widely identified, associated with an increased rate and range of deforestation which took clearance inexorably on to the 'wetlands', and eventually introduced fundamental and permanent changes in the vegetative balance.

Evidence for clearance on the uplands is scarce away from the Lake District in the second millennium. Northumberland has not been widely studied, in areas where human interference may have been unnecessary to stimulate deforestation on less well-drained soils. Studies of pollen cores in Upper Teesdale failed to provide evidence of human activity before *c.* 1000 bc (Turner *et al.* 1973). In Cumbria, the third-millennium clearances around Langdale made a very different backdrop, and clearance activity, in this area at least, continued in the early centuries of the second millennium. Wood from the base of the peat at Red Tarn Moss was dated *c.* 1940 bc (Pennington 1970: 71) and this seems to approximate to the major deforestation horizon, associated with a substantial and permanent increase in the pollen of grasses, sedge, *Calluna*, etc. The result was the permanent degradation of wooded uplands to the status of open moorland, accompanied by an increasing inwash to the tarns, carrying a more acid type of humus. At Rusland Moss, west of the southern tip of Windermere, small-scale clearances were identified in the second millennium, but these episodes were not dated (Dickinson 1975).

The worsening climatic conditions between *c.* 1250 and 800 bc had a particularly severe impact on the northern uplands. In these circumstances, it is surprising to find evidence of clearance, in some areas for the first time. In Upper Teesdale a series of short-term clearance episodes have been identified. High levels of pollen from grasses and grassland herbs alternate with forest species on the better-drained soils, implying periodic anthropogenic pressure of the upland woodlands. Around the Low Green reservoir, woodland had already been extensively lost by *c.* 1200 bc, but elsewhere in Upper Teesdale mid- to late-millennium clearances have been recorded. In Cumbria, upland woodland was cleared in the south-west uplands, around Devoke Water, Seathwaite Tarn and Burnmoor Tarn, and there are signs of similar activity in the valleys of the central Lakes (Thirlmere and Rydal Water) and on the fringes of the Eden valley at Haweswater (Pennington 1970: 72). At Seathwaite Tarn this episode was dated by carbon-14 *c.* 1080 bc. In each area a drop in the rate of deposition of pollen was recorded, implying increased erosion resulting in a faster rate of in-wash, coupled with an expansion of grassland pollen. At Devoke Water there were very definite signs of the increased erosion of mineral soils, symptomatic of a serious loss of topsoil and a dangerous acceleration in the rate of runoff. The consequence over wide areas was a spread of moorland vegetation on increasingly waterlogged and podzolized, acid soils incapable of supporting natural reforestation.

Population, settlement and subsistence

Population

Evidence of human activity in the second millennium is more widely distributed in the northern counties than is evidence for any previous epoch or culture, even including the mesolithic. The total artifactual record includes stray finds of metal-work, burial monuments, occupation sites for social or ritual purposes and monuments associated with land-use. Although there are significant differences in the distribution of particular types of artefact, the general pattern is of a broad spread of evidence throughout the lowlands, with early, strong concentrations in the Milfield basin, in the central Eden valley, and in Plain Furness. East of the Pennines the altitudinal range is greatest, up to about 427 m, but in western Cumbria the limit of monumental evidence is noticeably lower, thinning out rapidly above 274 m. In Northumberland there is a strongly riverine distribution, but this is less marked in Cumbria (see Fig. 3.3). The distribution of artefacts of all kinds is weakest in the historic county of Durham, and the south of that county, now largely Cleveland, represents a near total void, despite the limited palaeobotanical evidence of activity. It seems possible that this area was under-utilized, but the record may be artificially biased by problems resulting from the spread of industry in the nineteenth century and the poverty of local fieldwork. Generally, the evidence supports the hypothesis of substantial population growth, particularly between *c.*1800 and 1200 bc coupled with the expansion of human communities into areas previously considered marginal.

The second millennium opened with a human population which was highly selective in its habitat, and principally confined to the well-drained lowlands, particularly in the Milfield basin, the Penrith area and coastal Cumbria.

In the Milfield basin, at least seven hengiform monuments and a 'droveway' form the centre of a complex occupying at least 20 km^2 of alignments, standing stones, isolated pits and linear features (Miket 1976; Harding 1981; Fig. 10). While domestic sites have not been identified, this is probably because their comparatively superficial remains have not withstood the pressure of subsequent agricultural activity. The bias in favour of substantial monumental artefacts is therefore understandable. Nine carbon-14 dates provide a chronological spectrum from *c*. 1950 to *c*. 1590 bc, and the presence of pit alignments associated with grooved ware suggests further activity in the early second millennium (Miket 1981).

The scale of the evidence implies substantial reserves of manpower available for manual work over a long period on a series of projects, from some at least of which no immediate economic return was likely. Also implied, is a social and political organization capable of long-term planning and of controlling the subdivision of territory on what had been the preferred, and densely settled, sands and gravels. The presence of a substantial population at the end of the life-span of the henges is supported by the comparatively high density of burial monuments associated with all types of ceramic traditions throughout the millennium on the margins of the valleys and on the fellsides where a far higher incidence of survival has resulted from the concentration of modern agricultural activity on the valley floor. It is not yet clear whether the apparent absence of comparable sites from the Milfield basin is real or apparent, but on the north Cumbrian plains recent excavations have identified two lowlying cemeteries, one at Ewanrigg, Maryport, containing nine cremations (Bewley 1983), and at Eggleston (Durham) a bucket urn deposit has been excavated only 1 m above current water-level.

Evidence is less in the central Eden valley, where two henges survive as upstanding earthworks and a third may have been destroyed in the recent past, but no recent excavations have taken place (since Bersu 1940), and conditions are far less favourable for aerial reconnaissance, with a high proportion of sown pasture-land (Fig. 3.1). The presence of the Long Meg stone circle also underlines the apparent cultural dissimilarity between the east Pennine culture and the Lake District, where stone circles appear to perform a function equivalent to those of the henge elsewhere. In lowland southern Cumbria, the non-funerary stone circles were probably in existence in the first half of the second millennium, but these monuments have not been satisfactorily dated (Burl 1976). They are generally not concentrated in a manner comparable to the Milfield basin henges, and may represent a more scattered, though still substantial, population. Outside these preferred territories the evidence for human communities at 2000 bc is not totally absent, but is generally chrono-logically unsound and is thinly scattered.

By the third quarter of the millennium the practice of constructing substantial ritual monuments had been abandoned in all areas, and the geographical concentration of the population had broken down. Artefacts widely distributed in the lowlands, river valleys and on the lower fells support the scattered palaeobotanical evidence of a movement of communities on to terrain previously little utilized in both lowland and upland areas. The lowland environments now brought within the area of settlement are widely scattered, but in the uplands the most consistent and substantial evidence occurs adjacent to the nodal areas, on the Cheviot foothills and fell sandstone in northern

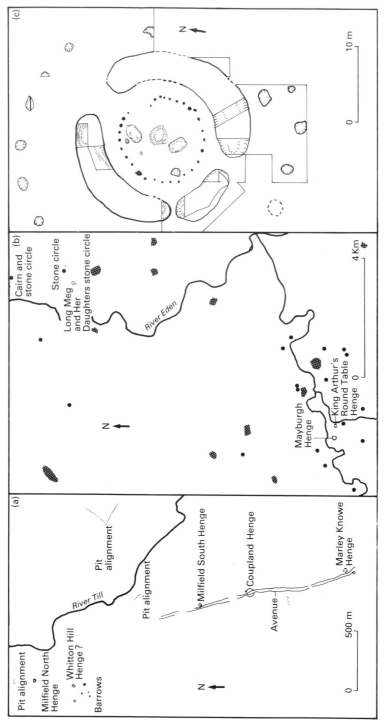

Figure 3.1 The henge complexes of the north: (a) The Milfield Basin Complex (after Harding, 1981); (b) Penrith Basin, henges, stone circles and settlement (possible settlement hachered and bronze age burials marked); (c) Milfield North henge, general plan after partial excavation (after Harding, 1981).

Northumberland, on the fells of southern and western Cumbria and in the marginal lands of the Upper Eden valley. While this is by no means infallible, and seems to neglect for example, the evidence for activity in the Upper Tees valley, the implication is that the colonization of the less favourable areas was fuelled by the growth of population in the nodal areas, where a resource crisis may have occurred. The most obvious, and least vulnerable, explanation of this movement of colonization is a climatically induced and long-sustained increase in population, due to a slight increase in the ratio of births over deaths and a slight improvement in life expectancy. A shift of only 1 per cent would have been adequate to achieve a population increase by *c.* 1200 of tenfold over the late neolithic, and the favourable climatic conditions of the second millennium created an environment in which such an increase was likely. Immigration is unlikely to have made a significant impact upon population, perhaps at most comparable to the addition of the one-quarter or one-half of 1 per cent made by the Normans to the English population in and after 1066.

The worsening climate in the late second and early first millennia may have seriously eroded the production capacity of the northern counties in general, and the uplands in particular, and it seems likely that this period saw a population crisis, as well as major social and economic changes closely dependent on these circumstances.

Settlement and subsistence strategies

Occupation sites of the second millennium have proved until very recently extremely difficult to locate, and even now few reliably dated examples exist. This has led to the widespread assumption that early-second-millennium communities were nomadic or at the least, transhumance pastoralists, who have left behind little evidence of habitative structures. This long-established view has now been discredited by fresh evidence deriving from fieldwork and excavation.

When, in 1969, Simpson discussed 'beaker period' houses in Britain, he was unable to point to more than a single dubious example from the northern counties – at Woodhead (Cumbria), where a circular, stone-walled structure approx. 8 m diameter was excavated before the war (Simpson 1969: 36; Hodgson 1940). In the interior were two post-holes and a shallow pit devoid of artefactual material, and only a single 'V' perforated, jet button implied an early Bronze Age date. Simpson suggested this might have easily represented a funerary monument rather than a habitation, and his case receives some support from the excavation of a similar structure at Levens Park (Cumbria), where a 'round-house' was thought to occupy the centre of an enclosed 'farmyard', but where skeletal remains and beakers were also present (Sturdy 1972).

The first incontrovertible habitative site to be excavated was that at Green Knowe (Peeblesshire). The site was distinguished by platforms created by terracing into the hillside, which had supported the foundations of round

Plate 3.1 A boat-shaped building at Dubby Sike under excavation in 1984 when the waters of Cow Green Reservoir (which normally cover the site) dropped during the drought. The peat which had covered it had been washed away, revealing a complex site with structures which included this building with an extrance in foreground and a substantial ring-cairn with two internal pits. The total absence of finds leaves the excavators reliant on carbon-14 dates for the site, but given the altitude at approximately 488 m, occupation in a neolithic or early Bronze Age context seems highly probable.

timber houses arranged in tiers and rows, in an unenclosed context associated with cairns and linear banks. On one excavated platform was found a stone hearth and traces of three successive superimposed huts, the largest of which was about 10 m diameter, each defined by an arc of stake-holes and internal posts (Feachem 1960; Jobey 1978b). Carbon-14 dates from the structures span a period of over 400 years from *c.* 1200 bc, and support the apparent longevity of occupation.

Since the identification and excavation of Green Knowe, comparable unenclosed hut groups have been found to be widespread on the northern fells, and a small number have in addition been located via aerial photography on the lowlands. By 1983, a careful policy of exploration and survey in Northumberland had identified about ninety sites, most commonly on open moorland between 210 and 380 m, but higher in places, with high densities on the slopes of the Cheviots (Gates 1983). The sites occur singly or in small groups, and range in size from 1 to 12 houses per settlement, although many have only 1 and more than 6 is uncommon.

Excavation of a typical group at Standrop Rigg centred on 2 of the 5 or 6 house stances identified, and revealed timber buildings with outer rings of stakes forming a wattle screen and inner postholes which had held more substantial roof supports. Both excavated houses had interior hearths, and one was dated *c.* 1050 bc, although earlier and later human activity was also recorded. Round the exterior of both houses had been piled stone to form a ring-bank approx. 2.5 m broad and 0.5 m high. This stone had presumably derived from clearance activity in the vicinity, and had continued after the abandonment of these houses, resulting in the blockage of the doorways (Jobey 1983b). Elsewhere, it has been suggested that stone-founded buildings may have replaced timber as the preferred vernacular style. Selective excavation on Black Law at the Houseledge site revealed timber huts which had apparently been replaced by stone-walled structures in a complex and long-lived settlement, associated with successive dispersed features in which the excavator identified three major phases of agricultural land-use (Burgess 1981). Other structures were probably not roofed over; high phosphate levels led to their interpretation as animal pens (Fig. 3.2). A comparable, stone-founded round-house formed the central feature of an enclosure at approx. 390 m above OD on Bracken Rigg above the Upper Tees (Durham). Inner posts supported the roof, or might represent a separate phase of construction utilizing the same paved and cobbled floor, and hearth site. Charcoal from the house was dated by carbon-14 to *c.* 1230 bc. A system of agricultural terracing at Simy Folds, in the same area, was also probably first commissioned in the second millennium bc [3].

Very recent, and as yet unpublished, excavations have extended the chronology of unenclosed sites back into the early to mid second millennium, and forwards into the mid first millennium. It is not surprising that the earliest dates have derived from a site in the valley of the river Till at Lookout Plantation. A series of ring groove timber houses of about 11.0 m diameter have been uncovered, which bear a close resemblance to the unenclosed sites of Upper Tweeddale and the Cheviots. At Hallshill near Steng Moss (Redesdale) occupation may divide into two distinct episodes, in the late second millennium and again in the mid first millennium, to coincide with the clearance episodes identified palynologically at the Moss (Gates 1983). Circumstantial evidence would suggest that the wooden stakes of a round-house located in the coastal peat beds at Hartlepool and probably associated with a Langdale axe should belong within the same chronological context as the Lookout Plantation site. Other probably broadly contemporary open sites have been identified by crop mark aerial photography in the lowlands, and now await excavation.

Whether or not traces of a stone building tradition are eventually substantiated, certain important conclusions are already available. Communities were occupying sites in less hospitable locations than at any later stage of human activity in the North. The habitations were distinguished by

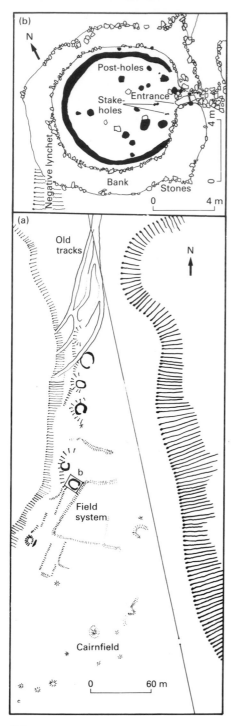

Figure 3.2 Houseledge: an upland settlement complex of the second millennium bc. (a) general plan; (b) excavated round house – see (a) for location (after Burgess, 1979).

carefully terraced or levelled foundations, permanent structures and a tradition of occupation which spread commonly over many generations. Each excavation has revealed pottery usage and possibly manufacture, and saddle-querns for grain preparation. It is difficult to avoid the conclusion that unenclosed, platform sites were both permanent and perennially occupied. The common occurrence of stone clearance implies agricultural activity, leading to land improvement as a cultivable medium, and probably to soil erosion.

This last observation finds support in the common occurrence of fields in direct and physical association with hut platforms. Boundaries are generally non-geometric in plan and plots are small – from less than 0.1–2.1 ha, but generally about 0.2 ha (Gates 1983). While the number of enclosures is variable, the average amount per house in Northumberland is approx. 0.6 ha, but stone clearance may have occurred outside these 'fields'. The boundaries generally consist of 'linear cairns' – walls comprised of clearance stone, and they are unlikely to have been effective barriers to herds, as was confirmed by excavation at Hallshill. The control of the latter was probably, therefore, very largely by herding, and the 'fields' were probably intended for hand cultivation, although residual furrows have been identified at Snear Hill. That grain cultivation was practised was confirmed at Hallshill, where houses yielded emmer wheat, barley, oats, flax and agricultural weeds.

West of the Pennines, survey is less advanced, and excavation almost non-existent on this category of site, despite the fact that many are known. On Heathwaite Fell, near Coniston, terraced hut platforms were first described, but wrongly interpreted, in the nineteenth century (Cowper 1893: 406). They can be identified in at least three separate groups within a complex and multiperiod pattern of field systems, cairns and settlements, within which they formed one of the earliest elements. Recent survey work by the archaeological unit based at Lancaster in the Ulpha Fell area has identified among the cairn fields enclosures or partial enclosures which are likely to fall within this context (Leech 1983). Surveys by the author elsewhere in Eskdale have been directed at numerous further examples. Among these a minority of enclosure settlements arguably belong to the late prehistoric/Romano-British reoccupation of the lower fells – as at Waberthwaite Fell and Barnscar, but most probably belong in an early- to mid-Bronze-Age context. Many of the enclosure elements are incomplete, and some are groups of disjointed stone walls which perform no enclosure function, but arguably acted as linear clearance cairns for the disposal of surface stone, or perhaps as wind-breaks, as is likely in the case of a linked group of three short stone walls radially organized around a single point on the apex of the west end of Eskdale Moor (Figs. 3.3, 3.4). The accumulation of stone at settlement sites and other nodal points bear witness to the twin process of erosion and agricultural activity on the uplands by which fine soil tended to be transported downslope, leaving an ever less attractive and stony till behind. The availability of stone made its use for construction a natural solution, particularly if local deforestation was a com-

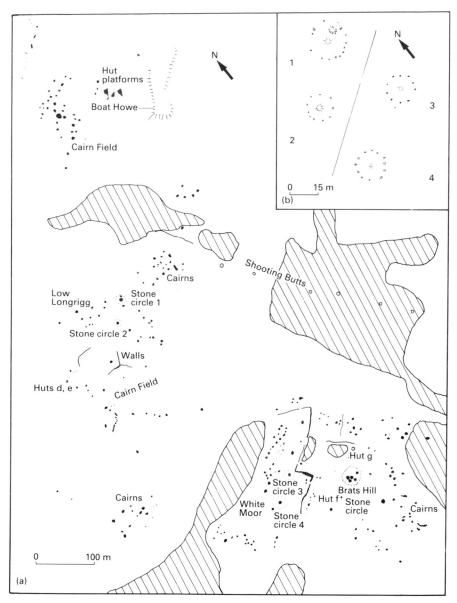

Figure 3.3 Cairns and the community: (a) dispersed landscape features predominantly of the second millenium bc on the south-west end of Burnmoor, Eskdale (Cumbria), showing the intimate association of stone circles, sepulchral monuments, clearance cairns and 'walls' (wetlands are hatched); (b) a detail of Low Longrigg and White Moor stone circles (after Burl, 1976).

mon product of human activity in the immediate vicinity of settlements.

If, as seems likely, the upland settlement model was one derived from the

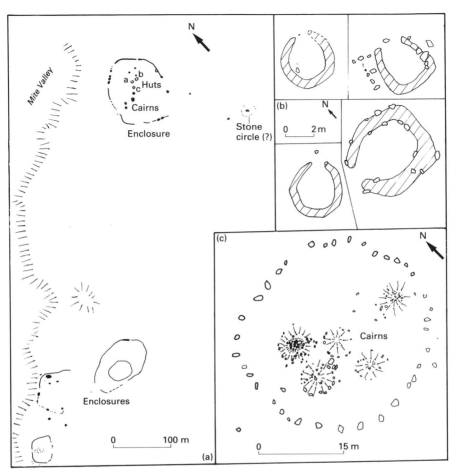

Figure 3.4 Cairns and the community: (a) dispersed landscape features predominantly of the second millenium bc on the north-east end of Burnmoor (being a continuation of Fig. 3.3); (b) details of hut circles (for location see Fig. 3.3); (c) the Brat's Hill Stone Circle (for location see Fig. 3.3; after an original survey, 1983).

adjacent lowland areas, it is reasonable to see the unenclosed, round or near-round-house as the ubiquitous habitative structure of at least the later second millennium, as it seems to have been elsewhere (Simpson 1969). This raises the possibility that major changes in vernacular architecture may have taken place since the rectangular structural traditions of the late third millennium and before, as exemplified in the North at Ronaldsway (Isle of Man) and at Balbridie, but round-houses may already have been present during the later neolithic, and it seems premature to argue for a clear break in tradition [4]. The construction of unenclosed groups of round-houses has now demonstrably a lengthy history, although it remains unclear the extent to which groups of sites were in contemporary occupation.

91

The land-use practised by man in the expanding territories of the second millennium probably always incorporated a large element of pastoralism (Fleming 1972–73). Other strategies were available throughout the period. Palaeobotanical evidence firmly supports the presence of cereal cultivation. Excavations in the Outer Hebrides have demonstrated that the ard was in use in the cultivation of barley and wheat in the twentieth century bc (Shepherd and Tuckwell 1976–77). Hand cultivation seems the likeliest strategy in the small enclosed areas associated with hut sites in the border counties, but occasional evidence supports the possibility that an ard or plough may have been used. It has been suggested that perforated axes were utilized as ard shares (Bradley 1972–73), but wear patterns have failed to support this interpretation (e.g. Rees 1981). In addition to the cereals found at Hallshill, grain impressions on pottery have come from two burials in Northumberland, in both cases from food vessels. That from Newton was associated with a carbon-14 date of *c.* 1685 bc (Gates 1981a; Collingwood and Cowen 1948), and was identified as bread wheat. The impression of a grain of hulled, six-row variety of barley was identified on a pottery sherd from the upper ditch fill of Yeavering henge (Harding 1981: 133).

In the uplands the most extensive and common remains are represented by cairnfields, with or without other evidence of activity which may include hut circles and stone walls. The piling up of clearance stone into cairns implies considerable disturbance of the soil, and a powerful economic incentive to undertake what must have been laborious and unpleasant work. The most obvious incentive must have been cultivation. However, there is a marked lack of support for the presence of cereals in the quantity that extensive cairnfields imply in the upland pollen diagrams.

Many large cairns were 'excavated' in the early days of antiquarian investigation, and many of these were shown to be sepulchral monuments, predominantly of the second millennium (e.g. Greenwell 1890; Soden Smith 1870). Where modern excavation has taken place, it is possible in some instances to distinguish between the relatively sophisticated structure of the sepulchral monument and the often smaller, unstructured 'heap' resulting from clearance. At Chatton Sandyford (Northumb.), a large cairn proved to be sepulchral, while of the five small cairns examined, four were probably clearance, although the fifth included a burial (Jobey 1968b). Clearly, burial mounds are present in many cairnfields and may be dominant in some, but the construction of sepulchral monuments does not exclude a secondary clearance function. A wide variety of developmental models are equally plausible, and cairnfields are likely to be multiperiod in origin (Fleming 1971). What is clear is that cairnfields are not explicable purely as cemeteries (Walker 1965a; Ward 1977; C. Richardson 1982), and while it is unsafe to assume that the absence of burials necessarily indicates clearance, it seems certain that many of the thousands of cairns on the northern uplands derive from the intentional removal of stone from the surface of fields. The scarcity of cereal pollen

Plate 3.2 A hollow cairn within the multiperiod complex at Heathwaite Fell (south-west Cumb.). This common form of cairn should be distinguished from hut circles, and may derive from the piling of clearance stone around the root ball of a tree, during cultivation and the consequent rapid soil erosion of the surrounding area.

suggests that cultivation in the cairnfields was never wholesale, and it is tempting to postulate irregular small-scale cultivation on the uplands, associated with the gradual colonization of fresh areas which slowly extended the cairnfields; soil exhaustion may have forced rapid abandonment. In general, cairnfields are selectively situated, both as far as altitude, but also with a preference for the comparatively level, better-drained soils more suited to agriculture, still in some instances visible in vegetational indicators. They are, however, absent from limestone soils, although various indicators suggest these may have been intensively used, but in circumstances in which the construction of cairnfields was unnecessary, presumably because of the general absence of stone in these thin soils.

It has been suggested that the construction of cairnfields was a relatively late episode in upland land-use (Fleming 1971), following a possibly lengthy phase of intense pastoralism which was directly responsible for deforestation. The method of forest clearance is unlikely to have been solely by hand, if only because of the inefficiency of the available equipment in stone, copper or bronze. However, at Barnscar pollen analysis of the old ground surface beneath cairns suggested that the cairnfield was developing at the same time as dramatic deforestation was occurring (Walker 1965a). Cairns commonly seal burning consistent with the use of fire, perhaps to clear brushwood, but at what stage is not clear, and doubt has recently been cast on the possibility of slash and burn in the northern forests (Rowley-Conwy 1981). Small pits are also not uncommon under cairns, but their function is not obvious. The sharp increase in humus and ultimately in base soils in upland sediments would support the general conclusion that deforestation only marginally preceded the sequence of soil erosion and stone clearance that led to the development of cairnfields. Initially, at least, cairnfields were broadly contemporary with that phenomenon, and both small-scale agriculture and clearance by intensive pastoralism seem to have been part of the economic strategy available to communities in the second millennium. Some hollow cairns may have resulted from the piling of cleared stone around the stumps or trunks of large trees – such occur widely in southern Cumbria, and many have an internal ground level which is lower than the surrounding area. Some cairns were built during or after the operational life of field plots, but in some cases they may have represented the first stage in marking-out fields, and the cairns may have been progressively robbed to provide 'walls' around fields and settlements.

Fieldwork and excavation at Black Law (Northumb.) has suggested that on the Houseledge site at least, clearance cairns derived from the first agricultural phase, and were followed by cultivation terracing and by rectangular fields, all within the same broad chronological context (Burgess 1981). Survey of the surrounding area suggested large-scale division of the moor by a boundary dyke between areas reserved respectively for agriculture and pasture (Burgess 1982). Comparable large-scale, but undated upland field systems have been located elsewhere, with Cumbrian examples on Crosby Ravensworth Fell and at Shap (Higham 1978a). The Crosby Ravensworth example at least may be associated with finds of second-millennium bc pottery in the vicinity [5].

When applied to the uplands, prevalent climatic factors at the end of the millennium meant that these strategies were likely to be ruinous. In many areas the environment was probably capable only of supporting a single episode, before the consequent erosion and soil deterioration rendered natural reforestation impossible. Where even temporary stability of soils occurred within an upland environment, this seems to have been sufficient to have attracted repeated or continuous episodes of human activity until the threshold of regeneration had been passed. Only the availability of wide expanses of forested uplands gave these strategies the appearance of success, and enabled the human population to retain them over a period of at least 700 years, and perhaps for most of two millennia.

The inefficiency of these strategies as applied to the uplands suggests they were originally developed and utilized in a more clement, lowland environment, and this is consistent with the presumed spread of the human population particularly during the mid to late second millennium from the well-drained lowlands into successively less hospitable lowland and upland environments. On well-drained lowland soils the same strategies would have been comparatively successful. Clearance by intensive grazing would have been an efficient method of deforestation and consistent with the development of substantial herds. Subsequent use of the cleared or partially cleared environment for agriculture probably incorporated ploughing and permanent field systems, and avoided the ruinous environmental repercussions that led to abandonment of the uplands.

That manuring was an available strategy is implied by the widespread scatter of pottery and flints in some upland complexes (e.g. Jobey 1978b; Burgess 1981, 1982), and this implies the concentration of livestock at the settlement for feeding over the winter months, perhaps in the type of unroofed structures found at Houseledge (Northumb.). The frequency with which numbers of artefacts and small features of likely second-millennium date derive from the excavation of later sites says much for the ubiquity of human activity during the period, particularly in the uplands. In the lowlands, the development of unacceptable levels of weed infestation may have been the limiting factor in determining the longevity of agricultural use of a field system, as it probably was on many soils in the medieval period (Harwood Long 1979). Such weed infestation is clearly visible on many of the Cumbrian upland sites. Barnscar, Heathwaite Fell and Eskdale Moor, to quote a few examples, are infested with bracken. The limited, relatively dry areas at Stainton Fell and Blue Quarry, Shap, are surrounded by wetland plants including rushes, which have probably encroached upon the cairnfields. Clearance episodes in any given area were generally of several centuries' duration. Without the need to practise stone clearance, lowland agricultural activity must have enjoyed a far higher productivity both per man-hour, and in the eventual yield, than was possible on the upland cairnfields, where agriculture was highly labour intensive, assuming it took place at all.

Pastoralism was certainly a major, and probably the major, economic strategy throughout the second millennium and much forest clearance may only have been a by-product of overstocking with domestic livestock managed as a direct food and capital resource (Bradley 1972). It seems likely that the worsening climate of the period *c.* 1250–800 bc would have led to abandonment of widespread agricultural land on the margins of productivity and its replacement by pasture. As a strategy this may have been forced upon the community by environmental factors, but it must have represented a substantial decrease in the food resources available to support a population vulnerable to such pressures after a long period of growth.

There are no relevant skeletal remains from the northern counties in quantities sufficient for statistical analysis, but nationally the indications are that the second millennium saw a shift of emphasis towards cattle and away from the pig, which had, for example, still been the most important meat source on the late neolithic site of Low Caythorpe, Yorkshire (Bramwell 1974).

By the beginning of the first millennium, ox bones comprised 58 per cent of the total skeletal remains at the Yorkshire hillfort of Grimthorpe (Jarman *et al.* 1968). Bones from the Heathery Burn cave (Durham) appeared to derive from domestic refuse and included those of young oxen, horses, immature sheep, pigs and a variety of wild fauna – red deer, roe deer, dog, fox and various small mammals, but the chronological context of these deposits is insecure (Greenwell 1892; Britton 1971). In the conditions prevalent on the acid uplands, skeletal remains are unlikely to be forthcoming in any quantity.

While herd management and agriculture were probably already the major economic activities practised by 2000 bc and were to remain dominant throughout the millennium, other food resources were utilized, where communities had ready access to them. On Walney Island, for example, profuse but poorly dated midden material associated with second-millennium ceramic traditions included a wide range of shellfish and the bones of an ox (Cross 1939, 1942, 1950). Elsewhere were found the bones of sheep or goat, deer and porpoise. At Eskmeals the dunes have yielded flint artefacts as well as a saddle-quern, and at Ross Links (Northumb.) beakers and food vessels came from a coastal context (Brewis and Buckley 1928).

Coastal resources continued to be exploited, both as a source of flint and in hunting and gathering, and man took advantage of the same richness of resources which had attracted mesolithic communities to the coasts and estuaries. The presence of flint arrowheads may imply both manufacture and use. There is every reason to believe that human populations in the second millennium acted with a degree of pragmatism in assessing and utilizing the resources of their particular territory.

Away from a marine or estuarine environment, these strategies were less available and less attractive. Even so, rivers or lakes were a normal part of the resources of many communities, and the exploitation of these were sufficiently important to maintain in use a specialist range of equipment. The hollowed tree-trunk boat was not a new invention, but surviving examples suggest widespread use. An example excavated at Branthwaite (Cumbria) displayed relatively sophisticated features including a carefully inset back-board, and was in use in the last century of the millennium (Ward 1974). Several comparable examples have been discovered on Humberside with a date range from the mid second millennium to the mid first millennium.

Technological change, trade and communication

The second millennium opened with positive evidence of renewed output from the Langdale axe 'factories', with substantial fresh clearance and the spread of moorland vegetation at Seathwaite Tarn at *c.* 1940 bc (Pennington 1970). This renewed interest in the Langdales probably resulted from population expansion not only in the northern counties, but also elsewhere in Britain in those areas where Langdale axes formed a normal element in the tool kit. The existence of a widespread demand for them is supported by the presence of Group VI axes on archaeological sites in lowland Britain in deposits as late as *c*. 1800 bc (Smith 1979). It is likely that in this respect at least, early-second-millennium technology and trade patterns followed closely that of the previous epoch.

However, by the middle of the millennium, exploitation of the Langdale tuffs may have ceased, and new metal and stone products had appeared. New designs of perforated stone axes were developed, and Langdale tuffs were discovered by experiment to be too fragile to allow perforation. The advantages in mounting that resulted led to the abandonment of non-perforated axes and development of new lithic resources and the production of a more specialized range of tools. A so-far unlocated source of quartz dolerite (Group XVIII) from one of the thicker deposits of the Whin Sill (possibly in Teesdale but a working site has been identified at Dunstanburg, Northumb.; Burgess, forthcoming) began to be exploited, with an industrial specialization in axe-hammers and battleaxes (Evens *et al.* 1962; Evens, Smith and Wallis 1972). These artefacts occur widely but in small numbers in southern Britain (about 2.2 per cent of all stone tools analyzed; Cummins 1979), but the source will probably prove to be more heavily represented locally, where axe-hammers are numerous stray finds in the lowlands. They are common in the Yorkshire Wolds where they form 9 per cent of determined axes (Manby 1979). A second northern source, of micaceous subgreywacke (a sandstone) probably derives from the Coniston Gritstone areas of southern Cumbria (Group XV), suggesting that local communities who had failed in efforts to produce perforated implements from Langdale material searched for, and found, a suitable alternative. Most of the small numbers identified in lowland Britain were found in the West Midlands (ten implements; Shotton 1959) with a single example in East Anglia, and these probably derived from 'trade' with Cumbrian communities.

Battleaxes are comparatively scarce in the northern counties, compared, for example, with the concentration of finds in eastern Yorkshire (Roe 1979). Axe-hammers are numerous (Fig. 3.5), particularly west of the Pennines, and finds on the lowlands bordering Furness and Morecambe Bay from the densest concentration in England.

Those few examples which have been petrologically identified are from the Group XV source, and local production was almost certainly responsible for the vast bulk of these artefacts.

There is every reason to believe that traditional coastal sources of flint continued to be exploited at least down to the second half of the first millennium, although changes in production techniques presumably dictated by demand led to the development of new designs, for example of tanged and

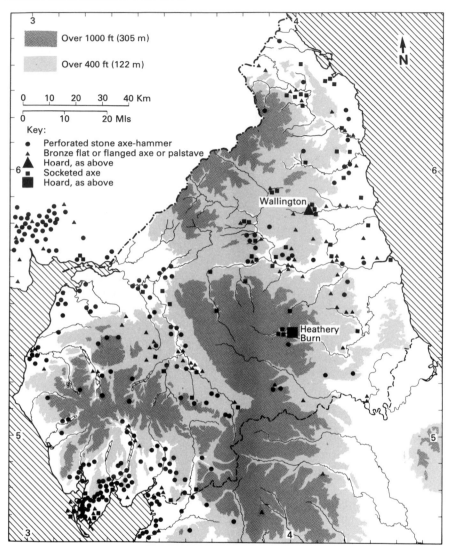

Figure 3.5 The distribution of stone axe-hammers and bronze axes pre-*c*. 800 bc in the northern counties.

barbed arrowheads. A range of scrapers and other domestic tools continued to be made and used, and the degree of continuity between the third and second millennia was such that most types of flint artefacts cannot readily be distinguished. The import of high-quality flint equipment, particularly knives, also continued presumably from the Yorkshire Wolds, and these were highly valued personal objects not uncommon as grave goods.

By the end of the millennium stone artefacts were also in use as querns for the grinding of grain, although querns are frequently found in a mixed or unstratified context, as at and near Skelmore Heads (Powell *et al.* 1963), or at Eskmeals (Cherry 1963). Two fragments of saddle-querns came from the excavation of one of the unenclosed houses at Standrop Rigg (Northumb.) along with possible hand rubbers (Jobey 1983a). Lithic material and jet seems to have been developed to perform a variety of functions associated with decoration (perforated discs of shale or other pendants are not uncommon grave articles) and whetstones, in some cases perforated, presumably for sharpening the novel range of metal equipment. Examples of each were found in a collared urn cremation cemetery dated *c.* 1440 bc at Howick Heugh (Northumb.), along with an artefact identified as a lathe core (Jobey and Newman 1975). Unfortunately, many objects which probably fall into these categories are unprovenanced or finds in some way out of context like the thirty-two jet beads which probably formed part of the necklace excavated by Greenwell from a food-vessel burial at Blawearie (Northumb.), and the various other jet objects and the spindle whorl from the same vicinity (Newbiggin 1941).

Less durable materials were probably widely used for domestic and personal artefacts, but with few exceptions these have not survived. The Branthwaite canoe was associated with a wooden 'crate' made of birch poles and oak and a 'landing stage' which included timbers, at least one of which had been sawn. The development of metal-working probably increased the uses to which wood, bone and leather could be put and many bronze artefacts may well have been used in their preparation. This period has also produced our earliest evidence of woven fabric, in the North largely evidenced in funerary contexts. Woollen cloth was being manufactured, and domestic sheep kept, but perhaps not in great numbers. Early excavation records from burial sites include references to a range of leather clothes, and these may have been common among the living as well as the dead.

Metallurgy

The introduction of metal-working is the one late prehistoric technological innovation which has attracted most attention, and which has provided that period of prehistory with a range of cultural tags. Despite this, it was probably not initially the most important development that occurred in the second millennium, and metal artefacts only slowly gained an ascendancy in little-understood but specific and limited spheres of activity. The earliest artefacts were treasured possessions which may have had a multitude of uses, but cannot be associated with any major change in man's ability to shape his environment. It is arguable that flint knives possessed some advantages over copper or bronze blades. However, flint of suitable quality was always a scarce resource in the northern counties. Subsequent developments in production technology eventually provided metal artefacts with a clear superiority in cutting, sawing or boring, and the adaptability and the malleability of the new material led to a wide range of uses beyond those in which stone tools had hitherto served. Even so, flint arrowheads and scrapers and other domestic, non-metal artefacts certainly held their own throughout the second and well into the first millennia, if not beyond.

The earliest range of metal products in Britain was of copper. Some southern examples were from ores of central European extraction: elsewhere, copper probably derived from Irish ores (Deady and Doran 1972), which seem to have been developed by *c*. 2000 bc. In the northern counties 'copper-age' metal-work is scarce. Only three copper flat axes have been found, one from each of the historic counties, and all were stray finds (Burgess and Schmidt 1981). It seems likely that these were 'trade' goods, introduced from neighbouring areas, and possibly from overseas. Other common products within the 'copper-age' range (e.g. tanged daggers, or flat, riveted blades) have not been found. Gold, in use in ornamentation by the end of the first half of the millennium, is similarly scarce in the North, but is represented by a basket-shaped ear-ring from Kirkhaugh (Northumb.).

By the second quarter of the millennium, bronze artefacts had penetrated the area, but the north of England was peripheral to the major areas of both production and consumption of early bronze artefacts, which have been found in greater quantities in both eastern Scotland and Yorkshire. Copper, flat, riveted blades were superseded by bronze knives and daggers, but none have been found in Durham, only one in Cumbria (Fell 1958) and six in Northumberland (Gerloff 1975), despite the wide chronological range of these typical grave goods from about the eighteenth century to the mid millennium, at least, when flat knife-daggers became common in female graves of the southern Wessex culture. The same pattern is visible in the distribution of bronze flat axes of the mid millennium, which are present in some numbers in Northumberland, but are scarce elsewhere (Burgess and Schmidt 1981). The Northumberland distribution is compatible with an exchange system which was centred on eastern Scotland with contacts with Ireland and the Continent, but in which northern England played only a peripheral role. Concentrations of early axes lie on better agricultural terrains, particularly on the Inverness and Aberdeen coastal plains. The scarcity of comparable artefacts in the northern English counties may be in part due to the comparatively low level of productivity, itself the product of a poor agricultural environment. At least some of this production was local, for moulds for flat axes have been found (Hurbuck, Durham, two finds; Cambro, Northumb.), but the styles are wholly derivative from those of neighbouring areas.

The communities in the northern counties failed to generate major cultural developments in metallurgy in their own area, but made copies or attracted small numbers of artefacts or artificers from neighbouring regions where cultures or artifactual traditions display a degree of initiative and originality.

By the mid millennium products of developed traditions of flat axe manufacture, sporting advantages in the hafting process, had reached the northern counties in small numbers, distributed comparatively evenly both sides of the Pennines, but the far greater density of these finds in east Yorkshire betrays again the relative poverty of the North. The same regional bias is present in the flanged axes which replaced them and which form the commonest and most widely distributed metal artefact of the second half of the millennium, present in numbers in all lowland and particularly riverine environments, excluding the southern part of Co. Durham and north Cleveland where they are rare.

The industries that produced the closed-mould flanged axe and rarer palstaves resulted in a wider range of artefacts than had previously been available. Manufacturing traditions in Britain generally exhibited a high degree of variability of form which may indicate highly localized production (Burgess and Schmidt 1981: 76) in itself perhaps the result of increasingly sedentary craftsmen. In the northern counties numerous types are represented, but it is arguable that most result from the import of either artefact, artisan or model from outside. The Bannockburn type of short flanged axe, for example, was probably of Irish origin, perhaps along with the typologically later Balcarry axes, while the Lisset type found inland in Cumbria and east of the Pennines are outliers of the major concentration in north and east Yorkshire. Palstaves are generally more common in the West than other forms and may derive from a north Welsh industry (Burgess and Schmidt 1981: 125). Contacts between Cumbria and Ireland via Man have already attracted attention, but it is interesting to note that throughout the Bronze Age metalwork in Man displays rather more contact with Ulster than with Cumbria (Bowen 1970; Clark 1935), and certainly greater vigour than the latter with a total of fifty-one items known in 1970.

The improvements in metallurgical methods, and particularly the development of clay moulds in the second half of the millennium, led to a wider range of bronze artefacts, and especially weapons, than had hitherto been available. Spearheads, rapiers and daggers became for the first time a common part of the smith's output. The centres for these industries were also predominantly outside our area, particularly in the Thames valley, but small numbers have been found in the North, and the presence of part of a stone mould for an early rapier at Kames (Northumb.) demonstrates that weapon manufacture was practised in the area. However, the proliferation of weapons came late to the North, with most examples and the large hoards dating from the end of the millennium. Again, there is a strong bias in favour of areas east of the Pennines.

The main side-arm in this developing weapon industry was the rapier, a thrusting weapon which may have been used in conjunction with a dirk in a fencing style of fighting, and which may have been suited only to combat between individuals (Burgess and Gerloff 1981: 113). The use of this weaponry survived in northern England until the end of the millennium when it was gradually replaced by a range of products which included more successful slashing swords and new types of axes. This regional survival was in marked contrast to developments in lowland England where the mass production of swords and of other related forms was introduced centuries earlier.

Throughout the second millennium, the introduction of bronze artefacts and bronze working to the northern counties was small in scale and retarded compared to developments in southern Britain particularly. Where material has been found, there is the same type of bias in favour of the east coast that is visible in the Scottish and Yorkshire evidence.

An important example of regional archaism is the presence of the Wallington tradition of metal-working in the first two centuries of the first millennium (Burgess 1968). In southern England, in the Penard phase, smiths adopted a new bronze-casting technique, by including in the tin–copper alloy small proportions of lead which gave greater ease of pouring, and consequently enabled craftsmen to produce hollow castings. Subsequent generations developed a wide range of numerous artefacts, drawing particularly for sword design on mainland Europe, but incorporating also socketed axes, in what has been named the Wilburton tradition after a substantial East Anglian hoard (Savory 1958; Coombs 1976a). Wilburton assemblages are almost entirely absent from the North, and the few finds that have been made are probably of late date. Instead northern England saw the development of a contemporary, and in some respects complementary, range of metal-work sharing descent from the Penard phase but lacking lead in the alloy, and with a clear archaism in some of the types present. A stone mould for a spearhead from Croglin (Cumbria) again demonstrates local manufacture, but rapiers and dirks probably continued to be made, while the new slashing sword was a rarity present only in a handful of hoards, including that found at Ambleside (Fig. 3.6). The Ambleside hoard, initially found in 1741, illustrates the early phases of the Wallington tradition, incorporating both a metal-hilted rapier and two swords with wide European associations (Needham 1982). The Wallington hoard itself, is very much larger, and well illustrates the mongrel nature of this tradition, including 8 transitional palstaves, 7 socketed axes, 2 rapiers, a dirk and fragments of spearheads (Burgess 1968).

Relative archaism in northern bronze-working traditions is an identifiable factor by the late second millennium, present not only in northern England but also in Scotland and other highland areas. While contact among these areas seems to have been normal, the increasing disparity between northern and southern England implies that a breakdown in the exchange of goods and technology had occurred by *c.* 1200 bc, if not earlier. 'Trade' contact was limited to a northern region which comprised Scotland and northern England, and perhaps other areas peripheral to both the Irish and North Seas, but was largely exclusive of lowland southern Britain, despite some overlap in Yorkshire and Lancashire. This regionalism replaced a 'trade' in Cumbrian axes which was universal until about 1800 bc, but which was not

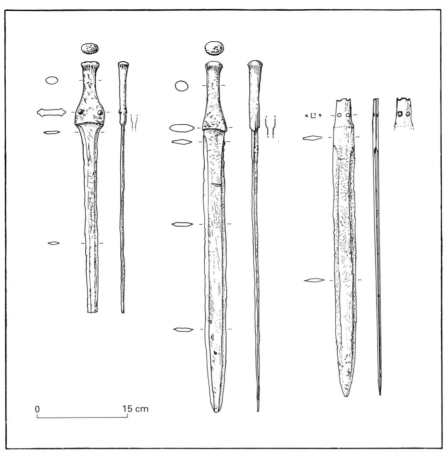

Figure 3.6 The Ambleside hoard: the swords and rapier (after Needham, 1982).

thereafter matched in the distribution of any artefact type, or single source substance whether of metal (with the single exception of tin) or stone.

Factors which contributed to this apparent decline in communication may have been incidental. The collapse in demand for Langdale axes left no northern product of general trade value in circulation. Perforated stone artefacts were readily obtainable from other sources, some of which were, aesthetically at least, more acceptable. Northern communities occupied terrain that was increasingly less productive than southern Britain, so that surplus production was likely to be less, and the attraction for exotic products or artisans from other areas consequently reduced. These factors were certainly not conducive to substantial trade contacts. The eastern bias in the distribution of northern metal-work is an indication of the higher productivity natural to areas on well-drained soils in the rain-shadow of the Pennines relative to communities in Cumbria, but even in those areas where bronze work is most

103

common, northern communities appear to have been conspicuously unsuccessful in competing for high-value products with more favoured areas. Therefore, by this standard, the populations of Cumbria, south Durham and northern Teesside were arguably impoverished communities. In Cumbria and south-west Scotland but not elsewhere, a sizeable local population seems to have developed the stone axe-hammer, perhaps as a cheap and locally available alternative to bronze equipment.

The poverty of the North is not surprising if we consider only environmental factors, but one major resource does seem to have been under-used if it was exploited at all. The exploitation of Langdale stone was a conspicuously successful strategy from the late fourth to the early second millennia, but there is no evidence that any comparable success was achieved in the exploitation of local copper reserves. Copper is present in numerous locations in the northern counties, in commercial quantities in central Lakeland, with major concentrations above Coniston and Ullswater and in the northern fells. The Lake District was Britain's leading copper producer in the sixteenth century AD (Firman 1978), and the Goldscope copper mine was already exploited in the early thirteenth century. Lead extraction was a successful industry in the nineteenth century, and it is a common mineral of the north Pennines (Dunham 1949). Although it is dangerous to argue from negative evidence it seems unlikely that the last two millennia bc saw any substantial exploitation of these resources in the northern counties. No evidence of prehistoric mining is known, and there are no indications in the distribution or typological development of bronze artefacts to support local extraction. While Cumbrian communities showed considerable versatility in adapting to new lithic resources, during the same period they displayed little or no innovative technological success in adopting or adapting metallurgy to their needs.

The extent to which stone and metal artefacts were mutual alternatives is not clear, since the functions performed by neither range of artefacts is fully understood. Some, at least, of the perforated stone implements seem to have been utilitarian, but in others, particularly the battleaxes this seems unlikely, given the high quality and undamaged nature of many examples. Each implement was the product of considerable expenditure of skill and time so that they should be seen as 'expensive' items of the tool kit, high in the relative value attached to them. Copper implements are less likely to be functional. A copper axe is unsuitable for carpentry or forestry, and copper implements may have performed purely social or hierarchical functions. The production of a harder metal implement by the use of a bronze alloy implies a function, but it is debatable whether even a tin–bronze axe was suitable for tree-felling, or would have been sufficiently expendable for this type of use. It has been suggested that axes were in part at least weapons, and that their role lay essentially in display or combat (Coombs 1976a). The growing dominance of bronze weapons (spearheads, rapiers, dirks, etc.) in the hoards of the first centuries of the first millennium implies that bronze products were to some degree at least the exclusive preserve of a social hierarchy. The increasingly frequent deposition of hoards and single items in wet locations may imply some religious or votive significance associated with water (Burgess and Schmidt 1981: 18), and this may also apply to the common 'wet' find-spots of battleaxes and other stone implements (e.g. Blake 1956; Fair 1943: 54).

If, as seems quite possible, the bulk of the products of bronze metallurgy were not utilized in the processes of wealth creation but were merely goods of high-status consumption, then there is little basis in arguing for any fundamental improvement in farming or domestic technology in the Bronze Age. A basket of strategies was already available at *c.* 2000 bc which enabled human populations to clear and utilize considerable tracts of land for food production. While changes in the balance between cattle, pigs and sheep, and between cultivation and pastoralism did occur, these resulted from changes in balance between the environment and the population, not from the impact of novel technologies which may have played only a very minor role in the farming community. Cinders betrayed the presence of copper-working at the Green Knowe settlement, undeniably a farm site, but generally metal objects are rarely discovered in this type of context, and the find of a part of a polished axe at Simy Folds (Co. Durham) may imply the survival of the stone axe in use among farming communities in the area well into the mid second millennium.

Pottery

Pottery forms the third common relic of second-millennium activity, deriving principally from graves. Pottery vessels were used either to contain cremated remains, or as containers perhaps for perishable grave-goods, principally with inhumations. Three related but distinguishable traditions of manufacture are present, and traditionally these have been associated with successive waves of immigration, initially by 'beaker-folk', and then by 'food-vessel-folk' and finally 'urn-folk'. Because so many grave sites were despoiled in the nineteenth century, few contexts have been securely dated, so that the study of ceramic traditions has been conducted principally on typological variables, resulting in a hypothetical and complex system of successive stylistic developments (Abercromby 1912; Clarke 1970). The traditional chronology of ceramic traditions has now been undermined. Beakers were acceptable grave-goods not only in the early centuries of the second millennium but as late as the twelfth and eleventh centuries bc, at widely scattered locations in Scotland. Food-vessels and cinerary urns of various types were deposited over much of the same period, although no examples have yet been dated in graves for the first few centuries. All three ceramic traditions were contemporaneous for long periods, and the revised chronology must have severe implications both for the typological assessment so far achieved, and for the cultural assumptions based on them.

Pottery identified as of early food-vessel type was found at Meldon

Bridge on the Upper Tweed in a late-third-millennium context (Burgess 1976b). Since this is the only non-sepulchral, northern site of the period so far excavated under modern conditions, we are not in a position either to support or contradict this evidence, but their appearance alone has suggested that food vessels derive directly from late neolithic ceramic traditions and particularly from the local Peterborough wares (Cowie 1978). It seems highly probable that a continuous tradition of pottery manufacture was maintained at least in the nodal areas such as the Till valley, and that both food vessels and the various types of cinerary urn derive from this (Gibson 1978). Few domestic contexts have been located, but it is at least arguable that the pottery found in burial contexts was only part of a wider range of domestic pottery. A shell midden at Archerfield (East Lothian) contained domestic wares, flint and bone artefacts (Curle 1908) with close parallels with the assemblages of beaker and food vessels from Ross Links (Northumb.) and Walney Island (Cumbria), both of which came from sand-dune sites. Pits at Yeavering (Northumb.) contained pottery, and sherds of beakers were also found, apparently unassociated with the cemetery. At Green Knowe (Peebles), about 350 sherds of 'flat-rimmed ware', fragments of bucket-shaped vessels and a large, undecorated urn with close affinities with sepulchral wares, all came from the unenclosed settlement site (Jobey 1978b). A thick, carbon encrustation suggested that these vessels had been used for domestic purposes. At Houseledge (Northumb.) a range of pottery fragments was found, particularly in the farmyard and nearby fields, many of which bore cord ornament, and these included one possible beaker sherd (Burgess 1982). Hand-built pottery came from Standropp Rigg, some of which had been decorated with scored lines (Jobey 1983a). In Upper Teesdale, comparable wares have come from the domestic sites at Bracken Rigg and Simy Folds. These sites demonstrate beyond reasonable doubt that the manufacture and use of domestic pottery was commonplace, at least by the last few centuries of the millennium. Previous to this, such use remains a matter of inference, but is at least highly probable, and the large numbers of sherds recovered from the excavation of the Yeavering henge monument strongly supports this (Harding 1981).

Beakers alone of these ceramic traditions, derived from a mainland European source, and their introduction and ready acceptance into northern Britain may have been associated with a 'package' of technological innovation and religious or cultural change. They are the least common of the local ceramic traditions, and in burial contexts are commonest in 'primary' locations beneath cairns, but this primacy may be due to a sociological rather than a chronological pre-eminence. Like the other ceramic traditions, the vast majority of the local beakers were probably manufactured in the general vicinity of their eventual find-spots. Pottery is one type of artefact which is unsuited to an itinerant life-style, or to long-distance trade over unmade tracks and the multiplicity of stylistic variations may derive from a local, and even a domestic, manufacturing tradition. Gibson believed an individual potter was responsible for vessels found at Roseborough, Beanley and Lowick (Northumb.), 32 km apart (Gibson 1978: 22), and this is perhaps the degree of movement that we should expect for the top range of a fragile and easily damaged commodity. Most domestic wares were probably used at source.

Social, ritual and territorial behaviour

The comparative retrenchment that seems to have occurred in the mid to late third millennium bc was reversed in the changing conditions of the early second millennium, and led to a new range of social artefacts. Environmental improvement may have stimulated population growth, but other factors were probably also important. This was initially felt in the old nodal centres where once again surplus labour was channelled into 'civil engineering' projects, comparable in scale to the long barrows that preceded them, and like them performing a social or religious, rather than a utilitarian function. The henge monument was an insular British development common in southern Britain in the later third millennium, but so far examples in the northern counties have only been dated to the period *c.* 1950–*c.* 1590 bc (Harding 1981). The form of these monuments is dominated by an earth bank and inner ditch, broken by

Plate 3.3 The henge at Milfield North (Northumb.) from the west. Under an arable crop, the interrupted ditches retain dampness and retard the ripening of the grain. An outer circle of pits is barely visible, although excavation by Dr Anthony Harding during the period 1975–1978 revealed substantial pits and a later re-use of the moment as a focus of burial in the Anglo-Saxon period.

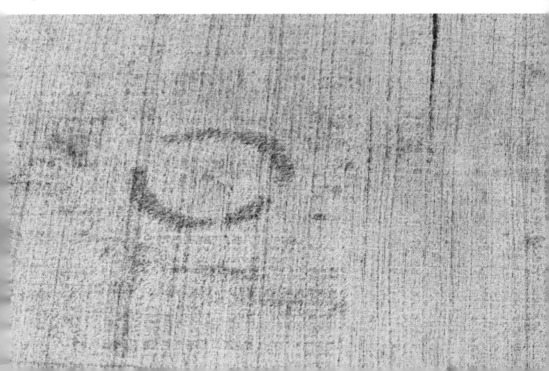

Plate 3.4 King Arthur's Round Table at Eamont Bridge (Cumb.) is the smaller of the two surviving henges of the central Eden basin. The site was in part excavated by G. Bersu in advance of construction of the roads that slight the north and east ditches.

one or two (but rarely more) entrances. Other features present are internal pits and circles of sockets, and external pits, all of which were present, for example at Milfield North. In the Milfield complex, an 'avenue' or droveway seems to play a unifying role, running close to (but in the case of Coupland henge, through) the majority of the henges and towards the smaller, northerly group.

In comparison with examples in southern England, the Northumberland henges are small, the largest at Coupland being 95 m in diameter across the crest of the bank. The Milfield North example is only approx. 40 m diameter *in toto* including the outer sockets, and the area within the ditch is only approx. 15 m diameter. With the exception of Coupland and Milfield South, all are type II henges, generally thought to be later, and typically the smaller type (see Fig. 3.1).

The Milfield henges were broadly contemporary, and presumably served similar functions. A study of their architectural peculiarities has failed to identify any obvious purpose in their form or siting, and the excavator could only suggest that their orientation on various local hills might be of significance. Some were used for burial purposes, but this may have been secondary, and the large internal pit at Milfield South henge yielded numerous fragments of bird and animal bones, rather than human.

Although we do not know the intentions behind their construction, the Milfield henges point not only to a numerous population but also to a group organized under a social and political hierarchy that was capable of planning, perhaps over several years or even decades, to develop individual projects and then to carry them through to a successful conclusion. The linear grouping of the henges and their apparent association via a ditched 'avenue' or droveway suggests that in broad strategy, this purpose was extended uninterrupted over a period at least as long even as several generations. This implies an enviable stability and a 'governmental' continuity of purpose in the nodal area.

A smaller, but otherwise comparable henge group is present in the central Eden valley close to Brougham (Cumbria). The Mayburgh is a class I henge (single entrance) 117 m in diameter, with a bank of small stone and earth, and no ditch. Four standing stones are in the interior. King Arthur's Round Table is a class II henge, with a bank external to the ditch approx. 85–98 m diameter. Excavation uncovered a 'cremation trench' (Bersu 1940) but no useful dating evidence. Other possible henge monuments are at Broomrigg, and at the Little Round Table (Burl 1970).

As at Milfield, these monuments were constructed in a rich lowland and riverine environment, largely devoid of orthostatic stone, where a substantial population probably developed early in the second millennium.

Other areas have produced comparable monuments. The context of the Hastings Hill complex (Tyne and Wear) could easily lie in the early second millennium. The Copt Hill and Hastings Hill barrows have certainly produced a range of Bronze Age material, but the possible *cursus* which appears to connect them has not been dated (Harding 1979). A stone version of the lowland avenue or *cursus* of Milfield or Hastings Hill was present at Shap (Cumbria), but has suffered from post-medieval agricultural improvement, and only one stone is now standing (Clare 1978). It is not clear whether one or two separate alignments were originally present, but the bilinear monument (or monuments) stretched over approx. 3.5 km. The granite boulders were probably in origin erratics, deposited by ice on this area of limestone and then collected and erected. As at Hastings Hill, the presence of a barrow, on Skellow Hill, appears to link the Shap 'avenue' with funerary ritual and this is a link common also with the reported, but now destroyed, 'avenues' and circle complexes at Lacra, Broomrigg, Moor Divock and elsewhere.

Stone circles are common in Cumbria. It has already been suggested above that the larger examples may have performed a social or ritual function, and some may already have been in use in the late third millennium. However, the *floruit* of even the large stone circle was probably in the early second millennium, when they should be seen in most areas as a direct parallel to the henge which is conspicuously absent in southern and western Cumbria. At the interface between these two cultural areas, in the Eden valley, the henges may have replaced the stone circle of Long Meg, which was then used as a funerary monument.

The association between stone circles, avenues, and burial mounds or cairns is a strong one, that apparently developed by the mid millennium, but only became common west of the Pennines, with examples in Northumberland apparently outliers of other Scottish regional traditions (Burl and Jones

Plate 3.5   The re-erection of the Goggleby Stone; the last orthostat of the Shap stone corridors was re-erected in 1975, under the supervision of Tom Clare of Cumbria County Council.

1972). The small stone circle with a central burial cairn occurs in the Eden valley and in west Cumbria, with examples also in the major Lake District valleys (Dixon and Fell 1948). It is unclear whether the circle and the cairn need necessarily be contemporary, particularly since the addition of a cairn to an existing circle or henge is evidenced at various sites like Cairnpapple (Scotland) and Long Meg. The flints, jet ornament and Group VI axe from the central cairn at Grey Croft, Seascale, for example, suggest use of the cairn in the first half of the millennium, but the circle may have predated this episode (Fletcher 1958). In many examples, as at Oddendale, Crosby Ravensworth, the interior of the stone circle is almost entirely taken up by a cairn, and in these cases the association appears somewhat firmer, although the possibility still exists of a stone-defined, mortuary space pre-existing the sepulchral monument.

Burial rites
Burial is the easiest understood function of the ritual apparatus of the second millennium. However, it is unlikely to account for the construction either of henges or large stone circles, which may, perhaps, be associated with the other major life crises, and this represents a departure from the much more direct funerary role played by civil engineering projects in the third millennium. In the second millennium, burial rites were responsible for a range of lesser monuments, albeit in overwhelming numbers. Until about 1200 bc burial continued to occur in or under barrows or cairns, and a considerable degree of

continuity may lie behind the interment of numerous deposits in existing sepulchral monuments like Hastings Hill and Copt Hill (Tyne and Wear). The numbers of burials beneath some long-used monuments, and the tendency for burial mounds to be grouped are such that the term 'cemetery' becomes obligatory; the twenty interments beneath a beach-derived, pebble cairn at Warkworth, for example, can only be described in this way (Greenwell 1890: 66). Similarly, thirty-two deposits of burnt bone were recovered from underneath a large cairn at Kirkoswald (VCH, I, 1901, p. 239).

Most sizeable cairns or barrows were opened in the nineteenth century, and many grave associations are now lost or dispersed. Worse, there is no opportunity to use objective dating methods, and the apparent inadequacy of typological dating of pottery styles means that most deposits are neither dated nor datable; nor in most cases is it possible to assess the life-span of any of the excavated, multiphase monuments. However, it is possible to point to a greater diversity of burial rites in the second millennium than were present in the first. The group burial practice of the long barrow tradition is absent (although multiple inhumations did occur in Scotland) but a bewildering variety of grave-goods are found in a wide range of combinations. In addition, both inhumation and cremation were widely utilized as methods of disposing of the dead, both making use of mounds, but with some divergence in grave goods, particularly in pottery.

It seems likely that some burials accompanied by beakers are among the earliest of these grave associations. At least, in no case does a beaker occur in a context demonstrably later than either a food vessel or urn, although this may be a social or cultural, rather than a chronological primacy (Megaw and Simpson 1981). The suggestion that beaker graves represent an individual of high status is supported by the relative wealth of these associations. Graves with several beakers are not uncommon, occurring for example at North Sunderland, Dilston Park and Amble Pier (Northumb.) and at Clifton and Brougham (Cumbria). Many come from well-made, if crude, capped stone cists normally at least covered by a low mound, and almost invariably associated with an inhumation. Other grave-goods are scarce, but where present do include metal-work which is among the earliest and richest in the area, including the Kirkhaugh gold ear-ring, a dagger from West Lilburn and a bronze pin from Clifton. Also associated in a few instances is archery equipment, although in the northern counties this is confined to barbed and tanged flint arrowheads, and does not include the range of equipment present in the South. Whetstones and jet buttons also occur. Although by no means conclusive, the evidence does give some support to the hypothesis that beaker grave associations derive from burial practices specific to a social élite, and the presence of child and female inhumations suggest that this élite is more likely to have been hereditary than personal. The purpose of the pottery is unclear, but may be associated with victuals, in which case there seems to be some evidence for a belief in an after-life. In many cases one or more burials accompanied by a

Plate 3.6 The Eggleston Urn; this recent example of second millennium bc funerary furniture demonstrates that burial sites already existed in comparatively poorly drained lowland situations before the abandonment of the traditions of accompanied cremations at the end of the middle Bronze Age.

beaker, form the primary deposit under a cairn, and in such cases the cairn may be of complicated construction. At Chatton Sandyford the first of three inhumations associated with beakers was deposited *c.* 1670 bc in a crouched position with two V-bored jet buttons (presumably on clothing) on a land surface which had been burnt, and into which four stakes had been driven. Two subsequent burials with beakers occurred in rock-cut pits and the cairn was constructed in a series of episodes on a well-laid platform of sandstone boulders placed on edge, to which was added a kerb of upright, roughly dressed stones (Jobey 1968a). Two cremations were added, one in an enlarged food vessel, and one perhaps originally deposited in a bag of perishable material, before the erection of the bulk of the cairn.

Food vessels are also commonly found with inhumations, although cremations are only marginally fewer. Most often they were deposited in cists formed by the excavation of a pit in the lowlands, or built of stone where soil cover was thin (Gibson 1978). Associated grave-goods are similar to those found with beakers, including a bronze knife at Amble, but most contained no other artefacts. Food vessels do occur in the context of secondary burials in barrows already covering beaker graves, but many have been found to have accompanied the sole episode of deposition (e.g. Broomhill, Prudhoe, Northumb.) or are primary deposits in monuments which were then reused. Like beakers, food vessels are scarce west of the Pennines, and absent on high ground. Both types are conspicuously scarce in southern Cumbria, where there may have been resistance to those cultural elements which these burials and henges represent.

Plate 3.7 Aldoth barrow, near Holme Abbey, Cumbria. A near-vertical aerial photograph, taken by a kite-suspended camera, of a ditched round barrow after excavation; in the centre the cremation burial had been placed in an upturned urn, in a shallow pit, prior to the construction of the barrow.

Cremation was widespread in the second millennium, was present in a wider range of environments than alternative burial traditions, and was associated to some extent with food vessels, but more importantly with a range of cinerary urns probably specifically developed to contain the ashes. Even so, many cremations were totally unaccompanied. The rite of cremation is securely based on local late neolithic practice, and the cinerary urn displays a similar parentage, including those forms developed from the food vessel (Cowie 1978). The cinerary urn is normally found under or in a mound, and many were protected by a pit or cist, but there was a strong tendency to reuse existing barrows. Where cremation in an urn constituted the primary deposit, others were frequently added, so that, for example, three cordoned urns came from a cairn at Appleby Slack, and two were associated with a pygmy urn and a bronze knife from Urswick, Cumbria (Fell 1958). In some cases substantial cemeteries developed, as at Kirkhill (Northumb.) where an inverted collared urn contained the partial remains of at least three adults and a child, deposited *c.* 1292 bc, and records exist of a further eight vessels from the immediate vicinity (Miket 1974). A mound within a stone circle at Howick Heugh (Northumb.) covered the cremation of an adult female and child with a collared urn, deposited *c.* 1440 bc, and possibly three additional cremations. Although our knowledge of most burials is neither age or sex specific, cremation of children and women was not uncommon with, for example, the cremated body of a child of three to six years found in a cordoned urn in a cist under a small barrow at Warden Law, Tyne and Wear (Ford and Miket 1982).

Not all burials were under mounds. 'Flat' graves may have been common, although it is difficult to distinguish a ploughed-away barrow from a flat grave. Rock shelters were also used, at Corby's Crags, Edlingham (Beckensall 1976), and Goatscrag (Northumb.) where four cremations were found, two in enlarged food vessels, amidst a complex of pits and post-holes (Burgess 1972), and elsewhere caves may have been favoured burial sites.

Second-millennium burial rites were diverse, but contained major elements which derive from the previous epoch, in some cases reusing existing monuments. Many barrows were probably always intended as places of multiple burial, or as cemeteries, and it seems likely that many served communities over long periods (Petersen 1972). Perhaps the most important development was the newfound, common practice of including grave-goods, and in particular pottery, but this represents an adaptation of existing burial traditions, rather than a cultural revolution due to mass migration.

The expansion of sepulchral monuments into new areas in the second millennium was accompanied by the innovative practice of relief sculpture, which produced a range of stylized symbols, but most commonly cup-and-ring marks. The affect was achieved by pecking, and it represents a time-consuming and skilled craft which provided an obvious outlet for religion symbolism or, possibly, some form of secular display. Although the symbols do occur on stone circles – as, for example, on Long Meg – their creation probably

Plate 3.8 A cup and ring marked stone at Weetwood Moor (Northumb.). Such decorative motifs are common on the Fell sandstones of Northumberland, but are only rarely found elsewhere in the northern counties. The distribution may be derived from the suitability of rocks found in this region, but may also represent the emergence of an economically more successful community in Northumberland than elsewhere in north England, in the middle Bronze Age.

post-dates these monuments, and they share some of the characteristics of the distribution of burial cairns on the lower fells, in some cases occurring on stones incorporated in cairns. However, although they are present in all the northern counties, over 90 per cent occur in the lower sandstone fells of Northumberland in a broad band from Hexham to Wooler, and there is no reason to think that this distribution derives from uneven recording (Hadingham 1974: 56; Beckensall 1983). The cup-and-ring marked stone and closely parallel forms appears to be a phenomenon even more closely associated with the communities of Northumberland than the axe-hammer was with the population of Cumbria, and both these distributions underline the cultural distinctiveness of these two areas, and the connections between Northumberland and south-east Scotland and Yorkshire on the one hand, and Cumbria and Dumfries and Galloway on the other. On the other hand, we should not ignore the physical constraints that the distribution of suitable sandstone surfaces placed upon the artists of the Bronze Age.

A social and political hierarchy

The construction of henges and large circles required the presence of organizers within society, and burial practices provide further tentative support for a social hierarchy. However, by the mid millennium the construction of new henges ceased in the Milfield basin, and this probably applied equally elsewhere, on both sides of the Pennines. The abandonment of the great communal structures coincides with the spreading out of human activity into areas hitherto under-exploited. It is tempting to see some causal association between these episodes. Population pressure in the henge-building areas may have led to social stress sufficient to destroy the influence of a ruling class which was no longer able to direct labour into non-productive engineering, nor restrict the emigration of the land-hungry. We do not know.

When evidence for a social hierarchy re-emerges late in the second half of the millennium it takes a different form, and is typified not by the wholesale organization of labour, but by the centralization of resources into the hands of a competitive élite who responded to the developing anarchy by using scarce resources to exchange for personal weapons. During the latter part of the second and into the first millennia, weapons became increasingly common, more specialized and made up an increasingly dominant part of the bronzesmith's output. Worsening environmental conditions and widespread land exhaustion were probably responsible for much of this technological spiral, as the defence of scarce farming land and mobile herds against human predators became a necessary survival strategy. Contemporary with the scramble for weapons, communities withdrew from monumental architecture. The scattering population of the mid millennium maintained, admittedly on a small scale, something of the monumental traditions of the earliest Bronze Age. Without the resources and probably without the ambition to construct henges, the scattered communities constructed and maintained sepulchral monuments which incorporated elements of the hengiform, but more particularly the stone circle tradition, and in Cumbria at least maintained a substantial degree of continuity albeit in diminished forms.

By the end of the millennium, the barrow or cairn burial tradition was abandoned. The method of disposal of the dead in the later Bronze Age is obscure, but the resources which had been used in the rites of the dead were now increasingly devoted to obtaining weaponry, and deposits of weapons commonly occur in circumstances reminiscent of votive offering, in wet locations. If the marginal productivity of labour also declined, this may explain why the social and political hierarchy probably hardened, and the gap between producer and protector or predator widened. By *c.* 800 bc cattle-reeving was probably endemic in northern society, and life had, perhaps, sunk to its least secure point since the neolithic revolution began.

Later Prehistory 800 bc–AD 100: The Re-emergence of a Settled Landscape

Climate and the environment

The climatic deterioration of the late second millennium reached its maximum effect by about 800 bc. The impact on the habitable environment in northern England was both considerable and detrimental, and was most severe in areas of naturally high rainfall – that is, a positive bias existed against upland areas and against exposed western hills. The result was a large-scale increase in hill soil wash particularly exacerbated where human interference had effectively deforested the upland landscape, and further wide areas with poor drainage were reduced to impoverished moorland or blanket peat. This amounted to a massive capital loss to prehistoric communities which had hitherto been able to rely upon an inheritance of virgin or near-virgin soils. Not only was expansion on to still unused high ground made impossible, but much of the marginal terrain of the lower fells, where widespread settlement and land-use had occurred, were now rendered uninhabitable. This loss of habitat was at its greatest in Cumbria, and particularly in western Cumbria where, in Eskdale, for example, abandoned cairnfields represent something approaching a third of the lowland or lower fell area which had been available to communities centred on the valley, and these occur at altitudes as low as 150 m. Even admitting that this third was the least productive and quickest to become impoverished, we are still dealing with a long-term crisis that can only have led to considerable pressures on the local community towards pauperization, mutual aggression and population loss. East of the Pennines/Cheviots the worst affected areas were the higher foothills, and the fell sandstones which were probably also largely abandoned by this time (Jobey 1981b).

In the lowlands pollen cores suggest that the pattern of clearance established in the second millennium continued well into the first, with discontinuous clearances used for mixed agriculture before eventually reverting to woodland. By the eighth century some clearances were beginning to be continuously maintained on the east of the Pennines, and particularly in Co. Durham (Haselgrove 1981: 76), but generally discontinuous episodes recur until the last two centuries before Christ. At Steng Moss (Northumb.), for example, the third recorded clearance phase peaked about 636 bc (Davies and Turner 1979), and at Camp Hill Moss the second began *c*. 720 bc. At Steng Moss the fourth episode was considered to be more continuous, if no different in scale, beginning *c*. 578 bc. At Neasham Fen (Teesside), fresh, but temporary, clearance on an unprecedented scale was recorded *c*. 750 bc. In the Cumbrian lowlands no significant break was noted in the pattern of generally discontinuous clearance until after Christ (Walker 1966: 200).

It has been argued that a climatic improvement occurred in the last four centuries bc and into the Roman period, with reduced rainfall and an improvement in mean temperature (e.g. Turner 1981: 261). If this is justified – and it seems difficult to envisage viticulture in the conditions prevailing in southern England at 1000 bc – improved conditions would naturally have spread from the South and East, reaching the north-west of England last of all. There is some evidence that this was the case. Over much of England there occurred a marked increase in the tempo of clearance. In the North this major and permanent deforestation episode was late in arriving, and in many areas, particularly in the uplands and in the West it remains elusive until after the Roman occupation. At Steng Moss (Northumb.) extensive clearance began *c*. 20 bc, but further south in mid Weardale clearance was under way by *c*. 110 bc (Roberts, Turner and Ward 1972), and at Thorpe Bulmer, near Hartlepool, a substantial episode began *c*. 114 bc although it did not peak until the third century AD. At Hutton Henry (Durham) it was dated *c*. 108 bc and at Hallowell Moss at *c*. 4 bc. At Neasham Fen, Teesside, an unprecedentedly long-lived and dramatic clearance episode began *c*. 538 bc.

This evidence suggests that the permanently cleared environment which had been typical of well-drained, particularly limestone soils for 1,000 years and more was now being extended to allow permanent settlement and exploitation on the lowland terrains and that the threshold of permanent clearance was reached first in the East, where rainfall was naturally less. There are far fewer traces of comparable activity in Cumbria where only the Rusland Moor pollen diagram in the south of the county has so far produced a substantial clearance episode beginning in the last century bc (Dickinson 1975). Elsewhere, Walker, working largely without carbon dates, has suggested a post-conquest date for full-scale clearance of the lowlands, and has suggested that it may even have reached maximum effect in the post-Roman period. When Pennington summarized the vegetational history of Cumbria, she identified a 'Brigantian' clearance episode occurring nowhere earlier than *c*. AD 200 (Devoke Water) and generally in the later Roman and early post-Roman periods (Burnmoor Tarn, Morecambe Bay). The bias of her evidence is to the Lake District as opposed to the Eden valley, where it seems likely that clearance may have been somewhat earlier.

That the uplands had been largely cleared by this time by a combination of human and climatic agents cannot be doubted. The Widdybank Fell site (Durham) failed to support reforestation after *c*. 620 bc, and at Moor House, close to the summit of Cross Fell, a final clearance episode was dated *c*. 262–255 bc (Turner 1981: 270). Much of the Cumbrian, Pennine and Cheviot uplands were open, but uninhabitable, with impoverished soils and flora. In addition, the major lowland mosses were fully established, involving major loss of habitat in the Cumbrian coastal lowlands and on Teesside. It was therefore, only the intermediate areas of better-drained lowland soils that constituted the remaining reserves of land with agricultural potential, in part shrouded still by deciduous forest. These reserves were already being eroded in the early millennium by anthropogenic clearance. While the inexact nature of carbon-14 dating makes it difficult to determine whether any one of the permanent clearance episodes was earlier than the Roman occupation, the cumulative impression is of a major clearance episode, with its origins firmly rooted in a late prehistoric context, continuing unabated into the Roman period. By the end, late in the Roman occupation or even beyond, human pressure was threatening some areas of lowland forest with extinction.

Settlement strategies, social hierarchies and the rural economy

The human response to what was probably an increasingly impoverished environment was highly complex, but two major features can be distinguished from the scanty archaeological record. The most obvious is the abandonment of widespread land in use in the preceding epoch, but now allowed to revert to waste or poor-quality pasture. The second, and more difficult, is the increased level of territorial awareness within the community, and the growing investment in basic physical security, from encroachment or outright attack upon persons and possessions.

In the first half of the millennium, palisaded sites make their appearance, frequently occupying well-drained situations on the edges of the uplands. In the northern counties there is a disproportionate concentration in the Cheviots, but this is probably due to particular conditions that render them visible as surface features (Ritchie 1970), and there is a strong possibility that examples in the lowlands have been lost under agricultural pressure. Palisaded enclosures or settlements were constructed over a very long period, from at least *c*. 700 bc probably into the Christian era so that the presence of a palisade alone is not a particularly useful chronological determinant. In broad, chronological terms palisaded settlements succeeded, and were over several centuries contemporary with, unenclosed and platform settlements. It is not clear whether this succession was immediate or broken by the adoption of some other, as yet unidentified, class of site, but the possibility of an unbroken succession is strengthened by the identification of what is thought to have been an unenclosed timber round-house preceding the palisaded settlement at West Brandon, above the mid Wear valley (Jobey 1962), and by the comparatively late dates now identified for some unenclosed sites such as Hallshill (Gates 1983).

Many of the earliest palisaded enclosures to be identified underlie late prehistoric hillforts, occupy defensible sites, and may therefore have had a defensive function. The type-site for this group is at Hownam Rings, near Roxburgh in the Scottish borders, marginally within Scotland, in the Cheviots to the south of the Upper Tweed, where a primary palisaded enclosure was replaced by a second, before being abandoned in favour of stone and then multiple earth rampart defences (Piggott 1947–48). This sequence, known as the 'Hownam succession', has been recorded with and without variation on several northern English sites, as well as others in southern Scotland including the complicated series of developments at Broxmouth, where the large number of carbon dates should eventually allow this settlement to replace Hownam Rings as the principal type-site in the area (Hill 1978, 1982c). The modern Anglo-Scottish border is irrelevant to this period during which Northumberland at least shows strong cultural affinities with its Scottish neighbours. The earliest palisade so far dated by carbon-14 in Northumberland is that at Fenton Hill (*c.* 680 bc), but so few have been excavated that this may be misleadingly late, given that Gledenholm (Dumfries and Galloway) has produced a date of *c.* 1010 bc, very close to the date of the earliest occupation of Mam Tor, Derbyshire (Coombs 1976). The other available early dates are in the sixth century bc, and it may be that the mid millennium saw the widespread construction of palisaded sites. Where a site succession has been identified, as on several hillforts like Yeavering Bell, the palisade invariably forms the earliest structural phase.

While there are variations in constructional technique, the majority consisted of one or two lines of close-set vertical timbers set in trenches normally 30–60 cm broad and deep, approximately square-cut to take a flat-ended tree-trunk – defining an enclosed space generally of subcircular form, the perimeter broken by a gate or removable fence section, defined by single-terminal post-holes. The size of the interior varies enormously. The approx. 50 m diameter of the Ingram Hill or Yeavering Bell palisades place them within the smaller bracket where single palisades are uniform. At West Brandon double palisades enclosed a single massive 17.5 m diameter round-house supported on four concentric rings of post-holes. In a few instances, the larger palisades enclosed larger numbers of hut circles, as at Hoseden (Northumb.) where nine hut circles have been detected, and a classification system has been proposed to distinguish between the 'homestead' with less than three huts and the 'settlement' with three or more (Ritchie 1970).

The construction of palisades represents a fundamental reappraisal of the needs of a society which had hitherto apparently been content to inhabit unenclosed settlements. The desire to delimit the habitative complex may have its roots in social or economic imperatives, but given the preoccupation of at least the upper sections of society with weapons, the provision of basic security seems an obvious factor. A palisade or timber fence is not an impressive method of fortification, but it is a possible method, one which is compatible with a well-wooded environment and one which could be erected easily using only local resources, and which, combined with guard dogs, could provide at least a warning system to alert the inhabitants to potential danger. The skeletal remains of dogs were found at Broxmouth, where the same interpretation was proposed (Barnetson 1982). The location of some, at least, of the upland palisades on sites commanding wide views is consistent with this suggestion. Some, but we do not know how many, were later developed into fully fledged defensive sites and it may only be the minority – largely in poor strategic locations – which were abandoned without development beyond the palisaded level. The need to provide a minimal barrier that will offer an alarm system should possible competitors appear, is totally consistent with the inferred overpopulated nature of the late Bronze Age, and the consequent sharpening of competition for control of resources. It is also consistent with the insights afforded by Irish literature which, although essentially 'post-Roman' in composition, describes a long-lived social structure occupying a hierarchy of enclosed sites with some obvious points of similarity with late prehistoric northern England. While it would be wrong to argue that the presence of a palisade necessarily implies a defensive function, we should not overlook the position that the palisade occupies on the first rung of a scale of defensive enclosure up which several hillforts can be shown to have climbed. That the palisade was also adopted to circumscribe the living space of a humble homestead does not detract from this point.

There is an apparent discrepancy in the distribution of palisades in Northumberland and those areas elsewhere both west and east of the Pennines, although it seems likely that this is in part at least explicable by the uneven pattern of research. Only one example has so far been identified in Cumbria, predating the rampart of the hillfort at Skelmore Heads, Furness (Powell *et al.* 1963).

The possibility that the few other hillforts in the county began as palisaded enclosures cannot be ruled out, particularly given that Burnswark (Dumfries and Galloway) to the north originated as a palisaded hilltop enclosure in the mid millennium (Jobey 1977–78). Even so, the apparent scarcity of palisades may be a reliable reflection of the true state of affairs, which is paralleled in Durham, where West Brandon is currently almost the sole candidate.

The adoption of the palisade points towards other important changes in the structure of the economy in the later prehistoric period. With the possible exception of Fenton Hill, the upland palisaded sites appear not to be associated with field systems. It seems likely that the occupants were pastoralists, and that palisades and timber fences may have played a role in corralling livestock, or in excluding them from areas specifically set aside for habitation (cf. Strabo, IV. 4. 5. 2). Those sites where double palisades provide a wide gap between inner and outer circuits (e.g. Harehope, Lothian) may have combined these functions, with livestock excluded from the habitative central area but safely corralled in between, held in by a fenced entrance-way between the two palisades. That many sites have been located on the upland margins – by this time abandoned by agriculturalists – implies a switch in these areas at least to a ranching style of extensive herding, paralleled widely in southern Britain, and cattle seem to have been the dominant species.

It is understandable that timber construction was the initial mode of enclosure and shelter in the north-eastern communities. The timber round-house had already a long ancestry, and building techniques seem to have been brought to a new state of perfection in the latter part of the first millennium, using both the isolated timber ring of supports to create very large houses, and the more common construction-trench technique for a fence or palisade-type outer wall capable of bearing a conical roof. A slight porch was added to the last phase round-house at West Brandon (Jobey 1962), but such architectural diversions are by no means common, and the excavation of a screen giving wind protection to the entrances of huts at Witchy Newk and Carey House (both Northumb.) has not been repeated (Hope Dodds 1940). Hut entrances generally face south-south-west, perhaps to avoid the dominant wet winds. The resultant structures were probably comparatively long-lived, and provided accommodation of anything from 50 to 120 m² floor area that was adequate for a family group, or in larger instances for more than a single family. The majority of homesteads held only a single round-house, in many cases repeatedly replaced.

Soon after the mid millennium, the major palisaded sites were being superseded by new defensive enclosures, conventionally recognized as hillforts of various types, and many new examples may have developed on new sites. Huts continued to be constructed of timber up to and into the Roman period. The gradual abandonment of the palisade as an enclosure system probably occurred against a background of increasing deforestation, which left specific localities in Northumberland devoid of the stands of timber required to rebuild a major palisade, and ultimately led to the abandonment of this enclosure mechanism even for a small homestead in north Tynedale by the early Roman period. The little structural evidence we have is consistent with this interpretation. The mid-millennium site at Huckhoe utilized oak for the palisade timbers, implying considerable deforestation by the axe. By the end of the life-span of the last of the three palisades at Kennel Hall Knowe homestead in north

Plate 3.9 Super-imposed timber-built houses at the Late Prehistoric/Romano-British settlement of Kennel Hall Knowe, North Tynedale. In the foreground can be seen the construction trench and packing stones of the phase II perimeter palisade. The phase I palisade runs at an angle across the round houses and was sealed by them. (photograph: G. Jobey)

Tynesdale, probably in the second or third century AD, the site was surrounded by impoverished open scrub and moorland vegetation. Not surprisingly, the enclosure that succeeded it was defined by a ditch and bank. The deforestation that was contemporary with the construction of a major palisade was sufficient to appear on a pollen diagram from an adjacent bog in the mid millennium at Burnswark. Modern estimates suggest that between 1 and 2 ha of prime forest had to be cut to build an average palisade (Hanson and Macinnes 1980).

The prehistoric community was running into a major problem of resource management. Retarded or even severely curtailed by grazing stock, convenient timber supplies were unable to renew themselves within the lifespan of the palisade. The abandonment of this resource-expensive technique may have become necessary to any community which was determined to remain in a particular location.

Determined these groups undoubtedly were, and the high incidence of multiphase sites creates a strong impression of rights over property and territory at all levels of society, whether or not strictly continuous. The mid millennium saw the beginning of the development of new systems of defence and enclosure, which progressively replaced palisades as the typical site architecture. The hierarchy of sites already present to some extent among palisaded enclosures became far more pronounced, as hillforts developed

123

substantial defences, but lesser sites remained weakly enclosed, within palisades or lesser ditch and bank systems.

Hillforts proper developed during this period, but the general lack of large-scale excavation on these often massive monuments makes even the broad chronology imprecise. In the most general terms, the Hownam succession seems to apply in Northumberland and southern Scotland. At Hownam the two phases of palisades were superseded initially by an approx. 3 m wide sheer-faced stone wall perimeter, then by multivallate defences, these in turn giving way to an undefended settlement on the site later in the Roman period. The sequence holds on other sites, but where it has been tested by excavation there have been fundamental differences in the chronology, with the defences at Broxmouth (East Lothian) for example, ending well before the Roman period (Hill 1978). The development of defences occurred on some sites early in the half-millennium, or even possibly before. At Burnswark the initial palisade was replaced by a timber-revetted rampart which incorporated charcoal, probably from the palisaded site, dated c. 525 and 500 bc. The chronology is dependent on estimates of the life expectancy of a major palisade, but this is unlikely to have been as great as a century (Jobey 1977–78). Yeavering Bell is one of a handful of large sites on the edge of the Cheviot uplands commanding the Tweed valley, spaced approximately one every 16–22 km, that is, something like a day's journey in rough country (Jobey 1965a). Most of these can reasonably be portrayed as minor *oppida*, inferior in status to the very largest hillforts of the area at the end of their development, but occupying a more senior position in the site hierarchy than the vast majority of hillforts. The very largest sites are peripheral to northern England, but Traprain Law has been claimed as a centre for the Votadini in Northumberland and the Lothians, challenged in size only by Eildon Hill (16.7 ha), the principal site above the Tweed valley (Feachem 1966). Elsewhere, sites that may have performed a comparable function are much smaller, Burnswark (7.1 ha) is the largest example of these, ranking in size closely with Yeavering Bell, Rubers Law or Hownam Law. Taken together, these hillforts represent the highest tier in a social and political hierarchy which was typical of the Tyne–Forth region where they probably acted as tribal centres, and the large numbers of hut circles require that they be classed as defended 'towns'.

Far more common in northern Northumberland are the univallate or, more frequently, multivallate sites, typically less than 0.4 ha in internal area and comparable in size to many palisaded sites (Jobey 1965b). Univallate sites like South Titlington or North Pike House tend to be sited with less regard to tactical advantage, and the enclosing earthworks are correspondingly weaker. It may be that these were among the casualties in the chronological development towards an ever more defensive model. At Harehaugh, at least, a single line was demonstrably superseded by a multivallate form, and at other sites, like Greaves Ash, surface traces suggest a development from less to more adequate defensive lines. Elsewhere, as at Huckhoe, a multivallate system directly replaced a palisaded enclosure, following lines dictated by the latter, and apparently without a break (Jobey 1959). Where any development is visible, it is initially from a less to a more defensive site, and most forts ended up as multivallate. The recent excavations at Fenton Hill have revealed a five-phase development from the initial small palisaded site dated in the seventh century bc, to a site enclosed by a box rampart and ditch in the fifth century. Enlargement of the site in the late third century involved the replacement of the perimeter with a new box rampart with bedding trenches rather than individual post-hole construction. The final phase of occupation involved a total remodelling of the defences, and the construction of a triple-dump rampart system with intervening ditches, which had apparently been abandoned by the time Roman artefacts penetrated the area in the second century AD [6].

Only a small minority of hillforts experienced a radical increase in internal area when univallate defences were replaced by multivallate. The inhabitants clearly placed a high premium on security – about half have three or more defensive lines. However, the small internal area and the general absence of a water supply mean that they can never have been intended to serve the community as points of resistance during a lengthy military campaign. The small hillfort was designed to deter the sudden or casual raid, not from distant tribes but from nearer neighbours.

Most are near-circular or oval, like Roughting Linn, Doddrington, occupying a site on locally raised ground, and in the Cheviots there is a strong preference for primary spurs overlooking the main valleys, as at Pawston Hill and Brandon Hill. Local conditions were probably responsible for the presence of stone ramparts on the Cheviots where ditches are necessarily rock-cut and consequently uncommon. Where conditions allowed – on deeper soils – ditches appear and systems of defence in depth could attain a breadth of as much as 45 m at Alnham Castle Hill, with ditches, berms and banks. The lack of recent excavation on the vast majority of these sites leaves us without a clear picture of the development of fort defences which may have been as complicated and contrary as the situation at Broxmouth or Fenton Hill suggest.

Timber huts predominate in fort interiors as they do on palisaded enclosures, visible on the surface as ring-grooves or ditches on sites like Corbie Cleugh, as circular, hollowed floors at Colwell Hill or scooped platforms at Gleadscleugh. There seems little reason to believe that these are other than permanent settlements, and numbers of huts, where ascertainable, even in small forts can be as many as fifteen, implying occupation of the larger sites by a community of several families. It is common to find terracing on the hillside to accommodate round-houses, since many forts occupy sloping ground. It is rarely possible from surface features to distinguish any distinctive hierarchy in house size or construction, although the group of ring-ditched houses at West High Knowe palisaded site may be an exception to this (Jobey 1966a). Small hillforts may have taken over the niche in the settlement site hierarchy previously occupied by the larger palisaded enclosures. Whether or not this is the

Plate 3.10 Dod Law West; inner and outer ramparts of one of the numerous hillforts of northern Northumberland during excavations in 1984; beyond – the Milfield Plain towards Yeavering Bell.

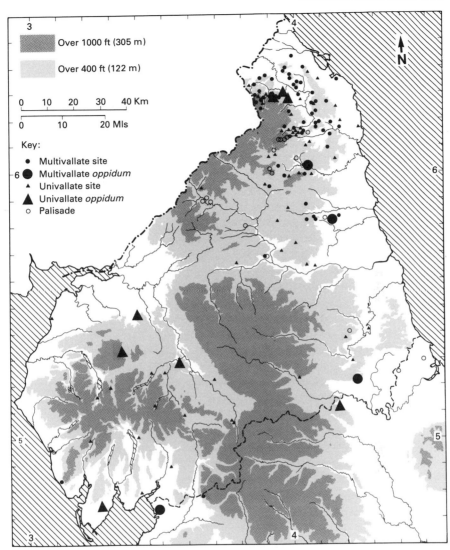

Figure 3.7 Palisades and hillforts in the northern counties.

case, their distribution is better known, and may imply a degree of awareness of agricultural resources which is unlikely to be coincidental (Fig. 3.7).

The pattern of defensive sites located along the upland fringes above the river Tweed, the Till, the Coquet and their tributaries may have acted as nodal points from which control of valley resources could be organized, and integrated with upland grazing. It is easy to imagine the degree of mutual antagonism resulting from competition for control in the margins between them and particularly in the management of unfenced grazing land on the fells. In such

Plate 3.11   The hillfort on Carrock Fell (Cumb.), is a rare western example of the stone rampart defended *oppida* of north Northumberland. Unlike Yeavering, there is here no trace of internal structures, and the remote and high location of the site makes it an unlikely candidate for permanent occupation, even in the ameliorating climatic conditions of Later Prehistory. A stone cairn occupies the summit, and medieval shielings utilize the little protection from the wind afforded by the stone rampart.

Plate 3.12 A two period, ditched enclosure at Castlesteads, Dobcross Hall, Dalston (Cumb.). The large outer ditch probably defines a Later Prehistoric, defensive enclosure; the small ditched enclosure in the centre was occupied during the Roman period. Faint traces of ditches radiating from the outer ditch can be seen on three sides.

circumstances the development of fortification systems is understandable, and the typical small hillfort of northern Northumberland probably played a fundamental role as the permanent home of a social and political élite and their dependants, that, combined, formed a numerically significant element within the community. If we move away from the Cheviots and their foothills the plethora of hillforts rapidly thins out. A handful of examples lie in southern Northumberland, with the only substantial site south of the Wansbeck at Camp House near Whalton (approx. 2 ha), but very few have been located, for example, in the Upper Tyne valleys. South of the Tyne, hillforts are conspicuously absent, with rare examples at Beacon Hill, Heightington, where a multivallate 1.3 ha site occupies a hilltop, Shakerton Hill near Bishop Auckland, or Maiden Castle near Durham City. Although there was some provision of defences on sites along the upland margins (Haselgrove 1981), the evidence for fortification of small sites is extremely thin. The situation in Cumbria is only marginally better. A single, *oppidum*-size fortification of approx. 2.1 ha is defined by a tumbled stone wall originally about 2.7 m thick on the irregular apex of Carrock Fell at the unusual height of about 650 m above OD. The total lack of hut circles and the remote and exposed nature of the site makes it probable that the fort was never permanently occupied (*contra* Collingwood 1938). Below Carrock Fell in the heart of Inglewood Forest a second site is a more likely candidate for permanent occupation, at Dobcross Hall (Higham 1981a). A scarp top, univallate enclosure of approx. 3 ha appears from aerial photographs to be the hub of several radial ditches – a situation with obvious parallels on the southern chalklands. Where sectioned, the perimeter ditch was slightly under 3 m deep and was 4.2 m wide with a near-vertical inner face, and a possible palisade slot was identified on the outer side. The centre of the enclosure is occupied by a small rectangular ditched homestead of the second/third century AD, which is thought to post-date the construction of the outer, more defensive perimeter.

Elsewhere in the north and east of Cumbria, defended sites are either very small – like Castlesteads, Yanwath Wood (RCAHM 1936: 254) and the scatter of sites in the Lakeland valleys – or they are unlikely to be of the late pre-Roman period. Such include the bivallate site at Petteril Green which produced Roman pottery (Spence 1933) and a bivallate, rectilinear enclosure at Kirkbampton (Bellhouse 1961a). The Solway plain is almost totally devoid of multivallate sites, in stark contrast to Northumberland. In southern Cumbria, four forts have been located, each sited in a distinct geographical area. A bivallate, near-circular site has been identified from aerial photography near Whicham on the coastal plain (Fig. 3.8). Otherwise these sites are upstanding. Skelmore Heads is a natural defensive site (approx. 1.3 ha) near Urswick, Plain Furness, which was successfully enclosed by a palisade, and then provided with a rampart only on either side of the main entrance (Powell *et al.* 1963). Warton Crag, near Carnforth relies largely on natural defences, but has three widely spaced banks on the north side, defining an enclosure in total about 8 ha. Between them Castle Head on the east side of the Cartmel peninsula is a small and simply defended bluff (Forde-Johnston 1962). Each of these sites occupied what can be described as a peculiarly favoured niche in the late prehistoric environment. Whicham is sited so as to exploit a wide range of coastal lowland and upland environments. Skelmore Heads and Castle Head occupy relatively sheltered sites on the east side of the two principal peninsulas of southern Cumbria with comparatively fertile lowland resources, and Warton Crag occupies a site on an important area of limestone terrain. It is attractive to view Skelmore Heads and Warton Crag at least as minor *oppida* sites with political significance over a wide area.

Multivallate defences are very rare in Cumbria, Durham and Cleveland, and small defensive sites of all sorts are only thinly distributed. These two factors offer a sharp contrast with the situation in Northumberland north of the Wansbeck. For whatever reason, the supply of labour made available for non-subsistence activity was significantly greater and better organized in the latter zone. It seems likely that the population of the old nodal area based on the river Till coped significantly better with the changing environmental circumstances of the middle Bronze Age, and emerged in the late prehistoric period with a denser population organized within a more competitive framework than their Cumbrian neighbours. The markedly drier conditions

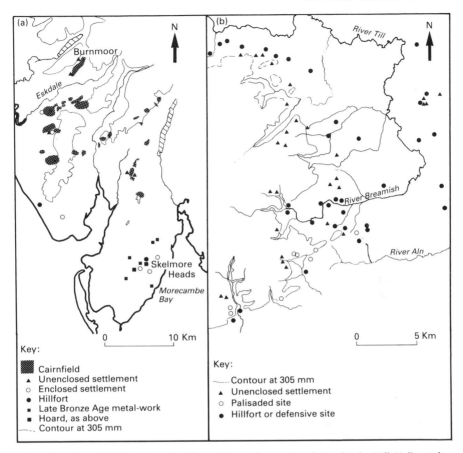

Figure 3.8 Later Prehistoric archaeology: (a) south-west Cumbria; (b) the Till Valley (after Jobey, 1983a).

and better farming land away from the Irish Sea may have been responsible, and the peculiarly base-rich soils of the Cheviots may be important. Outside Northumberland, the aristocracy appears to have been either sparser or less apprehensive, and the distribution of defended sites implies that a larger block of territory was 'administered' from each. Population density may have been lower, and wealth per unit area may have followed suit. By the second half of the millennium the central Northumberland waste lands had the appearance of a cultural frontier. Northern Northumberland displays a hierarchy of settlement sites comparable to the defence-conscious communities of central southern and eastern Scotland. Cumbria and the Galwegian peninsula were relatively under-defended, and the organization of settlement in Durham and Cleveland may have owed more to patterns in southern Brigantia than to Northumberland. The absence of the small defended site in the settlement hierarchy may point to a greater political authority at the tribal level south of

131

the Wansbeck, that may have guaranteed the community local security from an anarchic aristocracy operating without a massive investment in linear defences.

Even in northern Northumberland, the fortified sites formed only one tier in a settlement site hierarchy with at its apex a handful of *oppida*. The scale of multivallate defences makes it highly improbable that they were constructed solely by the residents of the site. Indeed, it seems unlikely that residents of high status would be present during the risky stages of site development, and even less likely that they would carry out the manual labour. The unfinished forts of southern Scotland make it clear that ditch excavation and rampart construction was done by gangs of labourers (Feachem 1971), and it seems certain that this manpower was drawn from the clients or estate workers of the aristocratic patron, who normally resided outside the ramparts in undefended or only weakly defended settlements. Such a pattern of small homestead enclosures is well documented in Northumberland in particular, and increasingly in the other northern counties as well, the major difficulty being to distinguish between sites of the late prehistoric and Roman periods. In Northumberland, it has been possible to arrive at some morphological distinctions, between the earth and timber sites with timber houses in the late prehistoric and the development of stone buildings in the second century AD (Jobey 1966a), but on some Cumbrian sites timber houses are present even late in the Roman occupation.

At Catcotes (Cleveland) a complex of enclosure ditches was associated with two circular houses, one with internal partitions and two pits of the type often associated with grain storage (Challis and Harding 1975), apparently in use about the time of Christ. At Ingleby Barwick on the Tees extensive crop marks with a subrectangular enclosure may date to this period, and similar extensive settlement was found at Dragonby. At Thorpe Thewles (Cleveland) ditches of a large, rectangular enclosure were backfilled within the late pre-Roman period and succeeded by extensive settlement which was apparently then abandoned at the Roman occupation (Haselgrove 1981). Elsewhere in Durham, the enclosed homestead appears the dominant form (Harding 1979). In Northumberland the numerous weakly enclosed sites, listed by Jobey in 1965, must be relevant, and, in addition, aerial photography subsequent to that date has revealed numerous ditched enclosures on the coastal plain (Jobey 1970a, 1980). In north Tyneside, excavations on a series of homesteads in advance of the construction of the Kielder Dam have revealed a group of palisaded enclosures with timber houses occupied in the last two centuries bc, then replaced by stone-built houses set in stone-built enclosures, or earth banks and ditches, in the Roman period (see p. 193).

Excavations on several ditched enclosures on the Northumberland lowlands has demonstrated late pre-Roman period occupation, utilizing the standard techniques of timber house construction. Enclosures are generally sub-circular or near square, and the basic shape owes nothing to the chronology of the specific site. The Roman–British farmer had no monopoly on the square or rectangular form, and the specific shape chosen had topographic or functional rather than chronological determinants. The rectilinear, ditched enclosure at Doubstead, for example, does not seem to owe its shape to construction in the Roman period (Jobey 1982). Without excavation, it is not generally possible to distinguish between the enclosed settlement of the late pre-Roman and the Roman period in any of the northern counties, and this obviously introduces considerable uncertainty to distribution maps. The major exception to this applies to those sites with stone houses which may not have developed until the second century AD (Jobey 1960), but it is by no means improbable that pre-Roman stone round-houses may be identified in the future. The converse regarding timber buildings does not apply, and the adoption of a stone-building technology was never universal, perhaps depending more on the comparative availability of stone and timber than any other factor. Timber houses were retained in some Cumbrian lowland sites through the period, in parallel with the stone-building tradition in the uplands, where stone was readily available. Perhaps the least chronologically reliable form of settlement is the so-called scooped enclosure, identified by a series of scooped areas and house platforms within an enclosure, sited on hill slopes in non-defensive positions (Jobey 1966a). The distribution of this demonstrably multiperiod type is centred west of the Cheviots, but examples occur in Northumberland above the river Till and its tributaries, and in north Tynedale, and similarities with other enclosed homestead forms suggest that most should be viewed in a late prehistoric or Roman context.

In Cumbria, aerial photography has revealed a plethora of both nucleated and extensive concentrations around Wigton and Penrith. Although no excavated settlement site has yet provided unqualified evidence of pre-Roman occupation, researchers working in the area have always been prepared to entertain the probability that a proportion at least of these sites may predate the Roman period. A comparable aerial photographic study on the Isle of Man has revealed a near-continuous complex of ditched boundaries with nucleated sites and enclosed ring-ditches across much of the fertile northern plain. It is tempting to see some at least of these groups of ring-ditches as hut circles, but where a Cumbrian example was tested by the spade, near Holme Abbey (Cumbria) it proved to be a burial mound of the second millennium [7] and at present it seems likely that the Manx examples largely conform to the same type. However, some of the large groups identified in south Scotland and Northumberland are more likely to be huts (Gates 1983; Maxwell 1983).

While the prevalence and chronology of unenclosed settlement remains to be demonstrated by excavation, the typical late pre-Roman farmer of the period in the North-east, at least, seems to have occupied a site delimited by any one of several enclosure techniques, the selection depending on the local availability of timber and stone and on the nature of the subsoil. He occupied the same type of round-house his forefathers had built over numerous centuries and had the facility to corral cattle in adjacent yards. He kept livestock within a territory that was long established and recognized, however grudgingly, by his neighbours. He might grow and his family might consume a grain crop, in part perhaps as a mildly alcoholic drink and he might have a plough or ard, with which to cultivate recognizable fields defined by ditches, banks or even hedges. He probably paid rent in kind to a landlord, but marketed little grain himself, and depended as much or more on his herds than on cultivation for a living. He had sufficient control over his resources to be able to anticipate in his turn handing over a functioning farm to his descendants, even over several generations, and the necessity to subdivide his holding may have been a greater risk than the ending of his blood line. While many sites like West Brandon seem to have been abandoned before the conquest after a lengthy or short occupation, other homesteads, like Kennel Hall Knowe, tended to increase in size and eventually to incorporate more or larger houses (e.g. Tower Knowe). The tenacity of this farming community is illustrated at Hartburn where thirty-six houses were identified, with a minimum of twelve replacement phases (Jobey 1973). In other instances small groups of enclosed homesteads like those on

Plate 3.13 A bivallate settlement, The Dog Mills, Isle of Man. This site is one example of several recently identified from the air; apparently dividing up the land between this site and its neighbours are ditches and tracks, which suggest the long and intense development of enclosures as a means of control of land-use over a wide area.

Doddington Moor (Northumb.) or Aughertree Fell (Cumbria) may imply population increase and territorial subdivision.

While much of this population expansion probably belongs within a Roman context (Jobey 1974b), its origins must be contemporary with the agricultural expansion of the late prehistoric period, and by the time of Christ, the north-eastern counties of England, and possibly the Solway plain and Eden valley were becoming increasingly infilled with farming units. In Durham estimates of site density based on aerial photography record up to one site per square kilometre in the best terrains, and settlement density reached higher levels than this in some areas of Northumberland and northern and eastern Cumbria, although the density of occupied sites at one time must always have been less. Although the real chronology of site development and the density of occupation may never be known, what is now apparent is that a considerable scatter of homestead or farm sites were present on all the better-drained, lowland areas, and penetrating well into the major river valleys. Whether or not these homesteads were the sites occupied by the lowest status group of the 'native' population, they do represent a numerous, low-status type of settlement that complements the provision of defended forts and *oppida* in northern Northumberland, and of the more isolated defensive sites elsewhere.

The rural economy

The initial identification and classification of late prehistoric settlement in Scotland and the northern counties led naturally to a view of economic strategies dominated by pastoralism. Encouraged by the development of the classic upland/lowland contrast in interpretation, the north and west of Britain were seen as profoundly separated from the south and east where the 'Little Woodbury' mixed farming economy had been identified, and was thought to have sheltered a mobile ranching community of late prehistoric cowboys summed up under the umbrella of a 'Stanwick' economy (Piggott 1958). Like most great truths, this contrast was exaggerated, and the process of reassessment has since led to a major rectification in the balance of the evidence in favour of sedentary communities with some at least of the strategies of the lowland farmer.

Despite this, cattle do seem to have been of major importance in the northern economy. Little statistically viable research on livestock has been possible because of the paucity of faunal remains, but on sites like Doubstead (Northumb.) ox and horse bones were dominant (Jobey 1982), and at Kennel Hall Knowe (Northumb.), Thorpe Thewles (Cleveland) and Dryburn Bridge (East Lothian) cattle were the most common species among sheep/goat, pig and possibly fowl (Jobey 1978a; Heslop 1984; Triscott 1982), and the same general pattern is evidenced at Broxmouth (Barnetson 1982). At Hartburn (Northumb.) young cattle were dominant among the butchered remains, followed by sheep and horses (Jobey 1973b). The dominance of cattle as a food source was probably a very real factor in the local economy, and is totally consistent with the ranching style of land-use already proposed. The primacy of beef cattle was probably long-lived. The stalling of cattle probably accounts for the ubiquitous stock corrals which form one of the commonest features of the homesteads of the late pre-Roman and Roman periods in Northumberland. At Catcote (Cleveland) sufficient faunal remains were recovered from a late pre-Roman and Roman site for detailed analysis (Hodgson 1968), but the total number of beasts was small. A calculated 78.6 per cent of meat consumed on the site derived from cattle, a high percentage of which had not yet reached maturity. Sheep, horses and pigs accounted for the remainder in descending order of importance, in contrast to the small sample at Tynemouth, where sheep amounted to some 50 per cent, followed by pigs and oxen in approximately equal quantities. It may be that Tynemouth had a bias towards sheep, utilizing coastal, marsh grazing. Sheep would have been more vulnerable to predators inland, where it is worth noting that the prevalence of wolves kept upland Lancashire almost devoid of sheep well into the thirteenth century AD. The inhabitants of Coxhoe (Durham) and Stanwick, further inland, both displayed a strong preference for beef over mutton or pork (Haselgrove 1981), and the consumption of wild fauna is conspicuously absent on all sites.

Despite this evidence of a bias in favour of cattle-rearing, the presence of sheep, pigs and horses support the view that cattle-raising was not the sole pastoral activity, and that a wide range of habitat was in use. Grain consumption was also present on most sites, at least in the late pre-Roman period. The apparent absence of arable farming – such a major plank in the early analysis – depended upon a misinterpretation of the role of the grain storage pit, then considered to be a *sine qua non* of Iron Age agriculture. More recent opinion has consigned the storage pit to a less crucial role, concluding that their use had more to do with storage against sale than the operation of a subsistence economy (Fenton 1983). Since the excavation of Staple Howe (East Yorkshire) it has been recognized that above-ground storage 'granaries' may have played an important role in all areas, and similar rectilinear settings of post-holes have been excavated at Huckhoe (Northumb.). Paired posts there and at West Brandon may have acted as racks for drying meat, skins or vegetable products (Jobey 1959, 1962). That no examples of storage pits are known north of Catcotes in Cleveland, is therefore, not detrimental to the presence of late prehistoric agriculture. Quernstones provide evidence of grain consumption at least from the mid millennium into the Roman period, and possibly beyond. Agriculture may have been centred on the lowlands, and may have been intermittent in any one area, but the evidence from the pollen diagrams demonstrated a quantitative increase in arable acreage and production at latest beginning about the time of Christ, and probably two centuries earlier. When a stone-walled enclosure was constructed at Tower Knowe (North Tyne) it replaced a palisaded, timber-built settlement, and seems to have been associated with clearance cairns, walls and a hollow-way

Plate 3.14 Plough-marks sealed by the phase III bank of the 'native' settlement of Belling Law, North Tynedale. The striations are probably the result of a single ploughing episode during which the plough or ard tip scratched the subsoil. Similar relics of plough activity are commonly found under the early Roman forts of the region; although some could belong in the context of land-use in the second millennium bc, most should probably be seen as the result of the re-emergence of intensive land-use strategies in the later prehistory. (photograph: G. Jobey)

(Jobey 1973a). The late prehistoric farming community extended ploughing on to marginal, heavy lowland soils, where the furrows have been sealed under later structures. Parallel ard- or plough-marks and ridge and furrow have been located under a barrack block and the Via Quintana at Rudchester Roman fort (Gillam, Harrison and Newman 1973), demonstrating the availability of the technology necessary to produce ridges. Similar remains have come from under the forts at Carrawburgh (Breeze 1974), Wallsend and Halton Chesters, and from under the Roman road at Walker (Jobey 1965a). Although the context supplies only a *terminus ante quern*, a late prehistoric date seems likely. The farmer responsible for the plough-marks outside the palisaded homestead on Belling Law might have occupied that homestead (*c.* 160 bc onwards), and those whose plough left marks under the hillfort rampart at Fenton Hill may have inhabited the palisaded settlement that preceded it on the site (Jobey 1977). Carbon from a drainage ditch overlain by Hadrian's Wall at Tarraby Lane, near Carlisle yielded a date of *c.* 130 bc, and was associated with plough-marks, demonstrating the presence of agriculture on heavy soils in eastern Cumbria, at least, in the ultimate pre-Roman period (Smith 1978).

No plough fragments have come from the northern counties of England, but they have from Traprain Law in East Lothian. In addition, wooden ard parts from Milton Loch (near Dumfries) were dated to *c.* 400 bc, and from a crannog at Lochmaben, close by, to *c.* 80 bc. This direct evidence for ploughing in adjacent, and comparable areas, provides artefactual support for the widespread and growing application of ploughing as an economic strategy in the northern counties in the last centuries bc.

It is possible to envisage an upland–lowland economic integration by the mid millennium, based on the products of lowland agriculture and upland grazing, brought together by the aristocratic occupants of defensive sites in the upland margins. Even so, we are far from demonstrating any such hypothesis that agricultural field systems were associated with many late prehistoric settlements (Halliday 1982), or even attempt to reinstate the possibility that some major linear earthworks, such as are present on Doddington Moor (Northumb.), should be associated with late prehistoric sites (Hogg and Hogg 1956).

Northern traditions of metal-working

The use of tin–bronze which had been retained in the area over the first few centuries of the millennium, gave way by about 700 bc to technologies utilizing a lead–bronze which had already been dominant in southern England for several centuries. The change made possible the adoption of a new wave of specialized production using hollow casting techniques and turning out weapons and ornaments (Burgess 1968). Swords of the carp's-tongue variety were part of a range of military equipment which included bucklers and spears. By far the largest hoard from the northern counties was that extracted over a number of years in the nineteenth century from the Heathery Burn Cavern (Durham) during quarrying (Greenwell 1982; Britton 1971). Tests on one of the nineteen socketed axes demonstrated a remarkably high (24.3%) lead content, placing the technological context of the hoard beyond doubt. Most of the axes were ornamented, creating further problems for those who would like to see these as having a function in forestry. In addition, there were two leaf-shaped sword blades and parts of a third, eight leaf-shaped spearheads and a range of lesser products – knives, a razor, chisels, gauges, pins, rings and armlets of which two were fashioned of gold. The presence of half of an axe-mould, tongs and raw and waste metal convinced Greenwell that the hoard was part of the stock of a manufacturer, but the non-metal elements in the hoard make its status doubtful. The most elaborate single piece was a bucket or cauldron of thin-sheet bronze 42.5 cm high and 35 cm diameter, made by riveting sheets together with the lip and base reinforced (Hawkes and Smith 1957). Comparable examples from Hatton Knowe (Lothian) and

Ranvenstonedale (Cumbria) demonstrate that the bucket or cauldron was widely distributed in the North in the mid millennium.

The bias in favour of aristocratic display in this type of assemblage is very noticeable. The bronze-smith's craft was turned into channels most likely to lead to lucrative reward, and his major, if not his only clients, lay in the warrior class. The general preponderance of items of display and ornamented weaponry over functional domestic equipment is overwhelming, and the farming population obtained little help from the changing bronze technology, which, in any case, produced a softer and less functional cutting edge.

Again, as among the middle Bronze Age products, there is also a geographic imbalance in the distribution of the smith's output. The distribution of the most typical product, the socketed axe, is a valid indicator of the basic trends. Apart from a small number, including the Skelmore Heads hoard, in Plain Furness, all the Cumbrian examples have come from the Eden or Lune valleys, and most from the Penrith area (Clough 1969). Southern Durham and Cleveland are devoid of examples, and with the exception of Heathery Burn and a handful of stray finds, the vast bulk have come from Northumberland, from the coastal plain in general, from the middle reaches of the Tyne and Cheviot valleys, where they form the southern end of a concentration spreading across southern Scotland towards Glasgow and up the east coast (Burgess and Schmidt 1981: Plate 113). The Yorkshire three-ribbed socketed axe is only one variant of this group of products (Burgess and Miket 1976). As its name would suggest, its distribution and probably its manufacture was based in Yorkshire, and the central Pennines and Lake District valleys and coastal plain failed to attract either artificer or artefact. The only hoards recovered from Cumbria are two from the protected, east-facing pocket of good agricultural land around Skelmore Heads in Furness from which also derived the only late Bronze Age sword (Ewart Park type) so far found in the country (Fell and Coles 1965). This distribution bias points once again to a relative affluence among the aristocracy of Northumberland in contrast to their neighbours west of the Pennines and south of the Wear, yet even they failed to attract the wealth of craftsmanship of eastern Yorkshire or Lincolnshire. The total absence of socketed axes from the Lake District valleys compares unfavourably even with the thin distribution of middle Bronze Age axes and palstaves in the same area, and it is arguable that a progressive pauperization of the community had occurred, even compared to Plain Furness and eastern Cumbria. We return to an appreciation of metal-work as an indicator of both aristocratic affluence and indirectly of rural productivity and find the northern counties generally, but Cumbria and Durham in particular, at the bottom of the English 'league'.

Some founding did occur in the North, and a school of metal-work has, for example, been proposed in the Eden valley. The diversity of regional types suggest that artificers were increasingly sedentary, but other examples seem to have been imports. The 'Meldreth' type of socketed axe, for example, has an overwhelmingly southern English distribution, but examples did reach both Furness and northern Northumberland.

Another characteristic of the period was the adoption of horse-harnessing techniques, again put to good use by the warrior aristocracy. The Horsehope (Peeblesshire) hoard contained horse fittings, and the Heathery Burn hoard included bronze axle mountings, discs and antler harness fittings suggestive of a well-appointed cart or even chariot, which in the context of the associated weapons must be seen as part of an aristocratic assemblage. By 700 bc, the well-off in northern English society rode or drove where they did not wish to walk. In addition, they adorned themselves with a wide range of personal ornaments including bronze or gold armlets, rings and a variety of brooches, beads and other forms in lignite, stalamite, amber and less pretentious pebbles, shells and teeth. The British inclination to import pretty baubles was noted with some disdain by Strabo (IV. 4. 5. 3) drawing presumably on the work of Poseidonius. Some of these items at least could come into the hands of the simple homesteader, as did the hinged bracelet and spiral finger-ring of the ultimate pre-Roman ditched farmstead at Doubstead (Northumb.).

Although the smith's work was dominated by the demands of the affluent, some products were available to the wealth-producing members of the community, at least to craftsmen in wood, who might have used the chisels and gouges in the Heathery Burn hoard, which also contained a possible flint and steel, and a dubious lead spindle-whorl. However, little was available to assist the peasant farmer in his tasks, and the lower orders probably relied still upon flint for a cutting edge, as seems to have been the case at the second century AD site at Milking Gap, and implements of bone and antler of the type that formed a significant part of the Heathery Burn assemblage, including 'spatulas', spindle-whorls, pins, buttons and a boar's tusk knife.

The gradual introduction of iron-working in the last centuries bc had major implications for the working farmer, for whom the provision of markedly stronger and more efficient equipment could considerably improve output per man-hour. There is some evidence that parts of the farming community took advantage of this potential. The extensive enclosure complex at Catcotes incorporated a clay furnace inside a hut (Challis and Harding 1975: 1, 16), rock-cut bowl furnaces were a feature at West Brandon (Jobey 1962) and crucibles and slag came from Dragonby (near Scunthorpe) and Traprain Law to the north. By the second century AD, a smithing hearth was incorporated at Huckhoe, and by the third century AD, iron was being worked at Witchy Neuk (Northumb.), and it may be that iron smithing was spreading from the South throughout the late pre-Roman epoch and into the Roman period. The scarcity of iron agricultural equipment from any area other than the military zone suggests that the use of iron never became as commonplace among the agricultural wealth producers of the North as it did in the South, although some post-conquest southern Scottish hoards were thought to contain a significant 'native' element and included a range of agricultural and related equipment including ploughshares (Piggott 1952–53; Rees 1979). Exceptionally, ploughshares came from Traprain Law and an iron adze from a Northumberland homestead (Jobey 1960), but both were probably from post-conquest contexts.

If iron implements were ever utilized in any quantity west of the Pennines before the conquest, they have left remarkably little trace, and the very existence of a pre-Roman 'Iron Age' is in doubt for Cumbria. Again the east–west contrast appears marked before the Roman period, when local coal and ore extraction rendered iron smithing a common activity on at least the Northumberland homesteads.

Even given the relative poverty of the late prehistoric cultures of the North when compared to other regions, there is still visible an enrichment in craftsmanship, and an unprecedented range of equipment and ornament. While the most exclusive and pleasing items, like a gold necklace of biconical beads from Fourlaws and the amber discs from Simonside, were the preserve of the aristocracy, indications are that modest display items were within the reach of the farmer by the end of the millennium. In addition, the great new potential of iron ploughshares, spades, etc. was beginning to present the better-off peasant farmer with new opportunities. This technological leap may even have played its part in the take-off of permanent clearance and cultivation that typified the ultimate pre-Roman period east of the Pennines.

The possibility of a quickening tempo to the northern economy in general terms should not be underplayed, despite the afforested picture painted by classical authors. Professional craftsmanship appears in areas other than metal-working, using precision metal equipment in the working of wood in particular. The building of wheeled carts, etc. required considerable craft skills, as displayed in the wheels found at Newstead and Bar Hill, and a shallow bowl found at Stanwick may equally have been a professional product (Wheeler 1954). In addition, querns emerge in the late pre-Roman/Roman period as a mass-produced artefact. Saddle-querns are thinly spread in the northern counties, and were probably complemented by about 300 bc by equally scarce beehive querns. However, the appearance of rotary querns at the end of the millennium coincided with a substantial increase in the numbers found, and querns become at that stage a mandatory and in some cases a frequently renewed piece of domestic equipment on almost every farm site. At Huckhoe (Northumb.), to take the best example, a single saddle-quern contrasts with over thirty broken, upper rotary quernstones, some of which were already redundant when an enclosing stone wall superseded the initial palisade around the settlement (Jobey 1959). In Cumbria, beehive querns may have enjoyed a longer life-span, and a single example from the unexcavated site at Castle Hill, Dufton, contrasts with the twenty to fifty pairs found during eighteenth-century field clearance of an ancient settlement site near Burton in Lonsdale (RCAHM 1936). Even so, rotary querns were present by the middle of the

Roman period on several sites. It seems likely that some quernstones at least were professionally fashioned both at the quarry and in the finishing stages, and they may have been traded over some distance. In addition, it has been suggested that defensive site architecture may have become a specialist trade by the end of the millennium.

If craftsmanship in metals, wood and stone was on a professional footing the scope existed for a simple exchange economy based on markets and specialist communities. In the North, coin never became a significant feature either in the market or as a display item as it had done among the southern and eastern tribes by about the time of Christ. However, a handful of sites stand out from the general pattern of hillforts and homesteads, on account of their size, and, where excavated, on account of the diverse wealth of their artefactual evidence. Traprain Law in East Lothian clearly fits into this group, although there are special problems of interpretation at the site (Jobey 1976). Forty items of late Bronze Age metal-work and ironwork of the pre-Roman period herald the early phase of the settlement as a distribution centre and manufacturing site with contacts with Ireland and mainland Europe. Its trading and metal-working survived the Roman occupation, and probably flourished in the new conditions, and a lengthy Roman coin series contrasts with the scanty coin evidence from contemporary rural settlements. Yeavering Bell may have served a similar function for the south side of the Tweed valley, and certainly attracted Roman wares (Jobey 1965b: 31–4), but insufficient excavation has occurred to be sure of its status. Further south, the current reinterpretation of the Stanwick defences suggests that this may have been an entrepôt site in the late pre-Roman period, handling the import and redistribution of fine wares, amphorae and their contents, and glassware (Haselgrove 1981), and this could have performed an important economic function both in Co. Durham and in the Eden valley over Stainmore to the west. Both the Catcote complex and the Thorpe Thewles site (both Cleveland) had successfully attracted imported Gallo-Roman wares before the Roman occupation. If any comparable entrepôt sites existed in Cumbria, Dobcross Hall is an obvious candidate with Roman coins found close by, and so too is the undated 3.5 ha, ditched enclosure at Clifton Dykes sited in the heartland of the scatter of late Bronze Age artefactual evidence in the central Eden valley. In the south of the county, the hillforts attracted some transmarine contact.

Specialist trading sites were not well established in the northern counties where they represent at most the first, tentative shift towards a market economy. Generally, both the economy and society were probably centred on the aristocratic household, where most crafts found their patronage and where most of the available agricultural surplus was consumed or used in exchange. The horizon of the late prehistoric farmer was very limited, depending upon local contacts with his peers, and overshadowed by local leaders who provided what little security was available. Within the area of patronage and client linkage, the economy was in most respects closed, and only the dominant minority had the means to maintain economic links with neighbours near and far.

There is in addition little sign that a rapid adoption of ironworking preceded the Roman Conquest, despite the presence of some activity east of the Pennines. In Cumbria, the enormous local iron deposits arguably attracted no more attention than the copper ones had done in the previous millennium and a half, and there is no evidence for local manufacturing of iron products at any level of society.

If there was some trade in imported pottery before the Roman occupation, the bulk of ceramic wares on 'native' sites were of local manufacture, uninfluenced by exotic imports, and standing at the end of a several-millennia-long tradition of domestic wares. The marked degree of uniformity from site to site over several centuries need not imply any central manufacturing organization, but probably resulted from an intense conservatism in hand-building techniques, and limited functional horizons. The numbers of vessels could be quite high, with 170 sherds of local wares at Burradon contrasting with only 9 sherds of Roman pottery (minimum 3 vessels), and comparable to the 130 sherds at Doubstead. In Northumberland, these undecorated local wares were a normal feature of occupation both before and during the Roman period. In Cumbria, to date, local pottery has only been excavated in a pre-Roman context at Skelmore Heads, and in Durham some pre-Roman sites seem to have been aceramic, as at West House, Coxhoe (Haselgrove and Allen 1982). Cumbrian farm sites do produce local pottery in the Roman period, and it is at least a possibility that this reflects the continuation of a pre-existing ceramic tradition in the area.

Ritual and burial activity

We have been able to demonstrate the development of a settlement site hierarchy for the late prehistoric period in the northern counties, suggesting the crystallization of a social hierarchy, with the emergence of a distinct propertied class in control of surplus wealth, and forming a warrior élite. There is far less archaeological evidence of specialists in ritual or religion, although the presence of local religious cults does emerge in the Roman period, with the cult of Maponus for example, centred probably in the Irthing valley (Cumbria). What is a very real characteristic of the period is the abandonment of recognizable burial practices such as typified the second millennium and their replacement by 'invisible' methods of disposal (Whimster 1981). In practice, this shift may have occurred in the last centuries of the previous millennium. Only in southern Cumbria, near Dalton-in-Furness in the hinterland of Skelmore Heads, has late Bronze Age metal-work been found in association with an inhumation burial in a cist (Fell and Coles 1965), and this only serves to accentuate the cultural archaism persistent in that area. A second, unaccompanied inhumation on Birkrigg may be of the same period (Erskine and Wood 1936). Elsewhere, slender, and often very questionable evidence may support the contention that rites that involved cremation deposited under barrows struggled on into the Iron Age, as at Alnham (Northumb.) where a single iron ring-headed pin was associated with scattered, calcined bone (Jobey and Tait 1966). A 'cemetery' under a cairn at Beadnell on the Northumberland coast may have been used during this period (Tait and Jobey 1971) and two unaccompanied extended burials were recorded at Catcote. Elsewhere, a scatter of cave burials have been found, such as the eleven skeletons from Bishop Middleham (Durham) some of which were crouched beneath large flat stones (Raistrick 1933), but the disarticulated condition of many of these imply abnormal ritual deposition. The Dog Hole deposit at Haverbrack (Cumbria) is not confined to a single period, and is again probably the result of unusual circumstances (Benson and Bland 1963).

In general, we do not know how the expanding communities of the later prehistoric period disposed of their dead. Even so, there is no reason to suppose that, like the Irish, they 'counted it an honourable thing, when their fathers died, to devour them' (Strabo IV. 4. 5. 4).

Notes

1. Examples of these are Simmons and Tooley (1981) and Megaw and Simpson (1981).

2. This approach has found its furthest development in the analysis of pottery and metal-work, at its best in Clarke (1970); it pervades regional surveys such as that by Challis and Harding (1975).

3. My thanks to Dennis Coggins for his correspondence concerning the site.

4. The mid-third millennium bc structure at Tatton, Cheshire, is of indeterminate shape, but a circular interpretation seems the most acceptable at present.

5. Information from Jim Cherry.

6. My thanks to Colin Burgess for his correspondence on Fenton Hill.

7. Unpublished excavation by Prof. Barri Jones, who kindly provided this information.

Chapter 4

Invasion and Response

The North on the Eve of Occupation

Mutually exclusive tribal groupings were probably already established in the Borders centuries, possibly even millennia, before the Roman invasion. As early as the late neolithic, core areas are identifiable, in the Milfield basin of Northumberland, the Eden valley of Cumbria and in Plain Furness. However, it is only via intermittent contact with Greek or Roman commentators that any of these groups cross the threshold of verbal identification. The picture that emerges is fragmentary, neither totally consistent nor entirely applicable to the area prior to the conquest. Even the most informative literary sources are subject to problems of interpretation that render them less than totally reliable [1], and epigraphic evidence is difficult to reconcile with the literature (Fig. 4.1).

The Brigantes emerge from these limited sources as the dominant group in northern England. There are seven altars known to the tribal deity, two stamps on pigs of lead of the reign of Domitian and the late-fourth-century rebuilding inscription from the Roman Wall (RIB 2022, now lost [2]). In addition, the name figures prominently, if infrequently, in the works of Tacitus and other historians and commentators. The cumulative impression is of a populus group, centred on Yorkshire, occupying a territory stretching from sea to sea, and broadly synonymous with northern England south of the Tyne, and north of the Humber (Fig. 4.1). A statuette from Birrens (Dumfries) has been repeatedly cited as evidence that parts of the north shore of the Solway lay within the tribal territory (RIB 2091). However, the statuette was dedicated by a legionary, perhaps from York, in the early third century – that is, exactly when the cult of Brigantia was being encouraged – and there is no particular reason to suppose that the dedication reflects a local ancient identity with the tribal deity.

The tribal name is not unique to northern England, appearing elsewhere as the root of a river or hill name (Rivet and Smith 1979: 278), and as a tribal name in Ireland and on the Continent. Given the meaning 'upland people' this is not surprising. The degree to which the name Brigantes represents a pre-Roman tribe is open to debate, particularly since most of the epigraphic evidence is third century or later. Tacitus applies the term variously to a wide territory with the apparent meaning 'the British peoples in the Pennine region' and more specifically to that group associated with Queen Cartimandua, almost certainly in Yorkshire. Alongside the latter group, other tribes can be identified, which may have at times been confederates within the greater

Figure 4.1   The tribes of Later Prehistory and their territories.

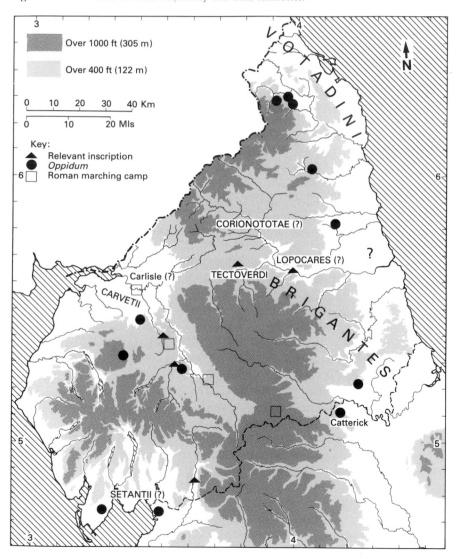

Brigantia, but at some stage in the late pre-Roman period emerge with a separate and distinctive identity.

In the North-west, the Carvetii have been identified from inscriptions at Brougham (Wright 1965b) and Old Penrith (RIB 933). The milestone from Middleton in Lonsdale may be relevant (Birley 1954b), in which case the southern boundary of the *civitas* should lie in the Lune valley near the Cumbrian county boundary. The root of the name is British 'stag' or 'deer', and the third-century *civitas* may reflect a tribe occupying the Solway lowlands and the Lake District, centred perhaps on the Eden valley. The emergence of this nomenclature coincides chronologically with the Birrens dedication to Brigantia and causes obvious problems to the traditional interpretation of that offering. Circumstantial evidence implies the name might be relevant in a local, pre-Roman context. Ptolemy (Geog. II, 3) named among the tribes of the Scottish west coast the Epidii (horse folk), Caereni (sheep folk) and Lugi (raven folk). The extension of this adoption of animalistic and possibly totemic nomenclature into north-west England is perfectly acceptable, and the pattern has been associated with the later development of Pictish art (Thomas 1961). Other tribal names with a similar basis may be the Gabrantovices (east Yorkshire) and Cornovii (on the Clyde and in the English Midlands).

The possibility that the Carvetii occupied part of the old county of Dumfriesshire is not unreasonable. Fordable rivers make poor boundaries, and the distribution of late prehistoric settlement in the North is such as to suggest that river valleys acted as foci rather than boundaries for tribal groups (e.g. Gillam 1958: Fig. 6). If this were accepted, the Roman fort at Birrens probably stood close to the western boundary of Carvetian territory north of the Solway, with this enclave centred on the hillfort at Burnswark.

The south-western boundary of the tribe is unknown. The only recent survey of the tribe (Higham and Jones 1985) assumed that Plain Furness was peripheral, but this is little more than a matter of inference. The Lancashire Setantii (Ptolemy, II, 3, 2) may have incorporated southern Cumbria. Alternatively, a quite separate but as yet unidentified group remains a possibility.

The north-east frontier of Brigantia is generally assumed to lie on the Tyne (e.g. Maxwell 1980). However, the possibility that the same tribe held both banks of the Tyne should not be ignored. Attention was drawn two decades ago to the dissimilarity between 'native' sites in northern and southern Northumberland (Jobey 1966a). The natural boundary lies along the poor-grade lands of Rothbury Forest from Otterburn to Alnwick. Against this must be placed the difficulty of fording the Tyne below Corbridge. In these circumstances, the tribal status of northern Tyne and Wear remains unresolved.

The possibility exists that a British tribal name is subsumed within the place-name Coriosopitum (Corbridge), and this has led to the cautious identification of the Lopocares (e.g. Rivet and Smith 1979). However, one

147

recent suggestion derives the latter part of the place-name from a separate but conflated entry in the Ravenna Cosmography, and this argument would require the abandonment of any tribal name, leaving Corbridge as one of the numerous *corio* names of northern Britain (Hind 1980).

As neighbours to the north-west the Carvetii bordered the Novantes of Galloway, and probably the Selgovae of central southern Scotland (Richmond 1958), although some debate has arisen concerning the proper location of this tribe (e.g. Breeze 1982). In the North-east, Brigantian territory marched with the lands of the Votadini. To them Ptolemy attributed the second-century sites of Bremenium (High Rochester in Redesdale), Coria (Inveresk, Mid-Lothian (?)) and Alauna (Low Learchild (?)). If these are correctly identified, all three lie close to the probable tribal frontiers. The Votadini were centred on two main areas of rich agricultural land. The Lothian lowlands provided the most extensive of these, but the Lower Tweed valley, the Milfield basin and the river valleys of Northumberland form an important southern nodal area. Traprain Law in Lothian stands out as the obvious tribal centre (e.g. Hogg 1951; Maxwell 1980), but the southern territory had important, if lesser, *oppida*.

Above the basin of the Middle Tweed the vast hillfort of Eildon Hill North has generally been identified as the 'capital' of the Selgovae, although there has been a recent cautious attempt at reappraisal (Breeze 1982a). If the identification is correct, the tribal frontier must have run north–south across the valley of the Tweed, and the resulting propinquity may have accounted for the nervousness apparent among the late prehistoric population on both sides of the Cheviots, and the consequent construction of ever more complex ramparts. The Selgovae may have been as fierce as their name suggests (meaning 'hunters'). Several pointers indicate that it was the Votadini who had the worst of this intimate relationship. It remains no more than an educated guess, but this tribe, or a section within it based on Traprain Law, may have been among the eleven tribes that submitted to Claudius in AD 43. No other tribe in the North can be credited with the consistent philo-Roman attitudes that appears to emerge among the Votadini from the Flavian period onwards.

The roll-call of tribes in the border counties is unlikely to be complete. An altar found at Beltingham, arguably originating at Chesterholm, recorded the *curia* (assembly) of the Tectoverdi (RIB 1695). This group is otherwise unknown and attempts have been made to identify them with a continental people, but the possibility remains that the name recalls a local tribal group centred in the Tyne–Solway gap. If such was the case, it is likely that every major river valley from the Tees northwards was the home of a separately named and identified pre-Roman tribe. At this level, a second but less well-established group, the Corionototae, were named by a cavalry commander in a dedicatory inscription, found at Hexham but presumably derived from Corbridge (RIB 1142). These references may help to explain the account of the Agricolan conquest given by Tacitus, where he refers to the many *civitates* which had previously maintained their independence (Tacitus, *Agric.* xx). The North on the eve of the conquest may have been as fragmented as was Wales during much of the early medieval period.

A Prelude to Conquest AD 43–70

The Roman Conquest of Britain was precipitated by political events far away in the centre of empire. Similar factors were to play their part – and arguably an overbearing part – in the major decisions taken concerning the province, and particularly concerning the location of its northern frontier (Breeze and Dobson 1976). Only within the broad strategy that these extraneous factors dictated had individual governors the ability to adopt tactics suited to the local arena.

The Claudian invasion and subsequent conquest began in the extreme south-east of Britain. Its major initial target was the Catuvellauni, dominant throughout south-east and south central England. Neighbouring tribes had suffered from the conspicuous success of this warlike group since the invasion of Julius Caesar, to the point whereby several had been subsumed into an enlarged political unit. Not surprisingly, those so subsumed, and those threatened with the same, saw Roman intervention as preferable to the progressive aggrandizement by which they were threatened. Eleven tribes entered into treaties with Claudius in AD 43. Among them were the threatened Dobunni to the west; the Coritani and Cornovii of the Midlands are obvious candidates (Frere 1978: 86), and both the Iceni of the Fens and the Brigantes to the north emerge as client kingdoms by the end of the decade. Of the remainder, the Parisi seem a sensible guess, and the case of the Votadini has already been put forward. Among the Brigantes, Queen Cartimandua seems to have considered that a Roman alliance was necessary to her security within the tribe and without, and with this attitude her husband Venutius seems initially to have been in accord.

Over the next two decades, the Roman administration failed to build upon the initial goodwill of the peripheral tribes, but squandered this resource through measures that did more than even Caractacus could achieve in stiffening resistance. The disarming of the federated and allied tribes by Ostorius Scapula may not have been attempted among the Brigantes, despite their client status, but led to resistance among the Iceni and probably the Coritani. A Roman attempt to force a bridgehead between the unconquered tribes of Wales and the North in AD 48 was abandoned as a result of mounting Brigantian resistance. Henceforth, the Brigantian aristocracy were divided in their attitude to Rome, and to Cartimandua who depended to a growing extent

149

on Roman influence and the occasional use of Roman forces to maintain herself.

During the 50s the balance within the Brigantes shifted inexorably against the client queen. Caractacus fled from north Wales in AD 51, and sought refuge in the North. That Cartimandua captured him by subterfuge (Tacitus, *Hist.* iii, 45) suggests he had made contact with her opponents and did not place that much confidence in the Queen. It may have been his betrayal to Rome that widened the breach between Cartimandua and her opponents, who gained the support of Venutius early in the 50s. It was he who subsequently led resistance to Rome in the North, and Tacitus goes out of his way for no very obvious reason to commend his military abilities. The Queen attempted to strengthen her hand by the seizure of her in-laws, but Venutius invaded her kingdom with a strong band of young warriors. Whether this invasion was from north of the Tyne–Solway, or from one of the northern septs of the Brigantes is unclear, although some commentators have been attracted to the latter. Cartimandua was succoured by Roman forces.

By AD 60, the Brigantes had had substantial opportunity to witness the activity of the Roman army in Wales and the Midlands, and to judge what sort of treatment they would eventually suffer, as one after another the client kingdoms or hostile tribes were incorporated into the Roman state. The case was put to the final test in that year. A renewed Roman thrust into north Wales threatened their near neighbours, and challenged whatever religious feelings were centred upon Anglesey. The campaign seems to have been conducted with ferocity on both sides (Tacitus, *Ann.* xiv, 30). It was interrupted by the 'Boudiccan' revolt in lowland England, triggered off by the cynical and callous methods adopted by the local administration (and by Roman financiers) in bringing the Iceni into the province. There is no record that the northern tribes became involved. Initially, at least, they may have been immobilized by Cartimandua and by the Roman forts on their eastern borders, and there was all too little time to resolve internal issues as well as mobilize. However, we should be in little doubt where Brigantian sympathies lay. The policies of repression adopted by Paulinus in the aftermath of rebellion can only have further injured native sensibilities in the North.

With increasingly little room for manoeuvre, Cartimandua divorced and deposed Venutius, and married in his place one of his prominent supporters, hoping, perhaps, thereby to divide the opposition. Venutius summoned 'outside help' and revolted (Tacitus, *Hist.* iii, 45). Roman auxiliaries rescued the Queen, leaving Venutius in undisputed control of the Brigantes. The anti-Roman faction had achieved a substantial victory, but it was largely the product of the bungling insensitivity and all-too-ruthless atrocities which must have appeared the hallmarks of Roman policy in Wales and southern England. The political élite of the Brigantes had viewed events for a quarter-century, during which Roman attitudes and actions encompassed a catalogue of diplomatic blunders. Polarization of Brigantian attitudes came at a bad time for Rome, with the Empire suffering the year of the four emperors, and a divided if not disloyal provincial army. There are, however, signs that the army was already involved against Venutius (Statius, *Silvae*, v, ii), and central control over the Empire was established sooner than he might have wished. Petillius Cerialis was appointed to the province in AD 71, apparently with instructions to conquer the Brigantes, and this he proceeded to do.

The Conquest of the North

Cerialis was not a stranger to Britain. As commander of *legio* IX he had made a rash attempt to suppress the Boudiccan revolt in AD 60, from which he had barely escaped with his life. However, his standing as an early supporter of the Flavian cause, as well as a member of Vespasian's family, made him a natural and safe choice as governor for a province with a substantial garrison. Vespasian required military victories with which to decorate and glorify his usurpation. Britain was an obvious theatre, and one in which Vespasian had already seen active service. Cerialis seems to have provided some success, however careless and headstrong his style (Birley 1973). His hand has been seen in the establishment of forts at Malton, York and Brough-on-Humber, aimed at the control of the most accessible area of Brigantian power in Yorkshire. There is still some debate as to the role of Stanwick, near Catterick, in the ensuing campaigns. The excavation of the site, published in 1954, revealed a hillfort rapidly and massively extended shortly after about AD 50, at greatest totalling some 300 ha (Wheeler 1954). Neither the dating nor the exact sequence of extension is secure (e.g. Dobson 1970), but it seems difficult to divorce this site from the changing political balance among the Brigantes. Venutius had already looked to help from the North to dispossess Cartimandua, and Stanwick is a reasonable hosting-place in such circumstances, to which Venutius could have called in his sympathizers from the West, the North-west and the North. No Roman general, however rash, could bypass Stanwick and campaign further north before taking it, and this Cerialis may have done supposing it was held against him. However, there appears to have been no decisive battle, but rather a series of many battles, some not without loss to the Roman side, as Cerialis operated, if he did not actually triumph over the major part of Brigantia (Tacitus, *Agric.* xvii). The marching camps on Stainmore, at Crackenthorpe (Richmond and McIntyre 1934) and at Plumpton Head may be relics of these campaigns during an invasion of the Eden valley from Yorkshire, and the first recorded push to the Solway. These camps are of a size (approx. 8 ha) sufficient to accommodate a legionary force on the march, and are evenly spaced at distances of a one-day

151

march from Catterick to Carlisle. On the basis of the *titulus* style of entrance defence, still clearly visible at Reycross on Stainmore, they are thought to be of comparatively early date.

An army base at Carlisle at this date remains an attractive but unproven possibility, despite the qualified support from early Flavian samian and coinage on the site (Hartley 1972; Shotter 1979). A well-preserved timber fort gateway has recently been identified and excavated (Charlesworth 1980: 210), but reappraisal of the site has led to the suggestion that the fort of which it formed a part lay not under the centre of the city, but to the north (Hanson and Maxwell 1983: 34). This fort need not have been so early, but the possibility remains that an earlier fort already occupied the city centre site when it was constructed, accounting for the antiquarian records of military structures under Tullie House and adjacent areas (Ferguson 1893).

The possibility that Cerialis campaigned beyond the Tyne–Solway gap should not be ignored, but as yet only the complex sequence of reoccupation at a handful of Scottish sites has attracted this interpretation which remains no more than a suggestion. Campaigning, as opposed to fort construction, was the preoccupation of Cerialis. The proliferation of local tribal groups may underlie his widespread and time-consuming campaigns, and the numerous battles. If the tribes attempted to use guerrilla tactics, the obvious Roman strategy was to harry the northern lowlands, and destroy the economic basis of resistance, in which case a march on the Solway was essential, and campaigns should also have been directed against southern Cumbria and Co. Durham, beyond Catterick.

Signs are that Brigantian resistance to Cerialis was intense, and support for Venutius widespread. The fate of the British leader is unknown, but one attractive possibility is his association with the place-name Venutio, recorded in the Ravenna Cosmography, and probably in the borders.

Cerialis was replaced as governor in AD 74; his successor was charged with responsibility for the completion of the conquest of Wales. Not until AD 78 was a governor appointed with a clear remit to extend the province northwards, and build upon the campaigns of Cerialis. Gnaeus Julius Agricola was only briefly delayed by problems in the West. In one short late season his troops annihilated the Ordovici and captured Anglesey. The implications of these events can hardly have been lost on the battered aristocracy of the Pennine vales, against whom Agricola turned his army in the following year. Chester may have served as the base for the new offensive – dating evidence is available for AD 79. Natural obstacles to the main campaign were estuaries and woods (Tacitus, *Agric.* xx), a description easiest reconciled with the route west of the Pennines, but it is at least likely that a parallel advance occurred from Yorkshire along the line of Dere Street. Agricola adopted the tactics of forceful persuasion, offering the various tribal groups the alternatives of devastation or surrender on his terms. The display of strength was enough, and the *civitates* put aside their resentment and accepted garrisons. The impact of the campaigns of Cerialis early in the decade, and the real threat of annihilation by Agricola brought the collapse of organized resistance south of the Tyne–Solway gap, and arguably south of the Forth–Clyde isthmus. The extent to which this amounted to a genuine change of heart among the northern tribes must remain highly dubious, but the apparent ease and scale of victory enabled Tacitus to point out that no fresh acquisition in Britain had ever come off with so little challenge as this. A reasonable conclusion must surely be that the decimated Brigantian aristocracy had neither the will nor the means to resist Agricola and the professional Roman army. They submitted rather than face either the annihilation suffered by the Ordovici or the economic collapse that would be the logical result of further guerrilla resistance. They were unlikely to recover their strength within a generation. It is applicable to bear in mind the speech placed by Tacitus in the mouth of Calgacus, leader of the Caledonians at Mons Graupius only four years later (Tacitus, *Agric.* xxx).

The arbiters of the new regime were the fort garrisons mentioned by Tacitus. Some of these fort sites have been identified but others may remain to be found (Hartley 1980). Agricola inherited a sound base in Cheshire and Yorkshire, but little further north. If Carlisle was not already built, the first timber fort must be Agricolan. Recent excavation has identified one of the gates of this large fort in an unusually fine state of preservation, in waterlogged conditions (Charlesworth 1980). In the interior, buildings, working areas and a bread oven have been identified, dated by large numbers of coins of the period AD 71–78 [3]. We must assume that communications were maintained with the south via the Lune valley, and via Stainmore to York, and that the major roads along these routes were at least put in hand under Agricola. Nevertheless, firm evidence of garrisons is hard to find. We should expect early occupation at Brough-under-Stainmore, for example, and at Low Borrow Bridge. At neither of these key sites has an early fort been identified, but both have produced sufficient Flavian and Trajanic pottery to support an early military occupation (Jones 1977; Hildyard and Gillam 1951). At Brough, the cemetery to the south-east of the fort was already in use in the Flavian period. In addition, Old Penrith had its origins in the late first century, and Kirkby Thore seems likely to have been of similar date. The close spacing of Roman forts in the central Eden basin may, however, imply a more complex developmental sequence than has so far been identified.

Several of the fort sites were established close to the sites of temporary marching camps, and reflect the strategic importance of the Eden corridor. At Old Penrith, three examples of possible temporary camps have been identified, although one has since been discarded after trial excavation as a probable 'native' site (Poulter 1982). A small temporary camp has been identified at Brougham.

Outside the Eden–Lune corridor, there is little evidence of Agricolan activity in Cumbria, and the Lake District and the south-west lowlands were

Plate 4.1   The construction trenches of open-ended, timber structures within the Agricolan depot at Red House, Corbridge, photographed during excavation. These short-lived buildings were probably used to store equipment and supplies for the army campaigning in Scotland.

probably ignored by Agricola and left to subsequent governors to tame and garrison.

East of the Pennines, the arguably more important route taken by Dere Street was laid out from York to Corbridge and beyond, via Catterick, Binchester and Ebchester. Some at least of these forts were probably Agricolan. At Binchester, timber phases of fort construction were sealed by a dump containing pottery of the late first and early second centuries (Ferris and Jones 1980). Piercebridge on the southern border is another contender. However, at Corbridge alone has there been uncovered large-scale and incontrovertible evidence of Agricolan activity (Hanson *et al.* 1979). At Red House, to the west of the major forts, a large timber complex, covering an estimated 8–9 ha has yielded evidence of a single phase of occupation within the period *c.* AD 75–90. Substantial timber-framed buildings, some with open ends, apparently served as warehousing for non-perishable supplies, shipped in via the Tyne and here transferred to road haulage. The context must be as a supply base for Agricola's campaigns in southern Scotland, so the likely date of construction lies in the autumn of AD 79 (Fig. 4.2).

Although more will probably be located and others verified, Agricolan forts do not at present form a dense network in the northern Pennines and,

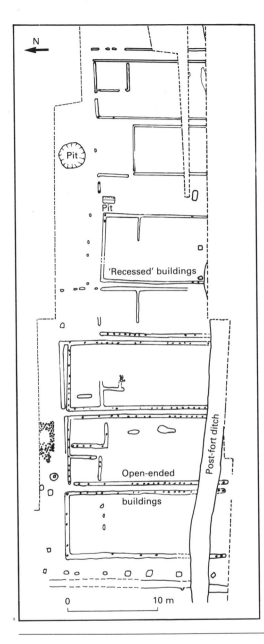

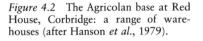

Figure 4.2 The Agricolan base at Red House, Corbridge: a range of warehouses (after Hanson *et al.*, 1979).

away from the two major arterial routes to the North, are conspicuous by their absence (Fig. 4.3). Tacitus records that the tribes received terms, which they accepted in order to avoid worse. The proper incorporation of the Pennines into the province was not undertaken at this stage; instead the Agricolan armies swept on in the following campaigning year, leaving behind them

155

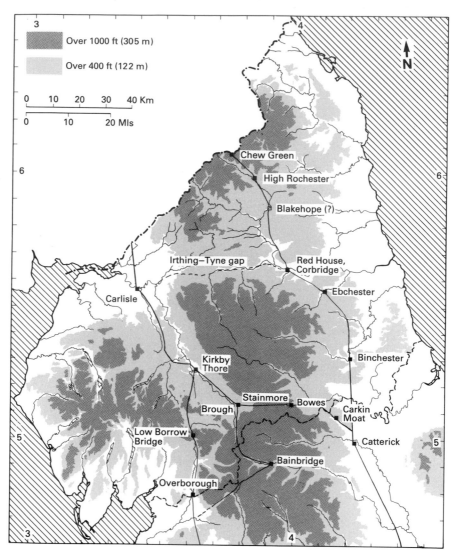

Figure 4.3 The military occupation of the North.

garrisons that may have been surprisingly light. In AD 81, Agricola moved his forces from the Tyne–Solway to the Forth–Clyde and even the Tay, apparently using as his springboard the new supply depot at Corbridge. The Selgovae seem to have been the immediate object of his attention, but Tacitus records that the tribes were too terrified to resist. The tribes of southern Scotland had witnessed the campaigns of the Flavian governors in the West and the North. Whether or not they had actively assisted Venutius is uncertain, but the destruction of their powerful neighbours, the Brigantes was probably sufficient discouragement for those who contemplated resistance. The Votadini on their flank were arguably already clients of Rome. The push northwards from Corbridge skirted their territory and the new extension of Dere Street, up Redesdale and into the mid-Tweed valley, provided a string of garrisons between them and their probable competitors, the Selgovae. The difference in treatment accorded these two tribes by the Romans has often been noted. Traprain Law continued in occupation in the Roman period, when arguably it was extended to its optimum size (approx. 16 ha). In contrast, a watch-tower (undated) was constructed within the ramparts of Eildon Hill North, perhaps as an outpost for the new fort at Newstead. Too much should, perhaps, not be made of this contrast, given the lack of excavation on particularly the latter site, from which second-century and later coins and pottery have been forthcoming (Breeze 1982). Although little excavation has taken place, there is very little evidence that the lesser *oppida* of either tribe continued in occupation. If Traprain Law became the seat of a client king, the provinces of his kingdom were apparently as thoroughly demilitarized as those of his neighbours.

In AD 82, Agricola was operating on the western seaboard of Scotland, and in AD 83 he advanced beyond the isthmus to force the Highland tribes to fight a conclusive battle, achieving this aim at Mons Graupius. The tide of military destruction had swept far beyond Brigantia, as the Flavian governors pursued a policy of expansionism designed to incorporate the whole of Britain into a single province. In contrast, the later 80s saw redeployment of Rome's military resources, drawing troops from Britain to new war theatres, and Trajan's wars in Dacia and the East were to involve new troop withdrawals over the next two decades.

The great legionary fortress of Inchtuthil was abandoned unfinished shortly after AD 86. The Gask Ridge watch-towers probably represent one stage of frontier organization in Scotland, in which for the first time in Britain a conscious effort was made to establish a visible and distinct frontier, but this was a short-lived stratagem, and by AD 90 the army had abandoned all positions beyond the Forth (Hartley 1972). For most of a decade sufficient troops were available to hold southern Scotland, with a network of garrisons pivoted on forts at Dalswinton and Newstead, but by the end of the century or the very beginning of the next, this too was abandoned and the army was back on the Tyne–Solway isthmus. Among the abandoned forts was High Rochester in Northumberland.

The final phases of withdrawal may have been due solely to manpower shortages (Frere 1981). However, a long-established view looked to a rising of the tribes in southern Scotland, based on fire damage at Newstead, Dalswinton, Glenlochar, Cappuck, Oakwood, High Rochester and Corbridge. Modern opinion accepts that garrisons frequently burnt the timberwork of demolished buildings before departure (Hanson 1978) and buried unwanted military equipment, and such may account for many of these destruction deposits, including the abandoned armour at Newstead (Manning 1972). No punitive expedition is known to have been launched against any putative insurgents, but at Corbridge, at least, destruction seems to have been unintentional. The first fort built after the abandonment of Red House, was burnt without any evidence of demolition, and subsequently rapidly reconstructed (Gillam 1977: 55). Accidental destruction cannot be ruled out, but some scholars still entertain as a real possibility a military disaster on the northern frontier in the reign of Trajan.

The Tyne–Solway frontier

The generals and armies of the late republic treated areas adjacent to Roman territory as potential or future provinces, only awaiting the act of conquest. In such circumstances permanent frontiers did not exist. After the vast conquests of Augustus, subsequent emperors allowed the momentum of expansion to slow, and the empire began to take on a permanent shape and structure. The conquests of Trajan in Dacia and Parthia constituted a major effort to re-establish that former momentum. It is ironic that the consequent drain upon imperial resources led, in Britain, to withdrawal from Scotland and the emergence of a permanent land frontier.

The Gask Ridge *limes* had constituted a road, and a string of observation posts by which those using it, or crossing it, could be observed. By AD 105 at latest, the permanent forts in southern Scotland were abandoned, and successive governors were left with the unenviable task of establishing an east–west frontier across an island in which the basic topography runs north–south. The Tyne–Solway gap was the only feasible alternative to holding southern Scotland; Flavian forts already existed at Carlisle and Corbridge, and a road connected them. This, the Stanegate, slowly emerged as a *limes*. The route had already served as an important link between the two major northward arterial roads, and early troop movements may have been responsible for the temporary camps at Seatsides IV and Moss Side I (Bennett 1980). The route may have offered political advantages, depending on the degree to which it formed the northern frontier of the Brigantes, but this is an open question on both sides of the Pennines.

Already in the 90s, Roman control of the route may have been strengthened by the construction of intermediate forts at Chesterholm (Birley 1977) and Nether Denton, and there are signs that the road was extended about AD 100 west of Carlisle to a new fort at Kirkbride (Bellhouse and Richardson 1982). The Flavian fort at Carlisle was demolished, and a second fort built over the slighted ramparts. Early in the second century the progressive infilling of forts continued. The process certainly included Old

Church Brampton (Simpson and Richmond 1936) and the small fortlets at Throp and Haltwhistle Burn; several other forts are likely candidates for inclusion, although the sequence of large and small forts suggested by Birley (1961: 132) has not so far been established. Beyond Corbridge in the east no sites have been identified north of the Tyne, but a fort located from the air at Wickham, south of the Tyne may imply an eastern extension of the Stanegate 'system' south of the river (McCord and Jobey 1971). In the west, the construction of a fort south of Burgh-by-Sands bisected the distance between Kirkbride and Carlisle (Jones 1982).

The Stanegate frontier still awaits major revision, but it is unlikely to be challenged *in toto*, although objections to it remain. Much of the route is strategically ill conceived, and it enjoys little overview to the north (Daniels 1970). It is difficult to argue that these difficulties were overcome by a series of watch-towers set up as observation posts to the north, since only two are known, and the only example to have been excavated produced no evidence to support construction before the reign of Hadrian (Charlesworth 1977). Both may simply represent an early stage in the development of the wall. The newly located fort at Burgh-by-Sands (south) was constructed over the site of a circular watch-tower base, associated with a ditched palisade line and this may be linked to the suggested primary military construction and use of the Fingland Rigg site adjacent to it to the west (Jones 1982). The inference may be that the stages by which the Stanegate frontier evolved were more complex than is, as yet, apparent. However, the full implications of that development involved the gradual concentration of military manpower within installations closely spaced along that route, with the capacity to maintain surveillance and control passage both along and across it. That the road did not lend itself to a frontier line is not relevant – it was conceived as a convenient route between garrisoned centres and the development of a *limes* was subsequent to that original use. It must, however, have been apparent to a man of Hadrian's experience that the Stanegate *limes* left considerable room for improvement.

In the hinterland of the frontier, the two decades after AD 90 saw the consolidation of Roman control, and the redisposition of the troops withdrawn from southern Scotland. Garrisons were maintained on both the main north–south roads, and along the Stainmore link between them. In addition, this period was crucial for the occupation of the Lake District, staffed in all probability by garrison troops withdrawn from north of the Solway. The role of these forces appears to have lain in surveillance and control of movement along the natural lines of communication. The new forts Caermote, Ambleside and Watercrook – were located on the crucial valley routes into the Lake District centre, in positions dictated by tactical considerations similar to those prevailing at the established sites at Low Borrow Bridge and on the Stanegate (Jones 1968; Potter 1979).

The new military dispositions of Trajan's reign may have been

Plate 4.2 A Roman fort, photographed for the first time in drought conditions, summer 1984, at Brackenrigg, west of Carlisle. Trial excavation in 1984 demonstrated occupation in the late first/early second century. The site was successively reduced in size.

undertaken against a background of widespread local resentment and occasional armed resistance, perhaps on both sides of the *limes*. *Cohors I Cugernorum* was awarded the title *Ulpia Traiana* at some stage between AD 103 and 122; the most likely context is success in war in the northern theatre. The biographer of Hadrian listed nations resisting the Romans at the outset of his reign (*Vita Hadriana* v.2), ending with the Britons who 'could not be kept under control'. The northern frontier must have been the war zone. Hadrian sent Q. Pompeius Falco as governor, and he recorded his suppression of the revolt on an inscription found at Jarrow. Whether this action was centred north or south of the *limes* is unclear; it is tempting to imagine that any trouble to the north might easily find support to the south. However, there is no archaeological evidence of fort destruction, and Corbridge II was evacuated peacefully during this period (Gillam 1977). Whatever the nature of the action, it may have proved costly to the Roman forces. It was probably this war that led Cornelius Fronto, in a letter to Marcus Aurelius a decade later, to compare the losses sustained in Britain to those of the Jewish revolt. A series of coins bearing the figure of Britannia began to appear in AD 119 and probably represent official use of the victory for propaganda purposes. Hadrian arrived in Britain in AD 122–23 probably bringing with him a new governor, Aulus Platorius Nepos. No emperor before him had shown such great interest in fixed frontiers, and his tour of the western provinces consisted very largely of a review of frontier dispositions in Germany and Britain. With the German examples of timber-built boundary lines firmly in his mind, Hadrian turned his attention to the British land frontier and commissioned the wall that bears his name (*Vita Hadriana* II, 2), to be constructed along the best tactical line available, using the heights of the Whin Sill.

As initially conceived and undertaken, the wall was a device by which the existing *limes* might be strengthened rather than replaced. A continuous barrier was to be constructed from Newcastle to Bowness-on-Solway (122 km) to the north of the Stanegate line, equipped with a regular allocation of mile fortlets and intervening turrets integral to the structure. The eastern and central sections were from the beginning in stone, but from the Irthing westwards the barrier was initially built of turf. The purpose of the wall was apparently to tighten control of native movements across the frontier. Henceforth all traffic would normally pass through the milecastle gates, under the close supervision of the border guards manning milecastles and turrets. This may imply that the Roman commanders felt that recent security problems derived from conspiracies hatched between groups on both sides of the *limes*.

Care was also taken to maintain surveillance along the exposed Solway coastline; the fort at Maryport defends a natural harbour and may have been designed as a marine base. Around it, and perhaps planned from the fort as the original nucleus of the system, a chain of watch-towers embraced the Cumbrian coast from Bowness as far south as St Bees Head (Jarrett 1976; Bellhouse 1969). The discovery of an early installation at Ravenglass may

161

Plate 4.3 Housesteads from the south-west: probably the most photographed fort on Hadrian's Wall; the Wall runs away from the northern corners; west of the fort a road runs away from the gates, linked by a hollow way running round the south-west corner of the fort to the *vicus* which occupies the south slope. Terraces to the south and west have been interpreted as pre-Hadrianic agricultural earth-works, but terracing for structural purposes is an obvious alternative.

imply that these watch-towers originally were to be extended even further to the south (Potter 1979: 48). At Silloth and along the Solway, the watch-towers and fortlets were set out between slight ditches, which at Silloth and Cardurnock at least supported twin palisades packed with clay. At Cardurnock three phases have been identified in the development of tower 4B which originated probably as a clay, or clay and turf, platform behind the palisade and ditch, designed to assist observation (Jones 1982: Fig. 3).

The construction of much of the wall in stone was a significant departure from the more usual timber and earth frontiers of Germany, and may be linked either to the Emperor's increasing preference for permanence in his dispositions, or to respect for the local opposing forces. An alternative possibility remains, that the local timber resources in the east and centre may not have been considered adequate, while plentiful supplies were available west of the Pennines (see Ch. 5). Whatever the cause, construction in stone was a major undertaking. Legionary units were drafted in to work on short sections in two gangs, the first laying the foundations and the second the superstructure (Breeze and Dobson 1976). The work must have continued unhindered by the local tribes.

During the process of construction, major changes were made to the design of the new frontier. The main garrison forces in the Stanegate forts were probably too remote from the wall to be effective. Perhaps more crucial to an army that was designed as an offensive force, passage through the wall to the north was severely inconvenienced by the necessity to pass through the milefort gates. It was probably as a result of these difficulties that the decision was made after about two years to move the garrison troops to new forts on the line of the wall, abandoning the Stanegate forts. In order to maximize access to the North, the new forts were originally designed to project beyond the wall, so allowing gates in three sides. This was eventually abandoned in favour of forts attached to the wall at the north-west and north-east corners, and the last to be built, such as Greatchesters, were to this plan. These alternatives to the basic design involved the commitment of new resources of manpower, expertise and time. Perhaps to compensate, the decision was made to reduce the gauge of the stone wall from approx. 3 m to 2.4 m. When the wall was extended to the east as far as Wallsend fort, the 'narrow' wall and fort were built as one (Fig. 4.4).

These changes in design explain many of the apparent anomalies along the line of the wall, including for example, the milecastles and turrets under forts like Chesters and Housesteads. The construction of the frontier dragged on. Greatchesters fort in the central section was not finished until after AD 128, and additional forts were inserted at Carrawburgh, Carvoran and perhaps Drumburgh.

Broadly contemporary with the major design changes came the decision to isolate the military cordon from the province with a massive ditch and double bank, known as the *vallum*. This was a major project in its own right, requiring a huge input of labour, and all the evidence suggests it was given a high priority and executed to a demanding specification (Heywood 1965; Williams 1983; Bennett and Turner 1983). The ditch was steep sided, about 6 m wide and 3 m deep. Separated from it on either side by a wide berm was a mound consisting of the upcast material, revetted by turf. The *vallum* was inserted into the design brief after the original choice of fort sites had been made, but before the insertion of Carrawburgh, under which the *vallum* had to be infilled. The purpose which this barrier served has been much discussed. It is not a strictly military design – hence the flat bottom of the ditch. It does, however, provide an effective observation ground, which could not normally be crossed without detection, and so adds to the surveillance role of the original wall design (Hanson and Maxwell 1983; 56). It may represent an official response to the continuing resentment among the tribes in the north of the province (Frere 1978: 157). Alternatively, it may have been conceived as a taxation barrier – a civil frontier manned by the procurator's staff (Breeze and Dobson 1976). Causeways were left in the line of the *vallum* equipped with gates on the north side, opposite the forts and some milecastles.

Even with the construction of the additional forts and the excavation of the *vallum*, the frontier was not complete. At the end of the reign, the western, turf section was rebuilt in stone, and the opportunity was taken to bring the new wall up to the front angles of Birdoswald fort (Breeze and Dobson 1976: 76). *In toto*, construction probably proved far lengthier and more expensive of resources than had been anticipated. However, by the end of Hadrian's reign,

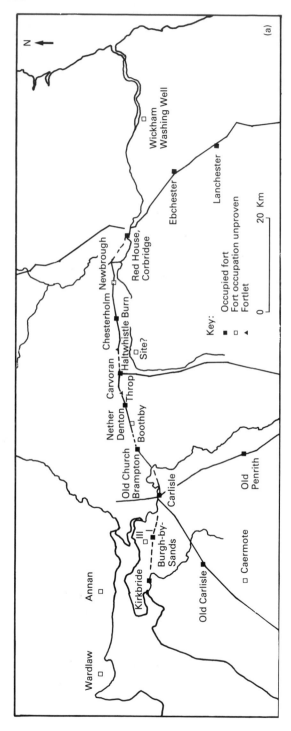

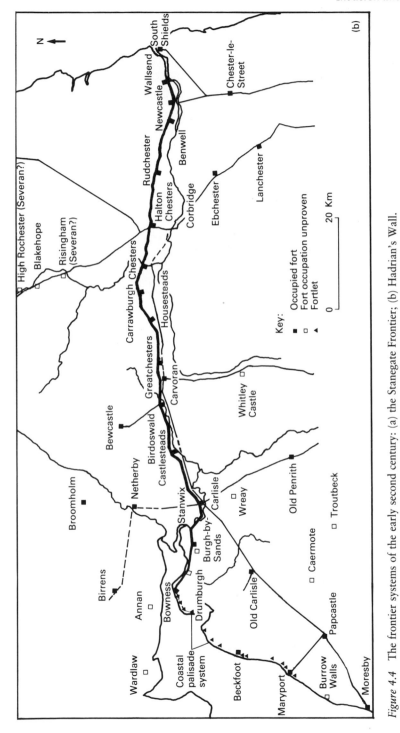

Figure 4.4 The frontier systems of the early second century: (a) the Stanegate Frontier; (b) Hadrian's Wall.

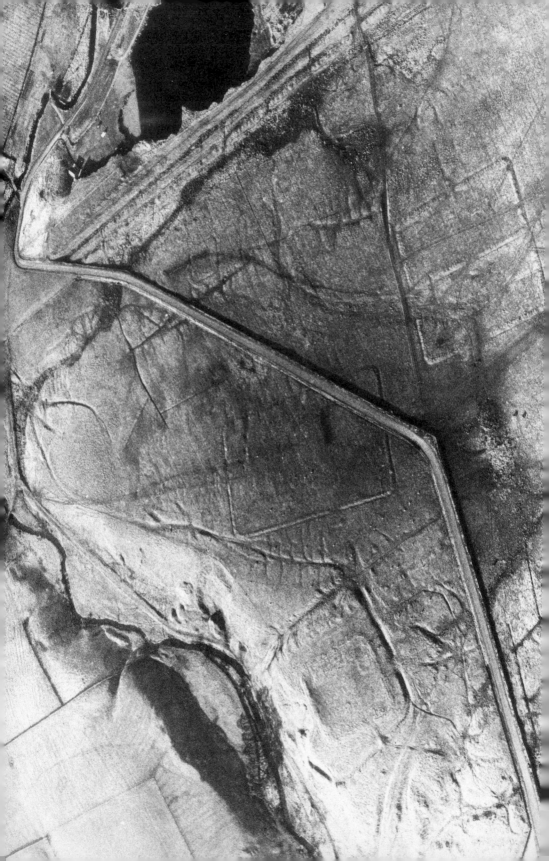

the British province had been provided with the most sophisticated fixed frontier so far conceived anywhere in the Roman world. Perhaps the scale of the project, in the last resort, owed much to outside factors.

In its final form, the wall was complemented by 16 forts with a full garrison strength of *c.* 9,500 men. Cavalry predominated at the extremities and infantry in the centre. Late in the reign of Hadrian, further efforts were made to strengthen the Roman grip on Cumbria. The coastal fort at Moresby was probably an addition to the observation system, still incomplete in AD 128 (RIB 801). Watercrook was unfinished in the 140s, and new forts at Hardknott and Old Carlisle give the impression that Cumbria was still considered newly conquered territory. Beyond the wall in the west, three outlying forts were constructed. That these were intended to defend an outlying part of 'Brigantia' seems ill founded (see above), but there is at least a contrast between the tightening of military control in the west and its apparent easing in the east. No Hadrianic forts exist beyond the wall in Northumberland, and only Dere Street was garrisoned to the south, with the solitary exception of Chester-le-Street. Even if, as seems likely, the Roman forces carried out regular training and surveillance exercises north of the wall, there is no trace of them in the Hadrianic period among the Votadini.

The Hadrianic frontier was no sooner at, or near, completion than it was rendered obsolete. Antoninus Pius was elevated to empire in AD 139, and almost immediately reversed the Hadrianic frontier policy in Britain, instructing his new governor to readvance to the Forth–Clyde isthmus. To some extent, at least, this must be seen as a response to Roman central politics. Antoninus Pius badly needed a military reputation, and exploited the British successes by minting coins carrying emblems of victory in AD 142–44. This does not explain why the British frontier was singled out for new expansionism, and it is possible that local unrest beyond the wall required a Roman expedition. The possibility remains that broch construction on the Clyde–Forth isthmus dates to this period, and may represent the immigration of a warrior aristocracy hostile to Rome, but examples so far excavated do not support this (summarized in Hanson and Maxwell 1983: 64). The brochs are more likely to represent structures commissioned by a local rather than an immigrant aristocracy.

The readvance was based primarily on Corbridge. Construction work on that site by contingents from *legio II Augusta* was already in progress in AD 139 (RIB 1147, 1148), and the advance proceeded along Dere Street, where

---

Plate 4.4 A panoramic view of Haltwhistle Common, near Haltwhistle, seen from the east. The low sunlight emphasizes the extensive Roman military remains surviving on the present moorland. To the left lies the Stanegate fort, known as Haltwhistle Common, with its irregular, outer defensive work highlighted by shadow; to the right run the twin banks of the *vallum* with the wall destroyed at this point by the water-filled quarry; in the centre can be seen two Roman temporary camps, probably to be associated with the construction of the various installations, the nearer example being subdivided.

Plate 4.5 View of Hadrian's Wall, looking east towards Housesteads along the Whin Sill, where it complements the natural barrier to north-south communication of the steep and rocky, north-facing incline.

Plate 4.6 Nick Castle, on Hadrian's Wall: an aerial view from the north. This is one of the better preserved of the milecastles on Hadrian's Wall, occupying a narrow gulley (or 'nick') in the Whin Sill; the two opposing entrances allowing controlled and regulated traffic to cross the mural zone where the wall was constructed along the apex of a steep and rocky descent that faces north.

High Rochester fort was recommissioned (RIB 1276). Henceforth, for most of a generation, Northumberland fell once more within the province, but the almost complete absence of military works might imply that client status was retained, under the watchful eye of the Dere Street garrisons and the fleet off shore. A new wall, of turf, was built from sea to sea, and many, but not necessarily all, the wall garrisons were redeployed and the gates on Hadrian's Wall were thrown open and the *vallum* slighted [4].

The expansion of the province drained troops from northern England. The garrisons concentrated in Cumbria were thinned. Watercrook was abandoned unfinished, and the Biglands milefortlet was demolished (Potter 1979: 360); there were probably further considerable troop withdrawals. Even so, there is some evidence of continuing activity at the (probable) naval stations at Maryport and Ravenglass, and, more surprisingly, at landlocked Ambleside.

The Antonine Wall and southern Scotland were briefly abandoned in the mid 150s, and Hadrian's Wall reoccupied in strength (Breeze 1980, for discussion). A commemorative coin issue of AD 155 may imply victory over a revolt and an inscription from the Tyne at Newcastle records the movement of detachments from the two Germanies for the three British legions (RIB 1322). Julius Verus, the Emperor's propraetorian legate named in the inscription was a highly distinguished soldier, whose name was also recorded on building inscriptions at Birrens and Brough (Derbyshire). The evidence is by no means conclusive, but it is consistent with a revolt in southern Scotland and the Pennines, although the suggestion has recently come under increasing attack. However, there is a strong regional bias, with evidence of damage to forts at Lancaster, Hardknott and Ravenglass reflecting those areas it was considered expedient to garrison securely in the 130s. The case for rebellion still exists, although it is by no means proven (Hartley 1980).

Whatever the cause of withdrawal, the Antonine Wall was rapidly reoccupied and the analysis of Samian pottery has demonstrated that the two walls cannot have been held in tandem for any length of time (Hartley 1972).

Final withdrawal to Hadrian's Wall was decided in the 160s, and probably mirrors political decisions made at the centre of the empire. The new Emperor, Marcus Aurelius, was faced by a series of frontier crises among which the problems of northern Britain were the least significant and most remote, and it is likely that troops were redeployed from Britain to the eastern empire (Breeze 1975). The distinguished general, Calpurnius Agricola, was appointed to the British province probably with instructions to redeploy the frontier troops on Hadrian's Wall and in the hinterland forts (*SHA* VIII, 7). Inscriptions recording the rebuilding work of the Governor are widespread.

The Hadrianic frontier was recommissioned in most respects: the forts were reoccupied and the *vallum* recommissioned, cleaned out and the breaks made good. Some changes may mirror experience on the Antonine Wall. During the latter part of the century, some turrets appear to have been abandoned and even demolished, and the milecastle gates were narrowed, or even in some cases blocked, reducing the ease of access across the frontier and forcing a higher proportion of traffic to pass under the more intensive surveillance of the forts. Behind the wall a service road was added, in places utilizing the northern mound and berm of the *vallum*. Supervision of the Cumbrian coast did not recommence at the Hadrianic level, but initially, at least, the Dere Street forts as far north as Newstead were retained, providing forward points from which surveillance of central Scotland could be maintained. This was an obvious strategy for an army that naturally responded to security problems by offensive action, and implies a partial rejection of the sedentary frontier of Hadrian. At the same time, the new dispositions represent a shift of emphasis away from south-west Scotland to the Upper Tweed basin (Hanson and Maxwell 1983: 194). Even so, the forts at Netherby and Bewcastle were recommissioned.

These dispositions suggest that southern Scotland was to remain under Roman control, even though excluded from the province (Breeze and Dobson 1976). The Dere Street forts provided an effective screen for the Votadini in Northumberland, and treaties with the Maeatae and Caledonii late in the second century provided the Scottish borders with some security. That these tribes were inclined to threaten the peace of the frontier region is at least one interpretation of the rumours of war in AD 170–72 (*SHA* xxii, 1), and the transfer of 5,500 Sarmatian cavalry to the province in AD 175 may have been intended to improve the mobility of the frontier forces.

The frontier dispositions broke down under pressure from the north in the 180s. Cassius Dio recorded an attack in which the tribes crossed the wall that separated them from the Roman garrisons, killed a Roman general and did great damage (Dio, LXIII, 8). Which wall was involved we are not told, but that it was the Hadrianic frontier that was penetrated seems at least a possibility. Destruction levels at Halton Chesters, Rudchester and Corbridge have been associated with this incursion. At Corbridge a new forum-like structure was under construction, when widespread areas of the undefended settlement were slighted by fire (Gillam 1974–1977 [5]), and a similar abortive stone building of the period laid out around a courtyard has now been excavated at Carlisle. The pattern of destruction that emerges is confused since several scattered forts in the hinterland may have been destroyed. However, the main thrust either at this stage or in the next decade was probably the responsibility of the growing tribal confederates from beyond the Forth.

The Roman government responded to the challenge, and Ulpius Marcellus campaigned beyond the frontier. An inscription from Carlisle may record one of his victories over a 'huge multitude of barbarians' (RIB 946). Despite the victories, the outposts beyond the wall were not reoccupied in strength: Newstead and Cappuck were abandoned, and there is some doubt whether Risingham and Birrens were retained (Robertson 1975: 284). Although Marcellus successfully cleared the enemy from the province, the Roman control of southern Scotland seems to have been far less secure than in the 160s, and the protection afforded the Votadini that much reduced. The possibility of abandonment at Traprain Law at exactly this period was suggested by Feachem (1956: 286), but remains unproven.

In the 190s central Roman politics once again rebounded on the provinces. The death of Commodus was followed by a struggle for power in which the Governor of Britain was a minor candidate. In AD 196, he crossed to Gaul with an army, but was defeated early in the following year at Lyons. To assemble a credible force it seems likely that Albinus took with him many of the auxiliary garrison troops. Those in the North were among those with experience of active service. This prospect has led scholars to seek evidence for renewed invasion of the province from the North, sweeping aside the denuded frontier defences, but there is little agreement as to the level to which the garrisons were reduced, or the nature of action if any taken by the northern tribes. Destruction deposits at Ilkley, Bainbridge and Bowes have been attributed to a Brigantian revolt in the later 190s (Hartley 1980: 6). Both suggestions remain viable, although recent reinterpretation of the evidence has reduced the possibility of widespread devastation (Breeze and Dobson 1976; Hanson and Maxwell 1983).

Whatever the exact nature of the frontier disturbances of AD 196/97, the first governor appointed by Severus, Virius Lupus, felt it necessary to buy peace from the Maeatae (Dio, LXXV, 5, 4), and his name is associated with widespread fort reconstruction throughout northern England, at Brough-under-Stainmore, Ilkley, Bowes and Corbridge. He and his successor, Alfenus Senecio, were active throughout the northern frontier, refurbishing military installations, as well as indulging in a certain amount of warfare (Dio, LXXVI, 10, 6), and a dedicatory inscription at Benwell (RIB 1337) may be relevant to this activity. Work is attested along the wall at Birdoswald, Chesters and Housesteads, as well as at Corbridge, and a quarry at Brampton provided stone for legionary masons in AD 207 (RIB 1009).

By AD 208 the situation on the frontier was bad enough to warrant an expedition led by the Emperor in person. Whether this was due to hostile action (Herodian, III, 14) or simply to Severus's desire to discipline his own family (Dio, LXXVI, 11) is not clear, but we must accept that real frontier problems attracted the imperial expedition, and led to the decision to incorporate all Britain within the province (Dio, LXXVI, 13, 1). This was a bold solution of what must have been an unsatisfactory situation.

As bases for the readvance, Corbridge and South Shields were re-equipped; the fort interior at South Shields was almost completely overbuilt with warehousing (Dore and Gillam 1979). The land forces pushed up the by now familiar Dere Street into Scotland, once more briefly incorporating southern Scotland and Northumberland within the province, and severely mauling the tribes beyond the Forth. The death of Severus robbed his son Caracalla of the opportunity to annihilate the Maeatae, since central imperial politics swiftly required his attention. The new Emperor probably took his expeditionary force away with him, and the first two decades of the third century saw the gradual abandonment of forts within Scotland. Only four outpost forts remained in commission, High Rochester and Risingham controlling Dere Street on the east, and Bewcastle and Netherby in the west. It is with these forts that we should associate the *exploratores*, with whom now lay responsibility for the maintenance of Roman interests beyond the wall.

Although the eventual outcome of the Severan campaigns was not as far-reaching as may have been intended, Roman security on the land frontier was not to be challenged for most of a century. In particular, the Severan settlement firmly consolidated Roman influence in the Tyne–Forth province, an influence which in the 180s and 190s had looked increasingly fragile. The credit for this must be given to the imperial expedition, and the campaigns in Scotland beyond the Forth. Throughout the third century, the Votadini and their neighbours enjoyed a high degree of security overseen by small Roman forces, but guaranteed by treaties underwritten by the memory of the Severan wasting in the North. Under that Roman umbrella, British communities south of the Forth escaped incorporation into the northern confederacies, and ultimately into the Pictish nation.

The Tribal Response

The Pennine region was the last part of Roman Britain to be permanently incorporated into the province, in AD 79, by which time the process of Romanization was well under way in southern Britain. Elements of this had already emerged as official policy before the disaster of the Boudiccan rebellion. However, the hearts and minds policy recommenced in the 60s under the governorships of Petronius Turpilianus and Trebellius Maximus, and was actively pursued by the Flavian governors (Tacitus, *Agric.* XVI, 21).

Romanization seems to have been attempted at more than one level of society. The local aristocracy was encouraged to learn the Latin language, become acquainted with Roman culture and spend its wealth on peaceful amenities such as arcades, baths and banquets. Another level of this operation, as described in the initial Romanization of Germania, was the Romanization of the general populace who 'were becoming accustomed to hold markets and were meeting in peaceful assemblages. They had not, however, forgotten their ancestral habits, their native manners, their old life of independence, or the power derived from arms. Hence, so long as they were unlearning these customs gradually and by the way, as one might say, under careful watching, they were not disturbed by the change in their manner of life, and were becoming different without knowing it' (Dio, LVI, 18, 2).

By the end of the first century, these policies had attained a reasonable level of success in the South. The countryside was studded with villas of varying quality, and most areas boasted a small urban community. By the mid second century, the construction of high-status town houses had begun (Walthew 1975). The province had been effectively civilized. Roman troops were almost entirely absent by AD 80, and when they reappeared in the third century it was in response to outside danger. The Roman administration had success-fully enlisted the active co-operation of the tribal aristocracies, and through them the tribes swiftly attained a degree of local self-government as *civitates*.

In the border counties this easy transition from conquered tribesman to Roman provincial did not occur. The area achieved only a limited degree of Romanization, and this took far longer than in the South. Active hostility to Roman troops was arguably still present several generations after the initial conquest, and it was not until the 130s that the occupation of Cumbria was complete.

The Agricolan conquest was achieved by the threat rather than the exercise of force. Presumably the terms he offered required the abandonment of native fortifications, some possibly still only half-built (Feachem 1971). This may have had important social and economic repercussions in Northumberland where fort sites were numerous, but south of the Tyne–Solway there were comparatively few. The abandonment of the latter need have had little impact on the bonds by which leadership of tribal society was exercised. Subsequent government exercised by the commanders of alien military garrisons was not likely to endear the tribesmen to Rome. Nor were the other 'benefits' of the Roman peace – extra-tribal taxation, enslavement, conscription to the army and deportment, or forced labour on the new road system.

The communities east of the Pennines had most reason to bow to superior Roman force and accept provincial status, and, with the exception of the Bainbridge and Ilkley destruction levels, there is little evidence of protracted resistance. The East was most vulnerable to Roman control. A port of entry on the Tyne and the philo-Roman Votadini isolated the Tyne–Tees community from potential allies and from possible refuge. Forest clearance had progressed further than in the North-west, and the community was, therefore, exposed to Roman supervision. The major part of its identifiable capital was invested in fixed dwellings, cultivated lands, harvested crops and livestock.

In contrast, west of the Pennines the process of deforestation was less advanced, and the valleys more heavily wooded. Very few sites have been identified which are even candidates for occupation in the initial conquest period; the Cumbrian communities were arguably more mobile pastoralists, less vulnerable to Roman activity. For a generation, the Lake District mountains and the valleys and plains beyond provided the sort of refuge available in north Wales to the Ordovici, into which dissident groups could withdraw with little risk of pursuit. Not too much should be made of the east–west contrast. Crops were probably grown on the Solway plain, and large herds grazed in the East, but these conditions help to explain the differing treatment of the two regions by the Romans. The problems of control and the level of garrisoning were consistently greater in north-west England than anywhere else in the province from *c.* AD 90 to the later second century. A useful parallel can be drawn with a similar situation in the two regions in the late Saxon period (Kapelle 1979: 35).

The Roman response was to delay the conquest of Lakeland. That conquest probably required several campaigns, via the route taken by the modern A66 from Penrith westwards (Fig. 4.5). A series of temporary camps at Troutbeck at the head of the pass bear witness to these armies. The largest at 16.2 ha was capable of holding a legionary force, and was sited on the highest ground available. A second camp of about 4 ha was located close by, and the strategic value of the site eventually led to the construction of an earth and timber fort, and a fortlet, probably in the Trajanic/Hadrianic period (Bellhouse 1956; Higham and Jones forthcoming). This was just one of a series of army posts sited so as to control and oversee the main lines of communication into and out of the Lakeland massif. Hardknott, Caermote, Ambleside, Watercrook and possibly even Papcastle fall into this category.

In addition, the complex sequence of coastal defences may have been designed to segregate Cumbria from potential allies in south-west Scotland. The Antonine re-advance allowed both shores of the Solway to be subsumed

Figure 4.5   The Troutbeck installations: successive military uses of a strategic pass into the Lake District.

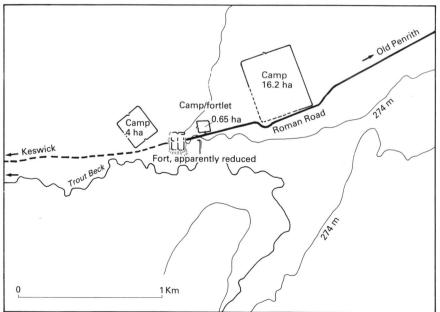

into the province, and it is noticeable that the subsequent reoccupation of the wall relied far less on this *cordon sanitaire* between the Carvetii and the Novantes. Presumably by the 160s links across the Solway had ceased to threaten Roman control on the southern shore.

The ease with which order was imposed is not known, and is probably not knowable. It may be relevant that the general level of inland garrisoning of the Lake District did not drop permanently until the Severan reorganization, at which point it became apparent throughout the North that the Roman frontier, and Roman control of southern Scotland, were permanent. Before that episode, the Roman presence in the North may have seemed rather less secure, and anti-Roman attitudes may have been consequently encouraged. Hardknott must rank among the least likely sites to be reoccupied without good, local cause under Marcus Aurelius. At some stage during the second century, the Cumbrian tribesmen became identifiable as Roman provincials. Exactly when is unclear, but there are some indications that it was rather later than Hadrian, and we should not discount the relevant palaeobotanical information which implies major clearance activity delayed until a context broadly contemporary with the Severans. It seems quite possible that the switch was based less on political attitudes than on expectations of economic opportunity, and as such was dependent to a large extent on climatic factors.

If the southern experience of Romanization had been relevant in the North, by about AD 100 or AD 120 at the latest, we should be able to identify traces of new, 'civilized' dwellings in the countryside commissioned by the native aristocracy. No such pattern has emerged, despite widespread aerial reconnaissance of the relevant areas. Few villa sites have been located; predictably all are east of the Pennines, and are concentrated around roads, forts and *vici* in the better arable areas of the Durham lowlands (Branigan 1980). If we extend this overview to the wider Brigantia, there is a peripheral scatter on the plain of York and in the lower dales. Compared even with the Yorkshire Wolds, the distribution has remained markedly thin. The little villa development that there was, occurred east of the Pennines, and much of it was in the post-Severan period. West of the Pennines, nothing resembling a true villa has been identified north of one isolated example on the Cheshire plain. The Romanized member of the Brigantian aristocracy is an animal elusive to the point of extinction. It is quite in order to argue in his defence that lower levels of productivity per unit area required a thinner distribution of villa sites. It cannot account for his near-total absence. Whether because of differences in economic or sociological hierarchies, or for political reasons, the border aristocracy do not appear to have made successful converts to the Romanized life-style and Roman provincial values. It is extremely difficult to argue that the families that had commissioned, inhabited and repeatedly refurbished the forts of Northumberland successfully replaced them with 'civilized' estate centres.

Romanization is undetectable among the aristocracy, but what of the population at large? If Dio's comments on Germany are apposite, we should be

Plate 4.7 A rectilinear, stone-founded building in the Roman *vicus* at Papcastle (Cumb.), during excavations in 1984.

looking for towns, market-places and places of peaceful assembly, under official surveillance. The obvious place to look is at extra-mural activity associated with early fort sites.

At least a minority, and perhaps a substantial majority, of early forts were associated with *vici* outside the gates. Such have been identified in timber in a Flavian or Trajanic context at Watercrook and perhaps Piercebridge, and sufficient finds exist to indicate Hadrianic examples at Housesteads and South Shields. The *vicus* could develop rapidly on the northern frontier. Examples are known outside some of the forts on the Antonine Wall. Among them Carriden was significant enough to be granted local government (Salway 1965). The speed with which they were constructed, and the regularity of layout may imply that they were laid out or even built by the military as a part of official policy (Casey 1981). In this case they are unlikely to have housed the dependants of active servicemen, but the plan of buildings end on to the fort access roads, jostling for proximity to the gateways implies that one major function lay in the provision of market facilities, particularly for the garrisons, and secondarily perhaps for the local community. It is even possible that the *mansio* buildings that remain a major element in the *vici* may have started life as *basilica*, intended to stimulate local trading, rather than as inns attached to the post service [6].

Only one *vicus* of the second century has been extensively excavated, at Chesterholm (Vindolanda). The site illustrates some of the current problems of interpretation. A series of buildings were laid out with stone footings end on to the fort access road immediately outside the fort ditch. Both the bathhouse and *mansio* were integral to the general plan, which betrays a high degree of planning and organization. One substantial corridor house has been provisionally identified as a butcher's shop (Birley 1977), but the burial of a rare example of chariot ornament under the floor has never been explained (Toynbee and Wilkins 1982). The extra-mural settlement was provided with a defensive ditch, implying that construction of a defensive circuit round such settlements may have been commonplace. This recalls a passage in Arrian's *Periplus* which describes a tour by a provincial legate of newly established forts along the Black Sea coast, where he judged whether or not extra-mural civilian settlements had reached a level which warranted a census, higher legal status and, where appropriate, defences (*Periplus* 7.4–8.1).

Sites like these were not a vehicle for the Romanization of the native aristocracy on the level attributed to Agricola, but they had considerable potential for the dissemination of ideas and trade among the local rural population. The widespread appearance of second-century pottery on native sites must reflect that function (Higham 1981b). However, the quantity of 'exotics' reaching native sites was always small, although levels were significantly higher south of the wall than in Northumberland.

In the south of the province, urban or market centres developed early, and were largely independent of the military market. In the border counties no such centres emerged, and market facilities remained in almost all cases heavily dependent on garrisons (Jones and Walker 1983). The site hierarchy of the Roman period was consequently not a complex one; fort, *vicus* and farm, or at most farming hamlet, was the normal extent of that hierarchy. Despite the appearance of a money economy in the forts and *vici*, little coinage has been found on the farm sites, and the money was arguably unable to make substantial inroads in the local economy. There is little evidence that *vici* were able to survive the removal of garrison troops. Piercebridge is an exception to this, but the site occupies a special niche in the south-east corner of the borders, where a

Yorkshire-style agrarian economy developed early. Nether Denton may also be exceptional; the Stanegate fort attracted a civilian settlement which survived the removal of the garrison to the wall, but the nearby Birdoswald garrison probably provided the necessary economic stimulus. Although both were arguably civilian sites, neither Corbridge nor Carlisle were economically independent of the wall garrisons.

The conclusion must be that Romanization failed in the border counties at all practical levels. Physical conditions and the disadvantages facing the local economy were probably more important factors than local anti-Roman sentiment, but the disadvantages facing the local community probably extended the process of conquest.

Only in very specific circumstances can we witness directly the disruption of local communities by the Roman military. Those who were in occupation of sites required by the army were expelled – probably without compensation. The classic example of this type of conflict occurred at Milking Gap, High Shiel (Tyne and Wear), where a native site was trapped between the wall and the *vallum* (Kilbride-Jones 1938). The site is a typical example of the undefended but enclosed stone-built homesteads common throughout the borders, and with five huts is among the larger type. Occupation occurred in the early second century, if not before, and it was probably abandoned as a direct consequence of the linear frontier in the 120s (Gillam 1958). We cannot generalize from this case, since further examples have not been identified along the line of the wall. Elsewhere, it can often be shown that pre-Roman occupation, or land-use, characterizes Roman military installations, but it is not clear whether the latter displaced the former. A ring-ditch, probably for a timber round-house, was identified immediately adjacent to the Agricolan base at Corbridge (Hanson *et al.* 1979); and Trajanic Samian was found with locally made coarse wares under the Hadrianic fort at Birdoswald (Simpson and Richmond 1934). In addition, the fort sites at Corbridge were superimposed over a native site which may have been a palisaded homestead, although no dating evidence was forthcoming, and the outer palisade trench appears rather broad to have fallen within the normal limits for a site of this kind. Evidence for cultivation has been identified beneath a growing number of military installations, now including turret 10A on the wall at Throckley, Tyne and Wear (Bennett 1983b) and predating the *vallum* at Wallhouses (Bennett and Turner 1983). Some of these examples may derive from clearance ploughing in the second millennium bc or earlier, but many probably derive from the redevelopment of the landscape by agriculturalists around the time of Christ, as forest clearance and cultivation rose towards a new optimum on the east of the Pennines. It is unlikely that plough cultivation was practised at a distance from the farm site, and it seems likely that many examples are now obscured by Roman and later landscape changes, particularly in the major route corridors.

In this context, the forts and other military installations may have had a major impact on the local community. The total land area removed from civilian access was very considerable, although the figure varied enormously over the Roman period. By the end of the reign of Hadrian, about 40 forts were located in the border counties, of which 16 were on the wall and about 24 in the hinterland. The installations in the hinterland occupied about 75 ha, to which should be added the areas utilized by *vici* and the major roads. In addition, an uncultivated *cordon sanitaire* was probably maintained around each fort several times greater than the area covered by the installation. Tracts of land may, in addition have been confiscated to provide the garrisons with certain resources like horse pasturage. Such *territoria* could be substantial if the 3,444 ha calculated for Xanten is a reliable estimate (Macmullen 1963: Ch. 5).

Provision of *territoria* on this scale could have involved the transfer of over 80,000 ha from civil use to military control. In addition, the wall–*vallum* corridor removed a substantial and continuous tract of land from civilian use. To calculate the area accurately would be extremely difficult, but it was probably between 85,000 and 120,000 ha, and this does not include a figure for *territoria* for the wall garrisons.

The exact requirement of land by the garrisons is not known. It was, however, very considerable. In addition, the weight of this resource realloca-tion fell on areas disproportionately. The comparatively well-developed east-ern lowlands escaped relatively lightly. The Tyne–Solway gap was, in contrast, almost exclusively military. In addition, fort sites in most areas occupy the best available agricultural land – a scarce resource in the border counties. The high density of fort sites in the Eden valley has led to the suggestion that resource consciousness played a part in their location. Like modern motorways, their construction removed from the local resource base crucial 'bottom land', and any substantial *territoria* in that area would have extended this impact over a wide area. In addition, forts such as Ravenglass, Low Borrow Bridge or Brough-under-Stainmore were sited within limited areas of agriculturally adequate land which they may, therefore, largely have controlled. In such circumstances, the absence of a native aristocracy may be easier to understand, and the basic functions of an aristocracy may have been largely subsumed within the Roman administration, at least in the second century.

Further problems are likely to have occurred. The wall and other *limes* probably separated communities from traditional resources, such as summer grazing, and crossing the frontier biannually with herds would subsequently have incurred a substantial tax liability. It may be that the authorities attemp-ted to minimize the problem. In the Irthing valley the wall was constructed along a line that maximized the area today designated grade 2 agricultural land to the south of the wall, but it is quite possible that this was an accidental by-product of strategic planning.

Away from the military sites, there is no evidence of deliberate damage perpetrated by the army on undefended, civilian sites during the conquest period. In the West, the current failure to identify ultimate pre-Roman settlements renders the question sterile. In the East, where evidence is available, the crisis of conquest left little mark.

Roman communities emerged after rebuilding on late prehistoric farm sites like Kennel Hall Knowe and Belling Law (Northumb.), but there is no reason to postulate military destruction, or any change in the inhabitants. The Tower Knowe site witnessed a sequence of four structural phases which began before the conquest, but there was neither sign of a significant break, nor evidence that the two reconstructions that occurred in the second century departed in any way from the pattern of periodic replacement already established. To the extent to which the archaeologist is competent to judge, the military interfered little with the farming community in Northumberland, but this could eventually prove to be a rash oversimplification. Between Tyne and Tees, a similar, but less well-documented pattern emerges. At Forcegarth Pasture (Upper Teesdale), one stone-walled settlement occupied in the first century AD was probably replaced by a second, with a carbon-14 date of *c.* AD 158 (Coggins and Fairless 1980). The Catcote site has produced evidence spanning the conquest, and the later Roman period. In contrast, Thorpe Thewles (Cleveland) was apparently abandoned broadly contemporary with the conquest (Haselgrove 1981). The excavation of individual sites is not likely to resolve the issue. More important is the palaeobotanical evidence, where signs are that the increasingly vigorous clearance episode that had begun in the last centuries bc progressed smoothly into the Roman period. No evidence of an economic crisis has been detected, in contrast to the palaeobotanical reflection of the Norman wasting of Yorkshire and Cheshire in the eleventh century. In these circumstances, we must assume that in the North-east, at least, the countryside was spared the heavy hand of Rome. There are some signs that the occupation may even have indirectly assisted the process of population growth with which it was broadly contemporary. In Cumbria, the process of permanent deforestation had made little impact when the conquest occurred; there are some signs that the conquest was both more traumatic and a longer undertaking than in the East, and it seems likely that garrison forces were active in the policing of the hinterland.

The Severan period witnessed the forceful redrawing of the frontier area, and the permanent extension of Roman control to the Tyne–Forth province. South of the wall or in Northumberland, the tribes were left in no doubt that the empire was there to stay, and whatever their attitude to it they had no option but to accept the political situation, and the umbrella it provided against hostile groups north of the Forth. Under that umbrella, the rural population were able to maintain existing developments and in some areas expand, and it was in the process of becoming a civilianized, even if not a Romanized, community. Even so, the future was one in which security depended solely on the substantial army presence, and consequently on the flow of taxation and other resources from the South and from Europe. The economy of the North had entered a phase of extraordinary complexity, which bore little relationship to the local resource base; were it ever to have to depend upon that base, it would inevitably collapse.

Notes

1. Both Ptolemy and Tacitus were guilty of gross understatement of basic topographical pointers. For a reconstruction of the tribal territories, see Richmond (1958); Breeze (1982); Rivet and Smith (1981); Maxwell (1980).

2. RIB is used here as an abbreviation for Collingwood and Wright (1965). Unless otherwise stated, the etymology of all place-names discussed derives from Rivet and Smith (1981).

3. My thanks to Ian Caruana for his helpful correspondence on this subject, which has materially contributed to the interpretation of Carlisle throughout Chapters 4 and 5.

4. For the Antonine Wall, see Breeze (1982); Hanson and Maxwell (1983) *et al.*

5. My thanks to John Dore for his assistance in the interpretation of Roman Corbridge.

6. My thanks to Prof. Barri Jones for his advice on this point.

Chapter 5

The Roman Interlude

The Environment

During the Roman period, the northern counties enjoyed a climate broadly comparable to, if not slightly more hospitable than, that of the modern day (Lamb 1972–77). Arguably, this represented a significant improvement upon conditions in the early to mid first millennium bc. Taking the agricultural potential of the modern period as a rough guide, these conditions should have enabled communities to utilize a bundle of subsistence strategies which included cereal cultivation. Such activity would naturally be most attractive within topographical parameters in the eastern plain and major valleys. West of the Pennines farmers faced then, as they face today, wetter conditions. Although the immediate hinterland of Carlisle has a rainfall of 914–1,016 mm, the total rises rapidly with altitude in the Lake District and the Pennines. Despite this, small-scale agriculture was then, as it was to be in the medieval period, a feasible strategy on well-drained upland soils up to c. 300 m. High rainfall rendered it a less successful economic strategy in the Lake District and on the low western fells, where the length of the growing season and the incidence of rain make conditions worse than on the eastern valley sides at a comparable altitude.

Those soils which were situated on base-deficient parent rocks which had supported wide-scale human activity in the second millennium bc were no longer attractive to large human populations. The fell sandstones in Northumberland had been abandoned by the Roman period (Jobey 1982), but of greater extent are the mudstone, gritstone and sandstone fells of south and west Cumbria where evidence of Romano–British activity is peripheral, and incapable of competition with the altitudinal range and density of the cairnfields. Other areas of unusable – or unsettleable – land continued to perform a role as barriers. The Cheviots above 300 m and much of the central and northern Pennines fall into this category, as do the mountains of the core of the Lake District. When all the areas are taken into account, it is difficult to escape the conclusion that the rural community was unable to reoccupy much territory that had been occupied a millennium previously. Despite voices of caution (Jobey 1981b), the loss of marginal territory was a general phenomenon, even where the threshold of waste land had moved downhill only a short distance. In total, the Romano-British community had lost parts of the habitat of their distant ancestors, measured in tens and probably in hundreds of thousands of hectares. Even so, in some areas the territory available to the farmer was marginally in excess of that considered today to be suitable for settlement.

This loss of habitat was largely the result of the pauperization of soils. It is arguable that soil condition had deteriorated over the last two millennia bc, in some lowland areas as well as in the uplands. Soil underneath the fort at Strageath (Scotland) had apparently been cultivated more or less continuously for a period of 1,700–1,800 years (Romans and Robertson 1983) and those inheriting such agricultural soils had to expect a consequent loss of organic matter leading to structural instability. The real extent of such long-lived cultivation on the eve of conquest cannot be known. That sections of the Antonine Wall consist largely of earth rather than turf might possibly be due to the ubiquity of cultivated soils in the vicinity (Maxwell 1983). In the wall area, the widespread occurrence of pre-Hadrianic ploughing has already been noted. However, while agricultural land was one element in the landscape at AD 100, it seems unlikely on present evidence to have covered a large area, or have been associated with many sites.

Upland soils had been subjected to severe erosive forces over several millennia, causing the wholesale truncation of soil horizons and the removal of organic and eventually of mineral soils to drainage hollows. The rate of accretion in the latter had dramatically increased at many Cumbrian sites in the second millennium, and the changes in the soil structure and in vegetation have proved to be irreversible (Walker 1966).

The extent of forest cover is not precisely ascertainable. A recent overview of the problem in southern Scotland in the Flavian period concluded that local supplies of timber were sufficient for the construction of all the Roman forts (Hanson and Macinnes 1980). This criterion is a very low one, demanding less forest than is currently available. Soil samples from beneath the first- and second-century forts provide widespread evidence of forest disturbance. At High Rochester (Northumb.), samples from the earliest ramparts revealed a landscape of grassland, with stands of birch, hazel and alder (Richmond 1936b). A similar picture emerged from Benwell, Risingham, Chew Green and Fendoch. Only Bearsden on the Antonine Wall was constructed in a landscape which can be described as wooded (Breeze 1977). Excavation of the *vallum* at Wallhouses revealed that plough cultivation had preceded excavation of the ditch, and that in the second century the area was open country, with only small amounts of alder and hazel scrub, and cereal cultivation was practised in the vicinity (Bennett and Turner 1983). The classical authors make frequent reference to woodland or forest in northern Britain, but among them only

Tacitus was specifically referring to woods south of the border – apparently in Cumbria (Tacitus, *Agric.*, xx).

East of the Pennines the limited data available supports the thesis that an episode typified by permanent and substantial deforestation preceded the occupation, gathered impetus during that period, and spread to adjacent areas where less advantageous conditions prevail, and where the environmental threshold of agricultural development was thereby retarded. Some recent commentators have counselled caution in the definite identification of pre-conquest clearance, arguing that carbon-14 assays are insufficiently precise for judgements over such a short time-scale (Gates 1983). This naturally places at the centre of the debate the role of the conquest in the stimulus of de-forestation.

While accepting words of caution, a wider view reveals a long-term phenomenon that arguably has little to do with the occupation. The heightened rate of deforestation is not peculiar to the North, but can be traced in southern Britain from about 400 years bc. If the limiting factors controlling the speed of deforestation were environmental, then we should expect the threshold to recede northwards and westwards, broadly in line with modern weather and crop geography. This it does. Clearance appears in the better-drained areas of the Cleveland and Durham lowlands, and the major valleys of the hinterland a century or more before Christ. At Steng Moss (Northumb.) large-scale clear-ance was not identified until *c.* 20 bc, and at Fellend Moss near the Upper Tyne not until marginally later (Turner 1983). The attack on the Lake District forests was delayed until after *c.* AD 200 at Devoke Water, and *c.* AD 390 at Burnmoor Tarn (Pennington 1970). The large number of pollen diagrams without the benefit of carbon dating support this late clearance (Walker 1966), but caution is necessary in the acceptance of this chronology, based as it is on a very small sample of carbon-14 dates. Further north the same pattern emerges. Extensive clearance was delayed at Flanders Moss on the Forth until *c.* AD 200, at Loch Lomond until *c.* AD 150 and at Bloak Moss, Ayrshire, until after *c.* AD 450.

This chronology implies a sensitivity to environmental factors, among which climatic conditions provided the most likely stimulant to change. En-vironmental rather than political factors governed the parameters within which subsistence strategies were changing. In other words, the intensification of clearance activity represented by the pollen data would have occurred within the same sliding time-scale even had the conquest not occurred. That it was climatic factors that were directly responsible receives support from the new retardation levels identified in the lowland peats of Morecambe Bay at *c.* AD 436, which were probably due to unusually low rainfall (Smith 1959).

It was similarly environmental factors that conditioned the local extent of forest clearance, and the use to which the cleared space was put. Neasham Fen has provided the only diagram where woodland remained the dominant land cover throughout the entire period, probably because of the lowlying, wet soils of the area (Bartley, Chambers and Hart-Jones 1976). Elsewhere in the lowlands of south-east Durham, cereal cultivation was more widespread than elsewhere, and may have been both extensive and important. Cereal pollen has been sporadically recorded further north and west, at Camp Hill Moss and Steng Moss in Northumberland, and in the valley of the south Tyne, but even where these diagrams record considerable deforestation, it seems to have been very largely in favour of open pasture. The Upper Teesdale diagrams reveal dominant moorland with widespread blanket bog already long established, and the extension of pasture-land at the expense of forest was only feasible on the better-drained soils (Turner *et al.* 1973). In Cumbria, the forest clearance was very largely to create pasture-land, but some cultivation was present, although rarely visible in the numerous Lake District diagrams, the dating of most of which is reliant on the synchronization of horizons (Pennington 1970). In the far west, Ehenside Tarn arguably suffered forest regeneration in the Roman period, with deforestation delayed until after AD 400, but once again no absolute chronology is available (Walker 1966), and this date may be rather late.

Parallels can be drawn between conditions in the period *c.* 1800 bc–1200 bc and *c.* 200 bc–AD 400, but it seems unlikely that conditions in the latter ever approached the optimum of the former, and the legacy of soil erosion was probably a major culprit.

The picture that emerges at the opening of the Roman period suggests that wholesale deforestation had already occurred in the south-east of the border counties, spreading during and after the occupation westwards and northwards. The status of the Cumbrian lowlands at *c.* AD 100 was not unremitting woodland, but clearances were not considerable. During the Roman period, existing clearances in most areas were vastly extended to the point where woodland was in specific localities close to annihilation. Even so, some of the wetter clay soils probably retained considerable forest cover. In the east, Neasham Fen appears to represent such a locality. In Cumbria, the area that became Inglewood Forest in the medieval period has failed to reveal the density of settlement that has been identified on its borders (Higham 1978c). The high uplands were already devoid of forest cover, and conditions on the fells altered little, although deforestation occurred where feasible to convert the drier areas to grassland. Clearance and subsequent interferences with the soil cover probably resulted in renewed erosion of soils in vulnerable locations, with the result that the threshold of settlement and intensive land-use may in places have shifted during the period, rendering some marginal terrains unhabitable within a few centuries. Consequent upon this, substantial soil accretion occurred in valley bottoms and drainage hollows. The contrast between upland and lowland was becoming more severe, and human strategies were more narrowly confined to terrains capable of withstanding a phase of clearance and land-use that was unprecedented in its extent and degree of permanence.

Rural Settlement

The local community inherited a package of strategies from their forebears in later prehistory, both social and economic. The Roman occupation possibly led to major changes in the social order. However, the economic strategies appear to have provided the basis upon which the community maintained the existing momentum of expansion without any identifiable sign of disruption in the political events by which the Roman period began and ended.

Settlement strategies

To the extent whereby it has so far been identified, the norm among Romano-British rural settlements favoured an enclosed habitative area. In this respect, as in most others, there is apparent a clear legacy of the late, pre-Roman rural strategy, and in some respects the types of Romano-British settlement enclosures that emerged are an obvious and logical end-product of the process of settlement enclosure first adopted early in the last millennium before Christ as palisaded sites. Given that the upper ranks of the site hierarchy represented by hillforts were not in use during the Roman period the enclosed form implies strong similarities in culture and in economic strategies bridging the conquest, and this is reinforced by the apparent continuity of occupation of some sites through the conquest period and beyond, for example, at Hartburn (Jobey 1973b).

A range of settlement site types have been identified over the last century. Fieldwork has been disproportionately concentrated, principally in the historic county of Northumberland but to a lesser extent also in Cumbria [1]. With the exception of a small number of specific projects, Tyne and Wear south of the Tyne, Durham and north Cleveland are under-represented [2]. In these counties, a substantial spread of opencast mining and industrial activity in the modern period has obscured significant areas, but it must be said that the incidence of upstanding sites is far fewer along the upland fringes where comparatively late ridge and furrow is dominant. The lowlands are less responsive to aerial photography (Harding 1979). Those sites that have been identified in this area can be assessed along with those of Northumberland (Fig. 5.1).

In the latter county, the first identified Romano-British site types were the small, stone-built, non-defensive, enclosed homesteads or farms that are the most obvious component of the settlement pattern in the Cheviot foothills and the upper valley sides of Northumberland south of the Coquet. In the southern dales the form is generally rectilinear. In the Cheviots this pattern

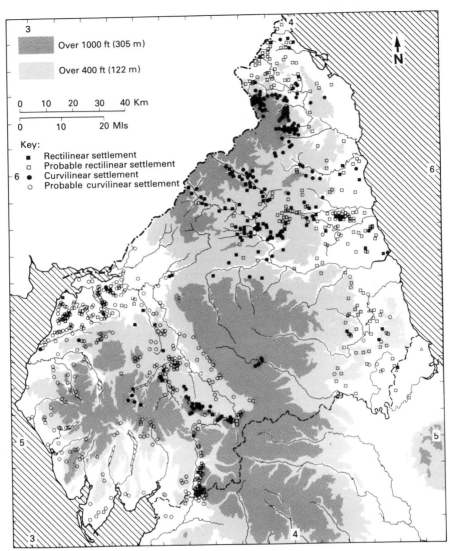

Figure 5.1 The distribution of rural settlement.

gives way to a predominate curvilinear form. The presence or absence of a single, non-defensive outer ditch depend on the nature of the subsoil. Ditches are present where sites occupy glacial deposits, but extremely scarce where they would require to be rock-cut. The ditch was not, therefore, conceived as an essential feature of enclosed settlement, but most communities exercised a preference provided the labour involved was not too excessive (Jobey 1966a).

These settlement forms are upstanding, and are therefore unusually accessible to fieldwork. They are absent from the valleys of Dumfriesshire, and

187

scarce in Upper Tweeddale, where 'scooped' enclosures of outwardly similarly form may be contemporary, although as a settlement type they may have enjoyed a broader chronology, and were not infrequently occupied in the medieval period (Jobey 1966b, 1981b). That some at least of these 'scooped' sites were Romano-British was demonstrated by excavation on the side of Burnswark Hill at Bonnies near Westerkirk (Jobey 1974a), and at Hetha Burn (Burgess 1970). The stone-built settlement of the Northumberland upland margins reveal a regularity of internal layout which implies a well-established and tested functional plan, from which some special circumstance was necessary to induce the inhabitants to deviate. The standard pattern common to both areas has one, or several, stone-founded round-houses situated towards the rear of the enclosure facing the sole enclosure entrance, often

---

Plate 5.1 A Late Prehistoric settlement at Burradon, south-east Northumberland, photographed by Prof. Norman McCord from the north during excavation under the direction of Prof. George Jobey in 1968–69. At the centre of a rectilinear, ditched enclosure is clearly visible a substantial round-house defined by a peripheral drainage trench and concentric rings of individual post-holes. In the southern half of the enclosure several, smaller round-houses are present, of which all but one are of the continuous construction trench variety. The parallel, dark lines running approximately north-south across the excavated area are the result of later ridge and furrow. The settlement site may be one in which there occurred conversion from an unenclosed, to an enclosed form, but other interpretations are equally possible.

oriented within the south-westerly arc. Fronting these are access paths between the houses and the entrance, and commonly cobbled, sunken, stone-walled inner enclosures on either side of the entrance (Fig. 5.2). The stone-founded houses vary between 6 and 15 m in diameter, but congregate around 10 m internally. The number present on sites varies. Homesteads with only one or two houses are the most common, but larger enclosures can contain as many as

Figure 5.2 The typology of rural settlement in Northumberland: (a) part of the settlement complex at Greaves Ash (after Jobey, 1966a); (b) (after Jobey, 1966b); (c) part of the settlement at Knock Hill, Reaveley (after Jobey, 1964).

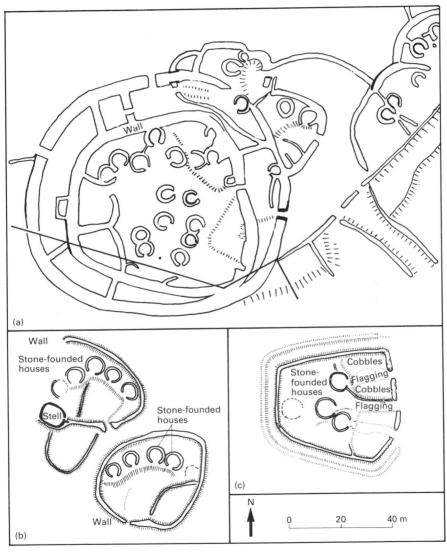

six houses as at Hartside, and the pattern of house construction outside the enclosed area can result in settlements of thirty or more houses, as at Greaves Ash, but these are rare in the south. It is possible to construct new patterns of settlement hierarchy based solely on roofed space, but without the additional factor of defence, such patterns are at best hazardous.

Some at least of the settlement voids, as conceived soon after the Second World War, have now been filled by a range of sites with at least a considerable potential for occupation within the Roman period. Aerial photography has revealed numerous small enclosed sites on the coastal plain and major river valleys, and this pattern is repeated south of the Tyne (Jobey 1981b; Harding 1979; Haselgrove 1981). These sites are revealed by their outer ditch lines, in most cases forming a rectilinear enclosure with a single entrance, rarely enclosing an area in excess of 1,500 m². Where these are visible from the air, or where excavations have occurred, one or two timber huts have been located in the centre of the enclosure, or in a few cases towards one side or the rear. At Marden, the small rectangular enclosure contained a single central round-house occupied in the Roman period (Jobey 1963), but a similar round-house in timber occupied a comparable near-central position within a ditch and palisade at Coxhoe, Westhouse, apparently abandoned before Roman pottery reached the site (Haselgrove and Allon 1982). At Burradon and Doubstead similar sites have been examined, and both may have been still occupied in the Roman period (Jobey, 1970a, 1982).

The proportion of sites excavated is very small, but of those types it is the stone-built examples in the upland margins close to the 300 m contour that are most securely Romano-British, largely because of the identifiable chronological relationship between many of these sites and the pre-Roman hillforts near the Cheviots.

It has already been noted that one at least lowland settlement type – the rectilinear, ditched, habitation enclosure – occurs south of the Tyne, on the eastern littoral (see Fig. 5.1). Similar enclosures have been located on the Solway plain and in the Eden valley (Higham and Jones 1975). An excavated example of a Roman period rectilinear homestead with timber internal structures is that at Silloth (Higham and Jones 1983), and another example was tested at Wolsty Hall (Blake 1960). In all, between twenty and thirty rectilinear enclosures of this type have been located on the Solway plain of Cumbria, but these are only a small minority of identified sites numerically overshadowed by circular or curvilinear enclosures in excess of 100. Excavation on a small sample of these invariably supports a Roman occupation date, and there are few if any significant differences in the internal layout between rectilinear and curvilinear sites (e.g. Higham and Jones 1983). There are no grounds for asserting that they are chronologically distinct as one recent fieldworker has suggested (Webster 1971).

On the Cumbrian uplands, numerous examples of extant settlements have been identified. The existence of a Royal Commission survey of Westmor-

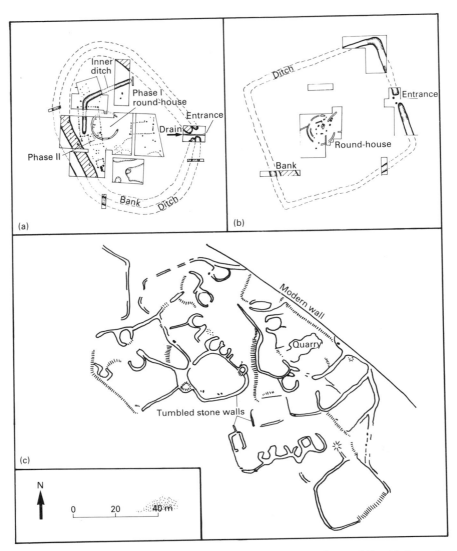

Figure 5.3 The typology of rural settlement in Cumbria and Durham: (a) Penrith farm after excavation (after Higham and Jones, 1983); (b) Westhouse, Coxhoe after excavation (after Haselgrove and Allon, 1982); (c) Crosby Ravensworth 31, an upland complex (after R.C.H.M., 1936).

land but not Cumberland or historic Lancashire has naturally prejudiced the distribution of fieldwork, particularly since both Webster and the author adopted the Royal Commission volume as a starting-place for their respective fieldwork programmes (Webster 1969; Higham 1977). The densest distribution of upstanding sites occurs at or near the 300 m contour on the limestone fells of the Eden and Lune watersheds and adjacent areas. Settlement forms are again less regimented than east of the Pennines and Cheviots. Examples of stone-built non-defensive enclosures are present, in many cases with extensive internal division, at Waitby or Middleton Hall (Higham 1978b, 1979a), but circular or curvilinear enclosures are at least as common in both these areas and in most others, and probably comprise the commonest upland settlement form. On the limestone fells of Crosby Ravensworth there are, in addition, small numbers of settlements which form agglomerate patterns which do not appear necessarily to have originated from an enclosed nucleus – in contrast to most Northumbrian extended sites. A good example among these is Crosby Ravensworth 31 (RCAHM 1936), where more than a dozen stone-founded round-houses are associated with, but not placed within, small rectilinear enclosures similar in form and probably in function to those within habitative enclosures elsewhere (Fig. 5.3). These partially unenclosed sites are peculiar to a group of parishes on the limestone fells, where they appear juxtaposed with numerous enclosed sites. At Ewe Close both a rectilinear enclosed settlement and partially unenclosed houses are present, which may conform to the extended type of settlement common in the Cheviots (Collingwood 1909). Other examples of a comparable settlement type have been located in Upper Redesdale at Barracker Rigg and Farney Clough (Charlton and Day 1978), but they are not widespread. One possibility would seem to be that they are the immediate successors of unenclosed hut complexes in areas where these continued in occupation down to the Roman period, and were rebuilt in stone. However, although they represent the most obvious departure from the omnipresent enclosed norm in the uplands of the border counties, further comment must await excavation. At present, there seems no reason to doubt that some at least were Romano-British in date, given the similarity of form with Ewe Close and Severals on the Cumbrian limestone fells.

Elsewhere in the Cumbrian uplands, rectilinear and curvilinear enclosed sites are common and most probably date to the Roman period. On dry subsoils they may be found in exceptional cases close to 400 m above OD, as at the Palliard site in the Stainmore pass, but elsewhere few exist above 300 m, and the ceiling of occupation of the gritstone and sandstone terrain in the exposed south-west is far lower. A Roman date for the settlements at Barnscar and Stainton Fell is likely, and for that at Heaves Fell, Sizergh seems certain (Hughes 1912), and a scatter of datable artefacts in the Esk valley implies rural settlements in that area (Cherry 1979). North of the Lake District massif, settlements have been identified up to about 300 m, and most of the upstanding examples conform to the near-square or circular form identified elsewhere (Higham 1982a).

In conclusion, settlement forms appear less regular, and specific types are less geographically exclusive west of the Pennines. Notwithstanding this, the major elements are consistent in all areas. The overwhelming majority of settlement sites are enclosed and all are non-defensive. The overwhelming majority of house sites are circular, and the distribution of ditches and of a stone-building tradition in all areas mirrors local environmental conditions. It seems reasonable to argue for a fundamental package of cultural forms common to all areas, but drawn upon in different ways as dictated by the interaction of local conditions and the pragmatism of an indigenous farming population.

The chronology of occupation

The study of the chronology of rural site occupation has tended to orientate around the chronological parameters of the Roman period, in an attempt to determine whether the identified, common site types are exclusive to the Roman period, or spread beyond it. Since artefacts commonly found on these sites are only useful chronological indicators within the Roman period, no approach from artefactual deposition is likely to succeed, and research efforts so far have led only to the accretion of a body of absolute dating evidence by carbon-14 in Northumberland. This is unfortunate, because the available palaeobotanical evidence would suggest that the intensive forest clearance with which these forms of habitation seem linked began only marginally before the initial conquest in that county. The obvious place to observe a securely pre-conquest rural community in enclosed settlements within the northern counties is the southern Durham and Cleveland lowlands; except at Thorpe Thewles where occupation apparently ended before the conquest (Heslop 1984), this has not yet been achieved (setting aside the excavation of Catcote, Cleveland, until it is published), despite the presence of attractive sites identified from the air. Given these circumstances we have to fall back upon the evidence of southern Northumberland.

A group of sites in the vicinity of the new Kielder Dam have already been noted in this context. At Kennel Hall Knowe the early, pre-conquest enclosures were palisaded, but close parallels exist with the established pattern of Romano-British homestead which then succeeded on this site, and which are widely represented in southern Northumberland and south of the Tyne (Jobey, 1978a). A regular rectilinear form is marked in all three palisaded phases; a circular round-house lies in the centre, or, in phase II and phase III towards the rear of the enclosure, and yard areas probably lay at the front. The last palisaded phase was not abandoned until after Christ, and the bank and ditched enclosure that succeeded it was utilized throughout at least part of the Roman period (dated *c.* AD 270), and contained three probable stone-founded round-houses (Fig. 5.4). Similar chronological development has been identified at Belling Law, Bridge House and Tower Knowe in the same area (Jobey 1973a, 1977; Charlton and Day 1974). Although it is foolhardy to argue from one remote valley to the reminder of the border counties, this alone is sufficient to demonstrate a comfortable and unquestionable pre-Roman ancestry for one at least of the basic and commonest settlement forms. The switch from palisaded enclosures to bank and ditch or stone wall is

Plate 5.2 Super-imposed timber-built round houses at Belling Law, North Tynedale. These are of the ring-trench construction, found frequently in Northumberland, in which walls of contiguous, vertical timbers were set in continuous trenches, and packed with stone. In the interior a scatter of stone-packed post-holes presumably supported the roof timbers of successive structures.

understandable in the changing environmental conditions (see above) in which grassland was becoming increasingly the dominant habitat, and building timber a diminished and less convenient resource.

A similar, pre-Roman ancestry has been rather less reliably indicated for the rectilinear, ditched, habitative enclosures of the lowlands (Haselgrove and Allon 1982; Jobey 1970a, 1982). East of the Pennines, at least, the vernacular architecture of the rural community appears to have been well established before the conquest. It requires special pleading to suggest that local farmers in the second century were in some respect taking inspiration from the totally inappropriate model afforded them by the military fort or fortlet. At Fingland Rigg (Cumbria) a compound was defined by ditches in the second century, and subsequently reoccupied by a farming community in the late Roman period who built and utilized a stone and timber round-house in the middle of what was an unusually small enclosed space (Richardson 1977; information from GDB Jones). This suggests a rational reuse of existing labour-expensive ditches, but the vernacular architecture of the reoccupation was profoundly conservative.

One possible caveat to this position is the development of the stone-founded or stone-walled house. No example has yet been securely dated earlier than the second century. It is, therefore, a prime target for those wishing to see

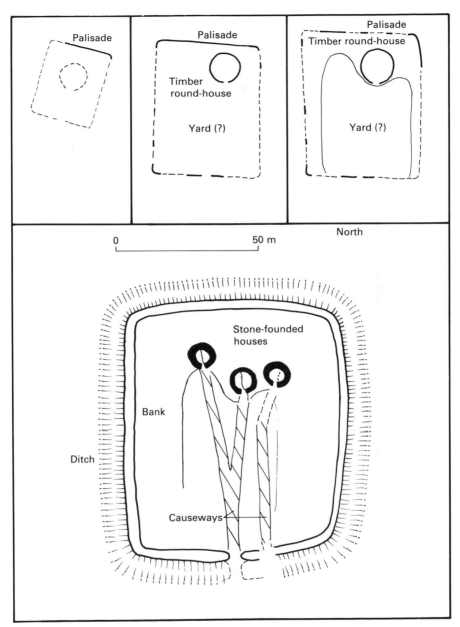

Figure 5.4 Kennel Hall Knowe, Plashetts: a four phase Iron Age and Romano-British homestead (after Jobey, 1978).

Roman influence on the rural homestead. However, the stone-built house is ubiquitous only in those areas where environmental conditions insured that woodland regeneration was vulnerable to the pressure of human economic strategies, and where stone was easily available in the soil or parent rock. Areas like the limestone fells in Cumbria or the lower slopes of Cheviot were arguably deforested by grazing pressure and other strategies in the preceding millennium, if not before. Even some lowland and riverine environments by the second century AD had become sufficiently deforested to tilt the balance of convenience from a timber to a stone tradition of construction, and to use the habitation site as a convenient location in which to deposit surface stone causing problems to the cultivator in the immediate vicinity. Parallels with the unenclosed settlements of the preceding millennium are obvious. Where stone was unavailable and cultivation soils comparatively stone free, as at Silloth (Cumbria), timber house construction was retained into the late Roman period, despite the propinquity of Roman military structures available to act as a model. To argue for Roman traditions influencing local communities in this respect is to ignore the widespread evidence for pragmatic decision-making on the part of the farming community within parameters set by environmental conditions specific to small localities. It is quite likely that the stone-founded round-house did, in fact, predate the conquest in areas where deforestation was early and widespread, and where stone was available.

That the communities of upland, northern Northumberland should have adopted a circular or elliptical site plan should not surprise us. The most obvious, recent and impressive local tradition of site construction lay in the numerous small defensive sites, in most of which the circular form was dominant for tactical reasons linked to those of labour economy. Although devoid of defences, the stone-built homesteads of the Roman period were presumably continuing an existing and well-tried tradition of economic strategies already closely identified with the pre-Roman forts, in which some at least of the new farmers may have been raised. The decline of the circular form south of the Coquet parallels the diminished number of fort sites in the south of the county and in the Tyne–Tees area.

The greater variability of form in Cumbria may result from the later adoption of enclosed settlement, and the consequent greater variety of prototype available. A pre-conquest tradition has already been invoked for the unenclosed sites of the limestone fells. The apparent longevity of Bronze Age traditions in Cumbria lend support to this suggestion, but it remains to be tested by excavation. At present, it is only apparent that these sites lie outside the normal parameters within which Romano-British communities designed, and redesigned their habitation sites. In the lowlands, sites such as Catcote (Cleveland) would seem to have maintained a similar tradition of unenclosed settlement from the late prehistoric into the Roman period. Even so, most identified sites conform broadly to an enclosure based on a near-circular or near-square form. Of the 5 per cent or so of identified Cumbrian examples of enclosed settlement so far tested by excavation, none has failed to produce stratified evidence of Roman period occupation exclusive of any earlier period. For the majority, settlement centred in the period after AD 200, although second-century and even late-first-century occupation is not uncommon in the lowlands (e.g. Wolsty Hall II, Blake 1960; Penrith, Higham and Jones 1983), or on the limestone fells (e.g. Waitby Castle, Higham 1978b). It seems likely that the change-over to enclosed settlement in Cumbria was later than east of the Pennines, and had barely begun (excluding the scarce hillforts) before the conquest.

The popularity of the square or circular enclosure is explicable by the labour efficiency of these forms for isolated enclosures. Rectilinear forms have a higher functional value when immediately adjacent to rectilinear field systems, and in the Cumbrian lowlands there is some evidence to suggest that a higher proportion of rectilinear than curvilinear habitative sites are associated directly with fields (Jones 1979). However, numerous examples of the latter do occur both in Cumbria and Northumberland (Gates 1983) and there are traces of field ditches running away from settlements of all shapes in the Durham lowlands (Clack 1982; Selkirk 1983).

The pattern of settlement that emerges is of an obstinately dispersed rural population, inhabiting comparatively long-lived and stable farmsteads or settlements at a distance from their neighbours. This distance may be small, and there are numerous instances of closely spaced groups of sites numbering from two to ten, apparently contemporary, but there is no evidence for widespread settlement nucleation in the lowlands, and only a minority of overgrown settlements in the uplands. The village was not a settlement form attractive to the indigenous population along the borders, presumably because of overriding economic rather than social factors. In this there is a clear contrast with southern Britain, and with the settlements developing outside the adjacent military sites.

Population

The low rate of artefact discard typical of rural settlements throughout the Roman period makes close dating impossible on many sites, and so data concerning population size are not readily comparable from one site to another. The special circumstances of Northumberland mean that the best that can be said on most sites is that occupation occurred within the second century AD, and more specifically within the Antonine re-advance into south Scotland, when political circumstances facilitated the distribution of exotic products. After AD 200, only a minority of the sites known to be occupied under Antoninus Pius can be shown to have continued in occupation, with the occasional find of diagnostic pottery or baubles, like the third-century glass bottle from Witchy Neuk (Hope Dodds 1940) or fourth-century pottery from Huckhoe (Jobey 1959). The comparative scarcity of artefactual evidence of the post-Severan period had led to the suggestion that areas north of the wall were extensively depopulated during the wars of the early third century, and that these people may have been among the British irregulars in Germany in the Antonine period. Despite this, it seems most unlikely that any real depopulation occurred and many, if not most, of these sites enjoyed a long occupation; the *pax Romana* of the third century is likely to have seen more occupied rather than less. In this context, it has been argued that a population expansion may have occurred in Northumberland in the Roman period (Jobey 1974b). This thesis is incapable of proof, as its author was only too well aware, but there is a growing body of circumstantial evidence in its favour. There is apparent on many sites, a tendency for the number of huts to increase, both within the original enclosure, and, as at Greaves Ash, also outside. This implies an increase in potential human accommodation at some stage after the initial occupation of the site. More speculative is the suggestion that the number of sites also increased, above those likely to have been occupied in the late prehistoric. This might be compensated by the need to find non-defensive site accommodation for the inhabitants of hillforts, and this factor could explain the large numbers of enclosed homesteads and settlements in the Cheviots, where greater numbers of stone houses are commonest (Jobey 1981b). In Durham, no evidence exists to support speculation on relative population size; in Cumbria, our inability to distinguish immediately pre-Roman occupation should not be thought to imply a massive rise in population density. When nucleated settlement emerges west of the Pennines, it utilizes the same well-tested strategies as are visible in the east, and there is no support whatsoever for any significant level of immigration into the countryside of the border counties.

Notwithstanding, what is clear is that the density of rural settlement reached high levels during the Roman period, even assuming not all sites were contemporary in any one area (see Fig. 5.1). Haselgrove (1981) noted a maximum site density in Durham of one site per 0.5 km^2, and greater densities are apparent in the upland margins of Northumberland and in the better-drained lowlands of Cumbria, around the rivers Eamont, Lowther and Wampool, and on the sands and gravels of the Solway plain. Although the rate of deforestation dropped in the Roman period in many pollen diagrams, in most, at least on the east side of the Pennines, it is within the occupation that the lowest levels of forest cover were recorded, and diagrams from Bollihope and Thorpe Bulmer noted clearance entirely within the Roman period (Clack 1982). That a link exists between increasing population and the development of cultivation finds support in the interdependence of those settlements with evidence for expanded numbers of hut circles and attached and presumably contemporary field systems. None of this evidence is conclusive, but the obvious implication is that the Roman occupation coincided with a population expansion which continued over several centuries, but which was rooted in improving environmental conditions beginning before the invasion occurred. The *pax Romana* may have facilitated this population growth; it did not, on present evidence, initiate it or provide the major stimulus.

Villas

The absence of villas in the North has already been noted. In Northumberland, no examples are known, and there was no compromise with alien house or settlement types throughout the Roman period. East of the Pennines but south of the wall, certain examples of villas or thoroughly Romanized farms have been identified only at Old Durham and Holme House, near Piercebridge. At the former, a well-equipped, small bathhouse built to produce both dry and

Figure 5.5 The Roman villa at Holme House, Piercebridge (after Harding, 1971, with additions after Clack, 1982).

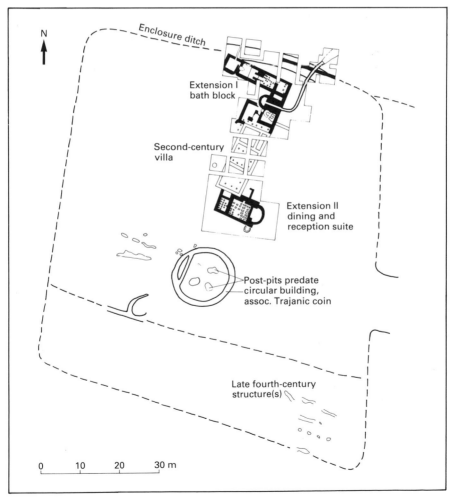

damp heat provided an enviable touch of comfort in the fourth century on a site apparently occupied since at least the second century (Richmond, Romans and Wright 1944; Wright and Gillam 1951, 1953). That the site developed from a ditched settlement system was suggested by the stratigraphic relationship between bathhouse and ditches, but the hurried later excavations did no more than record circular structures with rough-dressed stone footings interpreted as open threshing floors. In support, parallels exist at the villa site of Langton, Yorkshire, and on a farm site in Cheshire (Higham 1984).

At Holme House, occupying a position close to Piercebridge, a corridor villa developed early in the second century, and was later enlarged by the addition of a bath suite and heated rooms, and a large circular stone building, about 14 m diameter (Fig. 5.5). The whole complex was dismantled about the end of the century, although it may have been rebuilt on an adjacent site (Harding 1971).

Other possibilities have been offered. Apperley Dene has been interpreted variously as a fortlet and as a native farm (Greene 1978), so the suggestion that it was a villa (Clack 1982) merely broadens the options available. It should be said that it offers none of the architectural regularity of a villa, despite the tiles and large quantity of pottery on the site. Other examples have been suggested on the basis of aerial observation (Clack 1982).

All possible or proven villas lie east of the Pennines, south of the wall and closely adjacent to the major Roman roads, within 10 km of a fort and *vicus*. Holme House is immediately outside the civilian urban settlement of Piercebridge. This suggests that it is with the military markets and the urban communities that these sites are associated. They may represent the rural settlements of some of the aristocracy, or immigrants. Whichever, their business and their wealth was probably derived from cereal cultivation and large-scale pastoralism for a market economy.

In Cumbria, some novel architectural forms reached farm sites after the Severan period. The Penrith farm emerged from chronological obscurity in or only shortly before the second century, when a single round-house was in occupation at the rear of a cobbled enclosure defined by a ditch and inner bank, and within which the north end was segregated by an inner ditch, probably as a stock pen (Higham and Jones 1983). The round-house was superseded by a range of timber-framed, rectangular structures in use, at latest, by the late third century, and occupied well into the fourth century (see Fig. 5.3). Although the new buildings represented little increase in the roofed space available, the presence of paving suggests some improvements in living conditions, and a single perforated piece of sandstone of tile size may imply improvements in roofing. The change in life-style was not so great as to suggest that the occupant had disengaged himself from farming, and the yard area probably continued in use. Another example of a rectilinear structure in a farm enclosure is that at Risehow, near Maryport, built with stone footings and occupied in the late fourth century (Blake 1960). Smaller stone-founded buildings occupied within a similar chronological framework were excavated at Old Brampton (Blake 1960) and Dobcross Hall (Higham 1981b). This small group may represent the adoption of architectural styles common in the *vici*, and suggests a rural community more receptive to new ideas in the later Roman period than in the second century, and in contact with the urban markets. All examples are close to substantial *vici*, and most are within a one-hour walk. It may even be that these structures represent an investment in the countryside by members of the urban communities consequent on their abandonment of the *vici* in favour of rural sites. Flavius Martius, a senator in the *civitas* Carvetiorum and of quaestoran rank, was buried at Old Penrith, and commemorated by his daughter and heiress, Martiola (RIB 933, now lost). The known distribution of these Romanized farm sites is confined chronologically and geographically to the *civitas* based at Carlisle.

The rural economy

The major bones of the rural settlement structure owed their development to pre-Roman communities, and there is little evidence to show that the Roman period added more than a little meat to the skeleton. The rural economy was fundamentally enmeshed within existing settlement strategies, and the Roman period can only be said to have added more of the same in most areas.

Enough has been said above to establish that mixed agriculture was present in the area east of the Pennines, if not west, on the eve of the conquest. All the necessary components were already available, including cereals identified in pollen and as grain at Coxhoe (Van der Veen and Haselgrove 1983), rotary querns with which to process it at most sites, and the ard plough to prepare for its cultivation. In these circumstances, it is surprising that more recognizable fields with formal boundaries have not been identified in a late prehistoric or Roman context. Despite some recent adjustment of the balance (Gates 1981b), it is still fair to say that the majority of Northumbrian farm sites are devoid of evidence for associated fields. In many cases, the blanket occurrence of later ridge and furrow in the vicinity makes identification by fieldwork impossible, but the lowland sites located as crop marks from the air are likewise largely devoid of field systems. In these circumstances, it seems reasonable to argue that the basis of the Northumbrian economy in the Roman period was the keeping of livestock. In favour of this are the commonest site plans, with enclosed space within the settlement perimeter equipped as hard standing, of which the obvious and easiest interpretation is as stock pens (Jobey 1966a, b). An economic strategy that left such a powerful imprint on so many sites should not be underrated. In addition, many sites of this type occupy strategic positions within a pastoral resource territory, between high-level summer pastures and low ground suitable for winter grazing and a hay crop. In Northumberland, few permanent systems have been identified by which control of herds could be achieved. In contrast, it has been suggested that some at least of the dikes of the Kirkby Stephen area of Cumbria performed this function in the Roman period (Higham 1978b). Many dikes rationalize contours, at about 270–300 m, and seem to have been constructed in order to control livestock and exclude them from areas in which crops (including hay) were grown in the summer months. The method of construction, where tested at Waitby, was of turf, cut from the ground on the upper side of the barrier. Such turf walls are still employed to contain livestock in the Isle of Man, and the Roman military employment of the medium requires no comment. Although definitive dating is unlikely on such a linear monument, the close association between a group of dated Roman sites, field systems and several phases of dike construction establish the probability of a Roman date. Similar circumstances apply at Severals on Crosby Garrett Fell (Higham 1978a), and on Hartley Fell (Higham 1978b), although a later date is suggested for at least some elements of similar boundaries identified at Stainmore and Dufton. These boundaries are extra-manorial and extra-township as defined in the medieval period, and their reliance on sharply indented streams and other natural barriers in several instances bears a marked similarity of concept with those few field systems so far identified in Northumberland (Gates 1981b). Supposing them to be of the Roman period, they imply considerable co-operative effort by the rural communities, which can only have seemed desirable if a solid benefit was anticipated. The vast areas of summer grazing available to those communities may have led to a build-up of substantial herds and possibly of flocks. Arable fields below the dikes were laid out with slight banks, probably to a large extent comprising stone derived from field clearance. Parts at least of the area was lynchetted before the construction of one of the later dikes, and the field boundaries were not considered capable of excluding sheep or cattle. The dikes, therefore, had an obvious function to perform, in excluding from cultivated or protected areas the cattle, horses, sheep and red deer, the remains of which came from one of the settlements.

The detailed chronology of even the Waitby dike system is still unknown. Although dikes were arguably in use in the Roman period, it was suggested that the origin of the system should lie in the late prehistoric, and that abandonment of arable land was already in progress during the Roman period.

That cattle and other livestock were kept by most border farmers is well established. However, although many sites like Hartburn and Kennel Hall Knowe have produced faunal remains, particularly of cattle and horses, the general prevalence of acid soil conditions has deprived us of large deposits suited to statistical interpretation. That the cattle teeth from Hartburn, for instance, came from young animals implies but does not demonstrate a sophisticated slaughtering strategy. Support comes from local military sites, but there is no guarantee that a large proportion of those carcasses are of locally bred livestock, although it is an attractive possibility that the local farmers were assessed for taxation, like the Frisii, in oxhides (Tacitus, *Ann.* IV, 72). The dispersed nature of rural settlement, the demonstrable under-representation of permanent fields, and the prevailing climatic and environmental conditions should incline us to the view that local communities depended to a large extent on pastoralism for their livelihood, and lived within a settlement structure that had evolved on capital derived from this source. To the extent that the total land surface was put to economic use, by far the greatest area was arguably given over to livestock.

Notwithstanding all of this, crop cultivation was a widely practised strategy on rural sites during the Roman occupation. The scarcity of upstanding field remains in Northumberland suggests that there at least the practice of cultivation was centred on the lowlands, where later cultivation has eroded the evidence. Despite the ubiquity of querns, and therefore presumably of grain consumption on upland and lowland sites, only a small minority of settlements in the Cheviot foothills are associated with field systems, and many are arguably isolated from any evidence of contemporary cultivation (Gates 1981b). Where they do occur, there are marked similarities with the more widespread field remains located in upland Cumbria (Higham 1977, 1978a), but no evidence has been offered for lowland field systems in Northumberland except at Yeavering, and further south the status of complexes such as Catcote is still obscure (Challis and Harding 1975). Whether on the uplands or in the lowlands, the problem of disentangling Romano-British elements from other tiers in a complex landscape is an acute one.

Where they have been located in the upland margins, the majority occupy glacial drift in areas where this is mineral-rich, as around Cheviot and the Upper Eden valley. The absence of field systems from the thin soils above the level of drift deposit is general. Many, but not all, occupy broadly south-facing slopes. North-facing complexes occur, as at Aughertree Fell (Cumbria), although that is arguably a non-agricultural, enclosure system (Higham 1978a). The largest complexes spread across large areas; approx. 60 ha of fields are still visible in association with seven settlements at Eller Beck on the south-west-facing slope between about 120 and 230 m above OD (Lowndes 1963, 1964; Higham 1979a), but no complexes are complete. Although unenclosed land provides a boundary on the upper side, later agricultural destruction or forestry plantation are the normal limiting factors elsewhere. At Severals, Crosby Garrett, a case has been made for a definable arable field system identified in association with one of three settlements, but later ridge and furrow has encroached on parts even of this complex (RCAHM 1936; Higham 1978a). It was estimated that 16 ha of field space was available to each of two of these sites, along with about 50 ha per site of unenclosed grazing below the limiting dike across the fell. At Brands Hill North (Northumb.) about 25 ha of enclosed land was identified, with potential for a complex, before later plough damage, two or three times greater, associated with a closely spaced group of settlements. The complex at Butts in Redesdale was more complete, with 19.8 ha of land divided between fifteen subrectangular fields associated with three settlements, largely surrounded by moorland. At Coldberry Hill, Humbleton, two settlements were associated with a field system that incorporated at least two phases of development (Gates 1981b) (Fig. 5.6).

Figure 5.6 Field systems in the Roman North: (a) the Eller Beck settlement and enclosure complex, Lonsdale, Cumb.; (b) Yanwath Wood (after Higham, 1983); (c) Coldberry Hill, Humbleton, Northumb. (after Gates, 1981).

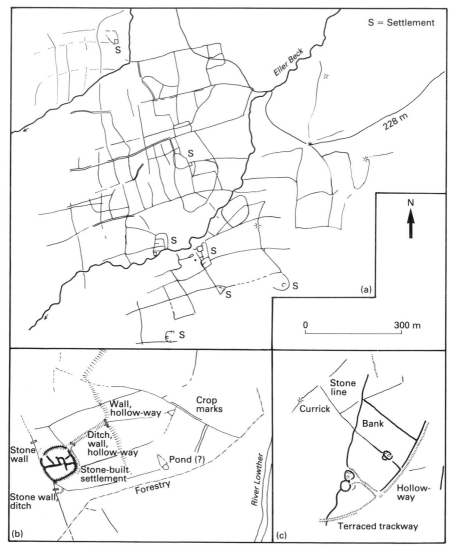

In the upland margins, the pattern of field remains implies in most cases piecemeal enclosure associated with specific dispersed settlements. However, south of the wall, complexes like that at Eller Beck imply a high degree of co-operation between grouped settlements, reminiscent of the remains at Grassington in Wharfedale, for example, and reflect a landscape where, in favoured locations, widespread and interlinked enclosure was commonplace.

Most fields were broadly subrectangular, defined by low walls of tumbled stone, lynchets, lines of boulders or cairns or earth banks and ditches, although the latter have not been identified to date in Northumberland (Gates 1981b) with the single exception of Yeavering (Hope-Taylor 1977). A complex certainly dated to the Roman period in which ditches played an important role was that at Yanwath Wood, on the edge of the central Eden basin. A Romano-British stone-based settlement was associated with fields defined by ditches and stone banks or walls, apparently derived from field clearance (Higham 1983). At Yanwath, and elsewhere where fields were laid out on even slopes, fields were commonly designed with long boundaries across the contours, with short cross 'walls' or lynchets dividing them into rectangular units. At Butts six or possibly seven roughly parallel strips were separated by three long lines of rubble, two walled trackways and the deeply indented beds of two burns, and even more strips were identified at Eller Beck. At Waitby Castle Hill strips defined by lynchets, and on lesser slopes by banks, ran diagonally across the contours, associated with at least two settlements (and arguably several more), and protected by dikes. In certain locations, as on scarp tops or knolls, sites can be associated with a radial pattern of fields, as at Hunterheugh Crags (Northumb.) or to some extent Severals or Ewe Locks (Cumbria).

In the Cumbrian lowlands, topography may have been less crucial in the layout of field systems, but most identified remains are fragmentary. The farm sites at Silloth and Penrith were both arguably associated with ditched boundaries; at Silloth a shallow, flat-bottomed field ditch ran away from one corner of the settlement. Aerial photography has identified a similarly intimate association between site and field complex at Petteril Green, Thursby, Sandy Brow and on the ridge of Holme Abbey South (Higham and Jones 1975; Higham 1978, 1981b). Where any system can be identified, the same rectilinear pattern emerges, as at Thursby East and Sandy Brow, with fields tending to be roughly twice as long as they are wide. The evidence for arable enclosures should be greatest in lowland Durham and Cleveland, where pollen data suggests cultivation was concentrated. However, perhaps owing to the higher incidence of ridge and furrow, evidence is scarce. Four examples were illustrated in a recent survey (Clack 1982). The Upper Teesdale complex at Force-garth Pasture has important parallels with Eller Beck, and the settlement site and field complex at Dyance, near Killerby, appears to be of at least two periods. Elsewhere, field systems are probably at present under-represented. Traces of slight field ditches are visible associated with two rectangular ditched enclosures photographed in the Langley Park area, north-west of Durham City (Selkirk 1983), and it seems likely that many more remain to be published.

Trackways are a common component of field systems occurring as an integral element, apparently within the original design. In many cases, bank or wall defined trackways form one or several of the dominant and lengthy boundaries within a complex, as at Coldberry Hill, Northumb. (Gates 1981), or at Eller Beck or Yanwath Wood, where the approx 4 m wide trackway was limited by a ditch and tumble of stone, and was well cobbled (Higham 1983). Elsewhere in the Cumbrian lowlands, ditched trackways are a prominent crop-mark feature, emphasizing the substantial nature of their ditches compared to the ephemeral field divisions around them. At Wolsty Hall and Parton they serve as access routes to the enclosed settlement, and elsewhere tracks have been identified running through enclosed areas, as at West Field and Biglands (Higham 1981b). The role of the trackways appears to be the provision of a controlled access to the settlement site from unenclosed land beyond the outer margin of adjacent fields (Higham 1977), and suggests a mixed economy, with crops or hay in the enclosed space, segregated from livestock on unenclosed land in the summer months. This pattern of land-use is exactly that suggested as the rationale behind dike construction in the Upper Eden valley where enclosed trackways are commonplace.

Plate 5.3 Settlements and associated field walls at Eller Beck, Lonsdale. The complex was in use in the Roman period, although it incorporates earlier elements, such as the robbed *tumulus* (top right). Top left is an example of a second phase of wall construction enclosing a paddock that slights the pre-existing, highly regular field system. These elements have been interpreted as an episode of agricultural recession that predates abandonment of the complex.

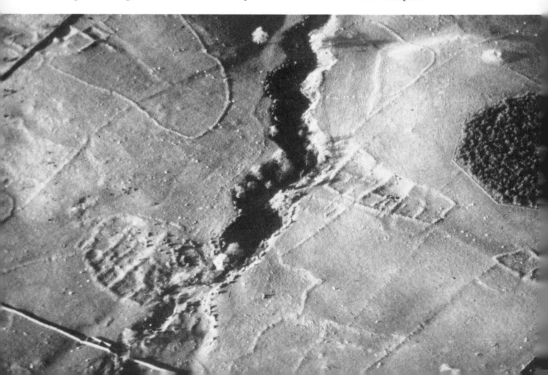

It is arguable that much of the enclosed land was cultivated. Lynchets are present on at least a minority of complexes in Northumberland and in Cumbria, and are arguably the result of soil movement during and after plough disturbance. In addition, on a small number of complexes, plough striations have been identified within the limit of the field boundaries (Higham 1977, 1978b; Gates 1981b). At Severals, ten small enclosures averaging 0.6 ha revealed traces of ploughing quite distinct from the later ridge and furrow that has obscured other parts of the complex, and similar traces were found in Northumberland at Brands Hill North, Knock Hill and Coldberry Hill, and at Waitby Castle Hill in Cumbria. The contemporaneity of these ploughing remains with the field systems within which they occur has not been demonstrated, but a substantial body of evidence now exists. In addition, ridges excavated under Rudchester Roman fort (Gillam, Harrison and Newman 1973) implies that some ridge and furrow could also be pre-Roman in date. At Yanwath Wood a cultivated soil horizon was identified adjacent to a field ditch and 'wall', and at Croftlands, near Bassenthwaite, agricultural erosion of the subsoil had occurred adjacent to a field ditch which produced a carbonized grain of barley and the seeds of weeds of cultivated ground, waste ground and pasture associated with Roman pottery (Higham 1982a). If field systems of this type were not always used for cultivation, it does seem clear that arable use was the strategy in mind when they were laid out. That the plough was the normal and intended method of cultivation gains support from the range of field size, as well as shape. Gates noticed that in Northumberland, Romano-British fields were generally between 0.5 and 1.75 ha, and markedly larger than the enclosures typically associated with unenclosed, prehistoric settlements. In Cumbria, this size range encompasses the majority of rectilinear fields (Higham 1977). That the Grassington field system in Wharfedale also has a numerous class of fields (78% of total) between 0.4 and 3.2 ha suggests that this size range is of regional importance and may relate to the area that could be ploughed in a day.

Most of these upland complexes occupy terrain on the margins of agricultural viability. An infield—outfield system may have been utilized in order to transfer via livestock manure the fertility of 'waste' grazing to the cultivated infield.

However, not all field systems appear to have been laid out with agriculture in mind. The Aughertree Fell complex has none of the common attributes of the arable field, except that at least one settlement was approached via a wide ditched trackway. The fields were large (many 2–6 ha) and irregular, north facing and ditched and banked. A pastoralist economy seems more appropriate on this mineral-deficient soil (Bellhouse 1967; Higham 1977, 1978a, 1982a). In the lowlands, a pastoralist function seems appropriate for the deeply ditched complex at Stone Carr (near Penrith), and the Tarraby Lane enclosure complex was interpreted as meadowland (Smith 1978). A part of this field group was ploughed, and cereals cultivated, but pasture seems to have

207

replaced the dominant alder and hazel scrub over most of the area, and the botanical evidence from ditch 837 suggested that hay was mown. This probably represents a typical use of badly drained riverine terrain. Elsewhere, only excavation will unravel the complex interrelationship between cultivation and pasturalism implied by the partially enclosed landscape of the Solway plain and the central Eden valley.

The apparent absence of agricultural complexes from the eastern lowlands may be illusory, as pollen and other botanical indicators suggest. Interpretation will depend heavily on the role field boundaries are thought to have performed. In most instances, the remains seem unlikely to have been capable of excluding livestock, and stone robbing has arguably been minimal on several of the larger, upstanding complexes. If the field boundaries had a tenurial significance or acted as divisions between convenient ploughing units, rather than as stock fences, the spread of evidence is more explicable. Stone 'walls' derived from the removal of stones from fields and developed as a side-effect of ploughing only where surface stone was present in quantity, that is, on the margins of the cultivable slopes or on soils derived from clay with boulders. The prevalence of boulder clay in the Eden valley explains the large quantities of stone found on sites in the lowlands, and their adjacent walled fields, but stone walls are not likely where clay was relatively stone free, or where sands and gravels were dominant. Ditched field systems in lowland Cumbria may reflect drainage needs, and their absence in Northumberland may reflect a lower rainfall, and a landscape where other forms of land division less susceptible to aerial photography may have been commonplace. It seems almost certain that the barley found at Doubstead on the Northumberland plain was locally grown on what would then have been recognizable fields (Jobey 1982).

It is impossible to balance the potential of the arable versus the pastoralist strategies in the native economy. The latter was arguably that which was associated with every rural site and involved the greater land area. Estimates of pastoral productivity suggest that this may have produced a substantial return (Higham 1977; Mercer 1981). Arable production on some sites may also have made a significant contribution, although we should beware of high yield figures based upon experience in southern England under experimental conditions (e.g. Reynolds 1980; Bennett 1983a). It was the experience of medieval and early modern farmers in the border counties that wheat was an unreliable crop in northern Northumberland and in most of north-west England. Reliance was placed instead on oats, barley and to a lesser extent in the North-east on rye – all spring-sown crops. Palaeobotanical evidence suggests that new crops had become available in the late pre-Roman period, including spelt, bread wheat, rye and oats, and the Celtic bean may also have been associated with the new wave of clearance and cultivation. The discovery of spelt wheat at Thorpe Thewles (Cleveland) provides confirmation in an arguably pre-Roman context (Heslop 1984). However, the extent to which these crops penetrated beyond the Cleveland Hills and the Teesdale lowlands is unclear. The recent suggestion that rice could have been grown locally (Selkirk 1983: 209) should be utterly rejected, and probably derives from a false interpretation of strip lynchets which belong in a context at least a half-millennium later. Similarly, the suggestion that large-scale Roman centuriation can be identified in the northern landscape (A. Richardson 1982) is insubstantial and relies wholly on post-medieval evidence, in an area which probably saw little use in the Roman period on account of unusually heavy soils.

While grain consumption was ubiquitous on rural sites, little storage facility seems to have been available, unless we assume that some round-houses acted as grain stores (Diodorus Siculus, 5. 21). A possible, four-post granary was located in a late Roman context in Penrith, but parallels are scarce in the border counties. Grain may have been the principal medium of provincial taxation (*annona*) as is implied by Tacitus (*Agric.* 19), but it seems unlikely that enough was grown beyond the wall to satisfy even the tax-collector.

Some readjustment between areas used for cultivation and for livestock, in favour of the latter, may have occurred during the Roman period. At Waitby, the dike system was progressively realigned so as to exclude ever more cultivated land from protected status, and at Eller Beck the regular field system was in two areas superseded by the construction of irregular walled paddocks apparently within the life-span of one at least of the farm sites (Higham 1978b, 1979a). These instances imply some readjustment towards pastoralism as a subsistence strategy, but both areas cited were marginal and abandonment may have been due to soil erosion stimulated by cultivation.

Other strategies were practised by the rural community, although they occupy a subordinate position. The skeletal remains of red deer at Penrith and Waitby Castle indicate that the hunting or trapping of wild species still occurred, if not, perhaps, on a scale to provide a significant food source. It seems likely that food-gathering was an important secondary strategy. The extent and rate of deforestation also implies that woodland management was necessary for many communities within the Roman period, in order to conserve supplies for fuel, building and equipment. However these strategies are poorly evidenced, and arguably played a small part in the subsistence of the rural community. Perhaps of greater local importance was the rearing of sheep and the production of woollen cloth, evidenced by a spindle whorl at Old Brampton (Blake 1960).

Once again, the Roman period witnessed the emergence of a complex body of subsistence strategies which included both pastoralism and mixed-farming techniques based on livestock and the plough. These operated within a landscape in which their distribution was ultimately limited by environmental factors, but fuelled by the increased subsistence requirements of an increased and increasing population. The extent to which, after the trauma of the conquest, political circumstances affected the farming community is unknown, but it is unlikely to have been great. The linkage between rural population and the adjacent military and 'vicinal' settlements is a sensitive issue to which we shall return.

The Military Frontier, AD 200–350

Whatever the motives that lay behind the Severan advance into Scotland, that advance proved to be the last major war fought by Roman armies beyond the wall, which henceforth was to provide the Roman provinces with a frontier, though not with a limit to Roman influence. The administrative division of the province into two coincided with the reorganization of the frontier. Henceforth the northern counties lay in the province of Britain Inferior, based on the single legion at York, but with the bulk of the British auxiliaries on or close to the wall. Some debate has surrounded the Middleton milestone and the possible implication that Carlisle was at some stage the capital of the province (Graham 1966), but it seems unlikely that that town exceeded the status of *civitas* capital before the later fourth century.

The frontier posts required and received considerable structural repair and improvement. Risingham south gate was reconstructed *c.* AD 205–208 (RIB 1234) on a plan reminiscent of military work of the fourth century, with projecting, polygonal towers (Richmond 1936b). Other gate reconstructions occurred at Chesterholm and South Shields (Welsby 1982), the Chesterholm example being poor-quality work perhaps by the auxiliary forces, *c.* AD 223 (RIB 1706). Elsewhere, on both sides of the wall, military works were under repair, documented both by epigraphic evidence and by excavation in a broad, Severan context. There is some rather inconclusive evidence that novel defensive strategies were incorporated into some forts at this stage, with the provision of a *ballistarium* – a clay platform for artillery – at High Rochester *c.* AD 220 (RIB 1280) and possibly another in a third-century context at Lanchester. *Ballistae* found at High Rochester weighed over 46 kg each, implying projectile machinery of considerable power. Whether or not these played a major role, the early-third-century reconstruction was large in scale, and very largely in stone. In some instances the new buildings differed radically in plan from their antecedents as in the case of barrack block 'c' at Housesteads (Wilkes 1961). In most instances, however, the general layout of the second-century fort was preserved, and it is arguable that reconstruction in stone was required not because of any damage by the enemy, but because the preceding stone or timber structures had reached the end of their useful life – as for example at Bowness (Potter 1975). A *principia* was normally still present, often rebuilt in stone, and it is during this period that the association between *principia* and armoury began, with some verandas being walled up to act as extra rooms. Granaries continued in use or were reconstructed, demonstrating that fort provisioning continued to be a matter for central authority throughout this period. Despite the absence of a fort, the two granaries begun before *c.* AD 185 at Corbridge continued in use throughout the third century, while, across the road, a range of military buildings were constructed behind the 'temples', and at some stage enclosed within a pair of walled compounds serving to separate military activity from the closely adjacent civilian settlement. Only at South Shields (and possibly at Birdoswald) were granaries apparently converted to other uses, but South Shields fort had temporarily served as a supply base to the Severan offensives, and the returning *Cohors V Gallorum* from Cramond had little option but to convert the now redundant warehousing to accommodation (Dore and Gillam 1979).

Elsewhere, many barracks and stable blocks were rebuilt in stone, or stone and timber, and in many forts new ranges of buildings were built into the back of the ramparts, not perhaps to provide accommodation but to provide covered space for service industries. Smithing appeared in such a context at Greatchesters and elsewhere, and ovens at Housesteads. Accommodation seems to have been at a premium in many third-century forts. The barrack blocks in many cases seem inadequate for the size of the garrison known. The outpost forts like Risingham, and some wall forts such as Burgh-by-Sands and Birdoswald are known to have been associated with as many as three units, apparently at the same time, and two units are on record at Greatchesters, High Rochester and Lanchester (Birley 1939c). Frisian *numeri* were at or near Birdoswald and Chesterholm (Gillam 1979) as well as Housesteads. In all cases, the barracks were inadequate for their accommodation, and it seems highly unlikely that significant numbers occupied either rampart buildings or the *vici* outside forts. The Chesterholm *vicus* appears to have been abandoned by about AD 270 in any case, and the suggestion that a part of the *vicus* in the second century had provided soldiers with married quarters (Birley 1977) has not been generally accepted (Salway 1965, 1980). This would seem to imply that large parts of at least some fort garrisons served for long periods away from their bases, perhaps serving on widespread patrolling duties, largely in the Tyne–Forth area. This suggestion receives some support from the discovery of two inscriptions from near Jedburgh near the line of Dere Street (RIB 2117, 2118). One was set up by a detachment of Raetian spearmen from Risingham, and the other by 1,000 Vardullians from High Rochester. By such means the Roman authorities retained control of Northumberland and southern Scotland. Even so, winter quarters may have posed problems.

While rank and file soldiers were accommodated in barracks, the accommodation provided for the garrison commanders was the finest house-building tradition of its day in the North. The commandant's house at Housesteads was initially constructed in the Hadrianic period, but was retained in the 'Severan' rebuilding as a substantial courtyard house of Mediterranean style (Charlesworth 1975). A similar structure at Binchester was occupied in the early fourth century, if not before, and was equipped with *opus signinum* floors, plastered walls and a bath suite (Ferris and Jones 1980). Where excavated this seems to represent the normal level of luxury.

The commanding officer would clearly be accompanied by his family, and his establishment served by retainers of both sexes. The discovery of small shoes, for example, has generally been put down to their presence. However, the large numbers from some sites seem impossible to explain in this context (Welsby 1982). The number from Bar Hill were thought to indicate that officers down to the rank of centurion might be accompanied by a family. The very high proportion of small shoes found in the pre-Hadrianic context at Chesterholm (Birley 1977) would seem to suggest that forts were far less exclusive male preserves than had been supposed, even before the Severan relaxation of rules governing the marriage of soldiers.

The third century saw several generations of peace on the northern frontier. Perhaps as a result, there is some evidence of troop withdrawals from the area in the latter part of the century, perhaps ordered abroad, or to garrison the newly constructed Saxon shore forts on the south and east coasts. The pirate menace appears to have initially affected the border counties little, preferring the richer pickings of the southern province. Only in the case of one fort is there evidence of possible enemy action – at Bewcastle north of the wall where the strong-room was broken open and violently ransacked (Richmond, Hodgson and St Joseph 1938). It is possible that this affair was associated with the adoption by the Emperor in AD 284 and 285 of the title *Britannicus Maximus*. However, if this is evidence of a clash on the borders, it comes within a period which saw the lowest levels of garrisoning yet achieved, and a significant shift in the military balance between the two provinces in favour of the South.

Archaeological evidence of abandonment is by its very nature difficult to establish, and to date. However, there does seem to have been a decline in the maintenance of those buildings not serving as accommodation. At Birdoswald, an inscription records that the *praetorium* had fallen into ruin before restoration *c*. AD 296–305, and this site may have been deserted during part of the late third century. Elsewhere, similar but rarely conclusive evidence provides a comparable picture. In all, at ten forts along the wall there is evidence of partial or total abandonment, and in the hinterland many others were abandoned. Watercrook shows no sign of occupation between AD 220 and 270, but it may have been reoccupied and enlarged by the end of the century (Potter 1979). Papcastle was arguably abandoned throughout most of the century (Charlesworth 1965), and South Shields had probably ceased occupation by the century's end, although a pottery kiln in a granary and an uninterrupted coin sequence suggests considerable civilian activity (Dore and Gillam 1979). However, the majority of the wall garrisons arguably continued in occupation, and the founding of Piercebridge fort about AD 260 implies that military resources were available if they were considered necessary. This site may have been an important link in the development of defence in depth on the northern frontier (Luttwak 1976). It may point to decreasing security on the coast and a consequent need to station troops in a position from which they could react to the north or towards the coast. Piercebridge occupied an important river crossing which had already attracted urban settlement and which may have been the upper limit of navigation on the Tees.

Some at least of the troop withdrawals may have occurred in support of the Gallic Empire of the 260s and 270s. More were probably the responsibility of Carausius and Allectus, after the creation of a British Empire in AD 286–87. The immediate interest of the commander of the Channel Fleet lay in the construction of the Saxon shore forts, and ultimately in the creation of a British field army capable of withstanding an Imperial invasion of the South-east. When that thrust eventually occurred in AD 296, the imperial forces triumphed over the provincial. Much of the northern garrisons may have been committed on the losing side, leaving the frontier only thinly manned.

There is some support for the possibility that attacks upon the northern counties coincided with the campaigns to the south, and this could be the proper context for the apparent damage at Bewcastle already mentioned. However, the shortage of coins at Carausius and Allectus along the frontier suggests that much of the damage hitherto explained in terms of enemy action was in fact the result of troop redeployment and consequent fort abandonment (Salway 1981: 313), and it is noticeable that the subsequent reoccupation of the North involved the refurbishment and reconstruction of some forts like Papcastle out of commission for most of a century. There is a single literary reference to enemy action (*Pan. Lat. Vet.* VIII. v. 11. 4), ascribed to the Hiberni and Picti, and this may have caused some damage on military sites. The refurbishment of the frontier was on a scale comparable to that in the 'Severan' period, and took place over several years. High Rochester received a third stone wall, and at Risingham the defences and official buildings were reconstructed (Birley 1961). At Birdoswald it was necessary to rebuild the north guard-chamber and the *principia* completely (RIB 1912). Elsewhere, modifications were made to a wide range of buildings, including the *praetorium* which at Housesteads was fitted with a hypocaust, and seems at Papcastle to have been provided with a bathhouse. The Bewcastle bathhouse, inside the fort from the beginning presumably for security reasons, continued in use into the fourth century and survived whatever late-third-century problems other areas of the site faced, apparently unscathed (Welsby 1982).

There are signs that the new garrisons were smaller in number than those of the Severan period. Some forts may not have been reoccupied. The Chesterholm *vicus* was arguably abandoned *c.* AD 270, and it seems likely that this followed the fortunes of the fort. Other sites probably followed a similar pattern. In some, areas appear to have gone out of use, as at Wallsend (Daniels 1976). In others, a new form of accommodation appears, although whether at this stage or later is not clear. At Wallsend (Fig. 5.7), seven (and part of an eighth) barrack blocks were totally demolished, and accommodation was provided in 'chalets', each totally free-standing but organized in a terrace formation (Daniels, 1980a: Fig. 28). Similar structures have been uncovered at Greatchesters and Housesteads, where they were considered to have provided accommodation for a garrison no larger than 15 per cent of that stationed in the fort in the second century. At Wallsend that proportion could have been even lower. It seems likely that these new buildings represent married quarters, and there is some evidence that fourth-century soldiers were expected by the authorities to be supporting families. It may also represent official acceptance of the move by the *vicani* into the forts when temporarily abandoned in the late third century – strip houses of the *vici* and chalets in the forts have some similarities. Certainly, some garrisoned forts were devoid of fourth-century *vici*, although there is so far no evidence of specifically civilian occupation

Figure 5.7   The Fort at Wallsend: the southern range of buildings: (a) in the Hadrianic era; (b) in the fourth century (after Daniels, 1980a).

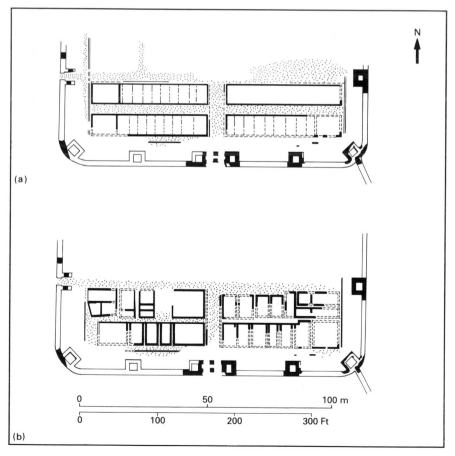

214

within the forts. Some at least of the northern forts may already have been taking on some of the characteristics of the 'fortified village' (e.g. Wilkes 1961). However, at other sites like Chesterholm, Maryport and Ravenglass, third-century barrack blocks and stables continued in use well into the fourth century without apparent alteration.

North of the wall, Constantius Chlorus carried out a brief campaign in AD 306 in which he probably crossed into northern Scotland, but upon his withdrawal, there is no evidence that any more forts were garrisoned beyond the wall than there had been in the third century. These forts now proved short-lived. Constantine visited Britain as emperor, probably on two occasions, and may well have been directly responsible for the withdrawal of those troops in AD 312, along with those at Piercebridge, Newcastle and Ebchester. The excavators of Netherby preferred occupation continuing until Diocletian (Birley 1954a) and the coin evidence from High Rochester would support the Constantinian date (Casey and Savage 1980). This abandonment may have been temporary – there are two phases of fourth-century occupation at Bewcastle, both before AD 367, which would suggest that the out-patrols were still operating when garrison strength permitted, and the apparent importance of the *areani* or *arcani* in the 360s, would seem to imply a continuing tradition of surveillance in the preceding decades. There can be little doubt that the frontier forces maintained control of southern Scotland at least until the middle of the century.

The coasts were also under increased surveillance. The fort at South Shields does not appear to have been rebuilt by Constantius Chlorus, but the civilian inhabitants were joined during the first quarter of the fourth century by *numerus barcarorium Tigrisiensium*, a specialist group equipped for work in the shallow waters of the Tyne estuary. A similar unit has been identified defending the Lune near Lancaster (Shotter 1973). On the Cumbrian coast new signs of activity are visible from the second half of the third century onwards, and the burning of Ravenglass may reflect this new threat from the sea (Potter 1979). Further south, Lancaster was arguably re-equipped during the reign of Constans as a Saxon shore-type fort, but the full development of the coastal system may post-date AD 350, with the renewed occupation of the second-century fort at Burrow Walls (Bellhouse 1955). These measures were designed to respond to growing threats from the Irish and Pictish fleets, and perhaps from the Saxons. Despite signs of growing pressure, the response appears to have been adequate to the challenge, at least until the mid century.

Certain broad conclusions can be drawn from the military occupation of this century and a half. There is no evidence of internal problems south of the wall. In addition, except in exceptional circumstances, the garrison was adequate for the protection of the province, and probably of southern Scotland. A breakdown in security may have followed the revolt of Carausius and his successor, but archaeological evidence of destruction is less widespread than has been thought, and the situation was quickly restored. There was a tial net loss to the garrison forces in the area from the Severan reoccupation to that of Constantius. The fourth-century garrisons were significantly smaller, and in some instances this may have been by a factor of 90 per cent. Despite this, there is little evidence of security breaking down before AD 350. There is, however, a significant break with the military strategy of the second century. The fourth-century garrisons were less mobile than their predecessors, and more prominence was given to defence, with strong walls and artillery assuming a central role. The defence-in-depth of the province can be said to have emerged. In the North, the fort walls performed the role of town walls in the southern province. In such circumstances the small size of the garrisons may not have been significant, and field operations were to be the business of a special mobile reserve, the *comitatenses* of the late fourth century.

The military market

The presence of large numbers of military units in the border counties from the Trajanic period onwards, made that area a net importer and consumer of wealth throughout the Roman period. The size of the British garrison fluctuated according to political circumstances, but generally declined from the Hadrianic period, when auxiliary forces stood at about 35,000 men (Holder 1982) to probably less than half that in the fourth century. The proportion of this force maintained in the North also fluctuated, but at most periods it was greater than half. Detailed estimates have been attempted on the basis of fort accommodation (Breeze and Dobson 1969), but before a higher proportion have been subjected to large-scale excavation, no exact conclusions are possible.

This army required provisions of all kinds. There is a marked contrast between the artefact discard rates on local native sites and those apparent within the forts and their *vici*. The latter are incomparably higher. Evidence would suggest that the soldiers not only had special needs but were also adapted to a life-style which required far more, and more expensive, equipment of most sorts. In short, the army was a massive engine of demand, fuelled by an equally massive subsidy provided, via the government, by other, taxpaying areas.

Much of this demand was met directly by the army. In return for a fixed reduction from wages, arms, cavalry mounts, basic foodstuffs and a uniform seem to have come to the individual via the fort store-rooms (Breeze 1981; Macmullen 1960). Foodstuffs could have been in part derived from taxation, either in corn or in animals. However most of this material would need to be requisitioned or purchased from civilian suppliers and paid for by the government. This traffic was enormous, as a recent survey has shown (Breeze

1982), requiring animals and animal products in vast quantities and considerable variety, sophisticated foodstuffs demonstrably including coriander and the seed of the opium poppy, clothing and metal-work and a wide variety of transport and other equipment.

The army units were capable of providing themselves with some of their needs. Each fort garrison was provided with an area of land which could be as large as the 3,444 ha calculated at Xanten (Macmullen 1963), and which might have been used to provide foodstuffs, or pasture livestock. Some local evidence for such *territoria* has come from inscriptions. At Ribchester, a *centurio regionarius* was recorded (RIB 583), and at Chester-le-Street, specific mention was made of a *territorium* in an inscription dated to Caracalla (RIB 1049). It is tempting to see the meadowland at Tarraby Lane as part of the *territorium* of troops at Carlisle or Stanwix. In the northern counties, the presence of native communities within the general vicinity of many forts would suggest that much of this area was leased to civilians, or perhaps that the system was not fully operated.

In other areas the units only involved themselves in the provision of artefacts when alternative supplies were unavailable. This seems to have been the case in the Trajanic period, when army potteries were in production in Cumbria. At Brampton, 8 kilns were examined, and about 800 fragments of pottery made on the site were retrieved, made by and exclusively for the unit occupying the Stanegate fort of Old Church Brampton (Hogg 1965). A less well-known tilery operated at Muncaster near Ravenglass, and a legionary tilery was discovered at Scalescleugh, 9.6 km south of Carlisle. None of these army factories produced pottery much after the accession of Hadrian, by which time civilian potteries in this area, but to a far greater extent in the south of the province, were able to satisfy demand. Only in building work did the army achieve self-sufficiency. Indeed, the army probably contained the vast majority of competent architects, engineers and masons in the area throughout the period. Although much major building work, such as the wall, involved the drafting in of legionaries, local forces were responsible for both building and rebuilding and took full credit for it on the ensuing inscriptions, such as at the Chester-le-Street example just mentioned, referring to the construction probably of an aqueduct or water-channel and certainly a bathhouse (see Selkirk 1983).

With these major exceptions, the garrisons obtained their supplies from the civilian community. It can easily be demonstrated that much of this supply depended on long communication lines. By far the best-documented example is that of pottery, which merits a fuller treatment.

In the aftermath of the Trajanic frontier dispositions, civilian potters, possibly from Wilderspool on the Mersey, began production in the Carlisle area, but by about AD 120 cooking pottery of the black burnished 1 variety was appearing in ever-increasing quantities from kilns on the south coast, probably shipped by sea into Carlisle (Gillam 1973). The push into Scotland under

Antoninus Pius coincided with new sources of pottery appearing from the Colchester area, via east coast ports, and Corbridge in particular received quantities of this black burnished 2 ware, besides providing locally made *mortaria* to the Scottish garrisons. By the late second century this local manufacture was in decline, and the factories supplying the garrisons appear to have been fewer in number, and entirely from south of the Humber. At the same time, continental wares such as Samian and Rhenish wares maintained or developed a place at the top end of the market (Hartley 1972; Brewster 1972). The third century saw a stable market, with existing southern manufacturers maintaining a share of the market, and Coritanian wares, Huntcliff and other east Yorkshire wares making an appearance. Only in the late fourth century, after 360, did the east Yorkshire factories achieve a near-exclusive dominance of the market.

Exactly how the distribution worked is not clear, whether via an army purchasing system, or via a private enterprise market and *negotiatores* to individual units or soldiers via the *vici*. If the latter, despite the 'pottery shop' at Corbridge, no example of a retail outlet has so far been identified. The distribution of Severn valley ware in the milecastles and turrets of the central section of the wall might appear to support a contract system (P. V. Webster 1972) but other options are open (Breeze 1977). The Severn valley wares distributed apparently via a Solway port northwards to the Antonine frontier could easily be the work of traders (Webster 1977). The suggestion that Samian wares were exclusive to the rank of centurion and above likewise

Figure 5.8 A schematic interpretation of the basic supply system for the Roman garrisons.

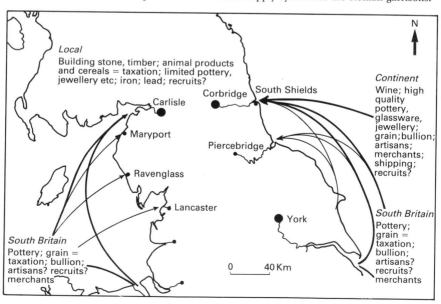

suggests a market situation in which higher-paid soldiers could, and did, afford a better class of table-ware than their subordinates.

The enormous demand for pottery that the military community generated was very largely satisfied by distant industries in Britain and beyond, and factory owners outside the area were the major beneficiaries of the market (Fig. 5.8). The same was probably true of other types of artefact. The mirrors found at Corbridge probably derive from the Nijmegen area of the Rhineland (Lloyd-Morgan 1977). The fine glass table-ware that graced the homes of the better off inside and outside the forts was imported.

Metal-working does seem to have been a normal activity outside many forts, particularly in the earlier period, but again much was probably imported, and the hearths at Carlisle or Kirkbride, for example, are unlikely to have been producing the plate armour of the kind found in the Corbridge hoard.

To service this very large and complex pattern of demand, we should expect to be able to identify a supply structure equal to it. Tombstones of traders are present from the extra-mural cemeteries, but not in large numbers. Ateco at Old Carlisle may have been a civilian trader (Davies 1977), as may Duvianus at Carvoran, but few are as explicit as the tombstone at Corbridge of Barathes of Palmyra, a trader in ensigns or standards (RIB 1171), or the mutilated altar from Bowness on Solway (RIB 2059). From Carlisle, the Greek Flavius Antigonus Papias is another probable candidate (RIB 955; Birley 1979). Clearly, these can only have been a small minority of the active traders in the area, most of whom presumably survived their visits. There is some corroborative evidence that the civilian settlements that developed outside the forts had as their primary function the provision of goods to the soldiers. The typical pattern of narrow strip buildings end-on to the roads, as close to the fort gates as possible, implies fierce competition for trade and a high premium on both street frontage and proximity to the gates, explicable only if they performed an economic function. Parallels with the medieval towns of England are obvious. In addition, several *vici* can be shown to have enjoyed occupation only during the life-span of the garrison. The Chesterholm *vicus*, for example, has three phases of occupation, with apparent abandonment between when a garrison was probably not in residence. In practice, many forts enjoyed a lengthy occupation, and substantial (but rarely extensively excavated) civilian settlements shared that occupation chronology at least until the late third century.

The occupants of these settlements were largely immigrant, to Britain or to the North, drawn by the prospect of markets for their services and products. The epigraphic evidence supports interpretation as a cosmopolitan community, drawn from all parts of the empire, in which recognizable Celtic elements make up only one-sixth of those identified (Salway 1965). It seems likely that immigration provided the vast majority of the *vicani* in the second century at least. Their economic role is less easy to identify. Many may have been dependants of the garrison troops – a role unlikely to be detected archaeologically. Alternatively, the easiest interpretation of most structures is as shops or workshops, and the *vicani* may have been to a large extent a community of shopkeepers, with contacts directly with the garrisons, and with suppliers at home and abroad. Even so, the wares offered for sale are rarely identifiable. The so-called 'pottery shop' at Corbridge suffered destruction by fire in the fourth century, on the evidence of a coin hoard, yet was 'stocked' with second- and third-century Samian, colour-coated wares and *mortaria* [3]. If this was the true turnover of a *vicus* shopkeeper, bankruptcy was certain, and the building was not of typical, workshop type, but perhaps a long-disused store containing archaic stock. Elsewhere, the evidence of their craft betrays workers in leather, metal and to a small extent pottery, and clearly stone masons and sculptors serviced local demand at Carlisle (Phillips 1976), Corbridge and elsewhere. The tombstones of Regina and of Victor at South Shields may have been the work of a Palmyrene sculptor (D. J. Smith 1959). Elsewhere, jewellery was being made to satisfy local demand (Charlesworth 1961).

The process of importation probably required capital equipment and considerable manpower, both skilled and unskilled. Artefacts from the South, or Europe, were carried by sea, as is clearly implied by the distribution of black burnished 2 pottery in Scotland which radiated from the ports on the Firth of Forth. On the West, Maryport was arguably an important naval and civilian port (Jarrett 1976) with a substantial *vicus* between the fort and the harbour, but the Solway was probably navigable as far as Carlisle which would have enjoyed substantial advantages in trade with the wall garrisons. Other natural harbours existed, at Ravenglass and elsewhere, but these were divorced by distance and bad country from the major markets. It may be that it was Carlisle's role as an entrepôt port that led to its pre-eminence as a town and as a third-century *civitas* capital. In the West, this site was the only one where civilian development after abandonment by the military can be demonstrated. The proximity of Stanwix, with its double-strength garrison, and access to any forces in south-west Scotland and the western wall forts almost certainly provide the commercial rationale. The limited deposits that have so far been examined imply a considerable and prolonged occupation, from the Trajanic period to the fourth century (McCarthy, Padley and Henig 1982). The name Luguvalium was in use by AD 103, and indications suggest a laid-out and organized town. Some houses, at least, were equipped with hypocausts and supplied with sewers and a running-water supply via an aqueduct. Recent excavation in The Lanes revealed a rectangular stone-built house, progressively enlarged during the third and fourth centuries, equipped with a channelled hypocaust, and associated with a metalled yard, ancillary structures and a stone-built well. A public bathhouse may have been present, and several exotic imports have been found, such as gold rings and a brass sea-horse (Charlesworth 1978). Even so, the incidence of dedications by the military found in the town but dating from its civilian phase suggests a strong army interest (e.g. RIB 946, 957), and recent excavations in Annetwell Street have identified military buildings in the town in the third century built in part at least by men of the XXth Legion which invite comparison with the military 'compounds' at Corbridge [4]. Carlisle may have been provided with defences, but no archaeological evidence has yet corroborated the suggestion found in the anonymous *Life of St Cuthbert*. The Middleton milestone implies that local government from this site extended at some stage to near the modern, southern county border.

Other *vici* in the vicinity developed to a considerable size. The surviving remains at Old Carlisle imply a substantial community, and crop marks suggest further remains to the south, perhaps including fields (Higham and Jones 1975) with similarities to those identified outside the *vicus* at Inveresk (Hanson and Maxwell 1983: Plate 9.5). Old Carlisle *vicus* enjoyed some degree of local self-government (RIB 899). The *vici* at Old Penrith and Brough-under-Stainmore likewise appear substantial and extensive (Birley 1946; Jones 1977). The evidence available suggests that all were at times prosperous, mixed and literate communities, but among them Carlisle does seem to have excelled.

East of the Pennines, the major ports of entry were probably South Shields and Corbridge. Until the civilian occupation of the fort in the late third century, the *vicus* at South Shields appears to have been substantial and prosperous, but Corbridge emerged as the pre-eminent site. The sequence of forts at Corbridge is linked to the strategic importance of the site as a supply base linked to the South by road and sea. Occupation intensified whenever major forces were committed further north. The abandonment of the last fort coincided with the post-Antonine withdrawal from Scotland, but the garrisons of the wall and Dere Street provided a market which the civilian community was ideally located to supply. Late-second-century industrial activity was discovered in 1980 on the site of the new museum.

In the 180s a substantial courtyard building, until recently described as a legionary storehouse or forum may have been the centrepiece of a new, model town, but work was interrupted on the site and this complex, like that at Carlisle was not completed. A range of buildings south of the road have been described as temples, although for no conclusive reason. Behind them the military compounds were in use throughout the third century and beyond, with probable workshops. The 'forum' was reoccupied piecemeal during the same period, and the roads in all directions have been shown to have been fronted by typical 'strip' buildings. Military and civilian appear to be closely interdependent at Corbridge. Two probable storehouses or granaries were constructed within the north side of the town, probably in the third century, and there is a distinctive military flavour to the community. There is better archaeological evidence for town defences here than on any other northern site. The gate on the north-east side was associated with ditched defences, but the chronology is unclear, although perhaps lying in the late third or fourth centuries.

Elsewhere, only at Piercebridge does a civilian community appear to have developed and maintained itself for substantial periods in isolation from a military garrison. The supposed Flavian fort(s) have not been identified, but seem at least probable. The extant and partly excavated fort which underlies most of the village was founded *c.* AD 260, but excavations on the *vicus* suggest continuous or near-continuous occupation from the first century until the late fourth (*Britannia* 1976). Special circumstances may account for this. The bridging point for Dere Street across the Tees was an obvious place for a town to develop, and there is the added possibility that Piercebridge may have acted as an inland port for the garrisons at Bowes and elsewhere (Selkirk 1983). The proximity of the Holme House villa emphasizes that Piercebridge represents an intrusion into the northern counties by the developed economy typical of the southern province.

Some trade must have used the road system. This was initially designed to facilitate the movement of troops, but represented a substantial capital investment in communications between forts and between producer and consumer. That the roads played a major role in communication is undoubted, providing the means by which the post service operated, and the presence of a signalling system across Stainmore implies that at some stage attempts were made further to improve communications (Richmond 1951; Higham and Jones 1975; Farrar 1980); these improvements may also have been applied to other major routes (Higham 1979a). Roads such as the High Street across the Lake District had no economic role to play, but elsewhere some goods at least must have been transported by road, even if only from ports of entry to the inland forts. The effort originally put into communications must have had an economic benefit. The construction of bridges at least on Dere Street (Dymond 1961) for example, or Pons Aelius at Newcastle greatly expedited contact between communities.

The writing tablets excavated from Chesterholm dating to the early to mid-Trajanic period are receipts, disbursement records or purchase orders (Bowman 1974; Bowman and Thomas 1974, 1983). The most commonly mentioned commodity was barley, used as an animal and human foodstuff and for brewing, and this and other grains are archaeologically attested at many sites, and presumably were the normal content of the omnipresent granaries. Grain is a bulk commodity, expensive to move over land. While it seems reasonable to assume that the coastal districts were provisioned by imports from further south, it has been suggested that some inland areas depended to some extent at least on local provisioning (Manning 1975). The Eden valley may, by the later second century have been producing a significant grain surplus (Higham 1981b), and environmental evidence would seem to imply that southern Durham and Cleveland were capable of supplying Piercebridge and its neighbours. The identification of a water-mill for grain processing on the Haltwhistle Burn implies that the administration took responsibility for provisioning the forts of the central wall in the third century (Simpson 1976). Whether the supplies to the mill came from near or distant communities is not clear, but grain can hardly have been cultivated in the immediate vicinity. It seems certain that much grain would have needed to be imported to the northern frontier at least until the early fourth century, and this may have been achieved via taxation.

Among the other commodities documented at Chesterholm, vintage wine and poor-quality wine must have been imported. The remaining products, including Celtic beer, could have been either locally produced or imported, and it seems likely that both means of supply existed. This includes goat meat [5], young pig, ham and venison. The weight of archaeological evidence suggests that these were quantitatively minor sources of food, and it may be that they represent special rations for religious festivals such as the Saturnalia. Meat was a normal part of the diet of garrison and *vicani* alike (Davies 1971), but the bulk of it in all cases was beef. At Corbridge cattle products comprised 96.5 per cent of estimated meat consumption, and at Chesterholm *vicus* 91.7 per cent (Hodgson 1977). The same pattern emerges in small deposits elsewhere at Carrawburgh, South Shields and on the milecastles and turrets. Other animal products are represented, principally sheep (Chesterholm 18.9% of minimum numbers), pig and occasional deer both red and roe, goat, horse and birds. Only among domestic pigs are young animals common. Cattle seem generally to have attained optimum weight, having survived two winters, and sheep were, likewise, over-wintered and apparently reared for meat, although the evidence is not entirely consistent, and turret 33B yielded remains of a disproportionate number of young animals of cattle, sheep and pigs. The mechanics of meat supply are not known. Common sense would indicate that stock reached the *vicus* or fort alive, and the butcher's shop at Chesterholm would seem to support this (Birley 1977). Some beasts may have travelled on the hoof considerable distances from southern Britain, but many were probably of local origin, either from the *territorium* of the fort, or from the civilian community as tax or via purchase. Deer and wild boar were certainly available locally and may have been hunted for sport as well as meat by soldiers, as is suggested by an inscription from Bollihope Common, Upper Weardale (RIB 1041). The assemblage of faunal remains from military deposits is mirrored in those from the local farming community – the dominant position of oxen is the overriding factor in both, and this would support local supply, drawing upon the excellent grazing of the northern counties.

The special place occupied by cattle may also owe much to the importance of leather, which is the commonest organic material found on military sites, most often in the form of shoes, but also as tent fragments or parts of garments (Charlesworth and Thornton 1973). Leather-working and tanning, like butchery, was probably concentrated in the *vici*, as is strongly suggested at Chesterholm, and elsewhere, as at Ambleside (Burkett 1965), but it was also evidenced from within the pre-Hadrianic fort at Chesterholm.

Other animal products include wool for the manufacture of textiles. While rarely abundant on native sites, except perhaps along the east coast, sheep were kept, and local suppliers could have been responsible both for the small amounts of mutton and lamb consumed, and for the textiles excavated in a late-first-century context at Chesterholm (Wild 1977).

To satisfy other needs, the garrisons seem to have helped themselves. A strong case has been made for local self-sufficiency in military timber supplies (Hanson 1978). The use made of local stone is documented by inscriptions and the doodles on a series of quarry faces, largely along the wall, for example, in the vicinity of the river Gelt. Some indicate the unit responsible, often legionary, but others provide less information, although the implication seems to be that the quarries were worked directly by the military rather than by a militarily organized, civilian labour force.

The military also appear to have taken a direct interest in metal extraction. Iron ore is found in many localities in the North, and was almost certainly being exploited by local communities both for their own use and for its commercial value (e.g. Potter 1979: 183; Penney 1983). Working hearths are not uncommon on native sites east of the Pennines (see above); an example has also been located on a farm site near Low Borrow Bridge (Cumbria) and haematite is a common site find (e.g. Penrith, Cumbria). Lead ores may have attracted the military to establish the fort of Whitley Castle in the heart of the mining territory of the Upper south Tyne, and to connect it by road to Kirkby Thore. The triple ramparts of Whitley Castle might be designed to protect silver bullion extracted from lead-working, and the site could be a sophisticated 'strong-room'. Lead ores in the Lake District may also have attracted attention. Metal-working in the *vici* would have added considerably to demands for timber or charcoal, and may explain the appearance of coal as a fuel on military sites in circumstances in which other fuel sources could be in short supply. Considerable problems surround the identification of ore extraction by the Romans, because of the similarity of technology used in the Roman and later periods. However, it is at least a possibility that military units exploited a variety of mineral resources in northern England which may have included copper as well as lead, silver and iron.

Roman and Native

The artefact-discard rates on the military/*vicus* sites and adjacent farm sites are as different as those of a modern Western city compared with a Third World village community. The military garrisons and bureaucracy spent most of the vast purchasing power at their disposal outside the region. Those supplies they exploited in the vicinity very largely consisted of materials for which they are unlikely to have paid, or which reached the forts as taxation. This receives strong support from the distribution of coinage, which has derived almost entirely from the military sites, their immediate vicinity, or from hoards probably deposited by immigrant traders or soldiers. Coinage is extremely rare from rural settlements, to the point where it seems unlikely that coins ever penetrated to the farming community with any degree of regularity. Coins from Traprain Law are exceptional because of the unique status of the site (Sekulla 1982), and in the Tyne–Forth region they are concentrated in the areas where regular army patrols seem possible – on the Clyde–Forth (Robertson 1960–61), and along the coasts. Even the Severan invasion of Scotland can only be thought to have introduced coinage over a brief period and little can be said of coin circulation in the post-Severan period (Reece 1980b). In Cumbria, almost no rural sites have produced coins; among these only the supposed monastic site at Ninekirks, Brougham, has produced more than one (Casey 1978).

However, despite the lack of coinage, some exotic artefacts did reach many rural sites. In Northumberland this occurred almost exclusively within the Antonine period. South of the wall, the discard of exotic artefacts occurred on farm sites from about AD 100, well into the fourth century (Higham 1981b), and on some sites assumed respectable, if still lowly proportions. Samian and coarse pottery occur, some of the latter produced locally. Low-quality glass, and particularly bangles, are common to farm and *vici* (Stevenson 1954–56, 1976). Other implements, tools and weapons which may have been trade articles also occur. It seems clear that many rural communities were occasionally able to trade surplus production, for imported goods of generally low value. The market facilities within which this operation occurred almost certainly lay in the *vici*, and it is important to note that farm sites identified from the air in the vicinity of Old Carlisle seem to have been connected via ditched trackways to the fort, *vicus* and major roads (Higham and Jones 1975). However, high-quality products are totally lacking; the contrast between glassware, for example, from farms and from *vicus* and fort is as considerable as the differences in discard rates would imply, and structural improvements such as hypocausts are absent. The *vici* could not depend solely on the rural market, with the apparent exception of Piercebridge, and it was this inability of the farming community to generate surplus wealth which doomed to extinction those *vici* outside forts abandoned by their garrisons. The apparent failure of new technology to reach the farming community is also worthy of note. Although the Piercebridge model of a plough at work has no particular relevance to actual plough cultivation, it is symptomatic of the distribution of metal agricultural equipment in the countryside. Of the large number of types into which metal implements have been divided, all are far commoner on or adjacent to military sites than elsewhere, and this applies not only to the turf cutters, entrenching tools and spades of the engineer or sapper, but also to reaping hooks, scythes and pitchforks (Rees 1979). With the exception of a tiny minority, represented by a sickle found at Old Brampton (Blake 1960), expensive metal equipment seems to be absent from the farm. Obviously, an explanation may be available, but the weight of distribution is ominous.

Outside the province, markets did exist, but were even less buoyant than in the hinterland of the wall. Those communities able in the second or third centuries to construct brochs were probably of relatively high status, and it is here that trade goods from the province make an appearance, associated with other high-status artefacts including weapons (Main 1979; Mackie 1979).

The inflow of trade to the northern counties was, therefore, almost entirely due to the presence of the large military consumer community, funded very largely by taxes from outside the border region. It replaced a trading pattern in which Cumbria and Durham in particular, and the North in general had progressively withdrawn from trade with southern Britain in the late prehistoric. The impression is of a novel boom economy, consuming vast quantities of products of all kinds, but the profit of the new business opportunities went to outside communities more able to supply the kind of commodities to which the immigrant army was accustomed. Local resources may have provided basic raw materials in some quantities, but not necessarily via a mechanism which benefited the local community. No economic revolution occurred in the countryside, despite the evidence of occasional and very small-scale market penetration. The majority of the economically successful *vicani* were probably always immigrants, although local communities may have provided unskilled labour, or even recruits for the army (Dobson and Mann 1973). With the exception of the tiny number of villas and probably of Piercebridge, all in the agriculturally developed area of southern Durham, town and country did not share an economy but belonged to separate economic systems with only limited points of contact. The military and urban communities were dependent on the payment of soldiers by the government, whether in cash or kind. The decline of cash payments under inflationary pressure had dire consequences for the civilian communities dependent upon the military purse for their own economic welfare. Of the three groups, the *vici* were probably the most vulnerable to economic pressures, and the rural population the least.

Religion and Burial

Religious preoccupations in the Roman period are better evidenced than for all earlier and most later periods. Religious observance demanded a literate outlet in a permanent form, and required a specialist architectural tradition. However, this is true of only two sections of the population – the military and the *vicani* who considered themselves members of an imperial community. It is not true of the rural proletariat, whose religious interests and whose burial practices are not generally accessible via archaeology, and who have produced no identifiable epigraphic record. In this they followed the example and the tradition of their ancestors in the late prehistoric. Traces of a multiple burial tradition reminiscent of the local neolithic came from Beadnell in Northumberland (Tait and Jobey 1971), where successive inhumations over a long period had terminated in the deposition of three individuals, one with a pennanular brooch, arguably of the Roman period. Parallels exist in a late prehistoric context at Dunbar, and on Ampleforth Moor, Yorkshire, the latter associated with carbon dates in the mid first millennium bc (Wainwright and Longworth 1970). Another local example of the late insertion of a burial into an existing mound was that at Chatton Sandyford (Northumb.) where associated finds included a sliver of glass and sherds of a rouletted flagon of the mid third century (Jobey 1968a). On Sizergh Fell (Cumbria) an enclosure wall sealed a low mound erected over a contracted inhumation with a bronze brooch and blue glass melon bead (Hughes 1912). Some concept of a cemetery may derive from the closely adjacent Bronze Age burials. Elsewhere, other cairns or mounds have been thought to have incorporated Romano-British burials, if only at a late stage in their development. It is noteworthy that isolated settlements of Romano-British forms in the Eden valley occur in close proximity to isolated mounds of burial type, for example at Yanwath and at Hackthorpe, and this may imply a continuing tradition of burial under barrows.

In the third century and beyond, it seems at least possible that rural communities shared cemeteries outside forts and *vici*, but this is by no means certain. Despite the likelihood of small-scale local immigration to the *vici*, dedications by civilians to local deities are scarce, perhaps because the epigraphic form of dedication is entirely foreign. Where such do occur, they are unlikely to have been dedicated by members of the rural community, where literacy can hardly have penetrated, but were most probably commissioned by soldiers or civilian *vicani*, many of whom were immigrants. Most recognizable dedicators were members, often high ranking, of the military establishment.

Even so, local deities have a distinctly higher profile than in the southern province, perhaps betraying the continued vitality of elusive, but well-established, late prehistoric cults. Gods such as Belatucadrus attracted numerous dedications in northern Cumbria and along the central section of the wall (Fig. 5.9). The six dedications from Brougham may imply that his worship was centred there (RIB 772–7). If we were to seek a divinity of whom recognition occurred exclusively in the heartland of *civitas* Carvetiorum, his would be the obvious candidature, and many of the dedicators were arguably civilian. These probably include the Lunaris who dedicated to the god at Brougham, and he or his namesake was responsible for an outlying dedication at Carrawburgh. In contrast, other local deities attracted military dedicators, and only their distribution may imply a local association with the godhead.

Thus Vitris (or Huitris) is found on the central wall and in southern Tyne and Wear, Cocidius almost exclusively at Bewcastle and on the west-central wall and Maponus, with a cult arguably centred in the Irthing valley or at *locus Maponi* in Dumfries and Galloway, has dedications on the wall and at Corbridge. All may derive from the desire of immigrants to propitiate local divinities.

Figure 5.9 Indigenous religious cults and the Roman army of occupation.

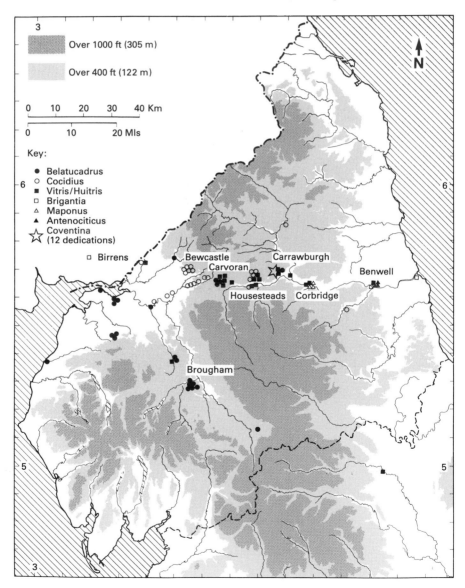

Some local deities attracted dedications at only a single site, and were, presumably, descendants of 'Celtic' spirits. At Carrawburgh, the shrine and temple of Coventina record a deity unique to that site, and dedications to Antenociticus are exclusive to Benwell (RIB 1327–9; Simpson and Richmond 1941), but the dedicators were soldiers. Elsewhere, dedications to the genius of a particular place are common, often requiring the production of an anthropomorphic representation of the spirit in a mode quite alien to late prehistoric religious observance – hence the genius from Burgh-by-Sands (E. J. Phillips 1979) or the several from Carlisle.

Two further godheads require mention. Dea Sattada was the subject of a single dedication by the curia Tectoverdorum probably originally from Chesterholm, and may be a dedication by a section at least of the local community (Stevens 1934; Salway 1965), and as such may be associated with a particular area, and a tribal group. Brigantia, by contrast, attracted widespread dedications in the border counties and elsewhere, but no recognition of the godhead occurred before the third century, when he attracted official dedicators, including a legionary centurion and a procurator, and was identified with Victory and other alien and imported divinities in a thoroughly Roman fashion. If local indigenes were among his followers, they may have found it difficult to recognize the form in which the official version was clothed.

Godheads associated with water do appear to have been common in Romano-Celtic religion, perhaps representing the survival of traditions first recognizable in the late second millennium deposition of weaponry in wet locations as apparent votive offerings. Votive deposits of metal-work in the first and second centuries AD have been identified at Carlingwark Loch, Eckford and Blackburn Mill (south Scotland), with obvious parallels with the Llyn Cerrig Bach hoard on Anglesey. Within the northern counties, it seems possible that some at least of the apparently isolated but chronologically diverse coin hoards may represent votive offerings at sacred wells, as was suggested at Kirkby Thore (Shotter 1978a). Some of the well-formed model objects found in the area may equally come from a votive tradition. Common forms are the wheel, lamp and axe, but a miniature pair of tongs came from Greatchesters (Green 1981). Small bronze animals have been identified in the valleys of the Upper Irthing and south Tyne, although the form is more common on the Firth of Forth (Thomas 1961).

The immigrant communities clearly found a rich and highly diverse religious framework already in existence when they established themselves. Parts of this they adapted to their own needs, with the accustomed ease of a polytheistic society. Other strands of religious observance they brought to the area from other provinces or from the centre of empire. The latter, official religions played an important role in the military community. In the late first and early second century, dedications to the Capitoline Triad were of considerable imperial significance, and played a crucial role in the official religion of the forts. The sixteen annual dedications to Jupiter Optimus Maximus by 1

Hispanorum in the Hadrianic period were carefully buried in pits beside the parade ground at Maryport, presumably after each had been replaced on 3 January (Jarrett 1976; RIB 830 ff). In addition, the imperial cult was already well developed by the time the conquest of Britain occurred, and not only received official support but may have attracted genuine popularity among the troops. Some emperors were recognized as having a special attachment to, or affinity with, specific deities, and religious enthusiasms were not above following the fashion of the day. One Carlisle inscription to the god Hercules associates his divinity with that of Commodus and Victory is ascribed to both. The Antonines specifically associated themselves with Hercules, but none more so than Commodus in his later years (Rostovtseff 1923).

Many of the vast pantheon of Roman or Greek gods attracted dedications on the frontier, in some instances associated with a local deity. The horned god (whether Belatucadrus or Brigantia) was, for example, variously associated with Mars, Mercury and Silvanus, representing a Romanization of the divinity in accordance with the attitude and needs of the dedicator. Other individuals and groups dedicated to deities of specific relevance to themselves. Dedications to Vulcan are common in the *vici*, underlining the importance of metal-working. It has also been suggested that the worship of Jupiter Dolichenus was associated with iron-working (Harris and Harris 1965). This cult is best attested at Corbridge, where a dedication by one Apollinaris, perhaps of Greek origin, attempts to combine Jupiter Dolichenus with Caelestis Brigantia and Salus. This altar and other fragments implies the presence of a temple, but none has been identified. Elsewhere, reference to the cult is common in the outpost forts, in a small minority of the wall forts and at Old Penrith, Old Carlisle and in the vicinity of Piercebridge. The suggestion that the Corbridge dedicators were interested in metal-work receives some support from the pottery from the site with applied decoration of a smith god, and it can be argued that Bewcastle and other practising cult centres were important in iron processing.

Other groups dedicated to divinities specific to their craft. Asclepius appears at Maryport, and the dedications to Oceanus at Newcastle were probably by traders or seamen before or after a voyage. Such dedications can and do derive from all parts of the empire and are the product of a cosmopolitan community with a diffuse 'Roman' culture.

Some provincials brought their own cults to the frontier. Some were unnamed, in the manner of *genii loci*. The Syrian garrison at Carvoran brought with them the cult of their home deities, Dea Hammia and Dea Syria, although the latter is mentioned in a lengthy dedication which has been identified with Julia Domna, the Syrian wife of Severus (RIB 1780, 1791–2). Corbridge,

Figure 5.10 The *Mithraeum* at Carrawburgh (after Richmond and Gillam, 1951): (a) initial structure in the third century; (b) extended structure, stage IIa; (c) extended and refurbished structure, stage IIc; (d) the rebuilt temple of the 4th century.

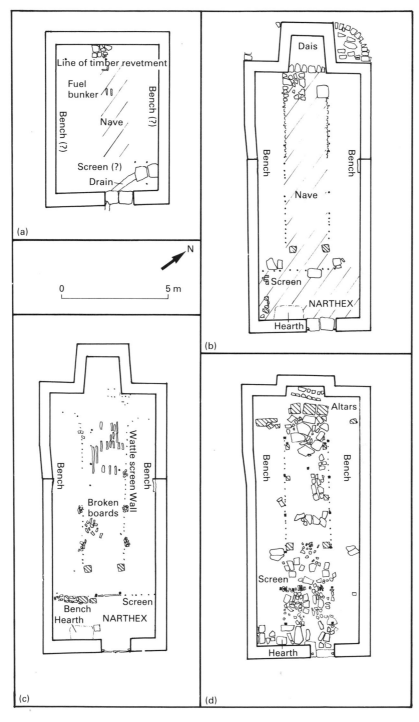

(a)

Line of timber revetment

Fuel bunker

Bench (?)

Bench (?)

Nave

Screen (?)

Drain

N

0   5 m

(b)

Dais

Bench

Bench

Nave

Screen

NARTHEX

Hearth

(c)

Bench

Bench

Wattle screen Wall

Broken boards

Bench
Hearth

Screen

NARTHEX

(d)

Altars

Bench

Bench

Screen

Hearth

again, is notable for eastern cults, perhaps emphasizing the peculiarly cosmopolitan nature of the frontier town where Barathes of Palmyra was buried.

Among these alien cults, that which has attracted most attention is Mithraism, appearing in Britain almost exclusively as a soldier's religion (Daniels 1971). It is the only one of the cults for which temples (*mithraea*), have been identified. With the exception of the London example, all of those so far located in Britain lie along the wall, or outside adjacent forts. It seems to have enjoyed popularity almost exclusively in the third century, when it was patronized by the officers of the auxiliary regiments. To what extent interest in this complex and demanding religion permeated the garrisons is not clear, but the extent to which it was an exclusively high-status cult may have been exaggerated. Even so, the excavated examples of temples are small, church-like structures. The first phase of the Carrawburgh *mithraeum* (Fig. 5.10), sited close to Coventina's Well, was a well-made stone building about 5.5 × 8 m, later considerably extended in the first of a series of major and minor reconstructions (Richmond and Gillam 1951). The dedication of the principal altars by commanders of the garrison betrays the attraction Mithras exercised for the leaders of local society, and this pattern is repeated at Rudchester and Housesteads. In all, ten altars were dedicated by military officers; the local civilian population seems to have taken little interest in the cult. This may explain the apparent discontinuity of worship at Carrawburgh. *Mithraea* have been excavated at Housesteads and Rudchester, and others are indicated by inscriptions at High Rochester, Castlesteads, and perhaps Corbridge, where it is possible that the building generally described as a *schola* was a *mithraeum*.

Traditional interpretations of the worship of Mithras have accepted the literary evidence for Christian hostility to the sect as sufficient to explain the collapse of the cult in the fourth century. Along the wall, enemy action has also been blamed for the destruction of *mithraea*, for example at Housesteads at the end of the third century. The apparent deliberate profanation of the main statues at Carrawburgh (Richmond and Gillam 1951) need not necessarily have been the responsibility of Christians, although it does suggest that vandalism is not a problem specific to the modern period. Caution is needed, because there is very little evidence of Christianity claiming converts among the northern garrisons before a generation of more after the worship of Mithras had declined. The London *mithraeum* appears to have enjoyed a new lease of life after Constantine, and the novel state religion was slow to permeate the frontier regions of the western empire.

No Christian churches have been located. Evidence of Christianity is confined to a handful of tombstones betraying in some cases dubious support from cemeteries at Risingham, Harraby Hill (Carlisle) and Brougham, and inscriptions of the Chi Rho monogram found at Maryport (Jarrett 1954) and Catterick (Wall 1965). Otherwise only portable objects betray an interest in Christianity, and the bulk of the evidence belongs after AD 350. The destruction of the main reliefs in the excavated *mithraea* does not look to have been the work of Christian bigots, although it may have resulted from imperial policy early in the century.

Religious observances had major implications beyond local or imperial culture. The majority of inscriptions were for religious purposes, and sculptors and masons seem to have congregated quickly in the towns and *vici* to supply the necessary skills. The vast majority of inscriptions were almost certainly local products, and the hand of individuals and groups have been identified (see above). In addition, the construction of temples required building materials and skills which were probably provided by the army, even where temples are found in the supposedly civilian contexts of Carlisle and Corbridge. Sacrifices required animals in large numbers. One recent estimate suggested that official festivals alone would have required the annual slaughter of 2,500 animals by the second-century British army (Breeze 1981). Remains of sacrificial meals found in the Carrawburgh *mithraeum* included the bones of lamb, kid and domestic fowl. All these aspects of religious practice must have had some knock-on effect in the local economy, although in other respects Roman religions may have made very little impact on the indigenous local community. Gravestones are one common, novel type of inscription introduced by the immigrant community and used very largely by them. They range in quality from the excellence of the work of the supposed Palmyrene sculptor at South Shields to the poorest and simplest local provincial work, and provide memorials to persons of varying status, sex and age. Tombstones of Barathes at Corbridge, and the *Lady with the Fan* from Carlisle contrast with the poor-quality lettering commemorating the death of the woman Tancorix aged sixty at Old Carlisle (RIB 908), or of Aicetuos and her twelve-year-old daughter at Old Penrith (RIB 936). The burials that these inscriptions commemorated were organized in the Roman fashion in cemeteries outside the forts and *vici*, commonly flanking the roads. Cremation is in some cemeteries the only rite identified, as at Brough-under-Stainmore where the majority were deposited in simple graves or, at most, with poor-quality pottery (Jones 1977). A minority were deposited in lead caskets or in a wooden box. Many cemeteries, like that at Brough, have suffered recent damage through the reconstruction of trunk roads. Such a fate has seriously affected the Brougham cemetery, 750 m east of the fort, which yielded 250 burials, mostly cremations, from a cemetery in use from the second to the fourth century. Others are known only through sporadic finds of tombstones. Cemeteries outside Carlisle have been identified on the north-east side, and on the west, including the Murrell Hill area, but the bulk of tombstones have come from beside London Road around Botchergate (Charlesworth 1978). A similar distribution surrounds the town of Corbridge.

Most, if not all these graves contain the remains of members of the garrisons, their dependants, or inhabitants of the *vici* or urban centres. However, a small minority of graves display a degree of exhibitionism and a command of resources far beyond the humble memorial stones or unmarked graves of the majority. Such mausoleums have been identified outside the fort of Brougham, but the most spectacular lay at the centre of the cemetery at Shorden Brae, outside Corbridge (Gillam and Daniels 1961). A central tower-like monument (nearly 10 m square) had been constructed above a burial shaft in the centre of a symmetrically planned precinct wall which had been ornamented with sculptures of lions crouching over stags at each corner of the exterior. The monument was raised probably in the second quarter of the second century, and may have acted as a focus for the lesser burials in the area deposited in the later Roman period. It was eventually dismantled, perhaps so that the masonry could be used in strengthening the town walls in the mid to late fourth century. It cannot have acted as a family crypt, and the date of construction suggests that it was an important member of the official community who was buried there, who may not have had any special association with the area, before the accident of his death. The cultural gulf between this man of empire and those tribesmen deposited in the Beadnell cyst was vast, and there is little evidence to suggest that it was ever bridged.

Notes

1. The enormous advance of our knowledge in Northumberland is almost entirely due to the work of Prof. George Jobey, who was prevented by outstanding commitments from joining with me in the authorship of this book. In Cumbria the Collingwood dynasty began a process of research which emerges in the work of the Royal Commission in Westmorland, and has been continued by Brian Blake, and then by Prof. Barri Jones and the author, with the assistance of many friends and colleagues.

2. The state of knowledge is summarized in Haselgrove (1981).

3. My thanks to John Dore for his comments on this site.

4. My thanks to Ian Caruana for his correspondence prior to publication of this site.

5. Not 'goat milk' as appeared as a misprint in Higham (1981).

Chapter 6

The Return of Tribalism (AD 350–685)

The late Roman Army and the North

By the mid-fourth century, the numerically reduced frontier army was faced by increasing pressure from tribal forces outside the empire. The military authorities responded to the new and increased problems of security by *ad hoc* means, but the frontier forces were eventually to prove inadequate in fulfilling their allotted task.

Some rebuilding or refurbishment on fort sites can be dated to the central decades of the century. The defences at Housesteads and Greatchesters were improved (Daniels 1980b) and the defence in depth of the frontier region was strengthened by the reoccupation of Piercebridge *c.* AD 350, although occupation there was not to be as intensive as in the very late third century (Harper 1968; Scott 1978; Scott and Large 1980).

Evidence for fort destruction during the period is less considerable than once supposed (Richmond 1958), when it was thought that the entire wall area fell to enemy action. Some sites do appear to have suffered significant disasters, but the exact chronology can rarely be established, nor the cause. At Corbridge, for example, three coin hoards have been identified from the central area of the 'forum', the granaries and the adjacent road [1]. All included coins minted no later than *c.* AD 340, and all had been burnt. All areas were subsequently reoccupied.

One of the lost books of Ammianus Marcellinus referred under the year AD 343 to an expedition to Britain by the Emperor Constans in some way associated with the role of the *arcani* or *areani*. The latter appear to have acted as scouts, or secret agents among the northern barbarians (Ammianus Marcellinus XXVIII, 3; Hind 1983). Some sort of service of this kind probably dates back to the Severan reorganization of the frontier, and may account for the presence of the Procurator Oclatinius Adventus at Risingham *c.* AD 205–7 (RIB 1234). The *exploratores* of the third century provide the obvious predecessors of the *arcani* of the fourth, but the former appear to have been exclusively concerned with security on the land frontier and the role was presumably abandoned during the later third century. Conditions in the mid fourth century required a more elaborate intelligence network, operating not only among the Britons of southern Scotland, but more critically among the Picts and Scots, and along the sea routes, in the North and Irish Seas. In this context, Constans's visit in AD 343 has possible links with building work at Lancaster and may have been important [2].

That the Picts and Scots were subject to treaties with Rome is evident from the account of their incursion in AD 360 (Ammianus Marcellinus, XXI, 1), when they were reported to be laying waste places near the frontiers. This presumably refers to the northern land frontier, and probably to raids on southern Scotland, where the tribal *loca* or meeting-places might have been the targets, but incursions into Cumbria or Durham should not be ruled out. The frontier forces were inadequate to meet the crisis, and the *magister armorum*, Lupicinus, crossed the Channel with a force of light-armed auxiliaries in midwinter.

Renewed incursions by the Picts, Saxons, Scots and Atacotti occurred in AD 365; the climax of the barbarian raids was reached in AD 367 when the tribes conspired together to overwhelm the British province (Ammianus Marcellinus, XXVII, 8). The main thrust of the conspirators may have bypassed the northern counties, and fallen instead on the wealthy civilian communities of the South, where the commander of the sea coast region was killed. The habit of accrediting AD 367 with all evidence of late-fourth-century destruction on the wall has now been abandoned, and, under recent reappraisal, evidence for enemy action has largely evaporated (e.g. Breeze and Dobson 1976: 221). However, Bewcastle bathhouse was completely destroyed during the 360s and there is a case for proposing destruction by enemy forces in this context at Rudchester, Haltonchesters, South Shields and Wallsend. The disabling of the *dux* in the North must imply considerable hostile forces in Yorkshire, and it seems likely that some areas of the Far North were also overrun.

The campaigns of Theodosius in Britain in AD 367 and 368 (Tomlin 1974), imply that, even if most of the raiders were encountered south of the Pennines, part of the responsibility lay with the *arcani*, who were, therefore, disbanded. We are not told where they were stationed (Ammianus, XXVIII, 3), but if they were long established, some at least ought to have occupied the outlying forts north of the wall, none of which have yielded pottery later than *c*. AD 360. If, however, they were also operating on the sea lanes, as circumstances would have required, some at least of this group must have been stationed in the coastal fortifications, and operated off shore. The Pictish raiders were arguably seaborne, and the Scots and Saxons were by necessity. It may be significant that Ravenglass fort – arguably a fleet base – was destroyed at approximately this date, and a tombstone found at Ambleside could be relevant, recording the deaths of soldiers within the fort at the hands of the enemy (Burkett 1965).

The Theodosian campaign had successfully repelled the raiders from within the province, but no attempt was made to launch counter-offensives in the North. Theodosius led his tiny field army back to the Continent, leaving behind him a part of Britain renamed Valentia, but an island if anything less defensible than he had found it.

The newly named province of Valentia was probably a part of the two provinces into which Britannia Inferior was already divided, namely Flavia Caesariensis based on York, and Britannia Secunda on Lincoln. Valentia has been identified with the pre-AD 367 Flavia Caesariensis, leaving, perhaps, a small part of the old province with the old name in the North-west administered from Carlisle (Hassall 1976). An alternative thesis has emerged from a reappraisal of the *Notitia Dignitatum*, suggesting that Valentia was a coastal command incorporating north Wales and north-west England, based presumably on Chester (Dornier 1982). Whatever the proper identification, the emergence of a fifth province is likely to represent a response by the Emperor's delegate to the increasing problems of guarding the northern coasts in the 360s. The consequent division of command most probably left Hadrian's Wall within a single command structure, but liberated from that structure control of the Irish Sea fleet and coastal installations.

Central to this response was the construction of the fort protected by the Wery Wall at Lancaster, another key coastal site (Potter 1979: 365), perhaps already commissioned by Constans in AD 343. The reoccupation of Burrow Walls (Bellhouse 1955) strengthened the cordon of defences around the Cumbrian coast, and a low level of reoccupation was recorded at Bowness-on-Solway, the terminal of the wall. Slight evidence exists for reoccupation of three of the second-century mileforts (5, 12, 20) and that on the Cardurnock peninsula may have re-emerged as an important observation post for the Solway estuary. Clearly the coast of north-west England absorbed considerable military resources at a time when those resources were already stretched, and the coastal dispositions may have been staffed by troops hitherto stationed in the hinterland.

On the east coast, no certain defences are known north of Malton, but a case has been made for installations at Seaham, Monkwearmouth, Jarrow and Hartlepool (Dobson 1970). Inland, there are signs that small units were used to link the frontier with troops in the Upper Eden and Lune valleys, and in the Dere Street forts. If Apperley Dene was a military site, its reoccupation after a century-long abandonment is significant (Greene 1978). In Cumbria new fortlets at Wreay and Barrock Fell may have acted as signal stations (Bellhouse 1953).

The wall was made more secure by widespread rebuilding, perhaps associated with the series of inscriptions recording work of the British *civitates* along the frontier. At Chesterholm patching on the fort wall may be attributed to this period. All the wall forts were occupied at some level and several in strength, but there is very little evidence to suggest that more than a few milecastles or turrets were in use. At Birdoswald, the programme of rebuilding utilized a series of third-century inscriptions, and at Housesteads, Chesters and Lanchester the blocking of gates and conversion of the gatehouses to accommodation signifies the reduced access needs of the garrisons and the increasing emphasis on defence.

Gradual changes emerge in the use of official buildings, although some *praetoria* continued to function as high-status accommodation until late in the century. That at Binchester received the addition of a private bath-suite after AD 367, but prior to abandonment was converted successively to communal baths and finally to a slaughter-house. The *principium* at Housesteads was used as an armoury, and bundles of arrows in large numbers were hung on the walls.

It has been suggested that changes in use may have resulted from the removal of *vicani* into the forts, but of this there is little archaeological evidence. The garrisons before and after AD 367 appear to have been of the same kind, accommodated in the same way. Where official buildings have been examined, they were converted to some new, official use associated with weapons, food processing or storage, or simply allowed to deteriorate and were then abandoned (Welsby 1982).

There seems to have been a marked decline in the occupation of *vici* after the 360s, even outside those forts like Housesteads where extra-mural settlement in the early fourth century has been identified (Birley, Charlton and Hedley, 1932). Outside the fort at Chesterholm, building lxxxvi was of crude construction but was associated with Huntcliff and Crambeck wares, diagnostic of the period after AD 360. This final phase of occupation was distinguished by a great depth of domestic and industrial rubbish within the building, and seems to represent a squalid vestige of occupation, far removed from the well-organized *vicus* of the third century (Birley 1977). At Corbridge and Carlisle urban occupation continued until the end of the century or perhaps beyond, but urbanism was a long-spent force on the frontier. The decline and abandonment of the *vici* exposes their economic vulnerability. During the fourth century, an increasing level and variety of army provisioning was undertaken directly by the government, shipping equipment from government factories on the Continent. The value of cash payments to the forces had been adversely affected by inflation since the heights of the Severan period. In addition, the army had declined numerically from the levels maintained in the second century and early third century. These changes spelled disaster for the civilian communities which had been attracted to the area by economic opportunities created by the army. The constraints on the flow of cash and goods in the vicinal market-place rendered their decline and eventual demise inevitable.

A symptom of the increasing economic malaise is the changing pattern of pottery supply in the North. Wares from east Yorkshire had already penetrated the border counties early in the century (Gillam 1973), but after about AD 350–60 they became dominant. The importation of black-burnished wares from southern England ceased. In practice this implies that importation of pottery to the Solway declined dramatically. In future, only the products of a small number of Yorkshire factories reached the North in any quantity. They were technically a retrograde product, but from a comparatively close source and on both counts likely to have been cheap (Welsby 1982). The dominance of Yorkshire wares represent a market in decline already by the mid century, with quality and choice sacrificed for price. There is, therefore, every reason to see the civilian support system in decline.

Despite the unhealthy economic trends on the frontier, there is little evidence of soldier-farmers acting as a self-supporting militia. Until the final collapse of the organization, the frontier forces continued to be paid and provisioned via *annona* by the state (Holder 1982), and there is no specific reason as yet to link the 'agricultural' platforms outside Housesteads with cultivation by the garrison. They may represent building platforms. The frontier guards were full-time soldiers.

Also under the command of the *dux Britanniorum* were the garrisons of the hinterland forts, listed in the *Notitia Dignitatum* as three units of *equites*, the *barcarii Tigrisiensis* and nine *numeri* of cavalry. Although the *Notitia* was finally compiled early in the fifth century, those lists relevant to Britain may already have been outdated by that stage. The troop dispositions are probably representative of the situation after AD 367 but before AD 383. Some units may have performed specialist functions. The *barcarii Tigrisiensis* have already been noted in this context. The unit at Brough-under-Stainmore may have served as a forwarding unit (*numerus Directorum*), linked perhaps to the lead seals that were found there (Richmond 1936). Sea scouts were based either at Papcastle, or more probably at Malton-on-Humber. The wall forts east of Birdoswald were occupied, but to the west the *Notitia* has proved resistant to interpretation (Hassell 1976a), and one suggestion has been that Cumbria was accorded the status of a client kingdom even before AD 400 (McCarthy 1982).

The barbarian problem continued to plague the northern frontier. Coins of Magnus Maximus are not common, but have been identified in a hoard of *c.* AD 385 found at Corbridge (Archer 1979), and as an isolated find at South Shields. These two sites had previously been utilized as supply bases for offensive action to the north, and it can hardly be coincidence that Magnus Maximus has also been credited with a war against the Picts and Scots (Casey 1979; Prosper Tiro, *Chronicon, Gratiani*, iv). The fiercely Christian general may, in addition, have been responsible for the use of pagan inscriptions as kerbstones at Corbridge. However, the major preoccupations of Maximus from AD 383 until his death lay not on the northern frontier but on the Continent, and it is likely that he was responsible for major troop evacuations. It has been suggested that Papcastle, Ambleside, Low Borrow Bridge, Water-crook and Ebchester were among the sites abandoned under Maximus (Frere 1978: 266). If this were the case, the northern frontier was seriously under-manned after the 380s, and defence in depth on the model argued by Luttwak (1976) became an increasingly hollow strategy.

The account by Gildas of the Pictish Wars of the late fourth and early fifth centuries is the most substantial source available. However, although the essential reliability of the sixth-century author has recently been re-emphasized (Miller 1975b), his description of this period remote from his own generation is chronologically imprecise and contains factual errors. Examples of the latter are his attribution of both walls to this period. Chronologically, the sequence of three periods of raiding by the Picts and Scots is limited by the Battle of Aquileia in AD 388 and the letter to Agitius, apparently Aetius, in AD 446. However, apart from the letter, a copy of which was apparently available to Gildas, the account derives from an oral tradition. The first of these wars should date to *c.* AD 389–90 by Gildas's chronology (Miller 1975a), and constituted a major British success, with imperial control extended beyond the wall, right back to the Clyde–Forth isthmus. However, this does create significant problems of chronology and interpretation. It would be more acceptable to credit Maximus with the success achieved in the first of these wars. Between AD 380 and AD 398, he alone was of sufficiently senior rank and he alone commanded sufficient forces to achieve the reintegration of south Scotland into the Roman sphere of influence. Such an attribution was resisted by Gildas, perhaps as part of his general vilification of Maximus whom he considered a tyrant and usurper, and the source of many of Britain's problems (Gildas, 10).

The second period of barbarian raids must, by this chronology, have begun after AD 385, and probably rapidly followed the disastrous Battle of Aquileia in AD 388, when it became obvious that neither Maximus nor his opponents and successors could protect Britain. Imperial priorities elsewhere left Britain to its own devices until AD 398 when an expeditionary force under Stilicho or his lieutenant cleared raiders from the province, and probably undertook naval action against the Irish, Picts and Saxons (Claudian, *de consulatu Stilichonis*, II, 250–5). However, Gildas makes it clear that south Scotland and Northumberland were not wrested from the barbarians, and Hadrian's Wall served as the new frontier between the province and the hostile tribes. Compared with the preceding campaign, that of Stilicho was a disastrous failure equivalent in results to that of Theodosius (Miller 1975a), and the withdrawal of his expedition probably saw yet more units transferred from the frontier.

By the end of the century, troop evacuation had reached a dangerous level. The poverty of coin finds post-AD 385 only underlines the problem. The events of AD 406–10 may have led to the removal of any effective forces that remained, although it is noteworthy that Gildas ignored the usurpation of Constantine III in his account of the northern frontier. Constantine was elevated to the purple by the British army, and crossed to Gaul to confront a Vandal invasion. In his absence, the Saxons raided southern Britain in AD 408, In AD 409 the rural proletariat of southern Britain revolted against both the local aristocracy and Rome (Thompson 1977). Constantine perished in

AD 411, and henceforth Britain was ruled by usurpers.

On the northern frontier there is no evidence that country folk joined the South in rebellion. The presence of the rump of the armed forces, and the very different social and economic conditions both weigh against it. However, the collapse of organized government in the South was disastrous in the North, where occurred the final and irrevocable disruption to the flow of pay and supplies. Throughout the Roman period the maintenance of the garrisons on the northern frontier relied upon massive and regular injections of resources from other parts of the province and the empire. In receipt of these, the frontier army had performed the tasks demanded of it more or less satisfactorily. Even with diminished resources and seriously reduced manpower, the late-fourth-century army continued to act as a professional force, but the consistent outflow of men and equipment during the century had seriously weakened the garrisons. By AD 410, those which remained were abandoned by the support structure and most units must have found their position untenable. The inadequacy of the northern army at the opening of the Third Pictish War was highlighted by Gildas (15).

At some date between *c*. AD 402 and 410, pottery from Yorkshire ceased to penetrate the frontier area, presumably because effective demand fell below the threshold of economic production, and the industry collapsed (Fulford 1979). The pottery industry was a casualty of the collapse of the organization, and the consequent inability of the provincial authorities to supply and fund the army. It is likely that all other commerce based upon the same military markets was affected by the process of disintegration, and experts in the movements of goods by land or sea must similarly have ceased operations.

In such circumstances, units were forced back upon the local resource base. In many areas the army could not have hoped to respond by cultivating land adjacent to the forts. The troops which had been in occupation of forts in the heartland of the ploughlands of the frontier zone had, in some cases at least, been withdrawn from the province decades earlier. The final distribution of forces on the frontier line is unlikely to have assisted in any transition to a peasant militia, and units are not likely to have responded to the collapse of provincial organization in time. In the event, it is extremely improbable that any recognizable units of the late Roman army still occupied their posts on the northern frontier by AD 420. The army did not ultimately fail to protect the province, but the province failed in its support of the army, its resource base and manpower. Without that support, the remaining military units probably disbanded themselves by desertion, in the face of new hostility from the North. The structure of local society had to readjust to a reduced economic basis, dependent on local resources, without the subsidies from outside that had supported an artificially inflated economy throughout the Roman occupation (Mann 1979). In many respects the resultant adjustment was brutal, but it was no less necessary for that.

The Successor States

The problem of evidence

The collapse of provincial government in the North left the local community face to face with fundamental political issues, including future relations between the Scots and Picts and the erstwhile provincials. The end of the artificial, Roman, economy has deprived the archaeologist of diagnostic, artefactual evidence on all but a small minority of sites, and has left us dangerously dependent on documentary sources, the interpretation of which is unusually difficult.

During the last decade, substantial monographs by prominent scholars have attempted to write, or rewrite, the history of Dark Age Britain, both with and without the central character of King Arthur [3]. These works have provided an important stimulus to historical research in the period, but may have given a misleading impression of knowledge. In consequence, a more critical reappraisal of the manuscript sources has already challenged some of the interpretations so recently offered, and has resulted in the separation of numerous pseudo-historical episodes and personalities from history [4]. The casualties include King Arthur himself, who had, in any case already been divorced from the northern British arena. Among the northerners, most important is Cunedda, the supposed chieftain from Manau in Gododdin and founder of the royal lines of many Welsh kingdoms, who is named in no document earlier than the *Historia Brittonum* compiled in the ninth century. Given that the compiler of this work was actively systematizing and restructuring the genealogies of the Welsh princes for political purposes, Cunedda has, regretfully, to be rejected as a probable fabrication (Chadwick 1958; Dumville 1977b). Likewise, the Harleian genealogies of the northern kings are arguably unhistorical before the generation of Riderch of Strathclyde (Miller 1975c). This at least frees many genealogies from that derived from Coel Hen (Old King Cole). There is consequently no reason to follow Morris in attributing Coel to York (Morris 1973: 213).

The historian is left with a small and not entirely consistent body of material. For the fifth century the *de Excidio* of Gildas is the sole, relevant, chronologically organized and near-contemporary account, dealing with the North in Chapters 14–21. Bede owed much to the work (Miller 1975b). In addition, the writings of St Patrick are relevant to this area and are contemporary with major political events. Within the work of compilation associated with the name of Nennius, the *Annales Cambriae* contains no relevant political information before the Battle of Armterid in AD 573, and in the *Historia Brittonum* nothing before the mid sixth century when an account of Bernicia begins, apparently from English sources. Before the generation of

Riderch in the late sixth century, British sources appear to rely on oral or poetic traditions. After that time, official documentation in Latin appears to have become accessible, and the genealogies of the Celts and English become increasingly reliable. Some lost poetry appears to have been available to the author of the *Historia Brittonum*, who arguably derived information from the lost work of 'Talhaern Tataguen' (*Historia Brittonum*, 62). Reputed to be of the late sixth or early seventh century are the *Gododdin* attributed to Aneirin (Jackson 1969) and a handful of lesser works by Taliesin (Williams 1968), but any or all could owe much to later hands over several centuries.

To set beside these sources are a handful of inscriptions and a very limited amount of archaeological evidence, much of which is of questionable value if only because of chronological imprecision, to which must be added the evidence of place-names and palaeobotany. Not much perhaps, yet few areas in Britain can offer historical sources in the fifth and sixth centuries the equal of those of the border counties of England and Scotland.

The resource base

The environment, population, rural settlement and subsistence
The political upheavals of the late Roman and sub-Roman periods were insufficient to leave traces in the palaeobotanical record. Those areas where extensive clearance already existed in the fourth century retained that level throughout the fifth and until late in the sixth century. This is an impression gained not from a small number of pollen diagrams but from almost all of the considerable number available. To offer specific examples, evidence from Hallowell Moss, near Durham, indicated that tree pollen declined below 5 per cent of the total during a clearance phase that began within the early Roman period, but which achieved maximum impact after AD 400 (Donaldson and Turner 1977). In south and east Durham widespread agriculture continued. Although the cultivation of the specialist cash crop of hemp declined at Thorpe Bulmer from the 19 per cent peak, *c*. AD 220, it continued to be grown throughout the remainder of the first millennium, dying out finally in the Norman period (Bartley, Chambers and Hart-Jones 1976). Its decline in the post-Roman period allowed the community to expand grasslands, and presumably herds, but the agricultural phase that began here before the Roman Conquest, survived all the political upheavals of the Dark Ages. The same pattern was present at Stewart Shield, Weardale, although this and other pollen diagrams from the uplands suggest that the priority given to pastoralism in the Roman period continued in subsequent centuries. Among Northumbrian pollen diagrams, economic stability over the fifth and (less certainly) the sixth centuries is the norm (Davies and Turner 1979). At Steng

Moss cereal cultivation was increasing in the late Roman period, but a rise in tree pollen ends the period of buoyancy *c.* AD 500. Local conditions clearly continued to play an important part in the encouragement or discouragement of clearance activity. The wet lowland hinterland of Neasham Fen remained obstinately wooded throughout the Roman period, but by AD 700 clearance had gathered momentum, and the extent of local forest had fallen to a level comparable to that elsewhere in south and east Durham and Cleveland. West of the Pennines much of the clearance phase occurred in the post-Roman period, starting at Burnmoor Tarn *c.* AD 390, but at Devoke Water *c.* AD 200 (Pennington 1970). This late horizon for clearance activity appears widespread in the Lake District and western coastal lowlands, where climatic improvement was arguably long delayed by high rainfall. Walker (1966) argued from this widespread (but poorly dated) series of pollen diagrams that the period after AD 400 and before about AD 800 witnessed the first 'permanent' and vigorous clearance of much of the area, following a period of retrenchment during the Roman occupation. This expansion was marked at Ehenside Tarn, the hinterland of which was virtually deforested, and extensively cultivated, with the novel appearance of *Linum* (flax) and *Cannabis* (hemp). To this horizon, Pennington was able to trace the first appearance of cereals in data from ten tarns. In addition, clearance activity associated with cereal cultivation was identified in Morecambe Bay peat *c.* AD 436 (Smith 1959).

Interpretation of the Cumbrian data is dependent on dating large numbers of non-carbon-14 dated diagrams by comparison with a small number which are dated. This means that the clearance horizon is chronologically imprecise, and we should not rely on the synchroneity of clearance throughout the region. Much probably began well within the Roman period (as at Devoke Water). Elsewhere it was late Roman/post-Roman, but until further dating is achieved it will not be clear where the weight of this horizon should be placed.

The available data are easiest interpreted as evidence for a continuing buoyant population enjoying a period of hospitable climate. The carrying capacity of this environment was either increasing, or at least stable, and capable of sustaining a population equivalent at least to that of the central Roman period. It is not possible to argue from the evidence for wholesale population decline before the late sixth century. At that stage there is revealed a dramatic decline in human activity in some localities. At Fellend Moss forest regeneration reached maximum levels *c.* AD 620, at which point the total herb pollen was reduced to about a third of the total. At Hallowell Moss an abrupt change led to the abandonment of wide areas of farmland, succeeded initially by hazel scrub and ultimately by woodland, although small amounts of grassland survived and it was arguably grazing pressure that kept the woodland canopy open. Little cultivation occurred throughout the remainder of the millennium. Forest regeneration had already occurred at Steng Moss in Northumberland, but the vigorous activity typical of the Lake District may have continued somewhat later in some areas. At Bolton Fell, forest regeneration was dated to *c.* AD 780, but at Devoke Water was rather earlier at *c.* AD 580.

The end of maintained clearance may not have been synchronous in all areas – the gap between AD 580 and 780 is a considerable one even given the margins proper to carbon-14 dating. Much will depend on the factors which caused it. In considering these, no firm conclusions are possible; specific causes may have affected particular but isolated localities, but an increase in rainfall in the mid millennium may provide the context in which local factors played their part.

Population

Documentary sources note several outbreaks of pestilence in the mid sixth, and again in the late seventh and early eighth centuries, when plagues afforded an opportunity to hagiographers to attribute yet more miracles to their patron saints (e.g. St Cuthbert, Anon. IV, 6 (Colgrave 1940); Bede, *Vita*, 8, 33; Eddius, 18; Adomnan, I, 103b). Plague has been discarded as a major factor in the decline of the Roman city in the fifth century (Todd 1977), perhaps because those cities had already declined beyond redemption (Reece 1980a). In the sixth century the *Annales Cambriae* records only the pestilence of AD 547 which killed Maelgwn of Gwynedd; in the seventh century mention was made of a plague which killed Cadwaladr in AD 682, and the pestilence which affected Ireland in AD 683. Clearly, major epidemics did occur, and it is likely that the plague that struck the Mediterranean world *c.* AD 543–47 also affected Britain, where it probably arrived in AD 547 and where it may, for example, have accounted for the deaths of the two sons of Liberalis, remembered on the Yarrowkirk stone in Upper Tweeddale. If parallels with the AD 1350 epidemic be allowed, the latter was the first of a series of endemic plagues which died out in the countryside no earlier than AD 1480, and in the towns and cities not until the late seventeenth century. During the century following the initial outbreak, a critical change in the age structure of the population hindered the replacement of lost generations, and the consequences in the countryside were widespread abandonment of less attractive holdings, and dramatic changes in the pattern of land-use in favour of pastoralism [5].

Some of these patterns emerge in late sixth- and seventh-century Britain. Population decline was arguably not uniform and was least visible in the best agricultural lands, for example in south and east Durham. However, other catastrophes could have played a significant role.

The breakdown of Roman control in the North was accompanied by famine (Gildas, 16, 17), leading in turn to brigandage and the collapse of food

245

production. One response was an increase in candidates for slavery, and slavery probably grew to be of considerable importance in northern society. Slaves were a major component of the booty that attracted Scottish and Pictish raiders from the 360s onwards (Ammianus Marcellinus, xxvii, 8), and until the mid fifth century northern England was subjected to slave-raiding from that quarter. When Patrick claimed to have been one among thousands captured by Irish slavers in a single raid, he was no doubt exaggerating (*Confessio*, 1), but the process may have resulted in a significant pressure on local population levels. This is not apparent in the palaeobotanical record, unless it was slave-raiding that drove Cumbrian farmers into the fastnesses of the Lake District fells, and consequently led to widespread use of agricultural strategies in that area – probably on lowland and valley sites.

By about AD 450 local tyrants were also active in slave-raids. That of the soldiers of Coroticus on Irish communities is the best documented, but it seems likely that both slave and cattle-raiding were endemic among the British kingdoms and their neighbours. Northern England had entered a slave-trading economy which had originally been centred outside the empire but which now encompassed much of western Europe. The Coroticus incident reveals that slave-trading was international. In such circumstances, northern England is likely to have been a net exporter of slaves, given the poverty of the resource base, and the demand of the local aristocracy for exotic imports. However, the palaeobotanical record requires that neither disease nor raiding can have seriously drained the border counties of manpower before the late sixth century. Dark Age England was a fragile ecosystem, in which a large producer population supported a small, warrior élite. The health of great natural ecosystems can be measured by their capacity to support major predators – the jaguar, for example, in the Brazilian jungle. The ability of the northern counties to maintain a warrior élite should similarly point to a buoyant population up to *c.* AD 600.

Rural settlement and subsistence

Despite the apparent continuity of the subsistence strategies for which they had previously been identifiably responsible, the rural population after AD 350 is rarely detectable through archaeological means. The collapse of bulk trade meant that the flow of cheap exotics on to farm sites stopped at latest by AD 410. However, this resulted in a situation no more damning than that already present in Northumberland in a post-Antonine context. At few excavated native sites has the structural succession of round-houses supported or required interpretation of substantial or long-lived post-Roman occupation. This may mean no more than that the stone-walled round-house was resilient to the passage of time, and, given an occasional new roof, could last almost indefinitely. One site has produced artefactual evidence of occupation in the late fourth and fifth centuries, at Huckhoe in the Wansbeck valley (Northumb.) where a range of buildings of circular and rectangular plan were in occupation (Jobey 1959). A small, rectangular structure at Belling Law yielded a carbon-14 date of *c.* AD 280. At Ingram Hill a phase of rectilinear stone building post-dates the typically Romano-British occupation, but no diagnostic artefacts were identified. In Cumbria, comparable buildings have been detected late in the sequence of occupation on upland sites at and near Crosby Ravensworth (Collingwood 1909; Collingwood 1933b; RCAHM 1936: 85; Higham 1979b). However, until objective dating is attempted, these examples cannot be assumed to be either 'Dark Age' or 'Anglian', despite the ninth-century date attributed to a similar complex at Ribblehead (Yorks; King 1978). Many of them are probably post-Conquest shielings. At this stage it is no more than inference that many Romano-British type farm sites belong to the sub-Roman period, whether exclusively or not. Otherwise the pollen data become inexplicable, as does the mid- to late-fifth-century period of great prosperity described by Gildas (19).

The earliest post-Roman structures identified at Yeavering were of rectangular plan, based on individual post-holes and associated with 'native' pottery (Hope-Taylor 1977: 209). Given that they ought to belong at latest to the first half of the sixth century, it is difficult to believe that these forms were derived from Anglo-Saxon architectural traditions. Their appearance at Yeavering significantly predates the threshold of diagnostic Anglo-Saxon artefactual evidence, and the late-sixth-century hall at Doon Hill, Dunbar, provides a possible Celtic parallel (Hope-Taylor 1966).

Occasional references in the lives of the saints and elsewhere imply timber-built rural settlements. St Columba, when crossing the 'spine of Britain' (the Pennines ?) rested for the night in a deserted hamlet among deserted fields, and a hostile pursuer fired the buildings (Adomnan, I, 35b). This incident implies recent abandonment of settlement and fields, and may be relevant to our investigation of the population decline.

When Penda's troops attacked Bamburgh, they pulled down the neighbouring 'villages' and used the beams, rafters, wattled walls and thatched roofs in an attempt to fire the 'city' (Bede, *Historia Ecclesiastica*, III, 16).

Within the Milfield basin, this vernacular style had already permeated the lower echelons of society by early in the English period. Aerial photographs taken by Prof. N. McCord in 1970 at Thirlings revealed the plan of six rectangular timber buildings, aligned east–west on a sandy gravel terrace, on which excavations began in 1973, revealing the construction trenches of buildings, the post-holes of others, fence lines around them and a scatter of post-holes of which some belong to the earlier neolithic occupation of the site (Miket 1976) [6]. The carbon-14 dates so far available for these structures place them in a fifth/sixth-century context (*c.* AD 470 and *c.* AD 580), but structurally it seems that they belong in the sixth or seventh centuries (Fig. 6.1).

A timber architectural tradition seems established, at least in the eastern lowlands, and if this was associated with a near-aceramic culture and was less obviously enclosed than the Romano-British type farm, then the archaeological elusiveness of these settlements is explicable. We should not fall into the trap of assigning ethnic origins to building traditions in this period. Suffice it to say that the hall style of structure probably permeated northern society from the high status to the low, over a long period, but possibly with its roots in the Roman occupation.

Given the inability of archaeologists to identify rural settlements in the fifth and sixth centuries, we have no access to the rural economy at that point. The picture derived from pollen data is quite specific. Throughout the fifth and (less ubiquitously) the sixth centuries the northern community was engaged in the same kind and pattern of land-use as had been present during the Roman period. Most cereal cultivation occurred in the lowlands, but upland communities practised limited cultivation, even in the Lake District where condi-

Plate 6.1   The foundations of a trench-constructed, timber-framed building (structure C) at Thirlings (Northumb.) during excavation in 1976. Carbon dates suggest a date for the occupation of this structure in the sixth century, but the style of construction is closely comparable to seventh-century buildings at Yeavering and elsewhere.

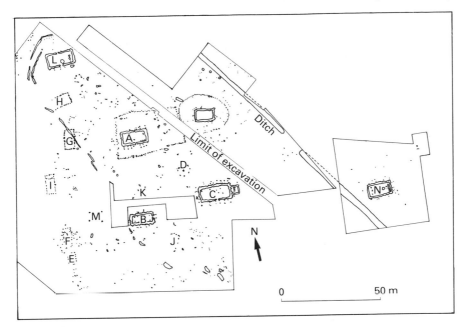

Figure 6.1   Thirlings: a post-Roman 'hamlet' (buildings lettered after Miket, forthcoming).

---

tions were least favourable. There is some evidence of decline in specific areas of the economy where cash crops had been cultivated, in particular hemp and flax, but the land did not go out of use, but was converted to pasture. Despite the lack of archaeological information, widespread land management appears to have been the norm. The faunal remains from an early-seventh-century building at Yeavering (Northumb.) suggested that the strong bias in the rural economy in favour of cattle continued – 97 per cent of bones were of cattle, and the others represented sheep, pigs, horses and humans. The age range of the cattle bones suggested two killing peaks, the first between 6 and 12 months and the second between 18 and 35 months, and this implies that systematic cattle-breeding for beef was practised in the area. Yeavering was a high-status site – a royal palace and centre of religious ritual – and the consumption here need not represent the normal fare of the Northumberland farmer. Even so, it seems highly plausible that cattle-breeding was the major economic activity, particularly in the northern uplands, throughout this period, and as such cattle played a natural, focal role in pagan religion at Yeavering.

In support of this, the tradition of taxation on cattle among the British and Northumbrian communities is known from sources of the Norman period. Similarities with the Welsh system may imply a common, and, therefore, an early ancestry. Transhumance may have been practised. This is the obvious inference to be drawn from the presence of thatched dwellings used only in spring and summer in the west Durham hills in which St Cuthbert was reported

249

to have taken refuge (Anon. 1, vi (Colgrave 1940)). References to other animal products occur haphazardly in the saints' lives, most of which are of seventh century or later relevance rather than sixth century. St Cuthbert greased his boots with swine lard (Anon. 3, v (Colgrave 1940)) and St Columba came across a sow fattened on hazel nuts (Adomnan, I, 71b). Other resources were utilized. Passing references occur to the slaughter of seals, salmon-fishing, a milk churn, a threshing floor, a boar hunt on Skye, the tradition of skin-covered boats and the consumption of venison. These references imply a continuing interest in food collection, culling and hunting.

Perhaps the most interesting reference to cereal cultivation comes from Farne Island, where St Cuthbert was unable to grow wheat, but found that barley produced a successful crop, even though the birds disputed his harvest. Climatic conditions are likely to have played a significant role in this 'miracle' (Bede, *Vita*, xix). At no stage in the medieval period was wheat to be a reliable crop in northern Northumberland or in north-west England.

British kings and their kingdoms

The local British aristocracy is notoriously elusive during the Roman period. However in the sub-Roman period Gildas makes it clear that 'tyrants' or kings emerged. Political conditions made it a matter of great urgency that competent and unchallenged leadership should come to the fore in northern society, in order to deal with the Scottish and Pictish raiders. The war associated with Stilicho left the barbarians in control of Britain down to the wall. When his expeditionary force withdrew in AD 401 the frontier army was inadequate to defend the wall frontier. Gildas described it as 'an army, slow to battle, unwieldy for flight, inept by reason of their quaking midriffs, which languished day and night in its sorry watch' (Wade Evans 1938: 140). The frontier collapsed, and for more than a generation raiders were safe to come and go in northern England almost at will. During this period Patrick and his 'thousands' of fellows were taken captive, arguably from the Irthing valley but possibly from the vicinity of Ravenglass. Slaves and cattle were probably the main lure for the barbarians, as they had been in the 360s. However, the apparent absence of major disruption in the pollen diagrams should prompt a degree of caution in accepting Gildas's account as factual. It is, perhaps intentionally, sensationalist. It was not the pathetic remnants of the Britons who eventually drove out the raiders, but a well-peopled community, within which the major problems had centred not on human and physical resources but on organizing the means of resistance. South of the wall, and to some extent also beyond it, Rome had created a civilian community within an international state. The re-establishment of sovereign, local, tribal communities required time, and ruthless management – a trait which attracted the condemnation of Gildas.

By about AD 450 this had been achieved. The Third Pictish War destroyed the last vestige of the frontier army but ended with the withdrawal of the Scots to Ireland, and the Picts to Scotland beyond the Forth. This satisfactory conclusion was achieved with local resources and by British arms. Henceforth, until the early to mid sixth century when Gildas was writing, the North was only troubled from outside by occasional Pictish raids. However, he makes it clear that 'civil war' (i.e. war between 'citizens') continued to plague the area (Gildas, 19).

The political and military leadership of the sub-Roman North had evolved in critical conditions, in which any ends justified the means by which the barbarian raiders could be repelled. Niceties concerning legitimate authority were not the concern of the strong men and their warrior bands, who responded to these circumstances by diverting to themselves the local taxation, and then strove to protect the local community which provided it, from outside raiders. By the mid fifth century, some of these 'tyrannies' had raised themselves to a level of considerable power. Coroticus must have been a northern British tyrant, whether or not he should be equated with the 'Ceritic Guletic' of the Strathclyde dynasty. He was able to launch a sea-borne raid on the Irish coast to capture slaves. North of the wall, the British had a longer tradition of self-government and self-protection on which to draw, but behind this shield 'tyrannies' developed also throughout the North of what had been the Roman province. Many of these new political units may have been very small, controlling only a single valley or a section of the coastal plains. Under the pressures of war and inheritance they may have been subject to frequent boundary changes, and it is not surprising that the names of only a few have survived. However, several of the old tribal areas may have emerged at this stage as successor states (Fig. 6.2).

Gildas makes it clear that the role of kingship evolved only slowly, with the 'anointers' – probably the war-bands – making and unmaking kings almost at will. In addition 'civil war' was endemic (Gildas, 19). This represents a resumption of the inter-tribal raiding that was probably common in late pre-Roman society. A king and his warriors could expect to be fed and provided with basic necessities from within the community, but the local resource base was not rich in valuable trade goods. Access to wealth could only be gained by drawing upon the resources of neighbouring communities which could be used to enhance those of your own, or exchanged in the limited international market for imports. The young female slaves of good birth and education whom the soldiers of Coroticus seized from Irish monasteries were destined for markets in Pictland. While this clearly enraged St Patrick, it is difficult to see how else northern British political leadership could have functioned, or could have protected the local community. Raiding, then, was a necessary evil among the successor states in which all indulged, and it mattered little if the raider and raided shared a Roman provincial origin. The economy after c. AD 410 was devoid of coinage, and the raiding of the early fifth century

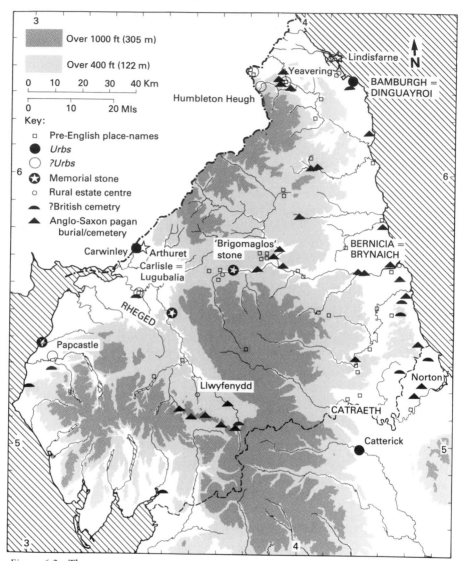

Figure 6.2 The successor states: a reconstruction.

probably led to the outflow of what bullion remained in northern England. Only slaves provided the northern British kings with an entrée to international markets.

Whatever its faults, this system had successfully established the independence of the northern Britons, and had underpinned that independence for most of a century by the time Gildas was writing. In most areas, no break occurred before the late sixth century. In addition, Gildas recorded a long period of prosperity in the late fifth and early sixth centuries, for which we must allow credit to the leaders of the successor states, however brutal their methods.

The political geography of the northern Britons only becomes recognizable, and then not uniformly, in the late sixth century, from which time have survived a Latin annal tradition, genealogical material in English and Celtic and a Celtic poetic tradition. However, the impression gained is of rapid change, with dynasties enjoying short-lived successes, and kingdoms subject to frequent boundary changes. Outside of warrior bands and the royal household, it seems likely that few communities enjoyed a well-established and long-lived political identity beyond the estate within which they lived. Even so, some of the protohistoric states betray broad parallels with the pre-Roman tribal territories, but in only one case does the name survive in recognizable form. The Votadini re-emerged as the kingdom of Gododdin, but only in the Lothians, that is, the northern half of that territory assigned to them by Ptolemy. South of the Lammermuir Hills, there is no evidence to suggest that Gododdin was ever an established, sub-Roman power. The emerging English kingdom in Northumberland had anglicized a Celtic name to Bernicia, presumably in origin a Celtic kingdom centred in part of the Tyne–Tweed lowlands (see below, and Fig. 6.3).

South of the Tyne, the Tyne and Wear and north Durham lowlands were probably part of Bernicia, including, perhaps enclaves of pagan English settled on the Tees estuary, as evidenced at Norton cemetery [7], although it is as yet unclear how early these should be placed. West Cleveland and the rich agricultural lands of southern Durham (below the Wear) make a discrete unit, contained by the Pennines to the west and the Cleveland Hills to the south-east, but open to neighbouring areas via Dere Street to the north and south, and the Stainmore Pass to the west. If the whole of this region was one political entity, it should be equated with Catraeth (Catterick(?)), known to us from poetic sources to have been ruled by Urien, and then, to have been the target of the expedition recounted in the *Gododdin* poem.

West of the Pennines, the south Cumbrian lowlands are not specifically mentioned, and Rheged, again associated with King Urien, should probably be identified with the Solway plain and the Eden valley. The place-names Dunragit in Galloway and Recedham (Rochdale in Domesday Book) have attracted the suggestion that Rheged encompassed at some stage a very substantial territory, uniting the various coastal plains from the Solway to the Mersey. The latter, at least, is unlikely to represent a genuine tradition. Until proved otherwise it is rash to see Rheged extending south of Tebay or, at furthest, Kirkby Lonsdale, and the kingdom may be broadly conterminous with the earlier *civitas Carvetiorum*.

The Rheged kings were not unchallenged in 'Dark Age' Cumbria; this seems at least to be the implication of the career of Pabo and his family. He was present at the Battle of Arthuret in AD 573, but successfully outlived Urien. His dynasty should probably be associated with Papcastle (Miller 1975d). If any

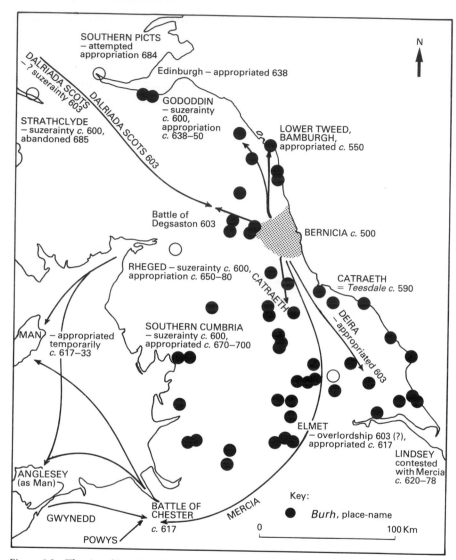

Figure 6.3 The rise of Bernicia, showing the extension of political influence and the expansion of the state.

credence can be given to the poems of Taliesin, there is at least a suggestion that Cumbria was subject to warfare and raiding before Urien gained control, and the implication may be that he seized Rheged in a period of doubt, striking from his existing power base beyond Stainmore identified as Catraeth.

Further north, Strathclyde was governed by a long-lived and successful dynasty from the stronghold on Dumbarton Rock. Although Coroticus may be properly identified with this dynasty, it is unlikely that the genealogists correctly identified its lineal descent before the reign of Riderch in the late sixth century (Miller 1975c).

The kingdoms that emerged into historical record in the late sixth century were ruled by kings who were locked into a competitive cycle of raiding, and defence of the home territory against enemy raids. For such a purpose did Urien post soldiers on his frontiers during the summer months, and fight off Pictish raiders in the Eden valley. He, in turn, led raids against the English and Gododdin. Success in war enabled the King to attract and reward warriors and other servants, including poets. Urien may have 'poached' Taliesin from Powys. Raiding not only involved the removal of the resources of rivals to territory held by the raiders, it required in addition, that the ability of neighbours to reciprocate be reduced by wasting. The language of eulogy employed by both Taliesin and Aneirin underlines this role, success in the raid, the theft of neighbours' cattle and the defence of the home base. Urien was portrayed as lord of Christendom, raider of cattle and a leader who burnt the homes of the English and took their 'attire' (Morris-Jones 1918). Cattle-raiding was a popular epic theme in contemporary Irish society.

The courts over which these warlords presided are known to us only from poetry, in which warfare eclipses all other activities. The fundamental bond was that existing between the lord and the warrior band who served him in the expectation of generous reward. If the *Gododdin* poem has any value as a historical document, it provides an insight into this relationship. The warriors of Mynyddog the Wealthy wore patterned cloth or silk, with a range of amber and gold ornament, and drank from horns, glass tumblers or gold or silver cups their mead, wine, bragget or ale, while reclining on a couch. The host that rode to Catraeth was accoutred with spears and swords, and protected by mail-shirts and shields, but apparently not helmets. The generosity of a prince was a suitable subject of eulogy.

Wine, glassware and silk had to be imported from European sources, and this required the movement of trade goods into the border counties, paid for by the export of small quantities of raw materials and slaves. Slaves could derive from criminals within the state – one murderer was recorded as having been sold to the kin of his victim (Adomnan, I, 87b) – but many probably came from neighbouring communities via raiding. The origin of those freed by Bishop Aidan is not stated (Bede, *Hist. Eccles.*, III, 5).

This limited foreign trade underlines the importance of water transport, which we have already identified as essential to barbarian raiders. The lives of the saints abound with reference to voyages, and the kings of northern Britain retained more than a passing interest in ships and the seaways. Sea communications were on a level that has enabled some to identify an Irish Sea culture province (Bowen 1969; Alcock 1970).

A historical account, albeit a fragmentary one, is feasible from the 570s onwards. The Battle of Armterid in AD 573 was known to the compiler of the *Annales Cambriae*. Armterid has been provisionally identified as Arthuret in the extreme north of Cumbria. In later tradition the principal leader on the losing side was Gwenddolen, whose name may be enshrined in the adjacent place-name Carwinley – Caer Gwenddolen. The battle was remembered for its ferocity, and the heroic constancy of the war-band of the dead leader (Miller 1975d). The real bone of contention may have been Wardlaw fort, above Caerlaverock (the 'city of the lark's nest'; Chadwick 1976: 100). There is, however, no evidence that the site was occupied in the post-Roman era. Both of the losing leaders are associated with areas linked with the Selgovae of late prehistory, Dingad son of Cynan with Powys in Liddesdale and Gwenddolen and his brother with lower Eskdale and Upper Tweeddale. Their opponents probably controlled wider territories. Cynfelyn of the Strathclyde dynasty was associated with Dunod the Stout, son of Pabo (of Papcastle?), but the chief members of the coalition were Gwrgi and Peredur, sons of Eliffer, presumably from northern England and arguably from Rheged. At the same time, there are hints that the Strathclyde dynasty had been successful in installing two of its own members, Clydno and Cadrod, in Gododdin at the expense of the Coeling dynasty.

The Armterid conflict may have been fought over control of the Solway, in which case the rulers of Cumbria may have sought to remove rivals on the northern shore who threatened their communications via the estuary. What remains to us is a tradition of ferocious conflict between two coalitions, the membership of which was exclusively British. The successful coalition consisted of several dynasties some of which were already engaged in aggression towards their British neighbours. The sons of Eliffer died in conflict with the English in AD 584, in ignominious circumstances, abandoned by their war-band, and it may have been in the aftermath that Urien secured Rheged. The Armterid conflict was not only the first recorded of these British struggles, it was also the last, and local political events after AD 580 were to be dominated by the growth of the power of English kings.

The Rise of Bernicia

Germanic troops were no strangers to the wall during the third and fourth centuries. A German *numerus* is, for example, well known at Housesteads, from epigraphic sources and from the finds of Frisian-style pottery (I. Jobey 1979). However, there is no evidence that these forces survived the break-up of the late Roman army, or provided a nucleus for the formation of English communities.

The only English kingdom to emerge in the border counties was that of Bernicia, known to *Brittonic* speakers as Brynaich, occupying, by about

AD 580, an area roughly conterminous with the modern counties of Northumberland and Tyne and Wear (see Fig. 6.3). Because little diagnostic archaeological evidence has been identified of English settlement before the later sixth century, modern, historical interpretation has tended to accept the tradition that the English settlement of Bernicia derived from Deira. That Soemil, the sixth ancestor from King Edwin (died AD 633) first separated the two kingdoms is a tradition reported in the *Historia Brittonum* (61), but this genealogy is not historical before the mid sixth century at the earliest, and should not be given much credence. Ida is the first Bernician king of whom the *Historia* offers any details, and his reign probably represents the horizon of Northumbrian historical traditions.

That Bernicia was ruled by English kings in the late sixth century is well established, but to suppose that this dynasty rose from captains of a coastal pirate stronghold at Bamburgh in *c.* AD 550, to be overlords of Britain early in the seventh century requires some explanation. An alternative account has been offered by Hope-Taylor (1977), whose reconstruction of the settlement chronology at Yeavering led him to postulate a Bernicia already independent of Gododdin by AD 500 and ruled by a separate dynasty. The arrival of the English may be associated with the tradition recorded in the *Historia Brittonum* (38) by which Vortigern despatched forty keels of the Saxons under Octha son of Hengist, and Ebissa his cousin, to fight the Scots (he presumably meant the Picts) in return for land 'in the North by the wall'. The account is of dubious historicity, although Octha's subsequent departure to Kent is at least mentioned, thereby retaining the internal consistency of the tradition. A cruciform brooch of Anglo-Saxon type made about AD 500 was found at Corbridge, and is the earliest of a small number of English metal artefacts lost in the Tyne area during the sixth century. Suffice it to say that pagan English warriors may have penetrated Tyne and Wear at the end of the fifth century or soon after. The political activity, as kingmakers, of contemporary British war-bands should be enough to render the subsequent elevation of English kings in Bernicia both plausible and likely.

The *Historia Brittonum* (61–3) utilized a Bernician genealogy, and the historical information associated with Ida and his sons may be correct, although the genealogy appears to break down in the late sixth and again in the late seventh century. Ida supposedly reigned for twelve years, was credited with two sons and joined Bamburgh (Dinguaroi) to Bernicia. The next entry records the valiant resistance of Dutigern (Euderyn) to the English, an entry possibly derived from a poetic source, given that the author next reviews the famous contemporary British poets. The sequence implies, but does not require, that these entries describe events which were associated in some respect.

The statement that Ida joined Bamburgh to Bernicia has been dismissed as a garbled reference to the later union of Bernicia and Deira. The author was well aware that the two provinces were later joined, and records it in the next passage. He knew that Bamburgh was almost synonymous with Bernicia by the early seventh century. It is only an implausible statement if we follow the view of Bernician history proposed by Stenton (1943: 74), in which the English colony originated on and around Bamburgh. In practice this is unlikely. The statement is a consistent element in an account that has English settlement initially in the Tyne area, but then encountering opposition from a British kingdom, situated between the central Northumberland hills and the Lammermuirs beyond Tweed, and based at Bamburgh, and in the Milfield basin.

The archaeological record is not substantial, but it is entirely consistent with this interpretation – Christian inscribed stones are almost entirely absent from Northumberland, but present throughout the periphery from the Lothians to Chesterholm, where the 'Brigomaglos' stone of *c.* AD 500 commemorated a member of the British aristocracy (Jackson 1982). Burials (see below) of the Christian British communities have been identified in all regions of south Scotland and northern England except southern Northumberland. A long cist cemetery immediately outside Bamburgh, found on the golf course south of the castle, reinforces but does not prove the claims of that site as a Christian, British centre (Miket 1980). The earliest inhumation cemeteries found at Yeavering may owe something to this tradition (Hope-Taylor 1977); both preceded the construction of a Christian church on the site by the recently converted English kings in the early seventh century. Close by, near Coldstream, is the only *eccles* place-name so far identified in the Tyne–Tweed region and the site of a newly discovered, Christian site dating from as early as the fifth century. These elements lend some substance to the existence of a British kingdom in northern Northumberland, conquered by Ida in the mid sixth century, and Dutigern or Outigern (Eudeyrn) is a likely candidate as the last British king.

Pagan Anglo-Saxon burials and cemeteries are scarce and impoverished in the North-east (Miket 1980). Those which can be identified as likely examples are scattered widely along the coast and in the upper river valleys between Weardale and Alnmouth (Northumb.). Outliers exist on Teesside near Darlington in the south, including the cemetery of eighty graves or more, recently identified and under excavation at Norton, close to the Tees estuary. A substantial group is concentrated on and adjacent to the known royal estates in the Milfield basin, but interpretation of the latter is difficult. One further piece of evidence may be of some significance. Blood groups identified in northern England have close parallels with those of upland Wales (Potts 1976). The slight divergence traced east of the Pennines, centres on Tyne and Wear and northern Durham. In both gene *p* and gene *r*, northern Northumberland is identical with southern Scotland. It therefore seems possible that a British community under independent kings did maintain themselves north of Alnwick until displaced by Ida, who could then be said to be 'first King of Bernicia' (*Historia Brittonum*, 56) or the founder of the royal family of the Northumbrians (Bede, *Hist. Eccles.* v, 24).

The union of all Northumberland, Tyne and Wear and northern Durham under one dynasty created a powerful resource base, arguably richer and more populous than those of its neighbours, in the control of a king whose success attracted ambitious warriors to his court. The reign of Ida was a critical step towards English dominance.

In the aftermath, we are ill informed as to events in the North-east in the 560s and 570s. However, Urien of Catraeth is said to have fought against Deo(d)ric (Theodoric), son of Ida, and his sons, and with British allies against Hussa, a Bernician king whose genealogical descent from Ida is not given, and possibly may well not have existed (*Historia Brittonum*, 63). Hussa was the predecessor but not the father of Aethelfrith (AD 593–617) who was a grandson of Ida, and may have emerged as a strong war leader of the Bernicians at a critical stage of the conflict with neighbouring kingdoms.

The only member of the Lindisfarne alliance certainly identifiable is Riderch the Old (died AD 614), son of Tudwal and King of Strathclyde (Miller 1975c). Urien is known from the poetry of Taliesin as King of Catraeth and of Rheged, and later Welsh systematizers linked his genealogy with that of Coel Hen. This link is unhistorical, but the tradition that associates him with the Cynferchyn war-band may be more reliable. Riderch was associated with the Cynwydyon war-band. Gwallog may be associated with Elfed (Elmet), in West Yorkshire leaving Morcant (Morgan) as the likeliest leader of the Coeling war-band, from Gododdin. The confederacy, therefore, seems to have brought together the neighbours of Bernicia from the north, west and south, and implies considerable alarm at the growing strength of the English kings. Urien, ruler already of two kingdoms and perhaps the overlord of Elmet to the south is the likely leader. His strongest association is not with Rheged but with Catraeth, and there is a hint in the poetic sources that his dynasty was not long established in either kingdom. He may, therefore, be seen as a warlord who was elevated by a war-band, welding together a substantial power base exactly parallel to that of the Bernician kings, but one which in the event proved less resilient, and which failed to long survive his own death.

Hope-Taylor suggested that the confederates launched a pre-emptive naval strike against the Bernician fleet, but this interpretation is not entirely consistent with the account we have, and both Rheged and Strathclyde would have experienced difficulty in concentrating a fleet off the Northumbrian coast. The likely course of events would have been substantial raids, particularly against the heartland of Bernicia in the south on the Tyne, forcing Hussa to withdraw northwards and take refuge on Lindisfarne. Urien was then murdered while on an expedition (presumably raiding for booty), at the instigation of Morcant. The obvious bone of contention would have been the lordship of Bamburgh and the predominantly British community of northern Northumberland. Urien's death ended the alliance, and left Hussa in control of all Bernicia and its resources.

The last British attempt to stifle Bernicia was the expedition launched by

Mynyddog the Wealthy of Gododdin against Catraeth. The latter had been one of Urien's kingdoms, but had apparently been lost to the English (presumably of Bernicia) in the 590s. An epic poem, accredited to Aneirin is the only source for the expedition which was a disastrous failure, and ended with the annihilation of the attacking force (Jackson 1969). Mynyddog assembled warriors from Gododdin itself, Pictland, Ayrshire, Elmet, Gwynedd, Anglesey and elsewhere in Wales. The army was numbered variously 300 and 363; the editor suggested that the real strength must have been about ten times greater, but the poem is obviously not reliable at this level. The number 300 is an all too common building brick in medieval Welsh poetry. It is an attractive hypothesis that the army may have been able to reach Catraeth by marching through north-west England and over Stainmore, but if Morcant should really be identified in Gododdin, then the sons of Urien in Rheged might be among its most committed opponents. There appears to be sufficient reference to historical personnel to justify treating the *Gododdin* poem as a historical document, but this may of course be an illusion. If it was historical, it may have been launched at King Aethelfrith of Bernicia soon after his accession in AD 593.

Whatever the relevance of the *Gododdin* poem, Aethelfrith quickly established himself as the dominant force in the North. His raids into neighbouring British territory destroyed all resistance, and robbed his rivals of the power and will to retaliate. The ruthlessness of his campaigns was still a powerful tradition in the early eighth century when Bede recorded his 'exterminating or enslaving the inhabitants, making their lands either tributary to the English or ready for English settlement' [8]. The likely direction of his activities lie in Gododdin and Strathclyde, where he caused such alarm among the Dalriada Scots, the near neighbours of Strathclyde to the north, that King Aedan led a Scottish army against him in AD 603. Aethelfrith destroyed the Scots at *Degsaston*, perhaps in Upper Liddesdale, near Dawston, but the two names are probably not etymologically connected. By AD 603, Aethelfrith was strong enough to intervene in Deira to the south. He seized the kingdom, married the daughter of Aella the last king and drove her brother into exile in southern Britain, and continued to do what he could to ensure that his dynastic rival met an untimely end. Northumbria was born. Despite the ensuing history of conflict between the two dynasties, the unity which Aethelfrith had imposed by force was a powerful political factor in succeeding generations, and Northumbria was immediately a power to be reckoned with throughout Britain.

The absorption of Deira by a Bernician king says much for the power and prestige he had accumulated by his decade or more of raids against the Britons. It was as the arbiter of the resources of the whole Tees–Forth province that he was enabled to move against the rich and populous kingdom in Yorkshire, and associate the Deirans with his own success as a war leader.

The Northumbrian Supremacy

The Northumbria of Aethelfrith consisted of three separate but integrated elements. He ruled as King in Deira and Bernicia. Other areas recently held by British kings were controlled directly, and English settlement was encouraged. Such may have included the Tweed basin. In addition, British kings were prevailed upon to follow his leadership, and almost certainly paid tribute. The account of King Edwin requires the King of Elmet to have been a tribute-paying subordinate of Aethelfrith (*Historia Brittonum*, 63); his death in AD 616 was recorded in the *Annales* after which his kingdom was absorbed by Edwin. It is at least likely that the kings of Rheged, Strathclyde and Gododdin were similarly subject to Aethelfrith after AD 600, when all hope of withstanding his forces must have evaporated, and the possibility exists that the Scots of Dalriada were similarly placed after AD 603. Henceforth, the major conflicts in which seventh-century Northumbria became involved were with more distant neighbours, very largely in the Midlands and north Wales. The political preoccupations of the kings required that the unity of Northumbria be maintained, and the northern resource base be protected.

Aethelfrith retained both kingdoms until his death, but it was probably in pursuit of his rival and brother-in-law Edwin that he launched the great raid on Wales that led to the Battle of Chester. Edwin sought support in Gwynedd, Mercia (where he contracted an early marriage) and East Anglia, and it was with military support from King Raedwald of East Anglia that Edwin seized the thrones of Northumbria in AD 617, driving the sons of his predecessor in turn into exile among the Picts and Scots. Between AD 617 and his death in AD 633, Edwin exercised enormous power and influence, and was listed among the Bretwaldas or overlords of Britain by Bede (*Hist. Eccles.*, II, 5; see John 1966). In addition he took control of Man and Anglesey, the keys to the Irish Sea, and clearly possessed a substantial fleet. Man was thereby drawn into the English area of influence for the first time. Among the court pedigrees of Hywel the Good, genealogy IV supposedly traces the descent of the Celtic kings of Man, one of whom (Mermin) in the seventh century is known from other sources. It was hitherto within the Scottish sphere of influence. Edwin's penetration of the 'Irish Sea Province' and, in particular, his seizure of Anglesey may have prompted the great raid by Cadwallon and his Mercian allies in AD 633 which resulted in the death in battle of King Edwin. His young children by his second marriage fled with their mother to Kent and eventually to Gaul. In the crisis, Edwin's cousin took over Deira and Aethelfrith's son seized Bernicia, but both were killed within twelve months. Oswald, a younger son of Aethelfrith restored the fortunes of his dynasty by success in war, and reunited the two kingdoms 'by diplomacy' (Bede, *Hist. Eccles.*, III, 6). His death in battle in AD 642 led to renewed separation, only ended in AD 651 by the murder of the King of Deira by Oswald's brother, Oswy. The circumstances of this confrontation imply that, of the two kingdoms, Bernicia was able to field the stronger forces, a situation only likely if the subordinate areas of British territory provided part of the resource base that fuelled Oswy's ability to attract warriors. Henceforth, Northumbria was ruled as one kingdom, but it is clear that Deiran and Bernician separatism revived as a significant political force as late as the ninth century, and it seems to have been a factor even at the level of the burial of St Oswald at Bardney Abbey (Bede, *Hist. Eccles.*, III, 11).

Disaster in war was the invariable precursor of dynastic conflicts in Northumbria, but disasters were inevitable given the expansionist ambitions of the Northumbrian kings from the reign of Aethelfrith up to the death of Ecgfrith. Except when in the direst straits, the English kings had no difficulty in exercising overlordship over their British neighbours whom they could dispossess almost at will. In the year AD 638 the *Annals of Ulster* noted the siege of Eten (Jackson 1959). This almost certainly represents the capture of Edinburgh by the troops of King Oswald and the final absorption of Lothian and all Gododdin into the Northumbrian state. The fall of Edinburgh extinguished the British kingdom of Gododdin, but that kingdom must have been tributary to the English overlord for a generation. The Edinburgh campaign represents not the conflict of equal partners, but the expulsion by Oswald of a subordinate whose resources he required to bolster the flow of royal patronage.

The major crisis of the Northumbrian monarchy between AD 603 and 685 came not from the north but from the south. In pursuit of Deiran interests in Lindsey and elsewhere, the Northumbrian kings entered into a long and bitter conflict with their southern neighbours. After Edwin and one of his sons had been killed at Hadfield in AD 633, Cadwallon and his allies set about the systematic wasting of Northumbria. Oswald of Bernicia killed Cadwallon at the Battle of Hexham in the following year, but the struggle for supremacy continued, and Oswald and his successors were hard pressed by Penda of Mercia. Oswald was killed at the Battle of Maserfelth in AD 642 [9] and his brother, Oswy, was placed under considerable pressure by them, pursued to the northern limits of his kingdom and there forced to disgorge booty to Penda and the Welsh kings. In the same campaigns, Bamburgh was attacked, although it withstood the Mercians. Oswy's son and daughter both married into the Mercian royal house, and Ecgfrith spent a period as hostage at the Mercian court. Oswy was probably at times a tribute-paying king, subordinate to Penda, but he did eventually succeed in killing his enemy in AD 657, and enjoyed a short-lived supremacy over his successor, and over southern Pictland (Bede, *Hist. Eccles.*, III, 25).

The conflict with the Mercians continued, with a battle near the Trent in AD 679, but a peace was negotiated by Archbishop Theodore which recognized the independence of both kingdoms. This peace represents the abandonment by the Northumbrian kings of their ambitions south of the Humber. In the aftermath, King Ecgfrith reasserted his supremacy in the North beyond the Britons, raiding Ireland and Dalriada, and was killed in AD 685 while attempting the same in Pictland.

His successor, Aldfrith, was unable to restore the fortunes of Bernicia. Despite renewed conflict with the Picts in AD 698, Northumbrian influence was withdrawn south of the Forth, and the King had to acknowledge the independence of the Scottish kings of Dalriada and the British kings of Strathclyde. Although Northumbrian control of north-west England and south-west Scotland was unshaken, the kingdom that entered the eighth century was relatively weak, and had lost the opportunity to dominate Britain, outfaced and outfought by the kingdoms in direct control of the wealthier resources of Britain south of the Pennines.

Cities, citadels and forts

The British and English kings have been identified with specific citadels or forts, often described by contemporaries as *urbes*. Thus the Strathclyde monarchy was linked to the rock of Alcluith – Dumbarton Rock on the Clyde, and Gododdin to din Eidyn – Edinburgh. From Ida's reign, Bamburgh is described as a fortified *urbs* (Bede, *Hist. Eccles.*, III, 16), and closely identified with the kings of Bernicia. It has been suggested above that this usurped a pre-existing identification between that site under a Celtic name and a British dynasty. The association of Carlisle with Rheged has proved to be generally acceptable (Thomas 1968; Chadwick 1976), but should be treated with caution (McCarthy 1982). The kingdom of Catraeth may be associated with an *urbs* of the same name, but identification has been disputed between the indefensible and atypical site of Catterick and the castle site at Richmond, although the fifth-century evidence and the crucial site of the former must tell in its favour.

The problem remains one of evidence. At some sites, subsequent occupation has destroyed archaeological horizons and limited access. The excavations at Bamburgh have never been published in detail, but a lengthy occupation sequence was identified, beginning before the Roman Conquest, and continuing during the occupation. An episode associated with 'native' pottery but later than the third century AD, was sealed by massive deposits of charcoal, possibly associated with Anglo-Saxon pottery, laid down before the seventh century (Hope-Taylor 1977: fn. 339). This sequence might represent the successive British and Anglo-Saxon royal occupation of the site. That it functioned as a citadel in the mid seventh century is clear from Bede's account, by which time the term *urbs* has none of the Roman connotations, but represents a high-status dwelling, presumably with accommodation for retainers and an extended household, within a fortification (Campbell 1978). The presence north of the wall even in the mid fifth century, of towns (*civitates*) operating on the Roman–British model is inconceivable. Only Corbridge and Carlisle are likely to have maintained a civic organization and identity into the fifth century, and at neither site is it likely that recognizable urban communities survived by AD 450, despite the evidence for late-fifth-century use of the cemeteries at Corbridge and elsewhere.

Opinion to the contrary has centred on Carlisle, and fed on the visit of St Cuthbert to the site in AD 685, when the city wall and a well or fountain built by the Romans were shown to him by Waga, the *praepositus* of the *urbs* of Lugubalia. These relics of the past are not evidence of continuous occupation, and the *praepositus* need be no more than a reeve, responsible for what must have been a recent ecclesiastical establishment within a fortified site under royal patronage. A fragmentary post-Roman structure has been identified on Blackfriars Street, forming, at minimum, a 12 m × 6.2 m rectangular building, defined by a construction trench containing closely spaced uprights, disregarding the alignments of the late Roman occupation (McCarthy 1982). This building is not dated, but a seventh- or eighth-century date would obviously be feasible (Fig. 6.6). The change of alignment would suggest a period of abandonment, since the early fifth century, long enough for all traces of pre-existing building alignments to disappear. The survival of the Roman place-name at least demonstrates continuity of settlement in the area, but much of Roman Carlisle can be shown to have been succeeded by black earth of the kind associated elsewhere with agricultural activity, and a shrinking population. Of Carlisle's churches the alignment of St Cuthbert's suggests it might have been initially constructed within constraints imposed by late Roman buildings, but this is far from certain. The presence of a Northumbrian queen in AD 685 need not imply a royal palace, since the recently founded and royally patronized religious house could have provided both her and St Cuthbert with adequate lodging. That Bede knew Carlisle as Lugubalia, a Celtic rendering of the Romano-British place-name, may imply that the *caer* prefix (fort) was not attached to the site until the renewed *Brittonic* interest in the area in the tenth century. Occupation of the site in the late fifth and sixth centuries is unproven, and although use of the site by the kings of Rheged must remain an attractive hypothesis, it is entirely speculative.

The households of the nobility were necessarily peripatetic, needing to move from one estate to another in order to consume the surplus. The economy after *c.* AD 420 was devoid of any recognizable medium of exchange, and taxation was generally in kind. Even if certain sites were considered defensible and could be used as a retreat at the last resort, kings necessarily spent most of the year elsewhere, on sites less heavily defended and less easily identified. Some, at least, of the 'citadel'-type hillforts in south Scotland were occupied in the post-Roman period (Alcock 1970). One of these has been identified in

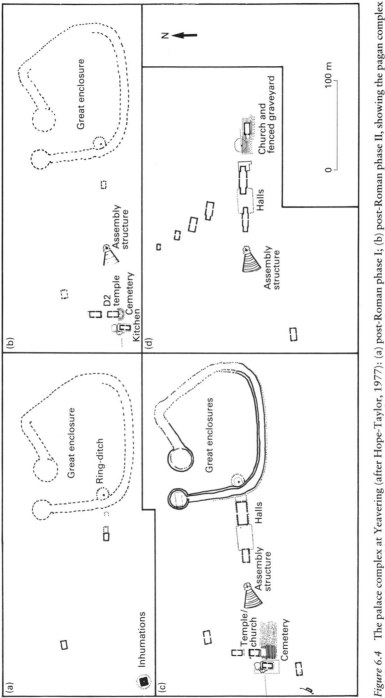

Figure 6.4 The palace complex at Yeavering (after Hope-Taylor, 1977): (a) post-Roman phase I; (b) post-Roman phase II, showing the pagan complex and the emergence of the assembly structure; (c) post-Roman phase IIIc (*c.* King Edwin), showing developments to the 'fort' structure, the emergence of major, secular timber halls and changes to the religious complex; (d) post-Roman phase IV (*c.* King Oswald) – the fort is not rebuilt, and is replaced by a Christian complex adjacent to the 'palace' buildings.

Northumberland, at Humbleton Heugh on the edge of the Cheviots, overlooking the valley of the river Glen and close to Yeavering (Jobey 1965b). Although it contains the typical late prehistoric quota of round-house stands, occupation or reoccupation of the site is an attractive possibility, entirely consistent with the case made above for a British kingdom in that area before the reign of Ida.

Most estate centres were probably not fortified. A favourite estate centre of Urien seems to have been a familiar subject for Taliesin who mentioned Llwyfenydd (Lyvennet, Crosby Ravensworth, Cumbria (?)) in three surviving poems (Williams 1968; Hogg 1946). One poem at least was arguably composed for recitation for his patron when present in his 'palace'. The *Eulogy of Urien* can be read as implying an outright gift of the estate to the poet, but a more attractive interpretation would be that Taliesin enjoyed its bounty rather by virtue of his position in the household of a generous patron.

> The lands of Llwyfenydd, mine is their wealth,
> Mine is their courtesy, mine is their bounteousness
> Mine are their feasts and their luxuries –
> Mead out of horns and good things without stint,
> From the best prince, the most generous I have heard of
> (transl. Morris-Jones 1918).

In the mid seventh century, the Northumbrian kings had numerous rural seats (Bede, *Hist. Eccles.*, III, 17). Yeavering was one such estate centre, in the Milfield basin in northern Bernicia (Fig. 6.4). A great defended or enclosed meeting-place was repeatedly and ambitiously reconstructed, in a sequence that began arguably in the fifth century or before, and ended *c.* AD 685 (Hope-Taylor 1977). Outside it, and totally undefended, was a long-lived estate centre, identified by Bede with the royal house in the reign of Edwin. The earliest phase of post-Roman occupation utilized small, rectangular, post-hole structures which may have predated the English Conquest (see Fig. 6.4). The first, identified English occupation incorporated a *Grubenhaus* style of building, upstanding structures in the 'Saxo-Frisian' tradition and the prototype of the great timber-built 'theatre', or political arena. These were succeeded by buildings of great size and of high secular status, presumably acting as an occasional residence of the Bernician monarchy. The great oak-built halls were associated with very few discarded artefacts, in itself a factor entirely consistent with occasional occupation. The royal household may have timed visits to the site to coincide with local assemblies using the 'fort' for social, economic or religious purposes. The 'theatre' surely implies that the kings expected to be seen and heard by the local population and the site may have been the scene of solemn, crown-wearing ceremonies accompanied by much regalia. The occupation of the palace complex in phase III occurred probably in the reign of King Edwin, and it is attractive to associate the fire that ended it with the campaign of Cadwallon in AD 632–33. If so, his forces were responsible for the deaths of the occupants of sixty-four graves. The site was rebuilt (phase IV) by King Oswald but once again destroyed by fire, presumably by Penda in the early 650s. Reoccupation of the site (phase V) was less substantial, with a small number of minor structures built with planks and nails. By about AD 685, the site was completely abandoned, probably in favour of the more enclosed palace complex at Milfield.

In contemporary literature, occasional oblique references to buildings of high status imply that the great hall of Edwin at Yeavering was not of a type exclusive to the English areas. The hall of Mynyddog at Edinburgh was reputed to be adequate to feast a war-band of 300 men or more for a year. The exact numbers are immaterial, but the impression is of a sizeable palace. One of the miracles associated with St Columba is linked to the problems of moving dressed timbers of pine and oak for a longship, and for a great house (Adomnan, I, 100a). The presence of a great hall of sixth-century date at Dunbar in Lothian implies that British kings, as well, could command the skills of architects and carpenters familiar with buildings more characteristically associated with the English occupation. The tradition of building great halls of the kind known from *Beowulf* may well have been a common tradition throughout north-west Europe, and not the exclusive preserve of any one race or language group, but they were the preserve of the wealthy and the powerful. Other important examples have been identified from the air at Sprouston, Borders, on the Tweed (Reynolds 1980: Fig. 7), and an equally complex group have been discovered by Prof. Jones and the author at Ronaldsway on the Isle of Man. Both could represent the extension of English influence and control in the North, but other interpretations remain possible.

English colonization and Anglicization

The border counties in AD 500 were arguably British in all important respects. By AD 800, British culture, leadership, language and religious organization had been eclipsed by alternatives that were in many important respects recognizably English. The process by which that revolution occurred is still a matter of debate, but, over several decades, that debate has drifted away from the ethnocentric interpretation by which the change consisted of complete or near-complete replacement of the earlier population by another, more successful one. Celtic survival in English Northumbria is not in question; what is, is the nature and extent of that survival.

Any survey of this subject must begin in the heartland of Bernicia. If substantial Celtic survival occurred there, then its presence elsewhere in the North is not in doubt. The basis of the reinterpretation offered by Hope-Taylor was that the English occupation of Bernicia required very small numbers of English colonists, who obtained control by inserting themselves into an existing social and political structure at the most influential and rewarding points – that is, into the secular and religious aristocracy. This type of high-status political revolution is exactly what was achieved by King William and his followers after 1066. The English settlement led to the replacement of most pre-existing estate names, yet the Norman Conquest hardly affected the place-names of England. From this type of comparison has derived the thesis that place-names reflect the proportion and status of a community made up by a particular language group (e.g. Gelling 1976). Quite clearly other factors must be involved, including the time-lag before place-names were committed to writing, but the density of English place-names in Northumberland requires comment.

Northumberland, Tyne and Wear, Durham and Cleveland fall within the middle group for the survival of pre-English river names (Jackson 1956; Ekwall 1928), with a concentration of surviving names for small rivers south of the Tyne, in limited areas only, comparable to the high survival rate in Cumbria. The majority of stream names in Northumberland are English with burns particularly common, and English place-names are in the overwhelming majority, except in those areas south of the Tyne where Scandinavian made a significant late contribution.

Since the chronological primacy of names in *ingas* has now been dismissed in southern England (Dodgson 1966), there is no reason to give any particular priority to the few in southern Northumberland. Place-names in -*ham* may be comparatively early, but there may be some confusion with -*hamm*, particularly in the case of Carham, Norham and Crookham on the major rivers in the north of the country, and Ovingham on the Tyne. Names with the suffix -*tun* are common throughout the county and may represent a comparatively late stratum of place-name construction. However, names derived from topographical features are the commonest groups, and may, as elsewhere, be among the earliest to have been incorporated into the English language. Among those names committed to writing before AD 731, they are certainly dominant (Cox 1975/76). In Lower Teesdale, where the substantial pagan cemetery of Norton has been located, the several -*ham*, -*burh* and *ing(a)ton* place-names may be relics of early place-namings.

For the tiny minority for which early sources exist, the process by which place-names came into being diverges radically from traditional interpretations of colonial activity. The *Historia Brittonum* (63) records the renaming of Dinguaroi as a direct consequence of the gift of the site by King Aethelfrith to his queen, Bebbab – hence Bamburgh. Bede reiterates the story of its naming in two passages (*Hist. Eccles.*, III, 6, 16). The obvious inference must be that English speakers and British speakers had used the Celtic name for half a century at least, before replacement of the name occurred, by the obvious and commonest stratagem of identification with an individual and the addition of a suitable suffix. The renaming of din Eidyn was more conservative, and did no more than add the same suffix to the pre-existing major element, hence Edinburgh. Bede, writing in the early eighth century, used the Celtic names for both the Anglicized place-name Yeavering, and Milfield (*Hist. Eccles.*, II, 14). These were, therefore, used not only by King Edwin and his household, but presumably as late as Bede's own generation in the early eighth century. It is at least plausible to suppose that the name Ad Gefrin – hill of goats – was transferred from the hillfort to the nearby palace complex (Hope-Taylor 1977).

These are high-status sites, important for defensive functions or as estate centres. No places can have been so frequently the subject of reference by English royal households as these, yet the English-speaking community apparently accepted for generations pre-existing Celtic names, before either Anglicizing them or replacing them with English alternatives. If such occurred among royal estate centres, surely a similar pattern should be expected among some at least of the numerous sites of lower status with purely English names; place-names derived from topographical features are obvious candidates in this context and many may, as Mawer suggested, be the result of etymological perversion.

Another area of England with a comparable level of Celtic river-name survival has recently been subjected to a critical reappraisal, from which it has emerged that a significant proportion of modern place-names contain elements that originate in the Celtic language (Gelling 1976). The possibility exists that a similar exercise might achieve comparable results in Bernicia, and reinforce the presence of place-names arguably of Celtic origin such as the numerous town, village and farm names (Mawer 1920) in addition to Farne Island, Coquet, Lindisfarne, and the Cheviot hillforts Ros Castle, Rosebrough and Cateran Hill (see Fig. 6.3). It has been suggested that a Welsh-speaking population survived in northern Northumberland at least as late as the eighth century (Watts 1976).

In Durham, an attempt has been made to associate the scatter of Celtic river- and place-names with Roman fort sites and roads (Watts 1976), but the problem in dealing with Celtic survival from this evidence is underlined by the case of Auckland (derived from Alclit via Auklint). It is arguable that Celtic place-names are most numerous in those areas of Durham where English settlement occurred earliest – a suggestion with parallels in east Kent. The succession of partial place-name survivals along Dere Street and other roads may imply that the forts or their *vici* found new life in the fifth and sixth centuries as estate centres and cemeteries (Thomas 1981: Fig. 44), but some, at least, of the name survivals quoted by Thomas are debatable, as in the case of Brougham (Brocavum).

Why did the Northumbrian community replace, or substantially alter, some Celtic place-names at some stage after initially accommodating them? A clue may appear in the *Historia Ecclesiastica*. Bede habitually translates names in *Brittonic* or *Goedelic* British into English (see C. Smith 1979). Inisboufinde was the Scottish name for an obscure island off the west coast of Ireland, for which no English name is likely to have existed, but Bede translates the name as 'Isle of the White Heifer' (*Hist. Eccles.*, IV, 4). Streanaeshalch (Whitby) was translated as, 'the bay of the beacon' (*Hist. Eccles.*, III, 25). The northern British section of the *Historia Brittonum* perpetuates Celtic versions of place-names. Dinguaroi is Bamburgh and urbs Iudeu is Stirling (?), both probably representing a genuine tradition, but the replacement of Hexham by Cantscaul is arguably a translation of an existing English place-name into Welsh by a bilingual Welsh author writing for a British audience. Penda met his death in battle on the field of Gai, which Bede describes as near the river Winwaed (*Hist. Eccles.*, III, 24) and Lindisfarne is Metcaud (*Hist. Eccles.*, III, 63), close to that in Irish Inis Metgoit; one must have derived from the other. Both authors were either bilingual or could at least draw upon sufficient linguistic expertise to transpose place-names from one language to another. This ability may not have been unusual, but the scarcity of our early texts makes it impossible to pursue, except among the kings themselves (see C. Smith 1979).

Of the kings of Bernicia, several in the seventh century were certainly bilingual. The sons of Aethelfrith fled in AD 617 to seek refuge among the Picts and Scots, with whom they remained until AD 633, and with whom communication would have been essential. Oswald had a perfect command of the Scottish language. His elder brother married a Pictish princess, and his son, a daughter of the King of British Strathclyde. His younger brother, Oswy, married a great-granddaughter of Urien of Rheged – at least according to British tradition (Chadwick 1976). The English partners to these marriages, and the children of them, were exposed to the Celtic languages and some at least must have been understood. King Edwin spent part of his formative years in exile in Gwynedd, and the same arguments apply. During the crucial era of contact, the highest stratum of English society in the North was less than ignorant of the Celtic languages, and the English Church was for a generation staffed with Scots. Presumably, once Northumberland supremacy had been achieved, it suited Celtic speakers to become familiar with English. Otherwise it seems difficult to explain the number of English place-names within the sometime client kingdom of Strathclyde. However, these conditions may have been peculiar to Bernicia; King Oswin of Deira had no knowledge of the Scottish language.

Even in the heart of Bernicia it is unreasonable to argue directly from the high proportion of English place-names to a substantial and ethnically near-exclusive English colonization. The degree of Celtic survival cannot be known from place-name evidence. Place-names were both more mobile and less permanent than we might imagine. The transfer of place-names from one language to another was already under way in the sixth century, and names like Ellingham, Beadnell, Pittington, Sockburn and Cocker may already have existed by AD 700 (Watts 1976). Despite the transfer, a minority of place-names or place-name elements survived, perhaps for peculiar reasons. At Dacre (Cumbria) and Melrose (in Tweeddale) British names survived from the period of bilingualism, perhaps because of the English monastic communities sited there. Some Celtic place-names were replaced very late: Penteiacob (James's cottages) was still extant in the eleventh century, but by 1189 had been replaced by Eddleston (Jackson 1956). The strategically sited Romano-British sites of northern Durham and Tyneside have already been noted, and these lay in the heartland of that part of Bernicia where English settlement occurred earliest. This might imply that it was the early contact that introduced a degree of bilinguality into Anglo-Celtic affairs, and later 'colonization' that witnessed the abandonment of the Celtic language. Pockets of Celtic place-names occur, however, in south Cleveland and the North York Moors, where a Celtic-speaking population may have survived the seventh century.

Priority was given to the assimilation of east coast districts into the Bernician state. Catraeth had fallen by AD 600, and the fall of Edinburgh (AD 638) allowed Lothian to be likewise incorporated. It seems at least plausible to suppose that English kings and their followers recognized the better agricultural lands of northern Britain, and intentionally extended their patronage into it, placing a lower priority on the central and western uplands and the more limited potential of the western lowlands. Galloway and Cumbria were a lower priority, as was Strathclyde. Perhaps the lowest priority of all attached to Plain Furness and other isolated tracts of southern Cumbria. Cartmel was still in the King's hands under Ecgfrith when it was given with all its Britons to St Cuthbert by his friend and patron, and the anglicization of local place-names in much of Cumbria cannot much predate this and similar grants. St Cuthbert may have received little income from it, but it seems likely, supposing it to be genuine, that it allowed a trickle of 'English' administrators to penetrate the area (Birch 1885: 101). It probably represents a pattern of royal grants west of the Pennines of estates measured not in *vills* but in scores or hundreds of hides, or measured in miles radius round the estate centre. The small numbers of English that such grants brought into the area are represented by place-names formed by Celtic speakers such as Pennersax (hill of the Englishman) and Glensaxon (glen of the Englishman) in Dumfries and Galloway (Jackson 1963b). In Cumbria, Carhullon (the fort of Holand) represents a similar construction, but its formation could easily be tenth century or later. Even west of the Pennines, the vast majority of pre-Scandinavian township names are of English origin; many of the numerous Celtic names are arguably of the Scandinavian period.

If English place-names represent the spread of one ethnic stock, then the evidence implies wholesale replacement of the Celtic by the English peoples. However, there are other, and, arguably, more plausible explanations of the English colonization.

No one would doubt that English was the preferred first language of the Bernician royal house, aristocracy and administration from the sixth century onwards. In such circumstances, the speaking of English, and conscious self-anglicization, became necessary prerequisites for any ambitious individual. The stock of English speakers was, therefore, likely to have expanded rapidly once it became clear at the end of the sixth century that patronage throughout the North was in the hands of an English cultural enclave. Even by the mid sixth century, Celtic communities in Northumberland, Tyne and Wear and northern Durham had already been confronted with a situation in which all advantages, and expectation of advantage, lay with the English-speaking community. By AD 600 it is at least arguable that the Celtic community in Bernicia had become identified with, and genetically inseparable from, the English community. Such would explain the references to raiding among the English in the poems of Taliesin, and also the undiagnostic graves from Yeavering, which were arguably of a native, albeit an anglicized community (Hope-Taylor 1977).

In such circumstances, recent studies in historical demography imply that a population increase might have occurred among the privileged section of the community in northern England [10]. A drop in the average age at marriage, and an increase in average family size, would be logical consequences of such a situation. Given that the advantages were available not only to ethnic English stock, but also to anglicized families of a single generation or more, the consequent surge in the 'English' population could have been considerable. In addition, the structure of the rural medieval population required that population stability or increase resulted from the over-production of children by advantaged sections within the community, compensating for the under-production of children among disadvantaged sections (e.g. Razi 1980). If the parallel is of any relevance, it would seem to provide yet another mechanism by which an English-speaking community could achieve numerical dominance within several generations, particularly given the stimulus that plague deaths afforded [11].

Given these alternatives the spread of English communities identifiable among contemporaries solely by language (and among modern scholars by the place-names they created) becomes a credible phenomenon. The mechanics of the operation depended on the assertion by the Bernician royal house of royal prerogatives in neighbouring areas, allowing them to use those estates in the purchase of service by English-speaking warriors and other servants. The grantee naturally chose to administer distant estates via English speakers and colonists, and estate centres and documentation were thereby transferred from one language to another. From these the English language gradually permeated local society, and English place-names replaced British, or new communities were named from the first in English. This process was under way in the Tweed valley and Catraeth within the sixth century. The extinction of the royal line of Gododdin followed in AD 638, and Rheged fell to Bernician patronage, probably by marriage. Southern Pictland was the last area to come under royal patronage, and English 'colonization' was in full swing there when the disaster of AD 685 brought about a sudden reversal of fortunes – many of the 'English' were killed and others enslaved or forced to flee. Among the latter was Bishop Trumwine, representative in the area of the English Church, but surely also of his royal kinsman (Bede, *Hist. Eccles.*, IV, 26).

The real extent of genocidal conflict appears limited, at most, to the reigns of Hussa and Aethelfrith, when some neighbouring British communities were expelled or killed. However, Aethelfrith attracted to himself a Celtic nickname that can be translated as 'the artful dodger' (Jackson 1955) – hardly the most odious pseudonym available to his victims. It seems highly unlikely that even Aethelfrith had the resources to treat the populations of large areas in this way. The evidence from Durham and Cleveland implies a catastrophic population decline in Lower Weardale, that is, on the borders of Bernician territory. Contemporary with this, an agrarian economy survived in the Tees basin. Lower Weardale could plausibly have been the scene of English genocide, but if so, it benefited the English little and the farming land was not recolonized but was allowed to fall into disuse, suggesting that the English community had no available manpower to take up the land. West of the Pennines the case for genocide is very limited indeed. If the decline of cultivation in the late eighth century at Bolton Fell was typical, then the drop in population associated with it can have had little to do with the absorption by Bernicia, arguably already completed within the seventh century.

The crude picture of genocidal conflict is a highly misleading interpretation of contact between Celt and English, and the mechanisms by which one language group was replaced by another are likely to have been highly complex. That comparatively little true ethnic replacement occurred is at least a defensible opinion, and support for this attitude exists in recent studies in nearby east Yorkshire (Faull 1977), and as far afield as Hampshire, as well as in the study of local blood groups (Potts 1976). All that is beyond argument, is that by the ninth century at latest, the presence of Celtic speakers in northern England had sufficient curiosity value for some at least of those communities to attract names in *W(e)alh-* given them by their English-speaking neighbours. Such place-names occur in two Walworths names in south Durham (Watts and Prince 1982), and Walton near Brampton, but they are conspicuous by their absence along the borders. The end result of the process of anglicization was the creation of Northumbria out of the competing minor kingdoms of the northern Britons. That they should have shared a northern land frontier versus the Scots and Picts is unlikely to have been a coincidence.

The drop in total population evidenced by the palaeobotanical record and broadly contemporary with the rise of the English-speaking community may have assisted the latter development, and have allowed the advantaged sections of the community to secure self-advancement comparable to that by which many late-fourteenth-century villagers elevated their families, along a road which took them ultimately into the ranks of the sixteenth-century yeomanry. The cause of this population decline is unlikely to have lain in political circumstances; among several unpromising options, bubonic plague or a similar epidemic disease is probably the most attractive. It has been confirmed that St Cuthbert survived contracting bubonic plague during his residence at Melrose Abbey in the 650s (Rubin 1975), and this would suggest that outbreaks in the 660s and in AD 682 and 683 might have been similar manifestations of the disease. In this context, the survival by St Adomnan of his visit to plague-ridden Northumbria may indeed have seemed miraculous; the less fortunate Bishop Tuda succumbed to the widespread and sudden plague of AD 664 which struck both in Ireland and throughout Britain (Bede, III, 27). In a wider context, this may be the proper background against which to view the widespread abandonment of Romano-British-style farm sites and hamlets which is a general phenomenon in all areas. If plague-induced population decline was the major factor in late medieval village desertion, there seems a reasonable chance that the same applied in the seventh century.

Christianity and Paganism

Ecclesiastical affairs dominated the interests of the monk Bede, and provided the mainspring of his historical writing. In the circumstances, we are fortunate that so much political and social history found a place in his work. Even so, despite the prominence given Christianity by Bede himself, his predecessors and his contemporaries, there is no reason to suppose that the general community was either more or less committed to particular religious attitudes than had been the Romano-British population. It is just that our sources derive from the small section within the community for whom religious convictions were an abiding and near-exclusive interest.

The British Church

Evidence for Christianity derives from the northern frontier region of the Roman province, but it is typically low-key and arguably late in date (Watson 1968). Two of the handful of tombstones reputed to be Christian rely on the exclusivity of Christian use of the formula *plus minus* (RIB 955, Carlisle; RIB 787, Brougham). That exclusivity is far from established. At Carvoran, the formula *sina ulla macula* has attracted the suggestion that the soldier Aurelius

Marcus may have been a Christian, but this remains no more than a possibility (RIB 1828). Only the chi rho monograms found on tombstones at Maryport and Catterick are reliable indicators (see Fig. 6.2). In contrast to the distribution of *mithraea*, no Christian, Romano-British church has yet been located.

All the remaining evidence relies on portable objects of dubious relevance to the frontier community, and even the rich finds of silver vessels from Corbridge need imply no more than the occasional appearance in the area of a wealthy Christian visitor or official (Wall 1965). Christian insignia on 6 of the 110 objects found in the Traprain Law hoard indicate Christianity, but not at Traprain Law but in the unknown locality from which they derived, and this may well have lain outside the British provinces.

Along the wall, most pagan temples ceased attracting votive deposits in the early fourth century. The sole known exception is that of Coventina at Carrawburgh. The pagan statuary used to mend the road at Corbridge may imply official hostility towards non-Christian religious observance, but the available evidence does not support any interpretation of religious attitudes more positive than, at best, local apathy towards Christianity.

The rise of Christianity corresponds chronologically with the demise of the Roman province, and may have owed much to that demise, as British and non-British rulers chose *Romanitas* and rejected the paganism of their Scottish and Pictish enemies. In this respect, Christianity performed a necessary function in the cementing of British self-awareness and self-identity, which may have been important in the fifth-century struggle against the aggression of neighbouring tribal groups.

In the North, the spread of Christianity is inextricably associated with St Ninian, who, by the age of Bede, was popularly supposed to have been a regularly ordained British bishop whose see was centred on Whithorn (Candida Casa, Bede, III, 4) and who was credited with the conversion of the southern Picts. The Church which he represented was not a monastically oriented Church, but an extension of the European Church, organized as sees but lacking a hierarchical structure. In northern England the Church was probably heavily dependent on the patronage of the royal dynasties, and it is at least likely that each of the fifth-century kingdoms constituted an ecclesiastical see along the same lines as many Anglo-Saxon kingdoms during the age of conversion.

That a conversion of the northern Britons occurred is supported by the evidence from the dug-grave cemetery at But on the Clyde estuary. Graves with a dominant north–south orientation were there overlain by the east–west orientation typical of Christian burials, and subsequently by an enclosure wall and stone chapel (Thomas 1968). An extended, oriented, inhumation cemetery was found at Whithorn, and another example may have been destroyed by quarrying at Eaglesfield, in that part of Cumbria associated with the sixth-century dynasty of Pabo. The place-name may recall a lost *eccles-* name (P. A.

Wilson 1978). East of the Pennines, a small number of burials and cemeteries have been identified. South of the wall, these are exclusive to Cleveland and Co. Durham south of the Wear, where they may be relevant to the sixth-century kingdom of Catraeth, and to the probable *eccles-* place-name Egglescliffe on the Tees. North of the wall, the only example of an *eccles-* place-name so far located in Northumberland lies inland from Bamburgh on the middle Tweed (see above) where it may be associated with a British Christian community north of Alnwick centred on Bamburgh and the Milfield basin. Further north, large numbers of cemeteries predate the medieval churches of Lothian and may represent a substantial and superficially Christian population in Gododdin. On Man, lintel grave cemeteries which predate the Viking Conquest have been identified at Peel Castle and Balladoole [12].

The British Church was neither monastically organized nor geared to missionary activity. Fifth-century British ecclesiasts allowed the Pelagian heresy to absorb their intellectual powers, while they turned their collective backs upon the pagan world (Morris 1968). Within this milieu, the career of St Patrick was exceptional. Forced by his early captivity to take note of the pagan Irish, he returned among his captors as a missionary. Yet his early disinterest in religion emerges from the *Confessio*, and may have been typical of the frontier area from which he derived (arguably northern Cumbria). His mission to Ireland caused considerable ill-will among the British bishops. The soldiers of Coroticus towards whom he addressed his famous letter were technically Christian, but did not allow their actions to deviate on that account from their own self-interest.

Most of the thin scatter of Christian memorial stones in south Scotland and the English borders commemorate members of the secular aristocracy – and these include the stone erected *c.* AD 500 near Chesterholm bearing the inscription 'Brigomaglos, who is also Briocus, lies (here)' (transl. RIB 1722; Jackson 1982). The exceptions to this are the small groups of commemorative stones at Whithorn and Kirkmadrine, some at least of which commemorate priests, and these lend substance to the Ninianic tradition, and imply a long-lived Christian community centred on the bishopric and on the only known example of a Celtic stone church or chapel in the border counties. The possibility remains of a Celtic bishopric centred on the household of the kings of Rheged, and, therefore, to some extent on Carlisle itself, but to argue for the lengthy survival of a late Roman Christian centre at Carlisle far exceeds the available evidence (McCarthy 1982). Some British religious centres may have developed as monastic sites by the end of the sixth century – it would seem strange if Cumbria at least failed to incorporate the Irish example. No certain example exists, but Ninekirk is still an attractive possibility given the coexistence of a Ninianic place-name, a riverside site, an adjacent cave and an unusual ditched enclosure revealed by crop-mark photography, although the 'Dark Age' date of the Ninekirk hoard has been pushed back to the Roman period,

Plate 6.2   A sixth-century warrior burial: one of over eighty skeletons so far excavated in the newly-discovered pagan Saxon cemetery at Norton-on-Tees, Cleveland, now in the process of excavation.

and the site may belong to that era (Casey 1978). Elsewhere, the presence of circular cemeteries may indicate early Celtic religious sites (O'Sullivan 1980), but the recent trial excavation of a ditch apparently forming part of the perimeter of such an enclosure at Ruthwell, north of the Solway, provided a carbon-14 date of *c.* 370 bc, and thereby failed to support this hypothesis [13].

During the sixth century and into the seventh, Bernicia was pagan and identified as such by contemporary Christian Celtic poets who contrasted the Christian British kings with their pagan English rivals. As a form of self-identity, paganism probably served the Bernician community well, serving the function of a tribal deity, and that community was at its most successful under the pagan King Aethelfrith and his (initially) pagan successor Edwin. Bernician paganism found an outlet both in forms of worship and of burial. The distribution of the burials has already been remarked upon above. They are widely scattered, but not numerous except at Yeavering and Norton (Cleveland). Grave-goods, where identified, are poor in quality and small in number (Norton excepted). The two cruciform brooches from Corbridge, made *c.* AD 500, may have been grave-goods, and there are other possible associations from the site. The recent find of a small-long brooch at Hylton (Tyne and Wear) provides another example from the same locality (Miket 1982). Elsewhere, few grave-goods are as diagnostic as the glass claw beaker found with an extended

277

inhumation at Castle Eden (Durham), which provides the only example of glassware from the fifth or early sixth centuries found in the border counties (Harden 1956). A bronze hanging bowl was extracted from a barrow cemetery at Capheaton (Northumb.), and a range of finds including weapons and brooches of late sixth or early seventh century type came from a cemetery at Darlington, Teesside (Miket 1980; Pococke and Miket 1976). The very recent excavations at Norton should eventually provide a substantial data base for the analysis of pagan burial in the sixth and early seventh centuries in northern England.

The burial sequence at Yeavering illustrates some of the problems of interpreting religious attitudes from burial traditions. The earliest historic phase of burials reused the site defined by a prehistoric ring-ditch, and radially oriented inhumations were grouped around a standing stone, and subsequent posts, within a rectangular mortuary enclosure or shrine. This phase was perhaps pre-English, but there is no reason to suppose it to have been Christian. This cemetery was superseded by an extended inhumation cemetery aligned west–east, which invites a Christian interpretation, but its association with building 'D2' does not support this. The building was a substantial example of rectangular, timber-frame construction, with a long history which included reconstruction after destruction by fire. An interior pit was entirely filled with animal bones, very largely consisting of ox skulls deposited in nine phases, and they were so numerous that it was suggested that they had originally been stacked well above ground level (Hope-Taylor 1977: 97 ff). If this structure is properly identified as a temple, then the Christian nature of the cemetery appears inconsistent, but the two were linked, and a small fenced enclosure adjoining the 'temple' south wall served as a focus for many burials. It is possible that the 'temple' was converted to a church in the reign of King Edwin, in which case the later phases, at least, of the cemetery may have been Christian. The excavator argued that the bulk of the graves contained the remains of members of the local Celtic community, in which case oriented inhumation even during the pagan period is more understandable. The Yeavering burials are still ambiguous in most respects, and reservations derived from this site must be borne in mind when dealing with all cemeteries of this period along the borders.

The last phase of pagan burial at Yeavering probably occurred during the short reign of the apostate, eldest son of Aethelfrith, and constitute the casualties of Yeavering's destruction by Cadwallon. Sixty-four 'string' graves were excavated, and bodies incarcerated, at the east end of the complex, in that area subsequently utilized for Christian worship and burial under King Oswald (Fig. 6.5).

The traditions of burial practised in the sixth and early seventh century at Yeavering have much in common with the cyst-burials found elsewhere in the North, and probably represent a strong, local and indigenous tradition owing little to English overlords, whether pagan or Christian. More reliable candi-

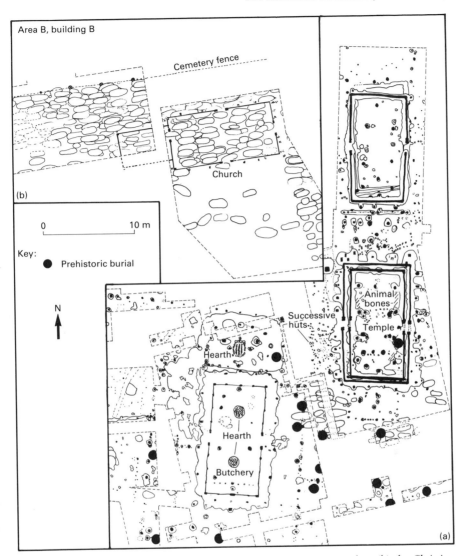

Figure 6.5 The religious complexes at Yeavering: (a) the Pagan complex; (b) the Christian complex that eventually replaced it.

dates for pagan English burials are those high-status examples accompanied by weapons found as isolated deposits or small groups under cairns, or inserted into pre-existing, prehistoric monuments. Those found by Greenwell at Crosby Garrett and the other possible Anglian burials in the Upper Eden valley may represent casualties among male warriors moving into, or raiding into hostile territory either from Deira or from Bernicia after the fall of Catraeth; a similar pattern emerges in the upper river valleys of Northumberland and

Durham. A group of burials within the henge monument at Milfield may be comparable (Harding 1981). A series of female burials have been found in the eastern lowlands outside the war zone as defined by Hope-Taylor, and several of these come from Roman sites which were, therefore, arguably still attractive to both British and English communities as cemeteries and religious centres (see discussion in Cramp 1983: 266–70). Such burials have been identified at Corbridge, Binchester and Newcastle, and pottery from Piercebridge might be relevant. The site's significance as a cemetery may help account for the survival of the first element in the place-name Corstopitum, ultimately joined with an English suffix to form Corbridge. Paganism was apparently deeply rooted, and the *Life of St Cuthbert* (3) recorded peasant hostility to St Cuthbert and the Christian monks, which apparently stemmed from a continuing attachment to the old religion.

The conversion when it came, owed a great deal to the personalities of the kings, and offers a cogent example illustrative of the intensely hierarchical nature of English society, and the powerful role of royal patronage.

King Edwin passed his most impressionable years in exile, perhaps in part in Christian Gwynedd, but also in pagan Mercia and in East Anglia. If his childhood was spent in Gwynedd he can hardly have avoided baptism into the Celtic Church. However, in East Anglia he probably came into contact with Augustinian, Roman Christianity. He married for political advantage, initially in pagan Mercia, and secondly a Roman Christian princess from Kent, and it was via the latter that the Roman Church was established in Northumbria. However, a British tradition repeated in the *Historia Brittonum* (63) states somewhat belligerently that Edwin was baptized by Rum (Rhun) son of Urien of Catraeth and Rheged following the baptism of his daughter Eanfled, and there then followed forty days during which the entire Northumbrian nation was baptized (Chadwick 1963). In contrast, Bede offers an account of a protracted and difficult conversion of the King by Bishop Paulinus (*Hist. Eccles.*, II, 12). These two conflicting traditions represent the rival claims of the Celtic and the Roman Churches, and may well properly record indecision on the part of King Edwin. It is quite clear that the new Bretwalda was besieged by would-be Christian missionaries, among whom Edwin may have had most sympathy for representatives of the Celtic Church, but the representatives of Rome, from his correspondent Pope Boniface downwards, were more importunate and offered the greater political advantages. As befitted a king of the royal house of Deira, Edwin was moved by political considerations centred in and to the south of his kingdom. Only after the conversion of the King did the Church make any headway in Northumbria, but once it achieved official status, the Northumbrian aristocracy fell over themselves to conform. Paulinus baptized the King at York in a hastily built wooden church in AD 627. In the aftermath he baptized many of the Bernicians in the river Glen below the palace at Yeavering. However, in Bernicia, at least, no church was reputed to have been constructed in the reign of Edwin, and Christianity remained at the most superficial level (Bede, *Hist. Eccles.*, III, 2). Paulinus was established at York in Deira.

The death of King Edwin in battle in AD 633 was a major crisis for Northumbrian Christianity. Paulinus fled with members of the royal household to the south, where he became Bishop of the rather less dangerous see of Rochester.

Leadership in Northumbria fell to the Bernician royal house, returning from exile among the Celtic Christians of Scotland and Pictland. The eldest undertook responsibility for the defence of Bernicia. Perhaps to reinforce the self-identity of that community he committed what Bede considered to be the ultimate crime – he apostated (*Hist. Eccles.*, III, 1). If this was a politically motivated gesture, as seems likely, it underlines the strength of paganism in Bernicia and the cosmetic nature of the official Christianity imposed by Edwin of Deira. Whatever the cause, it failed (to Bede's obvious relief) and the leadership of Bernicia fell to his younger brother, Oswald, who emphasized his own Christianity, of the Scottish variety, and led a Bernician force to victory at Denisesburn after firing the enthusiasm of his small force through prayer. The God of the Celtic Christians was thereby proved efficacious in battle, and Oswald naturally introduced that brand to his kingdom.

The reintroduction of Christianity to Northumberland represents the real basis of the northern English conversion. As befitted a king of the royal house of Bernicia, he looked to northern neighbours for inspiration, and particularly to Iona. The Christianity that Bishop Aidan brought with him to Lindisfarne in AD 635 was different in many respects to that of Bishop Paulinus. The major bones of contention between the Celtic and Roman Churches in the seventh and eighth centuries centred on the calculation of the date of Easter, and on conventions, such as the form of tonsure used. Underlying these differences were basic and deep-rooted divisions derived from the long and comparatively isolated development of Christianity in Ireland and Scotia from the Patrician period onwards. This Church had had to achieve a high degree of autonomous authority which was now threatened by the claims of the Romanists. It relied upon established hierarchies that were centred not within the ranks of the bishops but among the abbots of the great monastic houses. It was a monastically structured church that Aidan introduced, and Lindisfarne naturally developed as a monastic site, a daughter-house of Iona and in time a mother-house for the Bernician monasteries. Aidan himself, and most of his fellow missionaries were monks. When Aidan began to preach in Northumbria his English was inadequate to the task, and English translators had to assist him, including King Oswald himself (Bede, *Hist. Eccles.*, III, 3). The ability of a group of offshore Scottish monks to convert the northern English says much for the linguistic abilities of both communities.

The conversion was once again heavily dependent on the attitudes of the King, whose patronage of the Church was given great emphasis by Bede. The latter also had only good to report of Bishop Aidan whose missionary fervour and personal example he obviously respected, despite their differences over the date of Easter. The association between King and Bishop was a close one. Not only was the Bishop high in royal councils, but he was a natural and privileged member of the royal household (Bede, *Hist. Eccles.*, III, 6). It was the King who provided the means by which monasteries and churches could be founded. Lindisfarne was almost certainly royal land, and we find an early church in Bernicia at royal Bamburgh.

Both Oswald's successors maintained the Celtic Church in Northumbria, Oswy in Bernicia and Oswin in Deira, but it was with the latter that Bede initially associates the ageing Bishop Aidan. However, he was living as a hermit on Farne Island off Lindisfarne when Penda's forces first attacked Bamburgh in the 650s, and he eventually died, we are told, leaning against the wall of his timber church outside the fortress of Bamburgh. That church was a casualty of Penda's renewed raiding within a very few years (Bede, *Hist. Eccles.*, III, 17), and already by the early eighth century had had to be rebuilt a third time due to an accidental fire.

The establishment of the church was furthered by gifts of land, for the foundation of monastic communities, made by King Oswy, in thanks for divine support in the desperate battle in which Penda of Mercia was defeated and killed in AD 655. Six of these were within Bernicia, of ten hides each and five of these were probably Melrose, Abercorn, Coldingham, Norham and Gilling near Richmond (now in Yorkshire but arguably within Bernicia) (Fig. 7.2). Bede considered these grants rather frugal, in contrast to the foundation of Wearmouth (seventy hides) and Jarrow (forty hides) in the next generation. Royal patronage was exercised within secular constraints, and with at least a sprinkling of ecclesiasts from the royal family. Trumhere, the Abbot of Gilling, and later Bishop of southern Pictland, was a relative of Oswy, his sister became Abbess of Coldingham and his infant daughter was committed by the King to the religious community at Hartlepool, and proceeded thence to Whitby, as part of his thanksgiving. This last monastic site subsequently served as a royal cemetery for Oswy's family.

Church building was limited to a small number of sites throughout the century. Bishop Aidan's successor, Finan, built an episcopal church on Lindisfarne of hewn oaks thatched with reeds (Bede, *Hist. Eccles.*, III, 25), and the monastic site there was still no more than a tiny group of wooden buildings when Colman retired to Scotland after the Synod of Whitby. The monks of Hexham had founded a church on the nearby battle-site associated with St Oswald by the 730s.

The earliest English church site so far excavated is that forming an integral part of St Oswald's rebuilt palace at Yeavering (phase IV; Hope-Taylor 1977). Following the 'string' burials in the aftermath of the firing of the site by Cadwallon, an oriented Christian cemetery was laid out within a palisade fence, focused on a hall-like building which can best be interpreted as a church. In origin, this was a structure of rectangular plan aligned west–east,

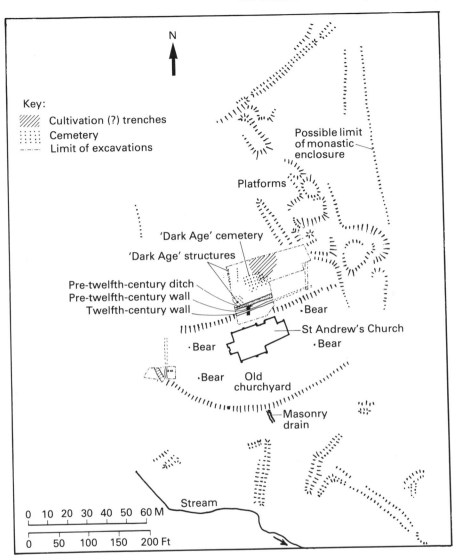

Figure 6.6 A general plan of Dacre (Cumb.), showing areas adjacent to St Andrew's Church where excavation has taken place since 1982 (after a survey by the Cumbria and Lancashire Archaeol. Unit).

approx. 11.3×5.2 m internally. Later fire damage, perhaps consequent on Penda's raids, was put right, and a western annexe constructed, probably under King Oswy or his successors, and the cemetery was heavily used for a considerable period, with graves identified in at least five phases (see Fig. 6.5). This church was arguably within the same Scottish tradition of timber construction as that at Lindisfarne, and probably also that at Bamburgh. Outside the wealthier monasteries, stone churches did not feature in seventh-century Bernicia, or in Cumbria, where the Dacre complex was built in timber with structures based upon secular models (Fig. 6.6).

The controversey over Easter came to a head in AD 664, when King Oswy presided over the Synod of Whitby with the intention of resolving which practice should be observed in Northumbria. His own staunch support of the Scottish Church was balanced by that of his wife, and a principal subordinate for the Roman – the under-king of Deira was already a generous patron of Bishop Wilfrid. The rival churches argued their claims before the King, who decided in favour of the Roman Church, which henceforth was in receipt of the undivided patronage of the royal family. Those of the Northumbrian Church who were unreconciled to Roman practice followed Bishop Colman to Northern Ireland, where a new monastery was founded with an English community of monks. However, these were few, and the main result within the Northumbrian Church was a transferral of patronage from the Scottish monks who had provided the first three bishops at Lindisfarne, in favour of indigenous churchmen led by those with European or southern connections. The Englishman Eata, Abbot of Melrose had been trained from childhood within the monastery of Bishop Aidan, but proved a pliable successor, after the synod, as Abbot and subsequently as Bishop of Lindisfarne. The synod, and the reorganizing of the church community consequent upon it, constituted a significant lurch towards the South, and towards the European continent for all Northumbria, natural enough, perhaps, for Deira, but alien to the established cultural and political contacts of Bernicia within the Scottish and Pictish worlds. It was a body blow from which the Scottish Church did not recover; Iona finally acquiesced in the Roman dating of Easter in AD 716. In the reign of King Ecgfrith, royal patronage was channelled towards men like Benedict Biscop, four times a pilgrim to Rome and inveterate visitor of monasteries on the Continent. The wealth of the endowment of Wearmouth and Jarrow (AD 672, 681) allowed him to bring artisans to Northumberland from Gaul, and thereby introduce a range of crafts, including glass-blowing, totally alien to the asceticism of Celtic monasticism. So ended the age of conversion in the North.

Notes

1. My thanks to John Dore for discussion of the Corbridge site.

2. My thanks to Prof. Barri Jones for discussion of the *arcani* and the *exploratores*.

3. See Morris (1973); Alcock (1971). Chadwick (1976) avoids most of the problems, but that work (and that of Jackson 1955) lean heavily on the Harleian genealogies, which are now considered to be less than reliable.

4. See Dumville (1977a, b); Miller (1975a, b, c, d).

5. See Hatcher (1977) for the most convincing analysis.

6. My thanks to Roger Miket for his correspondence on this subject.

7. My thanks to Blaize Vyner and S. J. Sherlock of Cleveland County Archaeology Section for information concerning the site and for Plate 6.2.

8. Quotation taken from the translation by Leo Sherley-Price, revised by R. E. Latham (1968).

9. The *Annales Cambriae* lists this event under the year AD 644.

10. See Wrigley and Schofield (1981: 240) *et al.*

11. My thanks to Dr John Peter Wild and to Dr John Smith for discussion of the demographic problem.

12. My thanks to David Freke for assistance with references on the Manx material.

13. My thanks to Chris Crowe for permission to incorporate this material prior to publication.

Chapter 7

The English and Anglo-Scandinavian Period, AD 685–1000

English Northumbria

The Northumbrian kingdom was forged in the decades after AD 600 under the leadership of capable warrior-kings. None were more aggressive than King Ecgfrith, under whose captaincy Northumbrian control was temporarily reasserted in the rich and populous province of Lindsey and among the southern Picts. However, his reign was not the opening gambit in a new era of Northumbrian expansionism. His defeat and death in AD 685 exposed the underlying fragility of the Northumbrian crown. His lineage, albeit via an illegitimate half-brother, provided the kingdom with two of the next three leaders, but his nephews proved unable to maintain control of rivals for the throne; King Osred was slain in AD 716. Henceforth the royal succession became the prize of first one then another cadet branch of the royal house, and at times even of powerful individuals with no known royal connections (Kirby 1974; Bede, Cont. AD 758).

In order to comprehend the subsequent weakness of Northumbrian political leadership, it is necessary to take account of several contributory factors, not all of which were providential. Specific crises were to some extent accidents. Ecgfrith left no son to follow him. Aldfrith left several sons but none of an age to rule effectively. Such crises endangered the dynasty and placed considerable responsibility on the political affinity of the dead monarch. Yet both these crises were overcome, and it was not until King Osred was slain in AD 716 that a representative of a rival, collateral line successfully established himself on the throne. King Ceolwulf (AD 729–37) founded the fortunes of this alternative dynasty which retained the throne until displaced by another usurping cadet line, led by King Alhred (AD 765–74). During the following century, kings were less likely to be succeeded by members of their own faction, but the progressive disinterest of the Anglo-Saxon chroniclers in Northumbrian affairs in the ninth century has rendered even its dynastic history obscure.

Underlying this dynastic fragility are visible substantial factors, to which we should ascribe the collapse of Northumbrian royal government. During the period AD 550–685, Northumbrian kings had reaped the benefits of a frontier status, by competing successfully with less able neighbours in southern Scotland and northern England. Thereby they had been able to attract and reward military specialists from within the kingdom and without. The attractiveness of service to the Northumbrian crown had been severely tested by the competition for supremacy with Mercia that dominated the mid century, but the Mercians, too, had suffered severe reversals. However, with expansion curtailed to the south by Mercia, and to the west by the Irish Sea, King Ecgfrith looked to conquests in the North to re-establish the momentum of expansion, and consequently of military recruitment. Their northern neighbours had proved less than dangerous to Northumbrian forces in the past, and Ecgfrith sent an army against the Irish mainland and campaigned himself into Pictland. His defeat and death in AD 685 was not merely a blow to his dynasty. It was the death-knell of Northumbrian expansionism; no longer could Northumbrian military superiority in the North be taken for granted. The Scots and Britons took the opportunity to seize their independence from the English, and were able to defend it throughout the remainder of the period. The initiative was lost to Northumbria. In the short term it was taken up by the Picts, who inflicted defeats on English forces in AD 698 and 710. Henceforth Northumbrian kings could not attract service by the promise of rewards extracted from successful campaigns, and the history of Northumbria in the period before AD 866 is the history of a 'possessor state', anxious to protect itself from its neighbours but led by kings without the resources to wage large-scale offensive action. King Eadbert (AD 738–58) came closest to breaking out of the strait-jacket imposed by his limited patronage. He attacked the Picts and successfully expanded the kingdom, but when he joined with them to launch an attack on the minor British kingdom in Strathclyde, the Britons defeated his army as it withdrew from Dumbarton. He retired to a monastery two years later, but his son and heir King Oswulf was murdered shortly after. We must beware of linking his military endeavours with the fate of his dynasty, but it is clear that Eadbert's expansionist policies achieved little and failed to underpin the authority of his family.

Devoid of the flow of patronage, tribute and booty available to a successful war leader, the Northumbrian royal house was forced back upon the resources available to it within the kingdom. There are signs that these resources were becoming dangerously eroded. The King was only so powerful as his ability to reward service. If his largesse included the irretrievable disposal of royal land, then subsequent generations in government had access only to a diminished pool from which service could be purchased or recompensed. In contemporary France the Merovingian dynasty underwent a resource crisis of exactly this nature. In Northumbria, monarchs in the late seventh and eighth centuries disposed permanently of large estates, and the recipients were less the warriors and aristocratic supporters of the royal household (the *comitatus*), than the monks and bishops of the new, Roman, Northumbrian Church.

The initial establishment of Christianity had been achieved by the Northumbrian kings extremely cheaply. The monastery at Lindisfarne as late as AD 665 constituted no more than a squalid huddle of sheds around a timber church. The monasteries established by King Oswy had each an initial grant of 10 hides – extravagant perhaps by contemporary standards given that Abbess Hilda began with a single hide (Hart 1975: doc. 138). After the Synod of Whitby the trickle of estates into the hands of the Church became a flood. The

Figure 7.1   Land-holdings of the community of St Cuthbert (after Morris, 1977).

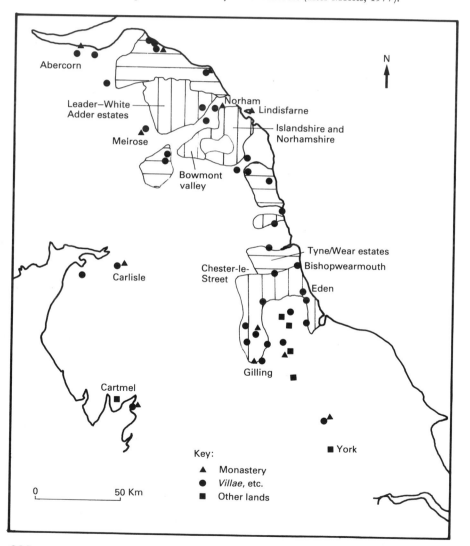

twin monastery of Monkwearmouth and Jarrow had a foundation grant of 90 hides (Hart 1975: docs. 144, 145). By AD 716 this had grown to at least 143 hides, not including any non-royal grants it may have received. St Wilfrid was enabled to found his splendid monastery at Hexham by a grant from the Queen's dower lands, arguably constituting an estate of approx. 3,550 ha (Roper 1974b). The endowment of St Cuthbert at Lindisfarne accumulated enormous estates, attracting from King Ecgfrith the grant of Carlisle with land 24 km in compass, the Bowmont valley in Northumberland, Cartmel and other large tracts (Craster 1954; Morris 1977; Hart 1975: docs. 146, 139, 147; Fig. 7.1). Ripon was equally well endowed with an initial 40 hides, and at the dedicatory ceremony, Wilfrid read out the royal charters that constituted his title deeds to wide estates in the mid Pennines (Eddius 17).

Along with Whitby, these constituted the wealthiest houses, but there were numerous others. The aggregated land endowment that they had received by *c.* AD 720 was very considerable indeed, and it increased substantially thereafter. Much of this land had been part of the direct resource base of the crown. The remainder came from the Northumbrian aristocracy in circumstances that suggest that they saw monastic foundations as a convenient strategy by which to minimize the obligations placed on their estates by the crown (Bede, *Hist. Eccles.*, v, 23; Letter to Archbishop Egbert). By both these strategies, the crown was in danger of losing control of a major proportion of the home resource base upon which it had more than ever to rely.

Contemporaries were well aware of the dangers; the reigns of Ecgfrith and his successors saw the growth of tensions between kings and leading members of the Church. The career of Bishop Wilfrid epitomizes these tensions, although they were by no means exclusive to him. His rise to eminence had already begun before the Synod of Whitby, under the patronage of a subking, Alchfrith in Deira, but during his first visit to the Continent to be consecrated bishop, his patron lost all political influence. There remained to him the friendship and patronage of the devout Queen Aethelthryth, who endowed Hexham, but subsequently removed herself from political life by her entry to a religious house (Farmer 1974). Wilfrid was left with enormous estates, patronage and power, but devoid of friends among the political affinity of King Ecgfrith. According to the biographer and close confidant of the Bishop, the subsequent rift developed out of the hostility of Ecgfrith's second queen, Iurminburh, probably fuelled by her ambition to retrieve the Hexham estates which were an important part of her dower lands. Those about the King were delighted at the collapse of Wilfrid's influence – 'smirking with delight at his defeat' (Eddius 24). The vast ecclesiastical empire over which he presided excluded them from sources of patronage to which their fathers would have had access. The Queen was not Wilfrid's sole protagonist. His rapid accumulation of monasteries and estates in Mercia were alarming to the Northumbrian dynasty, and Wilfrid's claims were met with considerable suspicion. He was temporarily reinstated by the new King Aldfrith in AD 686, perhaps in the hope that his political influence would help to underpin the succession, but by AD 690/91 he and the King were divided by further tensions over the lands and possessions of the Church, which his biographer claimed were unjustly appropriated by the King. His claims to wide estates was a key issue at the Council of Austerfield, and that and his political influence may have led King Eadwulf to bar him from the kingdom (Eddius 46, 59). Not until he was able to join the successful coup to elevate the child son of Aldfrith to the throne were his key estates restored to Wilfrid.

It is impossible to disregard the powerful political influence that Wilfrid's vast estates supported. The Bishop was sucked into dynastic politics whether he willed it or not. It is difficult to be sure of his dynastic preferences. Clearly, he was not a supporter of Ecgfrith. The close links between Hexham and the cult of St Oswald which the monks assiduously cultivated may betray a political interest by Wilfrid and his successors in that branch of the royal family, in which case the attitude of Ecgfrith and his successors becomes easier to understand (Kirby 1974: 28). If it is fair to draw parallels between the careers of Bishop Wilfrid and St Thomas à Becket, it is also apt to see in the former something of an eighth-century parallel to Warwick the Kingmaker.

The vast wealth and wide estates that became permanently attached to the Northumbrian monasteries made it increasingly necessary that the kings should retain control of the patronage they controlled via the key personnel. Ecgfrith's aunt Aebbe emerges as a powerful political figure as Abbess of Coldingham. She and Bishop Cuthbert were partisans of his dynasty. Wilfrid was not a partisan of the dominant group, and paid the price of his political unreliability. However, the eventual victim of this shift in the balance of patronage was the monarchy. The successive replacement of one dynasty by another in the eighth and ninth centuries led to the collapse of royal control over the Church. Individual monasteries and prelates linked themselves to the fortunes of specific dynasties. Hexham, for example, probably associated itself with the line of King Ceolwulf, and Lindisfarne with that of Alhred after AD 750. In the 790s both Hexham and Ripon supported Ealdorman Eardwulf who gained the throne in AD 796 (Kirby 1974). The political patronage was fragmented, and no king could muster more than a part of the whole. Each usurper was faced by the established church leaders appointed by his predecessors, who he might or might not be able to remove. Bishop Acca of Hexham may have been a victim of one such coup in AD 731/32. The most successful monarch in Northumbria in the eighth century was King Eadbert, whose brother was Archbishop of York, who presumably manipulated ecclesiastical patronage in his support. In addition his cousin and supporter was the ex-King Ceolwulf who entered the key monastery of Lindisfarne, in which he exercised considerable influence. Not even this control of ecclesiastical patronage was enough to save Eadbert's son and successor, who was slain by his own household on 24/25 July AD 758, but the dynasty retained control under Eadbert's brother, Moll Aethelwold until AD 765. The death of

Ceolwulf (AD 762) and the decline and death of Archbishop Egbert (AD 766 after thirty-seven years as a bishop) were damaging blows to the dynasty, which collapsed when confronted by the usurpation of King Alhred in AD 765.

Northumbrian kings were not blind to the wealth of the monastic endowments, and some sought to retrieve a part of the resources alienated by their more profligate predecessors. The case of St Wilfrid must be relevant to this context. In addition, St Boniface accused King Osred of interfering in church possessions, and Pope Paul I reproved King Eadbert for seizing three monasteries and granting them out to laymen (Roper 1974a; Hart 1975: doc. 153). Notwithstanding, no king was able to make significant inroads. Although they may have regarded the disestablishment of the monasteries as the only means by which the Northumbrian crown could recover its proper stature, no king enjoyed the power to achieve it. The monasteries were protected by religious sentiment as well as by the vested self-interest of the secular political élite.

On balance, the resources of the crown probably shrank considerably over this century and a half. The Church had accumulated vast new estates by AD 900. Kings were increasingly impoverished, unable to reward loyal service and subject to political coups by which the aristocracy exercised a growing influence over dynastic politics. In AD 774, the Northumbrians drove out King Alhred from York at Easter, and took Ethelred (Eadbert's nephew and Moll Aethelwold's son) as their lord. He was removed by a coup in AD 778 in favour of another rival, Aelfwold. In AD 796, King Ethelred was killed by his own people and in AD 806 another king was driven from his kingdom [1]. The status of kingship had fallen disastrously since the days of King Ecgfrith. The collapse of the resource base left successive kings competing as little more than equals with their rivals. When the Danish army seized York in AD 867, Northumbria was divided. The deposed King Osbert was contesting the crown with a rival devoid of any hereditary right but brought in as his replacement.

The Church was not the only successor to royal resources. Already during the reign of Ecgfrith, officials (*praepositi* and *prefecti*) were responsible for the royal *burh* sites, including Carlisle and Dunbar, where St Wilfrid was imprisoned (Eddius 32). In a local context, these officials resemble the counts to whom the Carolingian monarchy delegated royal authority in the provinces. By the end of the seventh century, ealdormen were undertaking responsibility for the defence of the northern marches of Bernicia – Brihtred was killed by the Picts in AD 698, and Brihtforth fought against them in AD 710. It would be flying in the face of all we know about the aristocracy in western Europe during this period if we were to ignore the probability that these officials were able, under the weaker monarchs of the eighth and ninth centuries, to pass on their offices and their power to their lineal descendants. Some of these men cross the threshold into the pages of history, pursuing political objectives often apparently distinct from, and at times opposed to, that of the king of the day – men like the 'high-reeves' Eadwulf son of Bosa, Cynewulf and Ecga in AD 778, and Sicga who slew King Aelfwold in AD 788. Ealdorman Beorn was burnt to death by the 'high-reeves' of Northumbria at *Seletun* on Christmas Day, AD 779. The nobles Aethelbald and Heardberht led the coup which replaced King Ethelred with King Aelfwold in AD 778 and Alric, son of Heardberht was among the casualties at the great internecine battle fought at Whalley in AD 798. Among this hereditary aristocracy were the cadet lines of the royal house, each assembling and maintaining political influence via marriage and patronage. From the aristocracy, individuals entered the Church and took control of ecclesiastical patronage in the interests of secular ambitions and expectations; it was very largely their initial status within the social and political élite that enabled men like Benedict Biscop, Wilfrid and even Cuthbert to attract lay patronage.

The ownership or control of estates was the *sine qua non* of the Northumbrian aristocracy, encompassing both the clerical and secular sections. Those few charters that have survived are almost all of royal land granted to the Church; the remainder record grants by ecclesiastical institutions to members of the secular aristocracy, or among themselves. Most are of substantial tracts of land, and the implication is that estates were transferred with the existing labour force, livestock and capital equipment intact. It was a functioning economic unit which changed hands, and the change in ownership need have had little impact within the estate, where men did not enjoy the liberty of choosing a lord. Many estates were described solely by the name of a central place. Monkwearmouth and Jarrow obtained an estate of twenty hides at *Sambuce* and another of ten hides at *Daltun* before AD 716. A grant to St Cuthbert included the estate of Cartmel with all the Britons belonging to it, and the *vill* called Gilling (North Yorkshire) with all its appurtenances (Hart 1975: doc. 147).

These grants transferred estates of the kind which have been described as 'multiple estates' (Jones G. R. J. 1961), typically consisting of a central place or estate centre through which were channelled the profits of land-ownership from the various, administratively subordinate communities occupying parts of that estate. Documentation from the Viking Age and the early post-Conquest period suggests that this form of organization was typical throughout Northumbria (Jolliffe 1926). Something of it survived into the 'shires' of medieval Northumberland, and into the Domesday survey for parts of Yorkshire and southern Lancashire (Kapelle 1979: 50 ff; Higham 1979b). The very large size of many of these estates implies that the land-owning section of society was highly exclusive. It was these men and these institutions who made up the political community of Northumbria. Below them, the main lines of organization within society were vertical rather than horizontal.

An example of this vertical organization and the exclusivity conferred by aristocratic birth is available in the leases of Bishop Cutheard early in the tenth century to two refugee nobles who had fled from pirates west of the Pennines. The estates provided for them encompassed a large part of Co. Durham.

Eadred received the lands between the Derwent and the Wear west of Dere Street, while Alfred received a group of estates stretching in a wide band along the coast from Easington to Hartlepool (Hart 1975: docs. 163, 162), a land-holding of roughly 150 km². No doubt it was intended that these grants should enable Alfred and Eadred to organize retinues with which to support the political ambitions of the St Cuthbert community.

Most of the estates named in the works of Bede and his contemporaries, and in the various charters, were termed *villae*. There is some reason to think the word was initially synonymous with a royal estate (Campbell 1978). Many of the documented examples were ecclesiastical estates derived from the crown. The name of the *villa* was in many cases used to denote both a specific settlement, and also the entire area tenurially dependent upon it. The *villa* named Gainford, for example, formed one element listed in a charter of Bishop Ecgred to the community of St Cuthbert in the first half of the ninth century. The place-name denoted a specific site, on which a church had been constructed, but also a wide tract of land from south of the Tees to the Wear, and from Dere Street to the high ground above Butter Knowle (Hart 1975: doc. 154). Similar 'multiple estates' based on Brainshaugh and Warkworth were granted to Lindisfarne by King Ceolwulf in AD 737 (Hart 1975: doc. 151). Other *villae* named in the same grant – including Whittingham, Edlingham and Eglingham – were not specifically associated with appendages, but the prevalence of -*ing(a)ham* names may indicate that these settlements also performed a central function. Other *villae* had names derived from topographical features, such as Gainford, but a small number were -*tun* names, originally with the meaning of enclosure or farmstead, but perhaps attracting in some cases the specialized meaning 'royal enclosure' (Campbell 1978).

The social and economic structure of these estates is not directly ascertainable, except to reiterate that many were very extensive, and encompassed numerous settlements. The majority of such settlements were probably small. With the specific exception of the larger monasteries, there is no evidence that large nucleated communities were either common or important in border society. On the contrary, the estates appear to have been structured so as to incorporate a non-nucleated pattern of settlement, in which communities larger than the hamlet were scarce (e.g. Bede, *Vita*, 32, 34). The green villages of Co. Durham and the planned nucleated communities visible today in all areas of the border counties did not emerge from this structure, but in general owe their foundation to the enterprise of landlords in the post-conquest period. Powerful economic disincentives existed to settlement nucleation that derived from environmental conditions and the consequent low profile of arable cultivation. If herding was the major subsistence strategy of this period, then a scattered population was better placed to exploit grazing resources. Parallels with the late prehistoric and Romano-British strategies are obvious. Despite the drop in total population in the period AD 550–700, there is no change so far identified in the basic social unit at the bottom end of society, except that fewer settlements existed. A great estate might include demesne land, and specialist employment. Such would seem to be the implication of St Cuthbert's visit to a well-peopled estate of Abbess Aelfflaed in order to consecrate a new church (Bede, *Vita*, 34). A shepherd of the estate was specifically mentioned, by name a certain Hadwald. This was at the estate centre; it is unlikely that the Abbess owned capital equipment or employed servants in the dependent communities round about. The same source (*Vita*, 29) refers to a member of the royal household – clearly a warrior and presumably a member of the aristocracy – who held a house in the country, in which his wife resided. It seems most likely that this also constituted an estate centre, but whether or not he had inherited the estate or received it from the King is not clear. The exclusivity of aristocratic society and the linkages and social contacts by which it was organized are stressed in the early chapters of the *Vita Wilfridi* (Eddius), and the basic tenets of that society probably pervaded both the secular and much of the ecclesiastical community.

Place-names represent the only substantial data base for the study of English settlement. In the northern counties, only a small proportion appear in documentary sources that predate the Scandinavian immigration, as in the case of Coniscliffe (*Ciningesclif*, AD 778) or of Sockburn (*aet Soccabyrig*, AD 780). Most are non-habitative names, derived from topographical elements, with the occasional addition of personal names. Other groups of place-names also most probably represent place-naming prior to AD 900 – including the *-ham*, *-ceaster*, *-tun*, *ing(a)ton* and *-wic* groups, but in all areas non-habitative names are at least equal in number to these habitative elements, and must have been an important element among the early name forms. Many non-habitative place-names are easily reconciled with estates as opposed to specific settlement sites; the possibility that they represent English translations of pre-existing British place-names of pre-existing estates has already been proposed (see Ch. 6).

Monks, masons and markets

The northern English kingdom was not a naturally wealthy area. Outside the East Riding, environmental factors rendered productivity per unit of labour and land lower than further south. In consequence, large estates were necessary to support an aristocratic élite. The donation of substantial estates to the new monasteries threatened the economic basis of royal government, but it also provided a new élite with wealth with which to pursue a different range of ambitions and objectives. The result was a permanent shift in the direction of Northumbrian aspirations, in favour of endeavours conceived within a religious framework. The 'Golden Age' of Northumbrian monasticism was short-lived, and it was probably confined to a minority of the religious houses.

Notwithstanding, those few hundred monks left an indelible print on the cultural history of western Europe.

The generation of Benedict Biscop and St Wilfrid led Northumbrian Christianity into the embrace of European, Roman and Christian orthodoxy. They drew upon the cultural heritage of Italy and southern Gaul and imported it, to mingle with the established cultural borrowings from English paganism and Irish Christianity. From these ingredients, the Northumbrian monks forged a cultural renaissance that was unique.

Figure 7.2   The Church of the Northumbrian Renaissance: a distribution map.

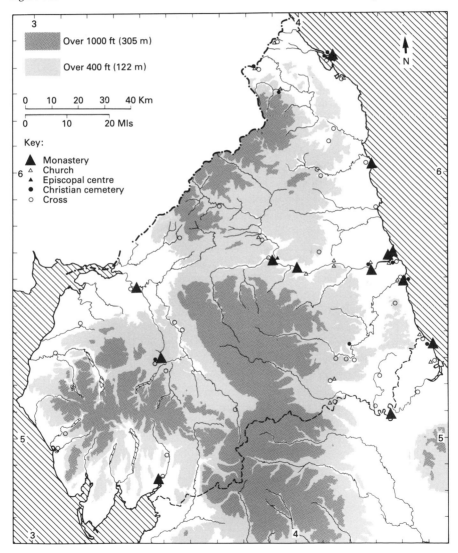

Before the reign of King Ecgfrith, churches had differed little from other buildings constructed in the 'timber hall' tradition, described by Bede as of the Scottish style. Benedict Biscop and Wilfrid brought back to the North a knowledge of Christian architecture in Rome and Gaul (Fletcher 1980). They used their new-found wealth to employ continental craftsmen to reintroduce to Northumbria the lost traditions of masonry, glazing and probably brick and tile manufacture. St Wilfrid set about the construction, or possibly the reconstruction of Hexham Church in AD 673 – there does seem to have been an earlier cemetery and a church is at least a possibility. Unfortunately, major excavations on this site occurred at the turn of the century, and were not of a standard to satisfy modern practitioners. As a result, attempts to reconstruct the fabric have since produced a wide range of suggestions (most recently see Gilbert 1974: 81–113). The original church was, in any case, substantially altered by Bishop Acca, Wilfrid's disciple and successor, and was eventually demolished in ruinous condition *c.* AD 1200. Remaining of the original is the crypt. This example and that at Ripon constitute irregular examples of the common European tradition of mausoleums, with their closest parallel in the mausoleum of King Dagobert's Church at St Denis, constructed as a burial place for the Merovingian royal house. Given the known link between St Wilfrid and King Dagobert (Dddius 28), the similarity is not surprising, however presumptuous may seem Wilfrid's use of the royal model. Whatever the exact form, Hexham Church and others like it made a massive impact on contemporaries. Wilfrid's biographer described the structure in terms of its huge size and the incomparability of the craftsmanship and ornament enshrined within it (Eddius 22). Along with similar buildings at Ripon and York, it stimulated a rash of stone-built churches in monasteries and within those rural estates where resources were made available. Masonry of some of these churches has survived. Others are only evidenced in decorated stones such as the lintels discovered at Moorhouses and Dalston, Cumbria (Cramp 1983). The Northumbrian monasteries became famous for their skill in masonry in the eighth century. The King of the Picts was converted to Roman Christianity in the early eighth century, and followed this up by requesting masons to be dispatched from Lindisfarne to construct a suitable church in his own territory. Despite the conflict between the secular leaders of the two kingdoms, a quiet conquest was under way, by which the Scottish and Pictish Churches were drawn into the Northumbrian cultural province. Despite the successes, glass-making was never well established in the North, apparently declining before *c.* AD 764 (Cramp 1969).

Within the wealthiest monasteries, some of the subordinate structures were constructed in stone [2]. Building 'A' at Jarrow was stone built, with plastered and painted walls within, a red concrete floor and windows illuminated with coloured glass (Plate 7.1). The roof was of stone slate and/or sheet lead. On this site and at Monkwearmouth the monastic buildings were laid out over a substantial area delimited by an enclosure ditch. Some buildings

Plate 7.1 The early monastery site at Jarrow (Tyne and Wear) during excavations in 1969, showing Saxon building B cut by later medieval Cloisters.

were apparently aligned on the church, and many were built in stone held together by mortar in the Roman fashion. The monastery in which Bede wrote was one of the most comfortable residential structures constructed since the fourth century, and to such structures the monks must have looked as a physical manifestation of their high status within society.

On other sites, masonry is less easily observed. Excavations at St Hilda's monastery (or nunnery) at Hartlepool revealed a group of four or five timber buildings constructed with foundation trenches, and a further three with individual post-hole construction (Cramp 1973; *Med. Arch.* 1969: 231). At Tynemouth, excavations by Jobey in 1963 and by Fairclough in 1980 revealed a complex of superimposed timber buildings, the earliest of which predate the Roman occupation. A probable five rectangular buildings were constructed using the sill-beam or post in construction trench technique (Jobey 1967; Fairclough 1983). While these buildings could be of any date between the Roman period and *c.* AD 1080, it seems at least possible that they formed part of the fabric of the known late-seventh- and eighth-century monastic site. Even

297

so, either or both of the Hartlepool and the Tynemouth excavations could have identified extra-mural or dependent structures rather than the core of the monastic fabric. Where we can be sure that excavations have uncovered a Northumbrian monastery, as at Whitby, buildings were more densely packed and in a more complex sequence, although the recording on that site was not adequate to recover the timber-built phases (discussed with refs. Cramp 1973). In 1982 and 1983 excavations by the archaeological unit based at Lancaster uncovered traces of a post-hole constructed rectangular timber-framed building at Dacre [3], but as yet the dating available is no better than for Tynemouth or Hartlepool. The site is probably that referred to by Bede (*Hist. Eccles.*, IV, 32) as a recent monastic foundation near the river Dacre, and an early masonry drain has long been known on the site (see Fig. 6.6). The timber-frame tradition clearly derived from vernacular building methods, and it is very doubtful if any significant differences can be identified between these structures and those of the apparently secular site at Thirlings.

Isolated churches are both more and less accessible to investigation. Many have preserved masonry of the pre-Conquest period, but excavation is rarely an acceptable research strategy. The investigation of early forms of the numerous pre-Conquest churches in north-east England is under way, at times via unlikely methods, some of which have yet to fully establish their credibility (Briggs and Bailey 1983). A network of churches and cemeteries emerged during the period of Northumbria's supremacy and are frequently to be found at advantageous lowland sites, particularly east of the Pennines where many estates enjoyed the facility of a church under the control of the landlord. Recent excavations have revealed such sites in Newcastle close to the river, and at the Hirsel, Coldstream, where grave-markers dating from the fifth century to the Viking Age have been identified within a wide enclosure which also contained buildings and probably a church of some size (Cramp and Douglas-Home 1977/78).

Contemporary commentators were attracted by the exotica and paraphernalia of the new churches as much as by the masonry. Church patrons accumulated precious metal-work with which to adorn their houses of God, coloured glass, furniture and hangings of purple and gold (Eddius 16, 17). Before Wilfrid died he presided over the division of what must have been a substantial treasure at Ripon, but few of these works of art have survived. The golden bowl found in Ormside churchyard (Cumbria) was probably made somewhere in Northumbria, and arguably at York in the late eighth century (illus. Pearson, *et al.* 1981: 41). There is nothing to connect this type of high artistic achievement directly with the monasteries, although this falls within a classical tradition of metal-working that English artificers re-exported to Rome and Germany in the wake of contacts within the Church (D. M. Wilson 1978). The pre-Conquest metal-work from the Hexham excavations is disappointing in quantity: a bucket of sheet bronze contained a hoard of coins of the latter half of the eighth century, a silver plaque was decorated with figure representation of the period AD 550–800, and a gold ring which was probably manufactured in the ninth century (Bailey 1974a).

Among the key possessions of churches and monasteries were sacred relics, a stock of which were imported by Wilfrid and Benedict Biscop. Although of little practical value, relics provided a crucial link with the divine. Although there is little evidence, an exchange system in relics was a European phenomenon. However, the Northumbrian Church rapidly established its own family of relics, following the canonization of St Cuthbert and other colleagues, and their corporal remains and associated artefacts were stored at the heart of the community. The pre-eminence of the relics of St Cuthbert gave the Lindisfarne community a crucial advantage over its competitors for patronage. When all else was lost in the ninth century, the corporal remains of the saint were carried to safety, and in turn ensured the survival of the institution.

The foremost monastic communities produced a range of literary material that surpassed in variety, literacy and illumination all else produced in early medieval England. The Lindisfarne scriptorium was responsible for the *Lindisfarne, Echternach* and *Durham Gospels*. Monkwearmouth and Jarrow produced the *Codex Amiatinus* and other manuscripts (reviewed D. M. Wilson 1978). Other works, like the *Book of Kells*, were probably produced outside Northumbria, but were stamped with the cultural influence peculiar to these monasteries. The production of texts was seen as a vital part of the monastic life, at least within the leading houses. Most works which have survived were produced within a period centred on the generation of Bede. Only those monasteries with major libraries achieved eminence in this area, and the classical and theological texts brought back from Europe by Benedict Biscop and St Wilfrid were a crucial stimulus. Manuscripts and books were among the most precious possessions of the Church. The devout and church-educated King Aldfrith was prepared to alienate a substantial estate (of eight hides) in return for a single manuscript. Charter books and land books had a special value, in addition, as title deeds. During this brief golden age, Northumbrian *scriptoria* produced and copied large numbers of texts, many of which were commissioned, or were destined for overseas markets, to support the missionary work of St Boniface and Willibrord in Germany, or for the use of brethren in Pictland and Ireland. The greatest artistic achievement was the work of illustrators based at Lindisfarne, but that centre never matched the intellectual creativity of Monkwearmouth/Jarrow, or of the later centre at York.

Sculptured stonework is a relic of the period more accessible to the curious, distributed widely across the whole of Northumbria. Unfortunately, little remains in its original position, with the exception of a minority of the great crosses such as those at Bewcastle and Ireby (Cumbria). Much has been reused in building work since the Anglian period, and much is not now widely accessible. It is, therefore, upon stylistic developments that we depend to distinguish Anglian workmanship from Roman and from that of the Viking Age. The detailed study of these artefacts began in the late nineteenth century,

299

but the first authoritative thesis was that of Collingwood between the wars. A recent reappraisal of the sculpture of the Viking Age (Bailey 1980) has provided a useful update, but the publication of the definitive study by Cramp, Bailey *et al.* is still awaited.

The most intricate pieces preserve, even in their often weathered and damaged condition, relief sculpture of the highest technical merit. Among these, the crosses at Ruthwell (Dumfries) and Bewcastle (Cumbria) excel. Both were probably worked in the early to mid eighth century – that is, within the most productive period of the monastic scriptoria. Some of the relief panels at Ruthwell were designed to illustrate the iconography of Psalm 90 (Farrell 1978). That both crosses should be associated with liturgical innovations introduced by Pope Sergius is one recent and attractive suggestion, which would also provide confirmation of the period of manufacture (Carragain 1978). It is arguable that such work was intended to encourage contemplation, and should therefore be associated with monastic communities, and both Ruthwell and Bewcastle are probable monastic sites. Many stone carvings incorporate inscriptions. Given the limited extent of literacy within North-

Plate 7.2   The dedication of the parish church of Jarrow, which is thought to date to the foundation in the reign of King Egfrith. In translation, the dedication reads (after a chi-rho) 'The dedication of the Church of Saint Paul was on the 23rd April in the 15th year of King Ecfrid (685) and the 4th year of Ceolfrid the Abbot and, under the guidance of God, founder of this same church'. (photograph: T. Middlemass)

umbrian society, these too should be associated with churchmen and arguably with monasteries. One of two examples from Monkwearmouth, extended, reads: *Hic in sepulchro requiescit corpore Herebericht presbyter* – 'Here in the tomb lies Herebericht the priest in [his] bodily form' (Okasha 1971: 92). Such inscriptions serve as memorials, and this is the commonest ascertainable function of the inscribed stones. Such must be the purpose of the slab found near Hartlepool Moor in 1833, bearing the inscription which, extended, reads: *Ora pro Vermund Torhtsuid* – 'Pray for Vermund [and] Torhtsuid.' Few texts are as lengthy or as historically significant as that still to be seen on the west-facing interior wall above the chancel arch of Jarrow Parish Church, which records the dedication of the church to St Paul on 23 April AD 685, and which is generally considered to have been inscribed as a contemporary memorial of that event (Okasha 1971: 61; Plate 7.2).

If many inscribed stones recall a monastic site, in many instances they provide the sole evidence for such communities, and should be seen as no more than indicators. In Cumbria only three or possibly four monastic communities (and a hermitage) are known from literary sources – at Heversham, at and near Carlisle and at Dacre. However, inscriptions have in addition been identified at Knells (significantly near Carlisle), Workington and Beckermet, while none have come from Dacre or Heversham. Important groups devoid of inscriptions have also been identified at Irton, Urswick and Addingham. All these sites are potentially the sites of Anglian monastic communities.

The total number of sculptured stones located west of the Pennines is not large, so far from Cumbria something between 25 and 30 from about 17 sites. East of the Pennines the resource base of the monastic communities was richer, and they were probably greater in number. Stonework has survived in profusion. At Hexham, for example, about forty-five fragments are arguably of Anglian date and derive from the masonry of the church as well as from memorial stones, from which two inscriptions have been recovered (Cramp 1974: 172–8). Other sites such as Carham and Norham have also considerable quantities of stonework.

The association between the Church – particularly monasteries – and the carving of stones was a close one. There is little evidence of direct lay patronage of sculptors or masons, and there can be little doubt that the literacy of the inscriptions derived from church learning. A minority of inscriptions used the ogham alphabet, and so point to Irish influence in the Northumbrian Church. Secular motifs are generally absent in relief sculpture, in contrast to the emergence of battle scenes, for example, in works of the Viking Age. The addition of inscriptions implies not only a literate craftsman but also a literate audience. Only within the religious community was literacy anything like sufficient to justify such expensive memorials, and it seems highly likely that the art of sculpting, like the craft of building in masonry, owed a great deal to the patronage and interest of the leaders of the Roman Church from the late seventh century onwards.

The monasteries were centres for other forms of craftsmanship, and arguably also for trading activity. Most of the wealthy monasteries founded in the late seventh and early eighth centuries occupy sites beside navigable waterways, with easy access to the sea (Cramp 1983). This is the case not only for those sites in a specifically coastal or estuarine location – Lindisfarne, Alnmouth(?), Jarrow, Monkwearmouth, Hartlepool, Carlisle, Heversham, Workington(?), Beckermet(?) – but also for those like Hexham or Norham on the major river network. It seems likely that there was a degree of preference for such a site among the founders. Communication by sea was of some importance, and imported artefacts make a hesitant appearance in eighth-century deposits on the north-east coast, although not with the persistence identified at Whitby where imported metal-work and ceramics underlined the wealth and sumptuous collective life-style of this most royal of monasteries. Excavations at Monkwearmouth and Jarrow identified very little in the way of personal possessions, as befitted a community following the Rule of St Benedict, but some use was made of riverine and estuarine resources; food debris was dominated by the skeletal remains of fish and shellfish (Cramp 1973), and we know that dolphin meat was an acceptable food source to a monastic community (Bede, *Vita*, ii). Monasteries were the wealthiest immobile consumer group within Northumbrian society north of the Tees. It is, therefore, likely that whatever market facilities did develop would have tended to cluster around monastic sites, much in the way that civilian *vici* clung to the Roman forts. This is not to suggest that the spending power of the monastic community ever approximated to that of the Roman army, nor was the structure of that purchasing power comparable: if the Rule of St Benedict was ever a significant factor then it was a highly centralized economic demand. Even so, monastic demand may have stimulated some local crafts, as evidenced by the local pottery found in rubbish pits and elsewhere at Hartlepool (*Med. Arch.* 1969: 231).

The Church was probably the sole source of patronage for exotic crafts such as glass manufacture, for which demand was insufficient to maintain the craft in existence into the later period. Clerics may also have attracted imports, such as the fine vestments and other personal and church adornments that appear sporadically in the texts. In this context, the availability of good harbourage may have been significant. Northumbrian monasteries were in contact via their own missionaries with Frisia and Saxony. Bishop Willibrord certainly came back to visit Lindisfarne (Bede, *Vita*, 44), and it is possible that Frisian merchants made regular visits to the Northumbrian coast, as well as to York. However, in those cases which are well documented, churchmen on their way to the Continent travelled to the south-east coast of England before braving the crossing. The long-distance system of gift exchange within the Church may have operated via the same route, and it is extremely difficult to point to any Northumbrian ports north of the Tees enjoying an entrepôt role independent of York and the southern seaboard.

Secular parallels to the coastal monasteries may be those sites which performed the function of defended centres within the estate structure, many of which began life as royal sites. *Burh* place-names are an important class, including the well-known royal site at Bamburgh, and other coastal centres at Lesbury by Alnmouth, Middlesbrough on the Tees estuary and elsewhere. However, most *burh*, and most *ceaster* place-names are grouped along the Roman road network and the latter at least are attached to pre-existing fortifications rather than to specifically Anglian sites. Given the itinerant nature of the Northumbrian kings, and the apparent growing identification with Yorkshire after *c.* AD 700, it seems unlikely that any significant market infrastructure could have been established or maintained solely by the demand from secular sites. By far the most consistent demand for imports should be associated with those pairs of sites where secular and church patronage were juxtaposed, as at Bamburgh and Lindisfarne (Cramp 1983). Elsewhere it is possible that the place-name element *-wic* may carry the inference of a market function, at such sites as Alnwick east of the Pennines and Warwick and Urswick in the west, but many northern names in *-wic* are arguably late, and of low status.

Coinage did not circulate widely in northern Northumbria before the Viking Age. Northumbrian kings began to mint a silver coinage in the mid eighth century, but had already ceased by *c.* AD 800, and subsequently issued a copper coinage known as *stycas* until the Danish Conquest temporarily interrupted the activity of the mint. The issue of *stycas* was peculiar to Northumbria, and the coinage did not circulate significantly beyond its frontiers. In one sense it was a highly sophisticated coinage, since it presumably enjoyed a value for the purpose of exchange significantly higher than the value of its base metal content, and in this respect it resembles a paper currency. If its value depended not on metal content but on royal authority, its limited distribution is understandable.

The coinage was minted under the authority of kings and archbishops of York. There is no reason to suppose that a mint operated in Bernicia, and coin losses diminish progressively north and particularly west of Yorkshire. West of the Pennines isolated coin finds are almost non-existent, and hoards, where analyzable, cluster around a deposition date *c.* AD 875; such include the substantial Kirkoswald hoard. At Carlisle, isolated coin finds from recent excavations include the only *sceattas* so far found west of the northern Pennines, and may imply a coin-using community within and around the monastery. Three coin hoards with varying claims to authenticity have been found in the Cartmel peninsula, including the 95 *stycas* reputed to have been found with a melée of Roman material at Castle Head, Upper Allithwaite (Watkin 1883: 215). Both Cartmel and Carlisle are peculiar for their known ecclesiastical associations. In eastern Bernicia the link between monasteries and coin hoards is even clearer. Hoards from Lindisfarne, Hexham, Jarrow, Monkwearmouth and Melrose constitute the majority of both hoards and coins. Of known secular sites, only

303

Bamburgh has yielded more than a single find. The group of coin hoards found in the Lower Tyne valley has led to the recent suggestion of commercial activity in that area (Cramp 1983), but the case is at best unproven, however attractive it may be.

The coin finds from Bernicia tell us much about the local economy. The rarity of single finds or small hoards implies that coinage played little part in the intra-estate economy. Links with the monastic centres imply that coinage was available to the social élite as a means of exchange, as a medium of the payment of rent or of taxation (whether to the clerical or secular arms), and as a medium of capital accretion – an activity which hoards such as that from Kirkoswald or Hexham probably represent (e.g. Pagan 1974).

Monastic communities were powerful institutions within Northumbrian society. However, their influence was not all pervasive. Kings and members of the lay aristocracy continued to pursue ambitions which were entirely secular. Bede strongly disapproved of the military adventurism of King Ecgfrith, and interpreted his sudden death in AD 685 as the result of divine retribution, but Bede had lived since the tender age of seven years in the most thoroughgoing of the new Benedictine communities, and knew little of the world outside the cloister. Not for him the political manoeuvring of Bishop Wilfrid, who eventually placed his political weight behind a king with a known predilection for fornication with nuns (Kirby 1974: 15), although, to be fair to the saint, this can hardly have been apparent when he became king at the age of eight.

The institutions of the Church were disunited in moral attitudes and in their own expectations of the religious life. The twin monastery founded by Benedict Biscop casts a long shadow over the lesser-known Northumbrian houses, but was itself atypical (e.g. Wormald 1978). The most important surviving manuscript produced in its scriptorium was sufficiently distinctive for the community to be interpreted as a Roman island in a Northumbrian sea; the manuscript was intended by the Abbot to be presented to the Pope. The insistence of Benedict Biscop and his immediate successor that they should not be succeeded by relatives highlights the normal practice in the Northumbrian monasteries, many of which were openly and unashamedly governed by dynasties of abbots and abbesses transposed from the secular aristocracy. Most communities were less committed to the collective life and more susceptible to secular ambitions than Bede would have liked. A letter from Alcuin of York in AD 797 to Hygebald, Bishop of Lindisfarne, was couched in language that implies that the latter community were rather less ascetic than the Primate would have wished (Whitelock 1955: 194). To the less austere communities among the English monasteries we owe the little that remains of literature in the Old English vernacular. To the ascetics we owe the ideological pressures that thereafter depressed the rate of survival of such texts to a very low level indeed.

The number of monasteries rose dramatically during the lifetime of Bede, to his obvious disquiet (Whitelock 1955: 170). The houses he criticized were the foundations of royal ministers under royal licence, in which they and their successors proceeded to live in a style no less secular than that to which they were accustomed, but within a legal and constitutional framework of great advantage to themselves. This was a form of patronage that the crown could not afford to dispense. That it did is a sign of the weakness of the royal resource base already apparent by the early eighth century. The hereditary principle lay at the heart of secular society; it provided the normal means by which privilege and possessions were transferred from one generation to the next. The powerful links between founding families and their monasteries ensured that the descent from one generation to the next of this important element of their possessions differed little from the remainder. The loser was the King, to whom access to those resources was entirely denied.

Whatever the intentions of the founder, the pressure of secular ownership on these communities cannot have encouraged the maintenance of a strict rule of collective life, and these communities were probably among the earliest to collapse under the pressure of secularism. Silence surrounds the fate of many of the great houses in the ninth century. Many were probably, like Lindisfarne, abandoned in the face of hostile raids, but Norham and Heversham were still described as monasteries *c.* AD 900, whatever the life-style of the resident community. However, most had probably ceased to practise a life-style compatible with the rule introduced by the founders before the Viking Age began, giving way slowly to the pressures of secular attitudes, and without either the opportunity or the will to distance themselves from the lay community. The letter of Alcuin to Calvinus and Cuculus makes it clear that senior churchmen were in many respects indistinguishable from the secular nobility (Whitelock 1955: 208).

The obvious exceptions are associated with the bishops, who provide a chain of contact with Deira and ultimately with Canterbury throughout the ninth century. The bishoprics were increased in number, despite the opposition of St Wilfrid, by Archbishop Theodore acting in collaboration with King Ecgfrith. Henceforth, the Bernician Church was organized by bishops based within monastic communities at Hexham, Lindisfarne and Whithorn (newly established in the lifetime of Bede). Under their jurisdiction were the monastic communities without special privileges, and the growing number of parochial centres established by estate owners for the use of local communities, to act as centres for burial and baptism and perhaps missionary work. We should not forget the peasants who jeered as the building timbers destined for Jarrow were swept past and out to sea, and whose lack of sympathy was ascribed to a preference for the 'old religion' (Bede, *Vita*, 3). Despite the increased numbers of bishops, Bede was concerned at their insufficiency and their worldliness when he wrote to Egbert at York in AD 734. The monastic communities had considerable influence on the bishop – most were elevated from the monasteries – but they arguably distanced themselves from the rural community, preferring instead to maintain a standard and style of living borrowed from the secular world, and indistinguishable from it.

Northumbrian society in the mid ninth century was organized via a hierarchical structure, at the head of which was a comparatively small élite, socially cohesive but politically fragmented, as is apparent in the competitions centred around succession to the crown. The role of the King had altered as the royal resource base disintegrated and kings became identified with factions and their partisans. The ability of this society to mobilize in its own defence was fatally eroded in step with the decline of the monarchy. Within the comparative peace which had pervaded the border area since the early eighth century, this was not a major problem. However, the secular order was ill placed to withstand the new pressures of war; much of it was swept away to reveal a growing kernel of theocracy within Northumbrian society that was to achieve a dominant position in some localities during the Viking Age.

The Viking Age

Scandinavian seafarers came first to the attention of the West Saxon chroniclers when they killed a royal official on the south coast in the year AD 789. This heralded a period of widespread raiding. In the North the earliest recorded attack struck at Lindisfarne only four years later: 'heathen men destroyed God's church with plunder and slaughter'. Further raids followed, and those which struck at the monasteries were at least sporadically recorded. The 'E' version of the *Anglo-Saxon Chronicle* mentions an attack on Jarrow in AD 794; excavation at Monkwearmouth and Jarrow revealed destruction of both sites by fire which was at the latter hot enough to melt window glass and lead (Cramp 1969). The guilt of the Vikings should not be assumed, but the coincidence of arson and a late-eighth-century context places them at the top of any short list of suspects. Both sites were abandoned, although Monkwearmouth was reused as a cemetery site during the Viking Age.

We do not know how many monasteries were the targets of raiders. Roger of Wendover may have been drawing on contemporary accounts when he recorded attacks on Tynemouth and Hartness in AD 800, but if so his source has not survived. Monasteries were easy and obvious targets for heathen pirates. Many were directly accessible from the sea. Few, if any, were in any sense defensible. They were staffed by the only wealthy but strictly civilian section of English society, yet the communities held considerable stocks of highly portable wealth in the form of precious metal-work and other costly furnishings. Those communities that survived to the late eighth century were certainly in danger from piratical raids.

These attacks were the work of Norsemen from the Norwegian fjords, and form one small part of the broad pattern of exploration, trade, piracy and settlement by which the Norse established themselves as the dominant maritime power in the north-eastern Atlantic, and settled widely in the Irish Sea basin. By the mid ninth century Norse settlement had occurred in the Western Isles, Man, Dublin and elsewhere on the eastern coast of Ireland, and the consequent mixture of the Gaelic and Norse languages and people had begun. No raids into western Northumbria have been recorded, but the area was largely beyond the threshold of literate comment, and attacks may well have gone unrecorded.

Along the north-east coast there is no evidence that the political community adopted a serious attitude towards these occasional raids. The pattern of internecine warfare was becoming more pronounced by the late eighth century, and worsened during the ninth. Only three years after the sack of Lindisfarne, King Ethelred was murdered. Osbald succeeded him for only twenty-seven days before Eardwulf was raised to the throne (Whitelock 1955: 199–200). Bishop Alcuin of York was caught up in these great affairs of state. It was the opinion of leading clerics like Alcuin that the raids were symptomatic of the wrath of God at the moral misdemeanours of the English, and attitudes of this sort did little to galvanize the community to effective defense action. Perhaps the speed and mobility of the raiders placed their destruction beyond the expectation of even the most determined English king. However awful for the victims, the activities of a few shiploads of heathen warriors were insufficiently alarming or predictable to stimulate the union of the fragmented Northumbrian leadership.

Within a generation, the problem disappears from recorded history. During the ninth century the perspective of the compilers of the chronicles was West Saxon and Mercian, and their horizons were severely limited.

The Scandinavian settlement

Substantial Danish fleets joined the assault upon England from the 830s onwards, and it seems unlikely that Northumbria was entirely free of incursions. The Danish attacks culminated in the arrival of a host of unprecedented size which reached East Anglia in AD 865. Later report had it that the 'Great Army' was led by Ivar the Boneless, Ubbi and Halfdan who had come to England to avenge the killing of their father Ragnar by King Aella of Northumbria. Whatever the truth of this, East Anglia was their landfall, and they may have been attracted to Northumbria not by thoughts of revenge so much as the news of civil war there (G. Jones 1968: 218 ff).

The arrival of the Great Army heralds the end of one era and the beginning of another. Hitherto Scandinavian fleets had raided widely, but had sought to avoid battle with the full armed strength of their enemies. The piratical raids had grown in scale and in duration, taking fleets to Spain, Africa and into the Mediterranean, but even the four-year cruise led by Ragnar was without major political consequences. In contrast, the leaders of the Great Army were less interested in booty than in the conquest of kingdoms over which they might then rule.

The first English kingdom to collapse was Northumbria. In AD 867 the Danes rode north, crossed the Humber estuary and took York. The civil war between Aella and Osbert prevented a prompt English response. The union of their forces was delayed until late in the year, by which time the Danish host had consolidated its position. The subsequent battle at York was an English disaster; many were slain including both kings and the survivors made peace with the enemy. The Danes overwintered at York, then campaigned in the following year in Mercia, leaving Deira in the hands of a client king. They returned to southern Northumbria in AD 869, and again in AD 873. In AD 875 the host divided, and Halfdan led part into Bernicia, overwintering on the Tyne and campaigning in northern Northumbria, Strathclyde and Pictland. It is possible that Halfdan's forces sacked Carlisle, but the source is less than reliable.

Halfdan probably intended to take control of all Northumbria as his own kingdom. A show of force in the North and West was essential to this purpose, and a demonstration of his power among the neighbouring kingdoms secured his northern frontier. During the same period the other part of the Great Army under Guthrum was establishing itself in eastern England and continuing the contest for control of the South with King Alfred. It was this contest that absorbed the interests of the West Saxon chroniclers who recorded only that in the year AD 876, 'Halfdan shared out the lands of Northumbrians and they proceeded to plough and support themselves' (Whitelock 1955: 179). The precise meaning of this entry is obscure to us, and it probably records an event only marginally within the perspective of the cleric who recorded it. It seems most unlikely that the victorious host entered local society as peasant cultivators, but rather as owners of the *villae* and estates of their vanquished competitors.

To these conquerors should be given responsibility for the numerous, so-called 'Grimston hybrid' place-names of eastern England, which derive from the renaming of existing English *tuns* (Jensen 1978; Cameron 1971; Gelling 1978). These place-names are scattered among those settlements with English place-names, and share with them the more advantageous terrains. The probability is that many of them were renamed after members of the host as they became landowners at the level of the *villa* as a result of the dispersal of estates by Halfdan in AD 876.

Such place-names are not common north of the Catterick gap, although several do occur in the Tees basin at and near Sheraton (*Scurufatun*, *c*. AD 1050; Watts 1976), and in the area between Sedgefield and Stockton-on-Tees (Fig. 7.3). If diagnostic elements occur, and this is increasingly challenged, the thin scatter of Scandinavian place-names in this area betrays a Danish rather than a Norse affinity, as in the form Coniscliffe (*Ciningesclif*, *c*. AD 778;

Watts 1976). Norse influence in place-names in Co. Durham is confined to the upper valleys of the Tees and Wear, where names in the area of Newbiggin may betray links with Norse settlement west of the Pennines, but which may be very late foundations. It is difficult to support the suggestion by Watts (1976: 216) that the 'Grimston hybrids' north of the Tees should be associated with the brief Hiberno–Norse conquest of the period AD 910–30. The more natural suggestion would be that these represent estates acquired by Halfdan's followers on the periphery of that area in which he was able to reward his soldiery – an area centred securely in Deira. If this were accepted, the scatter of names in -*by*(*r*) which occupy generally rather poor sites in the same area of Teesdale may represent the subsequent impact of Danish lordship, and the dispersal of lands to supporters and colonists in under-used terrain within estates in which the best sites and most profitable land was already being farmed in the lord's interest by English communities. There are a significant number of English place-names between Barnard Castle and the coast which betray evidence of

Figure 7.3 The Scandinavian settlement in the English Tyne-Tees province (based on Watts, 1976).

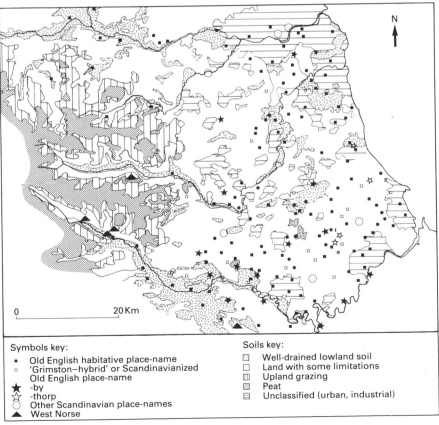

Symbols key:
- • Old English habitative place-name
- ▫ 'Grimston–hybrid' or Scandinavianized Old English place-name
- ★ -by
- ☆ -thorp
- ○ Other Scandinavian place-names
- ▲ West Norse

Soils key:
- ▨ Well-drained lowland soil
- ▫ Land with some limitations
- ▥ Upland grazing
- ▨ Peat
- ▤ Unclassified (urban, industrial)

0   20 Km

Scandinavianization, and these indicate that Danish speakers were present in significant numbers at least for a few generations (Mawer 1920). Conversely, Sheraton is one Scandinavian place-name in which an Anglicized pronunciation can be traced at an early date (Watts 1976).

Further north very little Scandinavian colonization occurred, despite the campaigns of Halfdan. To take over the Bernician estates was probably beyond the resources of manpower available to the Danish kings, who preferred to concentrate the host within the richer territory of Deira. However, the campaign of AD 875 was probably highly disruptive. Only via the community of St Cuthbert can we measure the reactions of the Bernician aristocracy. The community had already removed from Lindisfarne to the rather less vulnerable site of Norham upon Tweed during the tenure of the see by Bishop Ecgred (AD 830–45). They reconstructed there the church of St Aidan, and carried with them the key relics – the corporal remains of St Cuthbert and King Ceolwulf (Craster 1954). In AD 875 the community probably found itself in the path of the Danish thrust towards Pictland. Bishop Eardulf set out from Norham with the remains of St Cuthbert and a part at least of the community, travelling southwards or south-westwards. Western Northumbria was probably the obvious goal, and during seven years of wandering they reached Cumbria and were joined by Abbot Eadred from the Carlisle monastery, who henceforth led the refugees. Church dedications to St Cuthbert in Cumbria may correspond to the resting-places of the refugees.

During a succession crisis among the Danes in AD 883, Eadred lobbied successfully for the elevation of Guthred, a young candidate with Christian and English connections. This whole affair underlines the essential pragmatism of Anglo-Danish contact. The Danes were capable of appalling atrocities in the course of conquest when it suited their purposes – the death of King Edmund the Martyr may have had a northern parallel in that of King Aella of Northumbria. However, by AD 883 the Danish host was a satisfied power, absorbed in estate management and the dispensing of patronage, and was in addition in military decline. The warriors of the initial conquest of AD 867 were ageing, and had as yet been unable to raise a second generation. From AD 883, the Danish leadership was markedly less bellicose, and frequently forced back on to the defensive.

As a result of this successful intervention, the community of St Cuthbert was enabled to re-establish a permanent home east of the Pennines. King Guthred demonstrated his gratitude to Eadred by allowing him to purchase certain estates from the host in the Tees basin (Hart 1975: doc. 156), and granted him all the land from the Tyne to Wear between Dere Street and the sea, with right of sanctuary and with all customs (Hart 1975: doc. 155). The acquisition of this enormous block of territory, formerly largely held by Monkwearmouth and Jarrow monasteries, prompted Eadred to re-establish the community south of the Tyne at Chester-le-Street where he caused a wooden church to be erected (Symeon, II, 382).

The purchased land lay largely in the parishes of Easington and Hesleden near Hartlepool. Scandinavian place-names occur in both parishes, and by this purchase the community came to exercise lordship over Danish farmers as well as English; although the Danish lords may have retired into Deira, the preservation of the place-names implies a surviving Danish-speaking population in the area over several generations. This pragmatic approach to contact between Danes and English is exactly comparable to the 'Danophile' brother Edward who attracted the disapprobation of his correspondent, the author of a fragment of a letter written in the vernacular and copied into a Worcester manuscript (Whitelock 1955: 232).

As far as the Tyne–Tees province was concerned, the settlement between Guthred and Eadred formalized the end of the crisis of the conquest, with results satisfactory to both parties. The grant to St Cuthbert implies the recognition by that community of the authority of the Danish kings as legitimate successors to the Northumbrian throne, and Guthred could count upon the abbot or bishop to exercise royal authority in the area beyond the Tees on his behalf. For the bishops, the settlement allowed undisputed retention of the ecclesiastical estates, and the extension of those estates by substantial royal grants, in support of the elevation of his ecclesiastical authority to a *de facto* regal status, reinforced by jurisdictional privilege and by the distant threat of Danish support. In this period occurred the first stages by which the palatinate authority of the bishops of Durham was established.

Within this extraordinarily advantageous political climate, the community emerged as the major landowners in the whole Tees–Forth province. Membership of the community was highly prized. The priest Berrard donated the estate of *Twilingatun* (probably Willington, near Wallsend) as the price of membership (Hart 1975: doc. 157), and the refugee Abbot Tilred of Heversham purchased from them the abbacy of the dependent house at Norham at the price of the estate of Little Eden (Hart 1975: doc. 158).

Beyond the Tyne, Northumberland lay outside the normal control of Halfdan's successors, but not outside the influence of St Cuthbert. It was within this area that the monastery had attracted the earliest grants of estates (see Fig. 7.1), and the community was by far the most important landowner in Northumberland, the Merse and eastern Lothian. The settlement with the Danish monarchy established a regime under which the bishops of Chester-le-Street acted in a quasi-regal capacity throughout eastern Bernicia. The only significant rival for power was the aristocratic family based on Bamburgh, normally described as 'ealdormen'. The family did not emerge into history until the second decade of the tenth century, but it seems likely that the office derived from the English kings at some stage in the eighth or ninth centuries, and that the hereditary holders provided continuous secular leadership through the crisis of the Danish invasion, gathering about them the remnants of the Bernician aristocracy. During the tenth century they established themselves as an effective dynasty, largely independent of outside authority, and therefore assuming a semi-regal position. Although southern chroniclers never honoured them with the title of king, Ealdred son of Eadwulf was treated as a *de facto* monarch at the Eamont conference on 12 July AD 927. The dynasty at Bamburgh identified itself with the political attitudes and aspirations of eastern Bernicia, among which was a long-lived and deep-rooted hostility to the separate tradition of Northumbrian royalty established in AD 867 and enshrined in the Anglo-Danish Deira. In these attitudes, they looked towards an alliance of mutual interest with the southern English kings.

Having survived the political challenge of Danish conquest, the northern counties faced further disruption at the hands of Scandinavian armies and colonists early in the tenth century. As a result, the area fragmented, dividing along the line of the Pennines and Cheviots, and to a lesser extent in Cumbria on a line roughly identifiable on the rivers Derwent and Eamont. This second-wave immigration came not from Denmark but from the Norwegian and Gaelic colonies in western Britain. It was the misfortune of the Northumbrians that the Irish successfully (if only temporarily) evicted the Norse from their major coastal strongholds. Some groups were small, barely more than a handful of land-hungry refugees. Others were larger, and like that led into Wirral by Ingimundr were prepared to challenge for local control (Wainwright 1975: 131 ff). The largest was the host led by Ragnald, which raided Pictland in AD 904 and 905. By AD 914 Ragnald had assembled a force large enough to strike at Northumbria, and to contest control of both the English and Anglo-Danish areas. The attack came not from the North Sea but from the western coast of Northumbria, but no serious attempt was made to halt the Irish Norse until they entered Northumberland and seized the lands of Ealdred son of Eadwulf of Bamburgh (Arnold 1885: 208). Ealdred assembled a Bernician army and was joined by the Scots under King Constantine, but the First Battle of Corbridge was a Norse victory in which fell many of the Bernician aristocracy, among them Alfred, the ill-fated tenant of Bishop Cutheard of Chester-le-Street who had fled eastwards to escape the pirates in Cumbria and been granted estates in eastern Durham (see below). His death implies that the influence and affinity of the St Cuthbert community was thrown into battle against the Norse. A second battle occurred in the same vicinity *c.* AD 918, in which was killed Eadred son of Ricsige, another leading tenant of St Cuthbert in Durham. Despite the submission to Aethelflaed of Mercia in AD 918, the West Saxons and Mercians did not actively aid the Danes in Yorkshire, and Ragnald took the kingdom. Beyond the Tees he came to an accommodation with the family of Eadred Ricsiging by which they retained the poor upland holdings in western Durham (Hart 1975: doc. 163, note) but the more profitable and accessible lands along the coast he confiscated from the monastery by right of conquest and established two of his own protégés, Scule and Onlafball, in the Norse interest (Hart 1915: doc. 164). The scatter of Scandinavian place-names along the coastal plain suggest that they exercised patronage within these estates in favour of members of their host, and that some at least of these low- and middle-ranking estate holders survived the re-establishment of monastic overlordship in the 930s.

The death of Ragnald in AD 921 was a turning-point in Northumbrian politics. Although subsequent kings of Dublin exercised control over York, the influence of the West Saxon monarchy grew dramatically north of the Humber. The period from AD 921 to 954 saw a series of complex political manoeuvres by which the English kings successfully ousted the Norse influence, and established their own tenure of the Northumbrian throne (Whitelock 1959). The Norse could count on support from the Northumbrian self-determination and separatism centred in Yorkshire, led not infrequently by senior membrs of the church hierarchy like Archbishop Wulfstan (Campbell 1942). It should be remembered that Athelstan and his successors significantly increased the resource base of the Church in the North, and probably intended to use this as the basis of their own authority via their nomination of the bishops (e.g. Hart 1975: docs. 116, 120, 120a, 121). In addition the Norse could count on support from the Strathclyde Britons from the 920s onwards, and from the Scots at least until the disaster inflicted upon their cause at the Battle of *Brunanburgh* in AD 937.

The English kings lacked a secure resource base in the North, but could rely upon Danish anti-Norse feeling in Yorkshire, upon some senior religious leaders and upon the house of Bamburgh, with whom there developed a political alliance of mutual self-interest through which the politically ambivalent Danish community could be controlled. This alliance served the late tenth century monarchs well. Uhtred of Bamburgh allied himself by marriage successfully to the Bishop of Durham (formally of Chester-le-Street) and to powerful interests within the Anglo-Danish community. Through his network of alliances he held the North for Ethelred until his cause had utterly collapsed, and was subsequently murdered while under the safe-conduct of King Cnut, by his Danish rivals in Yorkshire. The Danish ascendancy drove an irreconcilable wedge between the Bernician and Deiran communities, and the area was practically ungovernable throughout the eleventh century (Kapelle 1979; Hart 1975: 143). The Bernicians were unable to protect their own territory against the rising power of the united Scottish–Pictish kingdom, and lost the Lothians after the disastrous Battle of Carham. The final consequence of this fragmentation was annihilation at the hands of the Norman conquerors in the winter of AD 1069–70 and during subsequent campaigns.

Settlement and land-use, *c.* AD 875–1000

There are some signs that the rural economy experienced the beginning of an upturn in the last century of the millennium. A vigorous renewal of clearance activity has been dated by carbon-14 at Fellend Moss (Northumb.) to *c.* AD 1000, when barley, rye and *Cannabis* re-emerged into the pollen spectrum. At Steng Moss, the reforestation that was a feature of the late mid millennium was relatively short-lived, and the climax of renewed clearance activity came in the mid tenth century (Turner 1983). Place-names local to both the mosses derive almost entirely from Old English or Middle English, so that there is no reason to suppose that any Scandinavian immigrants were responsible for the renewed economic activity. It has been suggested above that the decline in cultivation and land management that typified the late sixth and seventh centuries was due to plague-induced population decline, exacerbated by poor climatic conditions, similar to the situation between AD 1350 and 1480. If the parallel is apt, then the re-emergence of population growth in the tenth century is paralleled by a similar phenomenon in the sixteenth century. In the latter case the population was able to expand via internal mechanisms, without the stimulus of immigration. The same process arguably occurred in eastern Bernicia, from which the aristocracy successfully excluded other ethnic groups who sought entry.

The growth of population in this area was probably somewhat slower than in neighbouring areas of Northumbria into which colonists from outside successfully migrated, and this may help explain the comparative weakness of the Northumberland English during the Viking Age. Even so, we should envisage real growth in the rural economy, fuelled by local population growth under the impetus of a climatic improvement which probably included a decline in the level of rainfall. Growing pressure on resources pushed rural communities towards the higher yields per unit area available from arable strategies wherever these were feasible. There are severe methodological limitations to the establishment of a chronology for either colonization or place-name formation in the English areas of the North-east. Even so, there are indications that place-names do enshrine something of this process of colonization. The development of the western part of Co. Durham – west of Weardale – was accompanied by the creation of numerous woodland place-names, with elements, in *leah*, *hyrst*, *rydding* and *wudu*. Examples utilizing French personal names such as Frosterley demonstrate that some of these names derive from the twelfth century or later, but it would be natural to look to the late first millennium and the seigneurial activity of the bishops of Chester-le-Street/Durham and their tenants to see the inception of this colonizing initiative. Elsewhere, it is clear that much infilling also took place. Many names in -*tun* occupy poor-quality sites, and are likely to belong to a relatively late stage of colonization. Again the combination of -*tun* with post-conquest elements emphasizes the late use of the affix, as in the case of Nelson. Others like Newton and Morton advertise the secondary quality of the site. Other names generated in the ninth or tenth centuries may indicate, as do many Danish names, that proprietors were prone to rename settlements; the case of Rainton has been proposed in this context (Watts 1976).

There are hints that some Scandinavian immigration may have succeeded even within Northumberland, producing what are arguably Scandinavian elements in the place-name Rothbury and others in this and other localities (Påhlsson 1975/76; Mawer 1920). However, even were this the case, it is unlikely to have been of a scale to effect demographic trends. The pressure on land probably spilled over into the uplands, where summer grazing rights became of increased importance. Numerous sites of Romano-British farms occupying marginal terrain were reoccupied during the medieval period or even later, and rectangular stone buildings erected. Few if any can be dated to the tenth century, but the episode that generated this reappraisal of marginal resources certainly began before the end of the millennium, and then later was responsible for upland pasture names like Wether Cairn and Wether Lair, and the links between developing townships in the valleys such as the *-bothl* place-names between the Aln and Coquet, and elsewhere. In the west of the north-eastern counties, Norse and Cumbrian pastoralists were contesting control of the summer pasturage, the foremost contributing names derived from *-saetr* – a shieling or summer pasture, as in Earl's Seat, and the latter responsible for Glendhu Hill on the county boundary.

In some areas of southern Durham and Cleveland, Danish immigrants filled the crucial middle and lower ranks of land-ownership, and were able to consolidate their position by exercising patronage in favour of fellow country-men. As a result the immigration was probaby of numerical significance in some localities, and the *-by(r)* names such as Killerby, Cleasby, Ulnaby and Eppleby (North Riding) plus Dyance, Eggleston and Ingleton grouped around the Scandinavianized Gainford represent the influx of Danish colonists into under-utilized areas within those estates that came under Danish control (see Fig. 7.3). Around Sadberge, near Darlington, the immigrants were sufficiently numerous to form a wapentake. Even so, Danish did not survive as a spoken language in the North-east, and English lords rapidly re-established control over land-holdings in the area, including those estates in which an Irish–Norse aristocracy had taken control in the 920s. Danish landowners doggedly held on to estates at the local level, and it was probably their patronage that was responsible for the concentration of Viking Age sculpture in the Tees basin. The key centres lie well inland, on the Tees at Sockburn and Gainford – that is, at sites with existing links with ecclesiastical land-holding but central to areas distinguished by Danish place-names. These sites offer us a degree of continuity across the Danish invasion period, after which they re-emerge as proto-parochial centres. The stone sculpture which they exhibit owed much to pre-existing English traditions of craftsmanship, and commemorative stonework.

The continuity that was a key factor in the local schools of stone sculpture appears to have been the hallmark of the Danish colonization. Their initial impact on Northumbrian society was traumatic, but within a decade close contact between the immigrants and local ecclesiastical authority had begun the Christianization and anglicization of the Danes. By the early tenth century, all the evidence available suggests a community moving towards ethnic and cultural integration, and presenting a relatively united front to the Irish–Norse menace. In southern Durham integration was spurred on by the anomalous tenurial situation by which both English and Danes at the local level held land from the English aristocracy who were tenants of an English bishop and monastery operating in the political interest of a Danish monarch.

It is hardly surprising that in this political environment the permanent sites occupied by the St Cuthbert community at Chester-le-Street (and eventually at Durham), and the subordinate monastery at Norham attracted Viking Age sculpture with distinctive motifs of decorative knotwork (Bailey 1980: 194), which could have been commissioned by either clerical or secular patrons. In western Durham and throughout Northumberland the predominantly English estate holders preferred to avoid distinctively Viking Age sculpture; such cultural distinctions were based on the presence or absence of an intrusive social élite, and via this type of distinction developed significant local and regional subcultures in the Tees–Forth province.

Cumbria in the Viking Age

The collapse of the Northumbrian state in AD 876 left the area west of the Pennines dangerously exposed to the attentions of its neighbours. By the late ninth century communities with English place-names were scattered widely if thinly across the better-drained agricultural terrain of Cumbria. Excepting Keswick (cheese-*wic*), enjoying a limited area of adequate low land between Bassenthwaite lake and Derwentwater, English place-names are conspicuous by their absence in the central mountainous areas, and in the Pennines. The remainder are scattered on the coastal lowlands and within the major river valleys. At least half of the total are derived from elements denoting topographical features. This origin they share with many Celtic place-names, and it has already been suggested that some at least are the result of direct translation from one language to another. The remainder are habitative in origin. Names in -*ham* are not common (e.g. Addingham, Dearham), and the elements -*burh* and -*ceaster* are rare, generally occurring as descriptive suffixes at Roman fort sites (Brougham, Burgh-by-Sands, Brough) although no such site is known at either Hincaster or Burton. Most of the remainder are names in -*tun*, one of the commonest and longest utilized suffixes in all areas.

The best available agricultural land in Cumbria consists of permeable and semi-permeable marls, sands and gravels stretching in a discontinuous band around the lowlands. The distribution of English place-names is similar in broad outline to that of 'native' type-sites as identified from crop marks.

Where the two diverge, it is generally because the latter display a higher tolerance for marginal terrain, extending to altitudes where English place-names barely penetrate – as on the Eden–Lune watershed in the east of the county. The two distributions share an aversion for the wettest lowland terrains, avoiding for example, the area known in the post-conquest period as Inglewood Forest west of the Middle Eden valley, which was arguably a heavily wooded area throughout the late prehistoric–Roman–early medieval period. The place-names of this area betray Scandinavian influence, with numerous examples of *thveit*, meaning a woodland clearing, but many of these are linked to post-Conquest elements, and, with other late formations such as Johnby, represent Anglo-Norman or later clearance activity. However the possessive Old English place-name 'Englishmen's wood' may derive from the retention of grazing rights in this valley forest area by the surrounding and adjacent possessor communities – Dalston, Plumpton, Skelton etc. On the edges of the forest, groups of place-names such as the Huttons and Boltons imply large areas, or estates, associated with English place-names into which later settlement has intruded later names.

English place-names are not densely distributed in any area, even taking into account the probability of some casualties under the pressure of alternative languages during the Viking Age. The density of population was arguably lower than in the better terrain and the more advantageous climatic conditions east of the Pennines. The less advantageous climatic conditions, combined with the cumulative impact of ruinous subsistence strategies imply that productivity per unit of labour and of land was consistently low in Cumbria. Substantial tracts of land were under-utilized or totally unused. The prevalence of topographical names such as 'Uldale' ('Wolf-dale') imply that the central fells with their igneous rocks, shallow acid soils and inhospitable climatic conditions had been abandoned to the only natural competitor of man among the English fauna – the wolf.

English Cumbria was exposed to seaborne attack and immigration from the Irish Sea province along a considerable coastline. The 'possessor' community was disadvantaged by the broken, mountainous and underpopulated terrain which rendered communications between settlements difficult, and made the swift mobilization of armed forces next to impossible. After the removal of the umbrella provided hitherto by the Northumbrian state, Cumbria could not be defended by the indigenous community against determined and expansionist neighbours, of whom the most alarming were the seaborne, Irish Sea Norse.

Beyond the English areas of south-west Scotland, the minor British kingdom of Strathclyde/Cumbria was also under severe pressure from the Norse in the late ninth century [4]. Scandinavian armies passed through in AD 871, 875, 877 and on several occasions in the 890s. It was a small kingdom, unable to deny the Norse access to its own heartland, but as another of the possessor communities along the Irish seaboard, the British king was a natural ally of the English in western Northumbria. The proliferation of *Brittonic* place-names in north-eastern Cumbria, and the county name of 'Cumbra-land' point to the extension of British influence into the Solway basin which occurred during the subsequent two generations (Jackson 1963b). It may be that this British expansion occurred with the connivance of the English community who preferred the authority of a known, Christian neighbour long within the Northumbrian culture-province, to the menace posed by the heathen Gaels and Norse.

With or without English support, the period saw the establishment of *Brittonic* Celtic communities in the area, in sufficient numbers to have bequeathed a significant body of place-names (Fig. 7.4). It is impossible to distinguish in all cases between the survival of pre-English place-names (to which category belong Dacre and many river names), and the products of this late ninth–tenth-century reintroduction of the language. However, the distribution is such that the vast majority of place-names or area names must derive from this second episode. Through the communities which these represent, the Cumbrian kings used their patronage to establish a powerful local resource base with political interests identical with their own. This settlement was limited to the Solway basin, penetrating no further into the Eden valley than the Eamont river, and diminishing rapidly on the western plain beyond the Derwent. Within this area *Brittonic* place-names are common, and more numerous among parish and township names than are early Scandinavian compounds. The most common habitative element is *caer* (meaning a 'fort or defended settlement', or at this late date perhaps 'a farm') identifiable in such place-names as Carlisle, Cardew and Cardurnock. The element *tref* ('court') is present in Triermain. Some of these distinctive *Brittonic* names are identified with the physical remains of banked enclosures, for example at Castle Carrock. It is an attractive possibility that these represent the physical remains of occupation by immigrant British colonists, but none has yet been excavated. The similar remains of Dunmallard Hill (Ullswater) probably have a *Goedelic* rather than a *Brittonic* compound name. Some existing English and Scandinavianized place-names appear to have been Celticized – e.g. Carlatton and Cumwhitton – while the name Carholland implies the recognition of an Englishman's property rights by a British-speaking community (Ekwall 1918). In the west, British communities established and then maintained themselves in areas which were subsequently colonized by the Norse, who identified their settlements as Birkby (two occurrences) and Briscoe. In the east, the presence of *Brittonic* speakers was recognized by English speakers by the place-name Cummersdale.

In the central basin of the river Eden, British place-names generally occupy marginal sites within the most advantageous lowland terrains. The major exception is Penrith, which may either represent, like Dacre, a pre-English place-name survival, or a late place-name translation or replacement, but the presence of Anglian sculpture clearly forbids that it be a site unoccupied

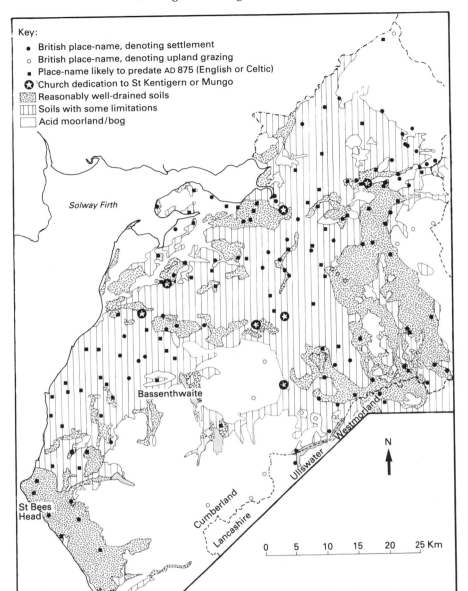

Figure 7.4 The Strathclyde Britons: settlement in English north Cumbria.

before the British re-advance. Penrith shares the well-drained soils of the area with sites such as Skelton, Stainton, Plumpton, Edenhall and Skirwith, all with English names, albeit that the last shows signs of Scandinavianization. On the edge of the well-drained soils lies the early monastic site of Dacre. This situation is less than advantageous, but the exact location of a monastery is less

319

directly linked to environmental factors than to the pattern of production within the estates it controls.

In similar locations lie the English Huttons, the Scandinavian Ousby and Langwathby and the Celtic Blencarn, Penruddock and Greystoke. On significantly poorer land are the Celtic Watermillock, Catterlen, Blencow, the late English Newton (Reigny), and the Scandinavian Lamanby. Along the eastern edge of the Eden valley, a string of fell-foot villages with Celtic names – Talkin, Castle Carrock, Cumrew, Lanercost – reinforce the impression that Cumbrian colonists were denied access to the best agricultural lands of the area. Instead they were established on under-utilized land and often marginal terrain within an estate structure that exhibits continuity of control and a capacity to protect the interests of the possessor community already in occupation of the most advantageous sites. The peculiarity of Penrith identifies this as the likely centre of an estate in the central Eden valley, perhaps one that was taken over by a Cumbrian lord from his English predecessor (Collingwood 1920). In the post-Conquest period Penrith emerged as the administrative centre of a small local honour; it is difficult to imagine that this is entirely coincidental.

Celtic place-names are not confined to the lowlands, but occur widely in the north-eastern fells – Barrock Fell, Carrock Fell, Penhurrock, Great and Little Mell Fell, etc. These place-names are attached not to settlements but to areas of waste land, and probably derive from their use as summer pasturage by the predominantly Celtic-speaking colonists moving into the margins of the adjacent lowlands at Greystoke and neighbouring sites. Transhumance re-emerged as a strategy by which limited lowland pasturage could be supplemented and conserved for the support of livestock during the winter months, and perhaps in addition for arable cultivation. Farmers from western Scotland would have needed little instruction in the management of livestock in such conditions, and it may be that improving climatic conditions encouraged them to establish themselves in an ecological niche otherwise unoccupied within the existing economic structure.

Those sites where conditions were most advantageous for cultivation were dominated with few exceptions by English place-names. Excavations in 1977 and 1979, designed to investigate a crop-mark site close to the Roman fort at Old Penrith near Plumpton Head, uncovered a circular, flat-bottomed pit which had been lined with clay-coated wickerwork supported on six internal stake-holes. In the lower fill were discovered carbonized grains of hulled barley, oats and flax which yielded a cargon-14 date in the mid tenth century (Poulter 1982). The lined pit has close parallels with several excavated at Tatton in Cheshire, where one yielded a carbon-14 date within the Roman period; it seems that this method of storage enjoyed a lengthy tradition in north-west England.

Even if Cumbrian kings and their aristocracy could draw upon the resources of these primary settlement areas, the identifiable colonists who settled under their patronage were excluded, and had to content themselves with marginal locations. Their settlement arguably gave a formidable impetus to expansion within the existing community, with the result that secondary place-names such as Newton (Reigny), and perhaps others were established during the period AD 875–1200.

The Cumbrians brought with them their own religious attitudes and preferences. Numerous church dedications in the Solway basin to St Kentigern (or St Mungo) reflect the extension of the ecclesiastical jurisdiction of the Cumbrian bishops of Glasgow in the wake of secular lordship. The limit of this jurisdiction in the tenth century probably lay on the Eamont river – arguably the acknowledged boundary of the kingdom in the 920s. With the exception of the *Brittonic* personal names enshrined in Mallerstang and possibly Melkinthorpe, place-names do not reflect any significant extension of royal patronage south of the river, and this situation is enshrined in the boundary between the old counties of Cumberland ('land of the Cumbri') and Westmorland ('land west of the moors' – presumably the Pennines), in the Eden valley and in the Patterdale area (see Fig. 7.4).

Relations between the Cumbrian kings and the English monarchy became increasingly strained after Athelstan assumed the crown of Northumbria. The Cumbrians had only recently annexed a substantial area that could be considered an indissoluble portion of the Northumbrian kingdom. The expansionism of the southern monarchy therefore posed a direct challenge to the British kings. Increasing tension led to an expedition from the South against the Scots in AD 934, and in AD 937 was fought the great Battle of *Brunanburh* between the southerners and an alliance of the Britons, Scots and the Irish–Norse. The alliance of mutual interests between the northern kingdoms and the southern English had served both parties well in the period AD 900–920, but had broken down as the latter became dangerously powerful in the 920s. Subsequently British kings in Strathclyde/Cumbria consistently allied themselves with the Norse, and were for that reason harried by the English kings – by Edmund in AD 945, and by Ethelred in AD 1000. A subordinate of the West Saxon kings in Yorkshire ravaged in Westmorland in AD 966, presumably attacking the Scandinavians beyond Stainmore. For this reason, it seems likely that Cumbrian kings were complacent concerning Viking settlement on their borders after c. AD 926. They alone were in a position to hinder Viking settlement of Allerdale and Copeland on the west coast, or of Appleby barony. Given that the densest primary Norse settlement in both areas occurred in the valleys immediately adjacent to Cumbrian territory, it seems that the Cumbrian kings actively encouraged rather than discouraged the influx of Norse colonists to the area.

After the demise of the Cumbrian royal house early in the eleventh century, the Solway basin was incorporated within the Scottish kingdom, which by this stage was a multiracial and multicultural state, united only by allegiance to a dynasty. In such circumstances, the separate Cumbrian language and culture declined rapidly, leaving the modern Cumbria within the cultural orbit of the Irish Sea Scandinavians as an enclave within a greater Scotland which marched with Deira in the Stainmore Pass, and included therefore, all the headwaters and valleys of the feeder rivers of the Solway basin.

Scandinavian settlement in Cumbria

Viking raids into Cumbria are not documented until *c.* AD 900, although it does seem likely that they may have begun a generation or more earlier, soon after the fall of York. In support of such a hypothesis is the Ormside burial which contained weapons with far-flung associations compatible with the burial of a much-travelled Viking warrior in the second half of the ninth century (Cowen 1934, 1948). The grave was located in a Christian cemetery and may have been constructed by a mobile group of raiders who sought thereby to guarantee the security of the grave.

A series of hoards consisting of Northumbrian *stycas* were deposited in the period AD 865–70, and this may also reflect local reaction to Norse raiding. However, these hoards contrast with the apparent coinlessness of Cumbria during the earlier ninth century, and may therefore, have been deposited by fugitives from the Danish Conquest east of the Pennines (Dolley 1966), and need not be linked directly to Irish–Norse raids.

At a date between AD 900 and 915 an English nobleman (*princeps*) named Alfred fled east to Co. Durham and the protection of the bishops of Chester-le-Street, fleeing from the activities of pirates. During the same period, Tilred, Abbot of Heversham abandoned his exposed monastery on the south coast, and retired eastwards with enough capital to buy an estate at Little Eden, and exchange this asset with the community of St Cuthbert for the abbacy of Norham upon Tweed (discussion, Stenton 1936). Both these leading members of the aristocracy may have come from southern Cumbria, beyond the reach of Cumbrian intervention, and their flight represents the lack of confidence within the higher social strata of the English community. Despite the desertion of the aristocracy, the scatter of pre-Scandinavian place-names demonstrate the determined and successful retention by local communities of many prime sites even in the most exposed areas subject to large-scale immigration.

The immigration of successful raiders fleeing from Dublin led to the deposition of distinctive hoards at Cuerdale (Lancs.) and Dean (Cumbria) in the first two decades of the tenth century. These contained Anglo-Saxon coins, but in addition Viking, continental and Kufic issues which betray the wide contacts of the Hiberno–Norse community (Dolley 1966). By the time the hoard found at Scotby was deposited *c.* AD 935, the exotic element was missing, and the horizons of the Cumbrian Norse were limited to Britain. The exotic element does not re-emerge, and by the mid millennium, Cumbria was probably once again coinless.

The coin hoards and the scarce documentary references make it clear that the Scandinavian immigration to much of Cumbria came from the Irish Sea, and from the Norse communities that occupied the coasts around it. They were pagans, and arguably even less sympathetic to Christianity than their Danish counterparts, and this factor is underlined by the series of early-tenth-century, furnished burials which have been identified. That at Heskett has been dated to the second quarter of the century, and probably involved cremation rites, as well as the deposition of weapons and a sickle (Cowen 1948, 1967). Yet despite the high profile of paganism and the large scale of immigration, the total number of pagan graves so far identified can be counted with ease on the fingers of two hands, including three examples which comprise no more solid evidence than grave-goods found in churchyards.

It is to place-names that we must turn to assess the scale of Norse immigration, to identify its source and the direction it took. Cumbrian Norse owed much to the Gaelic language —, borrowing from it large numbers of personal names, the practice of inverting compound place-names by the substitution of elements, and specific elements such as -erg ('a sheiling, farm') from the Gaelic -airigh. This heritage is shared by the Isle of Man, where numerous place-names such as Peel, or Dub- or -glas compounds underline the linguistic distinctiveness of the Gaelic–Norse areas of settlement from the colonization of Iceland direct from Norway (Collingwood 1895). In some instances almost identical place-names occur on Man and in Cumbria, as in Sulby/Soulby, Jurby/Ireby and Kneebe/Knipe.

This Irish or Goedelic component demonstrates that the immigrant community was of very mixed descent, within which the dominant Norse group had reinforced itself by substantial interbreeding with and recruitment from the Gaelic community (Ewall 1918). The Gaelic element is less pronounced in Appleby barony and the upper Eden valley. Scandinavian immigrants to this area may have derived as much from the Anglo-Danish Kingdom centred on Yorkshire as from Hiberno–Norse refugees. Indeed, Westmorland may at times have been considered a component of the York Kingdom [5].

Dense Norse settlement has left what can be reasonably interpreted as primary names in three distinct areas (Fig. 7.5). The west coast was exposed to immigration from the sea, and received large numbers of colonists. Southern Cumbria was remote from any possessor states, and, with Amounderness in Lancashire was extensively colonized. In addition, Appleby barony betrays a strong Scandinavian presence. Even so, in only narrowly defined and specific areas was the process of colonization on such a scale as to overwhelm the existing community, and to suppress existing major place-names. In Lonsdale the townships of Mansergh and to a lesser extent Kirkby Lonsdale stand out as

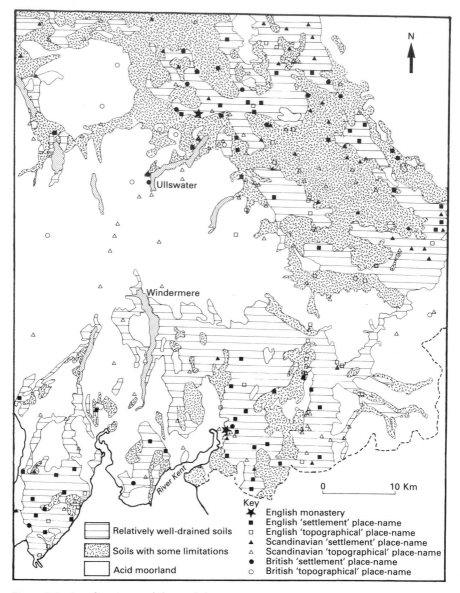

Figure 7.5 Scandinavians and the English community in south and east Cumbria.

centres of Scandinavian settlement, in an area in which all other township or parish names are pre-Scandinavian – detailed examination of Mansergh reveals that it is sited on the less advantageous, west side of the Lune valley, close to barren Silurian rocks and with only limited access to the better-drained bottom land. The resource base of this township has never justified the nucleation of the farming community or the creation of open fields. It is, therefore, a second-rate valley bottom site, occupied by a Scandinavian community within the estate structure that recognized existing place-names on the best sites (Fig. 7.5). Mansergh derives from an Old West Scandinavian personal name and -*erg*, a suffix which seems to have been reserved for poor-quality livestock farms. Within the township, minor place-names are almost exclusively derived from Norse or Old Irish, with examples such as Egholme Hall (*heggr* – *holmr*) and the inversion compound Rigmaden.

Many of the place-names where and elsewhere in Scandinavian Cumbria are names given to tracts of land rather than to settlements. Examples such as Rosgill (Shap) meaning 'ravine of horses', Setterah (near Helton) meaning 'hill with a shieling', Smardale (Kirkby Stephen) meaning 'valley with butter-producing pasture' and Grisedale (Patterdale) meaning 'valley where young pigs are reared' are descriptive terms relating to contemporary economic use. Others such as the several Uldales (probably 'wolves valley') refer to some of the disincentives facing the grazier or shepherd venturing into the waste. Many other Irish–Norse place-names derive from personal names and imply ownership of land – examples include Patterdale, Dailmaine, Aynerholme (Heversham) and Setmurthy. In the upland margins and the remote valleys, buildings were of sufficient rarity for their presence to be a factor in place-name formation, hence Boredale ('valley with a dwelling or store-house') and Fusedale ('valley with a cattle-shed').

The impression gained in much of Cumbria is of a major push into the under-utilized waste lands of the central Lakeland massif and other marginal areas. The similarity with the broadly contemporary British activity in the northern fells is a compelling one. Both immigrant communities may have been to some extent excluded from the majority of the most advantageous sites already occupied by the English settlements, despite the undoubted superiority enjoyed by Cumbrian and Norse aristocracies over all sections of the community. Even on the exposed west coast – the obvious landfall for many colonists – English place-names are identified with many of the most advantageous sites, such as Eaglesfield, Gosforth, Dearham, Whicham and in the Furness peninsula, Dalton, Aldingham and Stainton. Rottington occupies a central position in an area of well-drained soils based on sandstone. The adjacent Scandinavian place-name – St Bees – derives from the headland formed by the sandstone cliffs and is in origin a topographical as opposed to a settlement name, and a clear landmark to a seafaring community. Similarly, inland from St Bees Head, the English Frizington and Arlecdon occupy sites central to permeable and semi-permeable soils, with Scandinavian Asby, Kirkland and Cleator and the British Lamplugh occupying marginal sites on the periphery.

Further south, Corney and Bootle occupy the narrow strip of permeable soils, while Ravenglass (an inversion compound combining the Celtic *glas* with a personal name), Waberthwaite (a Norse clearance name) and Whitbek (a Norse topographical name) occupy less advantageous sites.

Within the most advantageous locations, some Scandinavianization of the pre-existing place-names took place; some names were partially or entirely replaced. Beckermet for example may be a compound of an Old English element (*mot* – 'a meeting') with old Norse *bekkr* ('a stream'), but it seems more likely that it is an inversion compound containing two old Norse elements, meaning 'hermit's beck'. The area is one in which much colonization was comparatively late, associated perhaps with the establishment of Calder Abbey. Place-names which betray a post-Conquest derivation include Ponsonby, Farmery and possibly Godderthwaite, but others were probably created in the tenth or eleventh centuries, and include the Old Norse woodland names Scaldersew and Briscoe ('wood of the Britons'), the shieling name Winscales and the clearance name Cringlethwaite. Other *thveit* names occur on the margins of the fells – Farthwaite, Brackenthwaite – but are probably the product of post-conquest name formation, by which time many common Norse elements such as thwaite and beck had entered the local dialect. The Beckermet area is dominated by drift soils, with the exception of two limited areas of better-drained soils. The larger of these is adjacent to Beckermet and occupied by the hamlet of Haile – derived from the Old English *h(e)alh*, a 'nook' or corner. The smaller supports only a single hamlet called significantly Carleton, a Scandinavianized place-name using the old English *-tun* and meaning a 'settlement of the ceorls'. In this case, at least, it seems likely that a low-status community should be associated with agricultural activity, and this may represent a settlement that predated the Norse immigration. Similar low-status communities occupy locally advantageous sites at Threlsgrope by Levens, Bondgate (Appleby) and Bombi (Brampton). Sites which indicate ownership by individuals of high status are less environmentally sensitive. Cunswick ('King's Wick') near Kendal is sited in an undistinguished location among a group of primary sites, but Yarlside ('Earl's *saetr*') on Shap Fell is an area of poor-quality grazing land high above the Crookdale Beck.

The widespread evidence for Scandinavian settlement in Appleby barony provides a further insight into the process of colonization. In this area, pre-existing place-names are concentrated not so much on the south-facing, north side of the valley (*contra* Bailey 1980: Fig. 2), but on the better-drained lowland soils which form a discontinuous but advantageous environment (Fig. 7.5). Within the best soils lie Brampton, Brough, Musgrave, Warcop, Kaber, Winton, Brougham, (Long) Marton and the Scandinavian Kirkby (Stephen). Pre-Scandinavian occupation of this last site, like that of Beckermet, can be demonstrated by the presence of distinctive sculpture. Other English place-names occupy less advantageous positions, close to the edge of the better-drained lowlands, such as Dufton or Hilton, and Scandinavian names also occur in this context – Knock, Nateby and Soulby. The high ground sites are dominated by Scandinavian names – Crosby (Garrett), Crosby Ravensworth and Asby – as are the poorly drained lowland areas – Kirkby Thore, (Temple) Sowerby, Crackenthorpe and Colby. Once again, a specific pattern emerges in which English place-names were retained in all but a very few of the best sites, and Englishmen shared the colonization of the wetter lowland areas (Meaburn, Bolton) and the drier uplands (Brampton, Shap) with Norse and Anglo-Danish incomers. The least advantageous tracts of land bear almost uniformly Scandinavian place-names, demonstrating the degree to which the immigrant community was exploiting the waste lands. A survey of woodland clearance names provides corroborative evidence. English woodland names are clustered within the valley, rarely at any distance from the river Eden and from the advantageous soils. Scandinavian woodland and clearance names are scarce in these terrains, but dominate the smaller valleys and the fell margins.

Scandinavian settlement names utilized the element *-by(r)*, meaning 'farm'. Examples such as Appleby ('apple farm') and Colby ('hill farm') derive from descriptive or 'village' terms. In some examples these descriptions are pejorative; we have, for example, Sowerby (farmstead on muddy or sour ground), Nateby ('nettle farm') and Waitby ('wet farm'). Many of these sites lie on the natural transhumance routes from the low valley farms to summer upland pasture. The Shap–Kirkby Stephen limestone fells provided by far the best summer pasturage in the area, with well-drained uplands offering a profusion of herbage. The routes into the summer pastures attracted numerous settlements on the edge of the cultivated land, as at Asby and Crosby Ravensworth. As a result, the limestone fells are dominated by names of the tenth century or later. Numerous examples of rectangular building foundations identify the probable sites of shielings on the summer pastures, and some may in turn have become permanent homesteads. Finds of Scandinavian metal-work on the Orton ridge link the exploitation of this area to Viking immigrants (Cramp 1964). However, no dates are available for any of the rectangular structures, and excavations at Ribblehead have demonstrated the dangers and difficulties in the dating of structures of this kind (King 1978). Even so, the presence of a 15 × 7 m 'longhouse' within the enclosed site of Castle Folds may imply reoccupation of a pre-existing site in the 'native' tradition. Close by, unenclosed 'longhouses' have been identified, including a 55 × 9 m example at Linglow Hill, and another of 32 × 6 m at Grange Scar, both of which are associated with other lesser structures (Higham 1979a). At Crosby Ravensworth, at least three of the group of 'native' sites contain evidence of rectilinear buildings which probably also represent shielings. The names given to these sites – Ewe Close, Ewe Locks and Cow Green – imply association with the pasturing of livestock. Even if these names are of the post-Conquest period, the expansionist episode that they represent began in the Viking Age.

The push into the Lake District fells has left the remains of graziers' huts high on Carrock Fell and elsewhere. Many are probably much later than the Norse migration, and it is impossible to say to what episode sites such as the Heathwaite Fell complex belong. The latter lies in an upland area south of Coniston, dominated by Scandinavian names, and is unusual in the evidence of ploughing in fields defined by the bases of stone walls associated with a complex of small enclosures that probably formed a farmstead occupying a substantial wind and drainage hollow. While it post-dates the cairnfields in the same area, the site is chronologically undiagnostic.

At Simy Folds in Upper Teesdale, examination of a group of farms with the foundations of rectangular buildings yielded a carbon-14 date of *c.* AD 780. The quantity of slag found outside, and the presence of a hearth with slag deposits suggested to the excavators that the site may have been in seasonal use for ore extraction and metal processing, but this kind of activity could easily have been combined with transhumance grazing (*Med. Arch.* 24, 1980: 219). In Kentmere (Cumbria), the subrectangular stone-founded hut recently excavated at Bryant's Gill may be broadly contemporary, but a range of artefacts included flints as well as spindle whorls, whetstones, iron equipment, and again, metal-working slag (*C.+W. Newsletter*, 2, 1984); a provisional carbon-14 date of *c.* AD 700 supports the identification of occupation in the English period [6].

Along the western edge of the Appleby barony, less advantageous soil conditions offered poor-quality upland grazing dominated by igneous rocks and blanket peat. Despite the disadvantages of this environment, some of the parish or township names derive from Old English place-names attached to sites occupying locally advantageous positions – e.g. Shap, Brampton. The area experienced considerable Scandinavian colonization, producing in Shap Rural parish, place-names such as Hegdale, Rayside, Selside and Rosgill. Along the Lowther river, Scandinavian colonists obtained entry to the better-drained lands, on which lie the communities of Lowther and its satellites Hackthorpe, Melkinthorpe and Whale, Askham (possibly a Scandinavianized Old English name) Helton (Old English) and Tirril ('a shieling built of tarry fir-wood' – *tyri-erg*). Away from the advantageous lowland sites, Scandinavian names are dominant, including an *erg* site at High Winder, and inversion compounds at Knottkanan and Cross Dormant as well as the descriptive names Bannerdale, Boredale and Fusedale. In Patterdale the Irish–Norse colonists met British pastoralists from Greystoke and Dacre, and the place-names accordingly derive from a mixture of all three languages, producing for example the inversion compound Glenamara (Park) with the *Brittonic glennos* and an unidentified personal name. The high profile of Irish–Norse place-names in this area may point to the importance of High Street as the route of entry to northern Westmorland for colonists initially reaching Cumbria by landfall on the western coast.

Throughout these marginal areas the emphasis was on the control of grazing lands, and we should envisage an upsurge in activity in the 'waste' as a direct consequence of both Cumbrian and Gaelic–Norse immigration into areas ill suited for cultivation – cattle, sheep, horses and pigs all contributed to place-name formation in the margins of usable land.

Graziers were increasingly eager to exercise rights of exclusive ownership

Plate 7.3 Bryant's Gill, Kentmere (Cumb.): looking east from the photographic tower in 1983 at the complex of wall footings and paving revealed after three seasons of excavation. The structure at the far end of the excavation, beyond the 2 m scale pole, has produced a carbon-14 date from an occupation deposit of ad 700±80 (uncalibrated: HAR 5944; photograph: P. Gilman)

– hence the common personal names attached to *erg* or *saetr*. On Orton Scar, the bases of limestone walls might date to this period – all that can be safely said of them is that they, and the earth dykes of Crosby Ravensworth predate the modern enclosure of parts of the fell. Elsewhere natural divisions of upland grazing were available, and most parish and township boundaries utilize the same swift-flowing streams and high ridges, but some of the new tier of place-name formation incorporate elements such as *stong* – a 'post' (e.g. Stangana in Mansergh, Mallerstang, etc.), and these may point to artificial boundary markers. The presence of meeting-places such as Thengeheved in Shap parish may also have played a role in the control of upland grazing land.

At the local level, it can be argued that English villagers and village aristocracies were generally able to maintain themselves throughout the era of immigration, although they were deprived of much land that had been available for extensive land-use, and placed under some pressure by colonists hoping to share in the agricultural lands. They had to become accustomed to an immigrant hierarchy, of Cumbrian, Gaelic or Scandinavian extraction, at the apex of local society, and the consequent dilution of English control of church sites, markets and assemblies. Beside them, considerable numbers of fellow farmers and pastoralists settled wherever resources were adequate for their subsistence and in some instances displaced existing communities. The various language groups established contact among themselves which led by the eleventh century to the creation of a distinctive, and ethnically mixed, Cumbrian community.

The distribution of Gaelic–Norse place-names is not uniform. If we are to identify a link between the areas where they are most dense, it would seem likely that they were all church estates in the ninth century. Monasteries are documented in heavily Scandinavianized Kentdale at Heversham, and in the Eamont valley at Dacre. Both were probably endowed with extensive local estates which are likely to have included parts of Lonsdale and the Lowther valley respectively. Cartmel was an estate of the Lindisfarne community. Pre-Viking sculpture at Workington, Beckermet and Brigham would seem to indicate that these sites may also have been estate centres attached to ecclesiastical institutions. The coincidence of Scandinavian immigration and the collapse of those institutions would suggest that their estates were seen as a prime target for the transfer of lordship and for colonization.

The majority of pre-Scandinavian sites where Anglian sculpture has been identified retained pre-Scandinavian place-names, although there were significant casualties at Kirkby (Stephen), Lowther and Waberthwaite. Most re-emerged as ecclesiastical centres in the tenth and eleventh centuries under secular, Norse or Scandinavianized patronage. Among the minority which have produced no evidence of Viking Age sculpture, Kendal and Heversham lie within an area of intense colonization distant from missionary centres, where paganism was probably relatively long-lived, and had economic and social advantages for the usurpers of monastic estates. Knells and Bewcastle were throughout the tenth century under Cumbrian control, and therefore, largely beyond the access of Anglo-Norse patrons during the crucial transition period. Scandinavian settlement names in the Carlisle area are arguably of the eleventh century rather than earlier, as is certainly the case at Scotby, Etterby, Harraby and Utterby. Between Carlisle and Penrith, along the Eden, it is possible that tenth-century Norse colonization occurred, resulting in the group of Irish–Norse place-names around Kirkoswald, Ainstable and Lazonby and the important group of crosses at Kirkoswald, but the place-names betray few of the forms typical of the primary colonization, and many, particularly of the formations from personal names, may be as late as the twelfth century.

In Appleby barony, pagan worship is probably evidenced in the place-name Hoff Lundr (near Appleby), deriving from elements denoting a temple and a grove. However, although this pagan influx may account for the discontinuity of place-names at Lowther and Kirkby Stephen, it is probably significant that the pagan centre was sited on poor terrain in the centre of probably the largest area of lowland forest in Appleby barony. It is distant from contemporary Christian cemeteries and probable church sites, and this choice of site implies a recognition of Christian rites among the English communities and a willingness to accept the two religions operating in tandem.

The account of the meeting at Eamont specifically states that the Cumbrian kings were expected to oppose idolatry, and presumably therefore, to take a lead in evangelical work among the colonists. Athelstan used the northern churchmen as a political counterweight to the pagans – as in his grant of Amounderness to the Archbishop of York in AD 934, an area which he had bought from the Norse with his own money. It is likely that Yorkshire churchmen stimulated missionary work among the colonists of southern Cumbria. The results were swiftly achieved, and dramatic in their implications.

Sculpture of the Viking Age has been identified at numerous sites from which no pre-Scandinavian work has been forthcoming. The discrepancy is on a scale that requires a real expansion in the number of centres attracting the patronage of sculptors in the tenth and eleventh centuries. This increase corresponded with the decline, if not the death, of ecclesiastical and monkish patronage, and the transfer of resources to a new aristocracy, dominant throughout the non-Cumbrian areas and sharing power within them. The new aristocracy was distinctively secular in its interests, and supported craftsmen who drew extensively upon pre-existing English traditions of sculpture, but added to these motifs drawn from the pagan world (Bailey 1980). The centres which attracted this patronage were cemetery sites, many of which were old-established settlements which retained pre-Scandinavian place-names – such as Dearham, Great Clifton, Gosforth, Harrington, Muncaster, Millom and Walton. Some of these are likely to have been pre-Scandinavian estate centres. The survival of the pre-existing place-names for sites serving as central places under a Viking aristocracy typifies the mechanics by which the Norse settlement occurred, within which pre-existing communities accepted new lordship above them and colonists beside them.

Elsewhere, sites with Hiberno–Norse place-names devoid of Anglian sculpture began to attract Viking Age memorial stones – as at Appleby, Aspatria and Bridekirk. The expanding pattern of settlement arguably required a denser network of cemetery and church sites, and the dispersal of the patronage of stone craftsmanship mirrors this development of what amounts to a parochial system within the lowlands and major valleys via the main-

Plate 7.4   Thor's fishing expedition: a panel of one of the several Viking Age relief sculptured stones at Gosforth (Cumb.), which demonstrates the use of a pagan theme within a christian cultural medium, probably executed by a christian Northumbrian sculptor in the tenth century. (photograph: T. Middlemass)

tenance of existing churches and the establishment of new ones by secular proprietors.

The best of this sculpture stands out as an artistic achievement of international importance. The Gosforth cross is undoubtedly the finest single product, but many others are more than competent examples. Few portray exclusively pagan motifs, such as the representation of Thor's fishing expedition on a Gosforth slab. The majority of scenes and motifs derive from the existing tradition of Northumbrian sculpture. The coincidence of location and the continuity in style demonstrates that many of the Norse leaders abandoned paganism within the first generation and enthusiastically patronized the local schools of craftsmanship hitherto heavily dependent on ecclesiastical commissions. The pan-Northumbrian uniformity of style and ornament that inter-monastic contact had maintained, broke down as a consequence of the Norse immigration. The result was a development of identifiable local traditions (Bailey 1980: 84). A specific workshop was responsible for the distinctive circle-head crosses of the coastal areas in north-west Cumbria, and close examination of specific motifs has led to the identification of close contact between specific communities such as Bromfield and Rockcliffe, where the same craftsman probably carried out commissions (Bailey 1980: 178 ff). The coastal communities were linked by sea with each other, and with sites further afield in Cheshire and Lancashire.

Other sites stand out for different reasons. The iconography of the sculptors at Lowther and elsewhere in the vicinity look to parallels in Scandinavia and the Isle of Man. In contrast, the bound-devil at Kirkby Stephen looks towards parallels in Yorkshire (Collingwood 1903).

Among the remarkable sculptured stones commissioned by the Norse aristocracy are the hogback stones, enjoying a distribution which is peculiar to those areas that formed the Irish–Norse kingdom of York in the early to mid tenth century. These represent a local development, modelled probably on pre-Scandinavian, Northumbrian traditions of stone, house-shaped shrines. Attracted by their link with the saints, the Norse aristocracy probably used them as grave-covers or perhaps as components in composite monuments such as that which can still be seen in Penrith churchyard. Their distribution allows us an insight into the cemeteries patronized by the tenth-century aristocracy. Many sites like Penrith, have non-Scandinavian place-names. They are significantly absent from the major areas of Cumbrian place-names in north and west Cumbria (with the exception of Kirkoswald), but occur on the coastal plain, at Aspatria, Penrith and in Appleby barony. East of the Pennines a strong concentration along the Tees reflects the Irish–Norse exercise of lordship in that area in the 920s, and the numerous Scandinavian colonists in the area, but here also most sites preserve their pre-Scandinavian place-names, despite the control exercised by an immigrant aristocracy.

By the mid tenth century, the immigration to Cumbria had slowed if not ceased. No new coins were entering Northumbria to compare with the hoards of the early decades. If the use of coins was retained it has left no trace, and Cumbria and Bernicia probably relapsed into an economy in which coinage played a minor role. In the Isle of Man a group of coin hoards were deposited in the tenth century in the south of the island, but by the end of the millennium coinage was in such short supply that the kings struck their own series early in the eleventh century, copying the latest tenth-century Irish copies of the Anglo-Saxon penny (Cubbon and Dolley 1980).

The trend towards coinlessness throughout England north of York implies that the area was unable to attract or profit from commerce; links with the merchant communities at York and Dublin were of small importance. The economy was not, however, stagnant, because a substantial and rising demand for foodstuffs was reflected in pressure on landed resources, and resulted in an expansion in all types of land-use. The resultant expansion of arable cultivation produced a spate of place-names referring to cereals, such as Haverthwaite, Corby, Cocker and Cockley derived from the Irish and Norse names for oats, Ruthwaite and Ruckcroft (rye) and Bigland and Biggar (barley). Those occupying less advantageous lowland sites supplemented their resource base by transhumance and eventually by permanent settlement in the waste lands of the Cumbrian fells and narrow upland valleys, where little human activity had occurred since the sixth century. The place-names that these groups of British and Irish–Norse created now dominate the upland areas. This economic expansion was necessitated by a population increase itself in part at least due to immigration. It did not result in an improvement in the standard of living, but arguably directly caused a real decline in conditions, as communities were forced by competitive pressure to occupy ever less advantageous niches in the ecosystem. The resultant decline in surplus wealth among the farming population was a real disincentive to commercialism.

The only group to benefit from the increase in population was the aristocracy. Successful in supplanting the English church landlords, the new secular aristocracy presided over the Viking Age, protecting elements of the possessor community in the advantageously sited valley estates and at the same time patronizing the incoming colonists in search of land to support themselves. The consequent expansion of arable and pastoral activity was to the advantage of the aristocracy, who exercised a vigilant control over rights of lordship, justice and particularly of grazing – as is implied in the mid-eleventh-century document known as Gospatric's Writ. One outlet for the wealth of this aristocracy lay in the adornment of their sepulchres, and these probably mirrored the normal residential pattern of the aristocracy within the more advantaged lowland terrains, where they were well placed to act as guarantors of an estate structure, the core of which they had inherited and on to which they grafted the economic activities of lower-status colonists.

The process of immigration artificially raised the population of Cumbria at a faster rate than could have resulted from internal demographic trends. The result represented a move to a population level numerically closer to the carrying capacity of the environment. Likely consequences include a rise in friction within society, and increasing bellicosity towards neighbouring communities. Something of the latter may be seen in the increasingly aggressive actions of Scottish kings after the absorption of Cumbria. The English of Northumberland were the normal target of Scottish raids, and the Tyne gap was a common access route for raiders in the eleventh century, to the point that the defence and control of the Pennine frontier was a major preoccupation of Earl Siward and his successors. The imbalance in population west and east of the Pennines rendered Northumberland susceptible to pressure from the North and West and contributed to the cession of Lothian and the Merse to Scotland in the eleventh century, as the price of political survival.

Notes

1. These references derive from the *Anglo-Saxon Chronicles* (Whitelock 1955), but only a single entry relates to Northumbrian events between AD 806 and 867.

2. Our understanding of Northumbrian monasteries is heavily dependent on the work of Prof. Rosemary Cramp and her students, without whose research this section could not have been written.

3. My thanks to Dr Roger Leech for his discussion of the site prior to publication.

4. For a full discussion of the name, see Wilson (1966).

5. For the discussion of place-name elements, this section draws extensively on Armstrong *et al.* (1950–52); Ekwall (1918, 1922); Smith (1967).

6. My thanks to Steve Dickinson for this information.

Postscript

The Anglo-Saxon border was to remain a volatile political frontier until the twelfth century. However, the existence of any such boundary line south of the Forth was inconceivable before the collapse of Northumbria in the late ninth century. Once the West Saxon kings had promoted themselves to direct lordship in the North, a political boundary could only be avoided by the absorption of all Britain by the English crown. Despite Athelstan and the more successful of his successors, this was never near, and the absorption of Pictland and Strathclyde/Cumbria by the Scottish kings and their subsequent conquest of Lothian raised up a powerful and relatively unified kingdom beyond the Tweed which at times appeared capable of the absorption of all England beyond York. Only the re-establishment of a powerful English monarchy by King William and his sons re-emphasized the claims that Athelstan had established in the North.

Beneath the political pressures from North and South, the border counties were divided by cultural and linguistic barriers that made co-operation between them difficult to achieve. Yet communities on both sides of the Pennines faced similar environmental problems. Despite the pressures of a population growth centred in the relatively disadvantaged terrain west of the Pennines, the community was forced to operate within parameters imposed by the ecological fragility of vast areas of inhospitable upland, where thin acid soils or accumulated peat were, and are, inadequate to support more than a low-density pastoralist regime. The strategies available to these communities were well tried and well tested. Both agriculturalist and pastoralist activity had in the past contributed to the degradation of the upland soils, and consequently to the accretion of the valley soils. The results defined the parameters within which Viking Age farmers were forced to operate – it is hardly surprising that they were unable to reoccupy upland terrain cultivated in the Bronze Age, nor re-establish settlements in the less advantageous fell margins occupied by Romano-British farmers. Theirs was but the last in a series of successive retreats from the fells that began at least a millennium before Christ, and arguably much earlier.

If we are to turn to a landscape in which this process is visible today, we could do worse than offer the example of Smardale by Kirkby Stephen. High on Ash Fell a robbed barrow reminds us of the well-drained, but now badly eroded, soils of the high ground. High in the 'dale', a 'native'-type farm with circular building platform is associated with a fragmentary enclosure system, now much damaged by recent cultivation. In the upper demesne pasture, a stone-walled enclosure system with near-square building foundations may represent a Viking Age site. Below it and contained within an earthen and stone dike system arguably of the Roman period is evidence of medieval cultivation on terraces ploughed across the valley as if to resist the errosive power of surface water. The modern hall, constructed about 1600 stands at the mouth of the dale on the natural transhumance route and close to the best agricultural land, which was in the eighteenth century substantially subdivided into strips still in many places today visible as lynchets. A late medieval pele tower graced the site, and traces of a shrunken village or hamlet and a chapel hang upon the skirts of the hall.

In fellside townships such as these is still visible the settlement history of a community that has pragmatically adapted itself to changing conditions and changing technologies, while retaining the same wariness of 'offsiders' with which locals faced the conflicting demands of Scottish kings and English earls, and at last the Norman armies by which kings in the South sought to press borderers into a cultural and political mould engineered to exacting standards in northern France and England below the Thames.

Further Reading

Because of the exceptional length of the bibliography and the shortage of general works on this subject, it was felt that the reader might appreciate having only a brief list of major secondary works extracted from the bibliography and organized by subject and chapter.

Chapter 1
Physical structure:
King, C. A. M. (1976) *Northern England* (Methuen).
Vegetational history:
Pennington, W. (1970) 'Vegetational history in the N.W. of England: a regional study', in Walker and West (eds) (1970).
Pearsall, W. H. and Pennington, W. (1973) *The Lake District* (Collins).
Turner, J. (1983) 'Some pollen evidence for the environment of North Britain 1000 BC–AD 1000', in Chapman and Mytum (eds) (1983).

Chapter 2
There is no general work available on the neolithic in northern England, but see **Burgess, C. and Miket, R.** (eds) *Settlement and Economy in the 3rd and 2nd millennia BC*, BAR 33.

Chapter 3
For henges see **Harding, A. F.** in *PPS*, **47**, 87–135.
For stone circles, see **Burl, H. A. W.** (1976) *The Stone Circles of the British Isles* (Yale).
For bronzes, see **Burgess, C.** (1968) *Bronze Age Metalwork in Northern England* (Oriel Press), and regional surveys by **Fell, C. and McK. Clough.**
For later prehistory, see **Challis A. J. and Harding D. W.** (1975) *Later Prehistory from the Trent to the Tyne*, BAR, 20, i, and the contributions of **Jobey, G.**

Chapter 4
For the conquest, see most recently **Breeze, D. J. and Dobson, B.** (1976) *Hadrian's Wall* (Allen Lane); **Daniels, C. M.** (1978) *Handbook to the Roman Wall* (Hill); **Hanson W. S. and Maxwell G. S.** (1983) *Rome's North West Frontier: the Antonine Wall* (Edinburgh Univ. Press)
See also **Potter, T.** (1979) *Romans in North West England* (C.W.).

338

Chapter 5
For the rural community, see articles by **Jobey, G.; Clack, P. and Haselgrove, S.** (eds) (1981) *Rural Settlement in the Roman North* (Durham) (C.B.A. Group 3); **Higham, N. J.** (ed.) *The Changing Past* (University of Manchester Extra-Mural Dept.); **Higham, N. J. and Jones, G. D. B.** (1985) *The Carvetii* (Suttons); **Chapman, J. C. and Mytum, H. C.** (eds) (1983) *Settlement in North Britain, 1000 BC–AD 1000*, BAR, 118.

Chapter 6
Hope Taylor, B. (1977) *Yeavering: An Anglo British Centre of Early Northumbria* (HMSO).
Bede *Historia Ecclesiastica.*
Kirby, D. P. (ed.) (1974) *St. Wilfrid at Hexham* (Oriel Press).
Gelling, M. (1978) *Signposts to the Past* (Dent).

Chapter 7
Cramp, R. (1973) 'Anglo Saxon Monasteries of the North', *SAF 5*.
Bailey, R. N. (1980) *Viking Age Sculpture* (Collins).

General
For sites, see **Clare, T.** (1981) *Archaeological Sites of the Lake District* (Moorland Press), and the various Dalesman series, region by region.

Abbreviations

Agricultural Hist. R. Agricultural History Review
Am. Journal of Arch. American Journal of Archaeology
Ant. J. Antiquaries Journal
Ant. Antiquity
Arch. Archaeologia
AA 1, 2, 3, etc. Archaeologia Aeliana, Series 1, 2, 3, etc.
Arch. Atl. Archaeologia Atlantica
Arch. Camb. Archaeologia Cambrensis
Arch. J. Archaeological Journal
Brit. Britannia
BAR (IS) British Archaeological Reports (International Series)
Bull. BC Stud. Bulletin of the Board of Celtic Studies
CBA Council for British Archaeology
CW (OS/NS) Transactions of the Cumberland and Westmorland Antiquarian and
    Archaeological Society (Old Series/New Series)
C.+W. Newsletter Newsletter of the Cumberland and Westmorland Antiquarian and
    Archaeological Society
Dumfr. and Gall. N.H. *and* A.S. *Trans.* Transactions of the Dumfries and Galloway
    National History and Archaeological Society
Ec. HR Economic History Review
EHR English Historical Review
Geog. Annlrs. Geographiska Annaler
Glasgow AJ Glasgow Archaeological Journal
Hist. History
Inst. Brit. Geog. Bulletin of the Institute of British Geographers
Int. J. Naut. Arch and Underwater Expl. International Journal of Nautical
    Archaeology and Underwater Exploration
J. of Arch. Sc. Journal of Archaeological Science
J. Cork Hist. Arch. Soc. Journal of the Cork Historical and Archaeological Society
J. Ecol. Journal of Ecology
JEPNS Journal of the English Place Name Society
J. Hist. Ecol. Journal of Historical Ecology
J. Inst. Wat. Engrs. Journal of the Institute of Water Engineers
JRS Journal of Roman Studies

J. R. Soc. Ant. Ir. Journal of the Royal Society of Antiquaries of Ireland
LCAS Transactions of the Lancashire and Cheshire Antiquarian Society
Lvpool. Manch. Geol. J. Liverpool and Manchester Geological Journal
Med. Arch. Medieval Archaeology
MOW Ministry of Works
N. Phytol. New Phytologist
NH Northern History
Num. Chron. Numismatic Chronicle
Pan. Lat. Vet. xii *Panegyrici Latini Veteres*, ed. R. A. B. Mynors, O.U.P., 1964
Phil. Trans. R. Soc. Lond. Philosophical Transactions of the Royal Society of London
Proc. Geol. Assoc. Proceedings of the Geological Association
PPS Proceedings of the Prehistoric Society
PPSEA Proceedings of the Prehistoric Society of East Anglia
PRS Proceedings of the Royal Society
Proc. Soc. Ant. N. upon T. Proceedings of the Antiquaries of Newcastle upon Tyne
PSAS Proceedings of the Society of Antiquaries of Scotland
Quart. J. Geol. Soc. Quarterly Journal of the Geological Society
RIB Collingwood, R. G. and Wright, R. P. (1965) *The Roman Inscriptions of Britain*, vol. 1, *Inscriptions on Stone.*
RCAHM Royal Commission on Ancient and Historical Monuments
SAF Scottish Archaeological Forum
Scot. Arch. Rev. Scottish Archaeological Review
Scient. Am. Scientific American
Trans. Arch. and Arch. Soc. of Durham and Northumb. Transactions of the Architectural and Archaeological Society of Durham and Northumberland
Trans. N.N.U. Transactions of the Northern Naturalists Union
Ulster J. of Arch. Ulster Journal of Archaeology
V.C.H. *Victoria Country History*
Welsh H.R. Welsh Historical Review
World Arch. World Archaeology
YAJ Yorkshire Archaeological Journal
Yorksh. Geol. Soc. Proceedings of the Yorkshire Geological Society

Bibliography

Abercromby, J. (1912) *A Study of the Bronze Age Pottery of Gt Britain and Ireland*, 2 vols. Clarendon Press, Oxf.

Adomnan *Life of St Columba*, ed. Reeves, W. 1857. Irish Archaeological Society.

Alcock, L. (1970) 'Was there an Irish Sea culture-province in the Dark Ages?' in Moore (ed.) (1970), pp. 55–65.

Alcock, L. (1971) *Arthur's Britain: History and Archaeology AD 367–634*. Penguin.

Alcock, L. (1979) 'The North Britons, the Picts and the Scots', in Casey (ed.) (1979), pp. 134–42.

Allason-Jones, L. (1980) 'Museum notes', *AA5*, 8, 153.

Ammianus Marcellinus *Historia*, ed. Page, T. E. *et al.* Loeb, 1935.

Anderson, W. (1940) 'Buried valleys and late-glacial drainage systems in north-west Durham', *Proc. Geol. Ass.*, 51, 274–81.

Ap Simon, A. M. (1969) 'An early neolothic house in Co. Tyrone', *J. R. Soc. Ant. Ir.*, 99, 165.

Ap Simon, A. M. (1976) 'Ballynagilly and the beginning and end of the Irish neolithic', in *Acculturation and Continuity in Atlantic Europe*, ed. de Laet, S. J. De Tempel, p. 15.

Apted, M. R., Gildyard-Beer, R. and Saunders, A. D. (1977) *Ancient Monuments and their Interpretation*, essays presented to A. J. Taylor. H.M.S.O.

Archer, S. (1979) 'Late Roman gold and silver coin hoards in Britain: A gazetteer', in Casey (ed.) (1979), pp. 29–65.

Armstrong, A., Mawer, A., Stenton, F. M. and Dickins, B. (1950–52) *The Place-Names of Cumberland*, 3 vols. C.U.P.

Arnold, C. J. (1962) 'The end of Roman Britain: some discussion', in Miles (ed.) (1982), pp. 451–9.

Arnold, T. (ed.) (1885) *Historia Regnum*, Rolls Series, vol. 75. Longman.

Arrian, Periplus 2 vols, transl. Brunt, P. A. (Loeb) 1976–83.

Arrian, Periplus *Arrianus, Flavius Arrian's voyage round the Euxine Sea*, ed. Falconer, T. O. O.U.P., 1805.

Ashbee, P. (1966) 'The Fussell's Lodge, long barrow excavations 1957', *Arch.*, 100, 1–80.

Ashbee, P. (1970) *The Earthen Long Barrow in Britain*. Dent.

Ashbee, P. (1982) 'A reconsideration of the British neolithic', *Ant.*, 56, 134.

Bailey, R. N. (1974a) 'The Anglo-Saxon metalwork from Hexham', in Kirby (1974), pp. 141–67.

Bailey, R. N. (1974b) 'The Sculpture of Cumberland, Westmorland and Lancashire North of the Sands of the Viking Period', unpubl. Ph.D. thesis, Durham.

Bailey, R. N. (1977) 'The meaning of the Viking-age shaft at Dacre', *CW*, NS 77, 61.

Bailey, R. N. (1980) *Viking Age Sculpture*. Collins.

Ball, D. F. (1975) 'Processes of soil degradation: a pedological point of view', in Evans, Limbrey and Cleere (eds) (1975), p. 20.

Barber, K. E. (1981) *Peat Stratigraphy and Climatic Change*. A. A. Balkema.

Barley, M. W. and Hanson, R. P. C. (eds) (1968) *Christianity in Britain 300–700*. Leicester Univ. Press.

Barnes, F. (1956) 'Pottery from prehistoric sites, North End, Walney Island', *CW*, NS 55, 1–16; see also *CW*, NS 54, 5.

Barnes, F. (1970) 'Microlithic Sites in Walney Island', *CW*, NS 70, 277.

Barnes, F. and Hobbs, J. L. (1950) 'Newly discovered flint chipping sites in the Walney Island locality', *CW*, NS 50, 30–42.

Barnes, F. and Hobbs, J. L. (1951) 'Flint implements from Plain Furness', *CW*, NS 51, 1–3.

Barnes, J. (1904) 'Ancient corduroy roads near Gilpin Bridge', *CW*, NS 4, 207.

Barnetson, L. P. D. (1982) 'Animal husbandry: clues from Broxmouth', in Harding (1982), pp. 101–5.

Barrett, J. and Bradley, R. (1980) *The British Later Bronze Age*, BAR, 83.

Barrow, G. W. S. (1966) 'The Anglo-Scottish border', *NH*, 1, 21–42.

Barrow, G. W. S. (1969) 'Northern English society in the early Middle Ages', *NH*, 4, 1–28.

Bartley, D. D., Chambers, C. and Hart-Jones, B. (1976) 'The vegetational history of parts of south and east Durham', *New Phytol.*, 77, 437–68.

Beckensall, S. (1976) 'The excavation of a rock shelter at Corby Crags, Edlingham', *AA5*, 4, 11.

Beckensall, S. (1983) *Northumberland's Prehistoric Rock Carvings*. Pendulum Press, Rothbury.

Bede *Historia Ecclesiastica*, ed. Plummer, C. O.U.P., 1966.

Bede Cont. – 'Baedae Continuatio', in *Venerabilis Baedae*, ed. Plummer, C. O.U.P., 1966, pp. 361–3.

Bede *Vita – The Life of St Cuthbert*, transl. and introd., by Webb, J. F. Penguin, 1965.

Bellhouse, R. L. (1953) 'A Roman post at Wreay Hall near Carlisle', *CW*, NS 53, 49–51.

Bellhouse, R. I. (1955) 'The Roman fort at Burrow Walls near Workington', *CW*, NS 55, 30–45.

Bellhouse, R. I. (1956) 'The Roman temporary camps near Troutbeck, Cumberland', *CW*, NS 56, 28.

Bellhouse, R. L. (1961a) 'An earthwork in Kirkbampton Parish', *CW*, NS 61, 47–56.

Bellhouse, R. L. (1961b) 'Excavations in Eskdale: the Muncaster Roman kilns', *CW*, NS 61, 47–56.

Bellhouse, R. L. (1962) 'Morecambe in Roman times and Roman sites on the Cumberland coast', *CW*, NS 62, 56–72.

Bellhouse, R. L. (1967) 'The Aughertree Fell enclosures', *CW*, NS 67, 26–30.

Bellhouse, R. L. (1969) 'Roman sites on the Cumberland coast, 1966–67', *CW*, NS 69, 54–101.

Bellhouse, R. L. (1971) 'Roman tileries at Scalesceugh and Brampton', *CW*, NS 71, 79.

Bellhouse, R. L. (1981) 'Hadrian's Wall: the limiting ditches in the Cardunock Peninsula', *Brit.*, **12**, 135–42.

Bellhouse, R. L. and Richardson, G. G. S. (1975) 'The Roman site at Kirkbride, Cumbria', *CW*, NS **75**, 58–80.

Bellhouse, R. L. and Richardson, G. G. S. (1982) 'The Trajanic fort at Kirkbride; the terminus of the Stanegate frontier', *CW*, NS **82**, 35–50.

Bennett, J. (1980) ' "Temporary" camps along Hadrian's Wall', in Hanson and Keppie (eds) (1980), pp. 151–72.

Bennett, J. (1983a) 'The end of Roman settlement in northern England', in Chapman and Mytum (1983), pp. 205–32.

Bennett, J. (1983b) 'The examination of turret 10A and the wall and vallum at Throckley, Tyne and Wear', *AA5*, **11**, 27–60.

Bennett, J. and Turner, R. (1983) 'The vallum at Wallhouses; excavations in 1980 and 1981', *AA5*, **11**, 61–77.

Benson, D. and Bland, K. (1963) 'The Dog Hole, Haverbrack', *CW*, NS **63**, 61–76.

Benton, S. (1930/31) 'Excavation of the Sculptor's Cave, Covesea, Morayshire', *PSAS*, **65**, 177–216.

Bersu, G. (1940) 'King Arthur's Round Table. Final report', *CW*, NS **40**, 169–258.

Bewley, R. (1983) 'Report on the Excavations at Ewanrigg, Maryport, Sept./Oct., 1983', privately circulated prior to publication.

Birch, W. de Gray (1885) *Cartularium Saxonicum I*. Whiting and Co.

Bird, J. (1977) 'African slip ware in Roman Britain', in Dore and Greene (eds) (1977), pp. 269–77.

Birley, A. R. (1967) 'The Roman governors of Britain', *Epigrapische Studien*, **4**, 6.

Birley, A. R. (1972) 'Virius Lupus', *AA4*, **50**, 179–89.

Birley, A. R. (1973) 'Petillius Cerialis and the conquest of Brigantia', *Brit.*, **4**, 179–90.

Birley, A. R. (1979) *The People of Roman Britain*. Batsford.

Birley, E. (1939a) 'Building records from Hadrian's Wall', *AA4*, **16**, 219–36.

Birley, E. (1939b) 'Roman inscriptions from Chesters (*Cilurnum*); a note on Ala II *Asturum* and two milestones', *AA4*, **16**, 237–59.

Birley, E. (1939c) 'The Beaumont inscription, the *Notitia Dignitatum* and the garrison of Hadrian's Wall', *CW*, NS **39**, 190–226.

Birley, E. (1946) 'Old Penrith and its problems', *CW*, NS **46**, 27–38.

Birley, E. (1954a) 'The Roman fort at Netherby', *CW*, NS **53**, 6–39.

Birley, E. (1954b) 'The Roman milestone at Middleton in Lonsdale', *CW*, NS **53**, 52–62.

Birley, E. (1956) 'Metalwork from Traprain', *PSAS*, **89**, 118–236.

Birley, E. (1959) *Chesters Roman Fort, Northumberland*. HMSO.

Birley, E. (1961) *Research on Hadrian's Wall*. Wilson, Kendal.

Birley, E. (1976) *Roman Britain and the Roman Army*. Wilson, Kendal.

Birley, E., Charlton, J. and Hedley, W. P. (1932) 'Excavations at Housesteads in 1931', *AA4*, **9**, 222–37, and *AA4*, **10**, 82–96.

Birley, E., Dobson, B. and Jarrett, M. (eds) (1974) *Roman Frontier Studies*. University of Wales Press, Cardiff.

Birley, R. E. (1977) *Vindolanda. A Roman Frontier Post on Hadrian's Wall*. Thames and Hudson.

Bishop, A. H. (1913–14) 'An Oronsay shell-mound – a Scottish pre-neolithic site', *PSAS*, **48**, 52

Blair, P. H. (1948) 'The Northumbrians and their southern frontier', *AA4*, 26, 98–126.

Blair, P. H. (1977) *Northumbria in the Days of Bede*. London.

Blackburn, K. B. (1952) 'The dating of a deposit containing an elk skeleton found at Neasham near Darlington, Co. Durham', *New Phytol.*, 51, 364–77.

Blake, B. (1956) 'An axe-hammer from Solway Moss', *CW*, NS 55, 317.

Blake, B. (1960) 'Excavations of native (Iron Age) sites in Cumberland, 1956–58, *CW*, NS 59, 1–14.

Blunt, C. E. and Stewart, B. H. I. H. (1983) 'The coinage of Regnald I of York and the Bossall hoard', *Num. Chron.*, 143, 146–63.

Bonsall, C. (1981) 'The coastal factor in the mesolithic settlement of N. W. England', in *Mesolithikum in Europa*, Proc. 2nd International Symposium on the Mesolithic in Europe, ed. B Gramsch. VEB Deutscher Verlag der Wissenschaften, p. 451.

Bowen, E. G. (1969) *Saints, Seaways and Settlements*. University of Wales Press, Cardiff.

Bowen, E. G. (1970) 'Britain and the British seas', in Moore (ed.) (1970), pp. 13–28.

Bowen, H. C. and Fowler, P. J. (eds) (1978) *Early Land Allotment in the British Isles: A Survey of Recent Work*, BAR, 48.

Bowman, A. K. (1974) 'Roman military records from Vindolanda', *Brit.*, 5, 360–73.

Bowman, A. K. and Thomas, J. D. (1974) *The Vindolanda Writing Tablets*. Newcastle. Graham, Northern Historical Booklets, 47.

Bowman, A. K. and Thomas, J. D. (1984) *The Roman Writing Tablets from Vindolanda*. Britannia Monograph Series 4, Sutton.

Bradley, R. (1972) 'Prehistorians and pastoralists in neolithic and Bronze Age England', *World Arch.*, 4, 192–204.

Bramwell, D. (1974) 'Animal remains from Rudston and Boynton grooved ware sites', in Manby (ed.) (1974), pp. 103–8.

Branigan, K. (ed.) (1980) *Rome and the Brigantes*. Dept. of Prehistory and Archaeology, Sheffield Univ., including, by the editor, 'Villas in the North: change in the rural landscape?', pp. 18–27.

Breeze, D. J. (1972) 'Excavations at the Roman fort of Carrawburgh 1967–9', *AA4*, 50, 81–144.

Breeze, D. J. (1974) 'Ploughmarks at Carrawburgh on Hadrian's Wall', *Tools and Tillage*, 2 (3), 188–90.

Breeze, D. J. (1975) 'The abandonment of the Antonine Wall: its date and implications', *SAF*, 7, 67–80.

Breeze, D. J. (1977) 'The fort at Bearsden and the supply of pottery to the Roman army', in Dore and Greene (eds) (1977), pp. 133–45.

Breeze, D. J. (ed.) (1979) *Roman Scotland: Some Recent Excavations*. Edinburgh. Duplicated typescript, not published.

Breeze, D. J. (1980) 'Roman Scotland during the reign of Antoninus Pius', in Hanson and Keppie (eds) (1980), pp. 45–60.

Breeze, D. J. (1981) 'Demand and supply on the northern frontier' in Clack and Haselgrove (eds) (1981), pp. 148–65.

Breeze, D. J. (1982) *The Northern Frontier of Roman Britain*. Batsford.

Breeze, D. J. and Dobson', B. (1969) 'Fort types on Hadrian's Wall', *AA4*, 47, 15–32.

Breeze, D. J. and Dobson, B. (1972) 'Hadrian's Wall: Some Problems', *Brit.* 3, p. 182–208.

Breeze, D. J. and Dobson, B. (1976) *Hadrian's Wall.* Allen Lane.

Brewis, P. and Buckley, F. (1928) 'Pottery and bronze from Ross Links, Northumberland', *AA4*, 5, 13–25.

Brewster, N. H. (1972) 'Corbridge – its significance for the study of Rhenish ware', *AA4*, 50, 205–16.

Briggs, H. D. and Bailey, R. N. (1983) 'A new approach to church archaeology: dowsing, excavation and documentary research at Woodhead, Ponteland and the pre-Norman cathedral at Durham', *AA5*, 11, 79–100.

Britton, D. (1971) 'The Heathery Burn Cave revisited', in *Prehistoric and Roman Studies,* ed. Sieveking G. de G. British Museum, pp. 20–38.

Brothwell, D. and Dimbleby, G. (eds) (1981) *Environmental Aspects of Coasts and Islands,* BAR, 94.

Bruce, J. R. and Megaw, B. R. S. (1947) 'A new neolithic culture in the Isle of Man', *PPS,* 12, 136–69.

Buckley, F. (1919–22) 'Early Tardenois remains at Bamburgh', *Proc. Soc. Ant. N. upon T.,* 3rd ser., 9–10, 319–23.

Buckley, F. (1922) 'Note on pygmy industry on the Northumberland coast', *Ant. J.,* 2, 376–7.

Buckley, F. (1925) 'The microlithic industries of Northumberland', *AA4,* 1, 42–7.

Bunch, B. and Fell, C. I. (1949) 'A stone-axe factory at Pike of Stickle, Gt Langdale, Westmorland', *PPS,* 15, 1–20.

Burgess, C. (1968) *Bronze Age Metalwork in Northern England,* Oriel Press.

Burgess, C. (1970) 'Excavations at the scooped settlement of Hetha Burn I, Hethpool, Northumb.', *Trans Arch. and Arch. Soc. of Durham and Northumb.,* NS 2, 1–26.

Burgess, C. (1972) 'Goatscrag: A BA rock shelter cemetery in north Northumberland, with notes on the rock shelters and crag lines in the region', *AA4,* 50, 15–69.

Burgess, C. (1976a) 'Britain and Ireland in the 3rd and 2nd millennia BC', a Preface, in Burgess and Miket (eds) (1976), p. i.

Burgess, C. (1976b) 'Meldon Bridge: a neolithic defended promontory complex near Peebles', in Burgess and Miket (eds) (1976), pp. 151–80.

Burgess, C. (1980) *The Age of Stonehenge.* Dent.

Burgess, C. (1981) 'Excavations at Houseledge, Akeld, Northumberland', *Univ. of Durham and Newc. Arch. Reps. for 1980.* Durham, pp. 7–10.

Burgess, C. (1982) 'Excavations and survey on Black Law, Akeld, Northumberland', *Univ. of Durham and Newc. Arch. Reps. for 1981.* Durham, pp. 4–6.

Burgess, C. (1984) 'The prehistoric settlement of Northumberland: a speculative survey', in Burgess and Miket (eds) (1984), *Between and Beyond the Walls,* Donald, Section 8.

Burgess, C. B. and Gerloff, S. (1981) *The Dirks and Rapiers of Great Britain and Ireland.* Prähistorische Bronzefunde, 4, 7. Munich, Beck.

Burgess, C. and Miket R. (1974) 'A bronze axe from Elsdon, Northumberland and the problems of the mid Bronze Age flanged axes', *AA5,* 2, 27.

Burgess, C. and Miket, R. (1976) 'Three socketed axes from North East England with notes on faceted and ribbed socketed axes', *AA5,* 4, 1–9.

Burgess, C. and Miket, R. (eds) (1976) *Settlement and Economy in the 3rd and 2nd millennia BC*, BAR, 33.

Burgess, C. and Shennan, S. (1976) 'The Beaker phenomenon: some suggestions', in Burgess and Miket (1976), pp. 309–27.

Burgess, C. B. and Schmidt, P. K. (1981) *The Axes of Scotland and Northern England*. Prähistorische Bronzefunde, 9/7 Munich, Beck.

Burkett, M. E. (1965) 'Recent discoveries at Ambleside', *CW*, NS 65, 86–101.

Burl, H. A. W. (1970) 'Henges, internal features and regional groups', *Arch.J.*, **126**, 1–36.

Burl, H. A. W. (1971) 'Two "Scottish" stone circles in Northumberland', *AA4*, **49**, 37–52.

Burl, H. A. W. (1976) *The Stone Circles of the British Isles*. Yale, reprinted 1979.

Burl, H. A. W. and Jones, N. (1972) 'The excavation of the Three Kings stone circle, Northumberland', *AA4*, 50, 1–14.

Burl, H. A. W. and Piper, E. (1979) *Rings of Stone*. Weidenfeld and Nicolson.

Camden, W. (1586) *Britannia, five florentissimorum regnorum, Angliae, Scotiae, Hiberniae, et insularum adiacentium* . . ., Londini per R. Newbery.

Cameron, K. (1965) *Scandinavian Settlement in the Territory of the Five Boroughs*. University of Nottingham.

Cameron, K. (1968) '*Eccles* in English place names', in Barley and Hanson (eds) (1968), pp. 87–92.

Cameron, K. (1971) 'Scandinavian Settlement in the territory of the Five Boroughs: the place name evidence, part III: the Grimston Hybrids', in Clemoes and Hughes (1971), pp. 147–63.

Campbell, A. (1942) 'Two notes on the Norse Kingdoms in Northumbria', *EHR*, **57**, 85–97.

Campbell, J. (1978) 'Bede's words for places', in Sawyer (ed.) (1978), pp. 34–54.

Carragain, E. A. (1978) 'Liturgical innovations associated with Pope Sergius and the iconography of the Ruthwell and Bewcastle crosses', in Farrell (ed.) (1978), pp. 131–47.

Case, H. (1969) 'Neolithic explanations', *Ant.* **43**, 176–86.

Casey, P. J. (1978) 'The Ninekirks (Brougham) Hoard; a reconsideration', *CW*, NS **78**, 23–8.

Casey, P. J. (ed.) (1979) *The End of Roman Britain*, BAR, 71, including, by the editor, 'Magnus Maximus in Britain', pp. 66–79.

Casey, P. J. (1981) 'Civilians and soldier – friends, Romans, countrymen', in Clack and Haselgrove (eds) (1981), pp. 123–32.

Casey, P. J. and Savage, M. (1980) 'The coins from the excavations at High Rochester in 1852 and 1855', *AA5*, 8, 75–87.

Chadwick, N. K. (ed.) (1958) *Studies in the Early British Church*. C.U.P.

Chadwick, N. K. (ed.) (1963) *Celt and Saxon: Studies in the Early British Border*, including, by the editor, 'The conversion of Northumbria: a comparison of sources', pp. 138–66, and 'Bede, St Colman and the Irish Abbey of Mayo', pp. 166–205.

Chadwick, N. K. (1964) *Celtic Britain*. Thames and Hudson.

Chadwick, N. K. (1976) *The British Heroic Age*. University of Wales Press, Cardiff.

Challis, A. J. and Harding, D. W. (1975) *Later Prehistory from the Trent to the Tyne*, BAR, 20, 1 and 2.

Chambers, C. (1978) 'A radio-carbon dated pollen diagram from Valley Bog, on the Moor House National Nature Reserve', *New Phytol.*, **80**, 273–80.

Chaplin, R. E. (1975) 'The ecology and behaviour of deer in relation to their impact on the environment of prehistoric Britain', in Evans, Limbrey and Cleere (eds) (1975), 40–2.

Chapman, S. B. (1964) 'The ecology of Coom Rigg Moss, Northumb.', *J.Ecol.*, **52**, 299–313.

Chapman, J. C. and Mytum, H. C. (eds) (1983) *Settlement in North Britain, 1000 BC–AD 1000*, BAR, 118.

Chapman, J. C. and Mytum, H. C. (1983) 'From prehistory to history: an outline of structural change in North Britain', in Chapman and Mytum (eds) (1983), pp. 1–12.

Charlesworth, D. (1961) 'Roman jewellery found in Northumberland and Durham', *AA4*, **39**, 1–36.

Charlesworth, D. (1965) 'Excavations at Papcastle', *CW*, NS 65, 102–14.

Charlesworth, D. (1975) 'The Commandant's House, Housesteads', *AA5*, **3**, 17–42.

Charlesworth, D. (1977) 'Turrets on Hadrian's Wall', in Apted, Gildyard-Beer and Saunders (1977), pp. 13–26.

Charlesworth, D. (1978) 'Roman Carlisle', *Arch.J.*, **135**, 115–37.

Charlesworth, D. (1980) 'The south gate of a Flavian fort at Carlisle', in Hanson and Keppie (eds) (1980), pp. 201–31.

Charlesworth, D. and Thornton, J. H. (1973) 'Leather found in *Mediobogdum*, the Roman fort at Hardknott', *Brit.*, **4**, 141–52.

Charlton, D. B. and Day, J. C. (1974) 'Bridge House re-examined', *AA5*, **2**, 33.

Charlton, D. B. and Day, J. C. (1978) 'Excavation and field survey in Upper Redesdale', *AA5*, **6**, 61–86.

Cherry, J. (1961) 'Cairns in Birker Fell and Ulpha Fell area', *CW*, NS **61**, 7–15.

Cherry, J. (1963) 'Eskmeals sand-dune occupation sites', *CW*, NS **63**, 31.

Cherry, J. (1965) 'Flint-chipping sites at Drigg', *CW*, NS **65**, 66–85.

Cherry, J. (1967) 'Prehistoric habitation sites at Seascales', *CW*, NS **67**, 1.

Cherry, J. (1969) 'Early Neolithic sites at Eskmeals', *CW*, NS **69**, 40.

Cherry, J. (1979) 'Sites in the Ravenglass area: the settlement evidence', in Potter (1979), pp. 6–11.

Cherry, J. (1982) 'Sea cliff erosion at Drigg, Cumbria: evidence of prehistoric habitation', *CW*, NS **82**, 1–6.

Cherry, J. and Cherry, P. J. (1973) 'Mesolithic habitation sites at St Bees, Cumberland', *CW*, NS **73**, 47.

Cherry, J. and Cherry, P. J. (1983) 'Prehistoric habitation sites in West Cumbria: Part 1, the St Bees area and north to the Solway', *CW*, NS **83**, 1–14.

Childe, V. G. (1932) 'The Danish neolithic pottery from the coast of Durham', *AA4*, **9**, 84–8.

Clack, P. A. G. (1982) 'The northern frontiers: farmers in the military zone', in Miles (ed.) (1982), pp. 377–402.

Clack, P. A. G. and Gosling, P. F. (1976) *Archaeology in the North.* Northern Archaeology Survey.

Clack, P. and Haselgrove, S. (eds) (1981) *Rural Settlement in the Roman North.* Durham. CBA Group 3.

Clapperton, C. M., Durno, S. E. and Squires, R. H. (1971) 'Evidence for the Flandrian history of the Wooler Water, Northumberland, provided by pollen analysis', *Scottish Geograph. Magazine*, April, 14–20.

Clare, T. (1978) 'Recent work on the Shap "Avenue"', *CW*, NS 78, 5–15.

Clare, T. (1981) *Archaeological Sites of the Lake District*, Moorland.

Clark, J. G. D. (1932) *The Mesolithic Age in Britain*. C.U.P.

Clark, J. G. D. (1935) 'The prehistory of the Isle of Man', *PPS*, 1, 70–92.

Clark, J. G. D. (1948) 'The development of fishing in prehistoric Europe', *Ant.J.*, 28, 45–85.

Clark, J. G. D. (1954) *Excavations at Star Carr*. C.U.P.

Clark, J. G. D. (1965) 'Traffic in stone axe blades', *Ec.H.R.*, 18, 1–28.

Clark, J. G. D. (1966) 'The invasion hypothesis in British archaeology', *Ant.*, 40, 172.

Clark, J. G. D. (1972) *Star Carr, a case study in bioarchaeology*. An Addison-Wesley Module in Anthropology, Module 10, pp. 1–42.

Clarke, D. (1970) *Beaker Pottery of Great Britain and Ireland*.

Clarke, D. (1976) 'Mesolithic Europe: the economic basis', in *Problems in Economic and Social Archaeology*, ed. Sieveking G. de G. *et al.* (1976). Duckworth, pp. 449–82.

Clarke, J. (1958) 'Roman and native AD 80–122', in Richmond (1958), pp. 28–59.

Claudian, de Consulate Stilichonis, in *Claudian*, trans. Platnauer, M. Loeb, 1922.

Clemoes, P. (1959) *The Anglo-Saxons*. C.U.P.

Clemoes, P. and Hughes, K. (1971) *England before the Conquest: Studies in Primary Sources, pres to D. Whitelock*. C.U.P.

Clough, T. H. McK. (1968) 'The Beaker period in Cumbria', *CW*, NS 68, 1–21.

Clough, T. H. McK. (1969) 'Bronze Age metalwork from Cumbria', *CW*, NS 69, 1–39.

Clough, T. H. McK. (1972) 'Recent Bronze Age finds from Cumbria', *CW*, NS 72, 44–52.

Clough, T. H. McK. (1973) 'Excavations on a Langdale axe chipping site in 1969 and 1970', *CW*, NS 73, 25.

Clough, T. H. McK. and Cummins, W. A. (1979) *Stone Age Studies: Archaeological, Petrological, Experimental and Ethnographic*, CBA, Res. Rep. 23.

Clough, T. H. McK. and Green, B. (1972) 'The petrological identification of stone implements from East Anglia', *PPS*, 38, 108–55.

Coggins, D. and Fairless, K. J. (1980) 'Excavations at the early settlement site of Forcegarth Pasture North, 1972–4', *Trans. Arch. and Arch. Soc. of Durham and Northumb.*, ser. 2, 5, 31–8.

Coles, J. M. (1971) 'The early settlement of Scotland: excavations at Morton, Fife', *PPS*, 37, 284.

Coles, J. M. (1976) 'Forest farmers', in de Laet (ed.) (1976), p. 59.

Coles, J. M. (1979) 'An experiment with stone axes', in Clough and Cummins (1979), p. 106.

Coles, J. M. and Simpson, D. D. A. (eds) (1968) *Studies in Ancient Europe. Essays Presented to S. Piggott*. Leicester Univ. Press.

Colgrave, B. (ed.) (1940) *Two Lives of St. Cuthbert*. C.U.P.

Collingwood, E. F. (1946) 'A prehistoric grave at West Lilburn', *AA4*, 24, 217.

Collingwood, E. F. (1961) 'A food vessel burial at West Lilburn', *AA4*, 39, 373.

Collingwood, E. F. and Cowen J. D. (1948) 'A prehistoric grave at Haugh Head, Wooler', *AA4*, 26, 47–54.

Collingwood, R. G. (1933a) 'An introduction to the prehistory of Cumberland, Westmorland and Lancashire north of the sands', *CW*, NS 33, 163.

Collingwood, R. G. (1933b) 'Prehistoric settlements near Crosby Ravensworth', *CW*, NS 33, 201.

Collingwood, R. G. (1938) 'The hill-fort on Carrock Fell', *CW*, NS 38, 32–41.

Collingwood, R. G. and Wright, R. P. (1965) *The Roman Inscriptions of Britain*, vol. 1, *Inscriptions on Stone*. Clarendon Press.

Collingwood, W. G. (1895) 'Some Manx names in Cumbria', *CW*, OS 13, 303.

Collingwood, W. G. (1903) 'Some ancient sculpture of the Devil Bound', *CW*, NS 3, 380–9.

Collingwood, W. G. (1907) 'The Lowther Hogbacks', *CW*, NS 7, 152–64.

Collingwood, W. G. (1909) 'Report on a further exploration of the Romano-British settlement at Ewe Close, Crosby Ravensworth', *CW*, NS 9, 295.

Collingwood, W. G. (1912) 'Anglian cross shafts at Dacre and Kirkby Stephen', *CW*, NS 12, 29–32.

Collingwood, W. G. (1920) 'The Giant's Thumb', *CW*, NS 20, 53–65.

Collingwood, W. G. (1927) *Northumbrian Crosses of the pre-Norman Age*. Faber and Gwyer.

Coombs, D. G. (1976a) 'Bronze Age weapon hoards in Britain', *Arch. Atl.*, 1, 49–83.

Coombs, D. G. (1976b) 'Excavations at Mam Tor, Derbyshire, 1965–9', in Harding (ed.) (1976), pp. 147–52.

Coope, G. R. (1979) 'The influence of geology on the manufacture of neolithic and Bronze Age stone implements in the British Isles', in Clough and Cummins (1979), pp. 98–101.

Corcoran, J. X. W. P. (1969) 'Multi-period chambered cairns', *SAF*, 1, 9–18.

Cormack, W. F. (1970) 'A mesolithic site at Barnsalloch, Wigtownshire', *Dumfr. and Gall. N.H. and A.S. Trans.*, 47, 63–80.

Coupland, F. and Coupland, G. (1935) 'Further Tardenoisian discoveries on the north east coast', *PPS*, 1, 154.

Coupland, G. (1923) 'A Tardenois or pygmy industry on Black Fell', *Ant.J.*, 3, 262.

Coupland, G. (1925) 'A microlithic industry in Durham', *PPSEA*, 5, 62–4.

Coupland, G. (1948) *A Mesolithic Industry at the Beacon, S.E. Durham*. Gloucester. Privately printed.

Cowen, J. D. (1934) 'A catalogue of objects of the Viking period in the Tullie House Museum', *CW*, NS 34, 166–87.

Cowen, J. D. (1948) 'Viking burials in Cumbria', *CW*, NS 48, 73–6.

Cowen, J. D. (1967) 'Viking burials in Cumbria – a supplement', *CW*, NS 67, 31–4.

Cowie, T. G. (1978) *Bronze Age Food Vessel Urns in North Britain*, BAR, 55.

Cowper, H. S. (1893) 'The ancient settlements, cemeteries and earthworks of Furness', *Arch.*, 53, 389–426.

Cowper, H. S. (1907) 'Bronze Age relics from Furness', *CW*, NS 7, 39–41.

Cox, B. (1975/76) 'Place names of the earliest English records', *JEPNS*, 8, 12–66.

Cramp, R. (1964) 'The Viking type pennanular brooch and torc from Orton Scar', *CW*, NS 64, 86–9.

Cramp, R. (1969) 'Excavations at the Saxon monastic sites of Wearmouth and Jarrow, Co. Durham: an interim report', *Med. Arch.*, 13, 21–66.

Cramp, R. (1973) 'Anglo-Saxon monasteries of the North', *SAF*, 5, 104–24.

Cramp, R. (1974) 'Early Northumbrian sculpture at Hexham', in Kirby (1974), pp. 115–40, and Appendix II, 'A hand-list of Hexham's Anglo-Saxon sculpture', pp. 172–9.

Cramp, R. (1976) 'Monastic sites', in Wilson (ed.) (1976), pp. 201–52.

Cramp, R. (1978) 'The evangelist symbols and their parallels in Anglo-Saxon sculpture', in Farrell (ed.) (1978), pp. 118–30.

Cramp, R. (1983) 'Anglo-Saxon settlement', in Chapman and Mytum (eds) (1983), pp. 263–97.

Cramp, R. and Douglas-Home, C. (1977/78) 'New discoveries at The Hirsel, Coldstream, Berwickshire', *PSAS*, 109, 223–32.

Craster, H. H. E. (1925) 'The Red Book of Durham', *EHR*, 40, 504–32.

Craster, Sir E. (1954) 'The patrimony of St. Cuthbert', *EHR*, 69, 177–99.

Cross, M. (1938) 'A prehistoric settlement on Walney', *CW*, NS 38, 160; see also *CW*, NS 39, 262–82; NS 46, 67–76; NS 49, 1–9.

Cross, M. (1942) 'A prehistoric settlement on Walney Island, III', *CW*, NS 42, 112–31.

Cross, M. (1950) 'A prehistoric settlement on Walney Island', *CW*, NS 50, 15–19.

Cross, M. and Collingwood, W. G. (1929) 'Explorations on Thwaites Fell, South Cumberland', *CW*, NS 29, 250–8.

Cubbon, A. M. and Dolley, M. (1980) 'The 1972 Kirk Michael Viking Treasure Trove', *Journal of the Manx Museum*, 89 (8), 5.

Cummins, W. A. (1979) 'Neolithic stone axes: distribution and trade in England and Wales', in Clough and Cummins (eds) (1979), pp. 5–12.

Cummins, W. A. (1980) 'Stone axes as a guide to neolithic communications and boundaries in England and Wales', *PPS*, 46, 45–60.

Curle, A. O. (1908) 'Notice of the examination of prehistoric kitchen middens on the Archerfield estate', *PSAS*, 42, 326.

Curle, A. O. (1923) *The Treasure of Traprain*. Glasgow, Maclehose, Jackson and Co.

Curle, J. (1911) *A Roman Frontier Post and Its People. The Fort of Newstead in the Parish of Melrose*. Glasgow.

Curle, J. (1931–32) 'Objects of Roman and provincial Roman origin', *PSAS*, 66, 359.

Daniel, G. F. (1950) *The Prehistoric Chamber Tombs of England and Wales*. C.U.P.

Daniels, C. M. (1970) 'Problems of the Roman northern frontier', *SAF*, 2, 91–101.

Daniels, C. M. (1971) 'The role of the army in the spread and practice of Mithraism', in Hinnells (ed.) (1971), pp. 249–74.

Daniels, C. M. (1976) 'Wallsend Roman fort, 1975 excavations', *Arch. News.*, 13, CBA Group 3, pp. 10–11.

Daniels, C. M. (1978a) 'Housesteads', *Brit.*, 9, 420.

Daniels, C. M. (ed.) (1978b) *Handbook to the Roman Wall*, 13th edn. Newcastle, Hill.

Daniels, C. M. (1980a) 'Excavations at Wallsend and the 4th century barracks on Hadrian's Wall', in Hanson and Keppie (eds) (1980), pp. 173–93.

Daniels, C. M. (1980b) 'Housesteads north rampart, 1978–9', *Arch. Reports for 1979*. Univ. of Durham.

Darbishire, R. D. (1874) 'Notes on discoveries in Ehenside Tarn', *Arch.*, 44, 273–92.

Davey, P. (ed.) (1978) *Man and Environment in the Isle of Man*, BAR, 54.

Davies, G. and Turner, J. (1979) 'Pollen diagrams from Northumberland', *New Phytol.*, 82, 783–804.

Davies, J. (1963) 'Some recent prehistoric finds of Lake District origin from the Yorkshire Pennines', *CW*, NS 63, 53.

Davies, R. W. (1971) 'The Roman military diet', *Brit.*, 2, 122–42.

Davies, R. W. (1977) 'Ateco of Old Carlisle', *Brit.*, 8, 271–4.

Deady, J. and Doran, E. (1972) 'Prehistoric copper mines: Mount Gabriel. Co. Cork', *J. Cork Hist. Arch. Soc.*, 77, 25–7.

Defoe, D., *A tour through the whole island of Great Britain*, introduced by Cole, G. D. H. and Browning, D. C., 1974 edn. Dent.

Detsicas, A. (ed.) (1973) *Recent Research in Romano-British Coarse Pottery*, CBA Res. Rep. 10.

Dewdney, J. C. (ed.) (1970) *Durham Co. and City with Teesside*. Durham, Local Exec. Committee of the British Academy.

Dickinson, W. (1975) 'Recurrence surfaces in Rusland Moss, Cumbria', *J.Ecol.*, 63, 913–35.

Dimbleby, G. W. (1962) *The Development of British Heathlands and their Soils*. Oxford Forestry Mems, 23.

Dimbleby, G. W. (1967) *Plants and Archaeology*. London, Baker.

Dio, *Roman History*, 9 vols, transl. Cary, E. Loeb, 1914.

Diodorus Siculus, *Library of History*, 10 vols, transl. Oldfather, C. H. Loeb, 1933.

Dixon, J. A. and Fell, C. I. (1948) 'Some Bronze Age circles at Lacra near Kirkstanton', *CW*, 48, 1–22.

Dobson, B. (1970) 'Roman Durham', *Trans. Arch. and Arch. Soc. of Durham and Northumb.*, NS, 3, 31–43.

Dobson, B. and Mann, J. C. (1973) 'The Roman Army in Britain and Britons in the Roman Army', *Brit.*, 4, 191–205.

Dodgson, J. McN. (1966) 'The significance of the distribution of the English place name in -*ingas* and -*inga* in South East England', *Med. Arch.*, 10, 1–29.

Dolley, R. H. M. (1961) *Anglo Saxon Coins*. Methuen.

Dolley, R. H. M. (1965) *Viking Coins of the Danelaw and of Dublin*, British Museum.

Dolley, R. H. M. (1966) *The Hiberno-Norse Coins in the British Museum*, British Museum.

Donaldson, A. and Turner, J. (1977) 'A pollen diagram from Hallowell Moss, near Durham City', *Biogeography*, 4, 25–33.

Donner, J. J. (1970) 'Land/sea level changes in Scotland', in Walker and West (eds) (1970), p. 23.

Dore, J. N. (1980) 'The fort at Red House and Flavian coarse pottery in northern Britain', in Hanson and Keppie (eds) (1980), pp. 113–18.

Dore, J. N. and Gillam, J. P. (1979) *The Roman Fort at South Shields*. Newcastle, Society of Antiquaries Monograph Series 1.

Dore, J. and Greene, K. (eds) (1977) *Roman Pottery Studies in Britain and Beyond*, BAR, Supplementary Series, 30.

Dornier, A. (1974) 'The reorganisation of the north-western frontier of Britain in AD 369: Ammianus Marcellinus and the Notitia Dignitatum', in Birley, Dobson and Jarrett (eds) (1974), pp. 102–5.

Dornier, A. (1982) 'The province of Valentia', *Brit.*, 13, 253.

Dumville, D. N. (1977a) 'Sub-Roman Britain: history and legend', *Hist.*, NS 62, 173–92.

Dumville, D. N. (1977b) 'On the North British section of the *Historia Brittonum*', *Welsh H.R.*, 8 (3), 345–54.

Dunham K. C. (1949) *Geology of the Northern Pennine Orefield*, vol. 1. Memoirs of the Geological Survey of Gt Britain. HMSO.

Dymond, C. W. (1893) 'Barnscar: an ancient settlement in Cumberland', *CW*, OS **12**, 179–87.

Dymond, C. W. (1902) 'An exploration of "Sunken Kirk", Swinside, Cumberland', *CW*, NS **2**, 53–76.

Dymond, D. P. (1961) 'Roman bridges on Dere Street, Co. Durham', *Arch.J.*, **108**, 136–64.

Eddius, Stephanus, 'Life of Wilfrid', in *Lives of the Saints*, transl. Webb, J. F. Penguin, 1965, pp. 131–206.

Ekwall, E. (1918) *Scandinavians and Celts in the North-West of England*. Lund and Leipzig, Gleerup.

Ekwall, E. (1922) *The Place-Names of Lancashire*. Chetham Soc., 81.

Ekwall, E. (1928) *English River Names*. O.U.P.

Elgee, E. (1930) *Early Man in North East Yorkshire*. Gloucester, Bellows.

Ellison, M. and Harbottle, B. (1983) 'The Excavation of a 17th century bastion in the castle of Newcastle upon Tyne, 1976–81', *AA5*, **11**, 135–264.

Erskine, J. S. and Wood, J. (1936) 'A Birkrigg burial', *CW*, NS **36**, 150–7.

Evans, Sir J. (1881) *The Ancient Bronze Implements, Weapons and Ornaments of Gt. Britain and Ireland*, Longmans, Green and Co.

Evans, Sir J. (1897) *The Ancient Stone Implements, Weapons and Ornaments of Great Britain*, 2nd edn. Longmans, Green and Co.

Evans, J. G. (1971) 'Notes on the environment of early farming communities in Britain', in Simpson (ed.) (1971), pp. 11–26.

Evans, J. G. (1975) *The Environment of Early Man in the British Isles*. London, Paul Elek Ltd.

Evans, J. G. Limbrey S. and Cleere, H. (eds) (1975) *The Effect of Man on the Landscape: the Highland Zone*, CBA Res. Rep. 11.

Evans, P. (1975) 'The intimate relationship: an hypothesis concerning pre-Neolithic land use', in Evans, Limbrey and Cleere (eds) (1975), pp. 43–8.

Evens, E. D., Grinsell, L. V., Piggott, S. and Wallis, F. S. (1962) 'Fourth report of the sub-committee of the south-western group of museums and art galleries on the petrological identification of stone axes', *PPS*, **28**, 209–66.

Evens, E. D., Smith, I. F. and Wallis, F. S. (1972) 'The petrological identification of stone implements from south-western England', *PPS*, **38**, 235–75.

Fair, M. (1932) 'A reconsideration of the lakeside site at Ehenside Tarn', *CW*, NS **32**, 57–62.

Fair, M. (1943) 'The Gosforth area in prehistory', *CW*, NS **43**, 50–4.

Fairclough, G. (1983) 'Tynemouth Priory and Castle – excavations in the outer court, 1980', *AA5*, **11**, 101–33.

Farmer, D. H. (1974) 'Saint Wilfrid', in Kirby, 1974, pp. 35–60.

Farrar, R. A. H. (1980) 'Roman signal stations over Stainmore and Beyond', in Hanson and Keppie (eds) (1980), p. 211.

Farrell, R. T. (ed.) (1978) *Bede and Anglo-Saxon England*, BAR, 46, including, by the editor, 'The archer and associated figures on the Ruthwell Cross – a reconsideration', pp. 96–117.

Farrer, W. (1900) 'The Domesday Survey of north Lancashire', *LCAS*, **18**, 88–113.

Faull, M. L. (1977) 'British survival in Anglo-Saxon Northumbria', in Laing (ed.) (1977), pp. 1–56.

Feachem, R. W. (1956) 'The fortifications on Traprain Law', *PSAS*, **89**, 284–9.

Feachem, R. W. (1960) 'Unenclosed platform settlements', *PSAS*, **64**, 79–85.

Feachem, R. W. (1963) *Guide to Prehistoric Scotland*. Batsford.

Feachem, R. W. (1966) 'The hillforts of northern Britain', in Rivet (ed.) (1966), pp. 59–88.

Feachem, R. W. (1971) 'Unfinished hill-forts', in *The Iron Age and Its Hill-forts*, eds Jesson, M. and Hill, D. Southampton University Archae. Soc., pp. 19–39.

Feachem, R. W. (1973) 'Ancient agriculture in the Highland Zone of Britain', *PPS*, **39**, 332–54.

Fell, C. I. (1940) 'Bronze Age connections between the Lake District and Ireland', *CW*, NS **40**, 118–30.

Fell, C. I. (1950a) 'The Beaker period in Cumberland, Westmorland and Lancashire north of the Sands', in *The Early Culture of North West Europe*, eds Fox, C. and Dickins, B. C.U.P.

Fell, C. I. (1950b) 'The Gt. Langdale stone-axe factory', *CW*, NS **50**, 1–29.

Fell, C. I. (1958) 'Middle Bronze Age urns from Furness', *CW*, NS **57**, 9–12.

Fell, C. I. (1967) 'Two enlarged food vessels from How Hill, Thursby', *CW*, NS **67**, 17–25.

Fell, C. I. (1972a) 'Neolithic finds from Brougham', *CW*, NS **72**, 36–43.

Fell, C. I. (1972b) *Early Settlement in the Lake Counties*. Clapham.

Fell, C. I. and Coles, J. M. (1965) 'Reconsideration of the Ambleside hoard and the burial at Butts Beck quarry, Dalton-in-Furness', *CW*, NS **65**, 38–53.

Fell, C. I. and Hogg, R. (1962) 'A food-vessel from Springfield, near Ainstable', *CW*, NS **62**, 27.

Fell, C. I. and Hildyard, E. J. W. (1953) 'Prehistoric Weardale. A new survey', *AA4*, **31**, 98–115, and 1956, *AA4*, **34**, 131.

Fenton, A. (1983) 'Grain storage in pits: experiment and fact', in *From the Stone Age to the Forty Five*, eds O'Connor, A. and Clarke, D. V. Edinburgh, Donald, pp. 567–88.

Ferguson, R. (1893) 'Recent local finds', *CW*, OS **13**, 57–67.

Ferris, I. M. and Jones, R. F. J. (1980) 'Excavations at Binchester, 1976–9', in Hanson and Keppie (eds) (1980), p. 233.

Firman, R. J. (1978) 'Epigenetic minieralization', in *The Geology of the Lake District*, ed. Moseley, F. Yorksh. Geol. Soc.

Fleming, A. (1971) 'Bronze Age agriculture on the marginal lands of north-east Yorkshire', *Agr.H.R.*, **19**, 1–24.

Fleming, A. (1972–73) 'The genesis of pastoralism in European prehistory', *World Arch.*, **4**, 179–91.

Fletcher, E. (1980) 'The influence of Merovingian Gaul on Northumbria in the 7th century', *Med.Arch.*, **24**, 69.

Fletcher, W. (1958) 'Grey Croft stone circle, Seascale', *CW*, NS **57**, 1–8.

Ford, W. and Miket, R. (1982) 'An urned cremation from Warden Law, Tyne and Wear', *AA5*, **10**, 53.

Forde-Johnston (1962) 'The Iron Age hillforts of Lancashire and Cheshire', *LCAS*, **72**, 9–56.

Forster, M. (1921) 'Keltisches Wortgut in Englischen', in *Texte und Forschungen zur englischen Kulturgeschichte*, ed. Boehmer, H. *et al.* Niemeyer.

Fowler, P. J. (1969) 'Early prehistoric agriculture', in Simpson (ed.) (1969), p. 153.

Fowler, P. J (1981a) *Later Prehistory*, Agrarian History of England and Wales, Vol. 1, Part 1. C.U.P.

Fowler, P. J. (1981b) 'Wildscape to landscape', in Mercer (ed.) (1981), pp. 9–54.

Frend, W. H. C. (1968) 'The Christianisation of Roman Britain', in Barley and Hanson (eds) (1968), pp. 36–49.

Frere, S. S. (1978) *Britannia*. Routledge and Kegan Paul.

Frere, S. S. (1981) 'The Flavian frontier in Scotland', *SAF*, **12**, 89–97.

Fulford, M. (1977) 'The location of Romano-British pottery kilns: institutional trade and the market', in Dore and Greene (eds) (1977), pp. 301–16.

Fulford, M. (1979) 'Pottery production and trade at the end of Roman Britain: the case against continuity', in Casey (ed.) (1979), pp. 120–32.

Garlick, T. (1970) *Romans in the Lake Counties*. Clapham.

Gates, T. (1981a) 'A food vessel burial from Wellhouse Farm, Newton, Northumberland', *AA5*, **9**, 45–50.

Gates, T. (1981b) 'Farming on the frontier: Romano-British fields in Northumberland', in Clack and Haselgrove (eds) (1981), pp. 21–42.

Gates, T. (1983) 'Unenclosed settlements in Northumberland', in Chapman and Mytum (eds) (1983), pp. 103–48.

Gaythorpe, H. (1904) 'Prehistoric implements in Furness', *CW*, NS **4**, 325.

Gelling, M. (1976) 'The evidence of place names', in Sawyer (ed.) (1976), pp. 200–11.

Gelling, M. (1978) *Signposts to the Past*. Dent.

Gerloff, S. (1975) *The Early Bronze Age Daggers in Great Britain*, Prähistorische Bronzefunde, Vol. 6, Part 2. Munich, Beck.

Gibson, A. M. (1978) *Bronze Age Pottery in the North East of England*, BAR, 56.

Gibson, A. M. (1982) *Beaker Domestic Sites: A Study of the Domestic Pottery of the Late 3rd and early 2nd millennia B.C. in the British Isles*, 2 vols, BAR, 107.

Gilbert, E. (1974) 'St. Wilfrid's Church at Hexham', in Kirby (1974), pp. 81–114.

Gildas, *The Story of the Loss of Britain*, ed. Wade-Evans, A. Church Historical Soc., 1938.

Gillam, J. P. (1957) 'Bewcastle', *JRS*, **47**, 204–5.

Gillam, J. P. (1958) 'Roman and native 122–197', in Richmond (1958), pp. 60–90.

Gillam, J. P. (1973) 'Sources of pottery found on northern military sites', in Detsicas (ed.) (1973), pp. 53–62.

Gillam, J. P. (1974) 'The frontier after Hadrian – a history of the problem', *AA5*, **2**, 1–15.

Gillam, J. P. (1977) 'The Roman forts at Corbridge', *AA5*, **5**, 47–74.

Gillam, J. P. (1979) 'Romano-Saxon pottery: an alternative explanation', in Casey (ed.) (1979), pp. 103–18.

Gillam, J. P. and Daniels, C. M. (1961) 'The Roman mausoleum at Shorden Brae, Beaufront, Corbridge, Northumb.', *AA4*, **39**, 37–61.

Gillam, J. P., Harrison, R. M. and Newman, T. G. (1973) 'Interim Report on Excavations at the Roman Fort of Rudchester', *AA5*, **1**, 81–5.

Godwin, H. (1943) 'Coastal peat beds of the British Isles and North Sea', *J.Ecol.*, **31**(2), 199–247.

Godwin, H. (1956) *The History of the British Flora*. C.U.P., 2nd ed. 1975.

Godwin, H. (1975) 'History of the natural forests of Britain: establishment, dominance and destruction', *Phil. Trans. R. Soc. Lond.*, B, **271**, 47–67.

Godwin, H., Walker, D. and Willis, E. H. (1957) 'Radiocarbon dating and post-glacial vegetational history at Scaleby Moss', *PRS*, B, **147**, 352–66.

Graham, A. J. (1966) 'The division of Britain', *JRS*, **56**, 92–107.

Graham, T. H. B. and Collingwood, W. G. (1925) 'Patron saints of the diocese of Carlisle', *CW*, NS **25**, 1–27.

Graham, T. H. B. (1933) 'Englewood', *CW*, NS **33**, 15–23.

Green, M. (1981) 'Model objects from military areas of Roman Britain', *Brit.*, **12**, 253–69.

Green, M. (1983) 'A Celtic god from Netherby, Cumbria', *CW*, NS **83**, 41–8.

Greene, K. (1978) 'Apperley Dene "Roman fortlet": a re-examination, 1974–5', *AA5*, **6**, 29–66.

Greenwell, W. (1877) *British Barrows*. Clarendon Press, Oxford.

Greenwell, W. (1890) 'Recent research in barrows in Yorkshire, Wiltshire, Berkshire etc.', *Arch.*, **52**, 1–72.

Greenwell, W. (1892) 'Antiquities of the Bronze Age found in the Heathery Burn Cave, Co. Durham', *Arch.*, **54**, 87–114.

Gresswell, R. K. (1958) 'The post-glacial raised beach in Furness and Lyth, North Morecambe Bay', *Inst. Brit. Geog.*, **25**, 79–103.

Grigson, C. (1978) 'The late Glacial and early Flandrian ungulates of England and Wales: an interim review', Limbrey and Evans (eds) (1978), p. 46.

Grigson, C. (1981) 'Mammals and man on Oronsay, some preliminary hypotheses concerning mesolithic ecology in the Inner Hebrides', in Brothwell and Dimbleby (eds) (1981), p. 163.

Grimes, W. F. (1951) *Aspects of Archaeology in Britain and Beyond*. Essays presented to O. G. S. Crawford. London, Edwards.

Guido, C. M. (1978) *The Glass Beads of the Prehistoric and Roman Periods in Britain and Ireland*. London.

Hadingham, E. (1974) *Ancient Carvings in Britain*. Garnstone Press, London.

Hall, R. A. (ed.) (1978) *Viking Age York and the North*. London, CBA Res. Rep. No. 27.

Hallam, J. S., Edwards, B. J. N., Barnes, B. and Stuart, A. J. (1973) 'The remains of a late glacial elk associated with barbed points from High Furlong, near Blackpool, Lancs', *PPS*, **39**, 100–28.

Halliday, S. P. (1982) 'Later prehistoric farming in south-east Scotland', in Harding (ed.) (1982), pp. 75–91.

Halliday, S. P., Hill, P. J. and Stevenson, J. B. (1981) 'Early agriculture in Scotland', in Mercer (ed.) (1981), pp. 55–65.

Hanson, W. S. (1978) 'The organisation of Roman military timber supply', *Brit.*, **9**, 293–306.

Hanson, W. S. (1980) 'The first Roman occupation of Scotland', in Hanson and Keppie (eds) (1980), pp. 15–43.

Hanson, W. S., Daniels, C. M., Dore, J. N. and Gillam, J. P. (1979) 'The Agricolan supply base at Red House, Corbridge', *AA5*, **7**, 1–88.

Hanson, W. S. and Keppie, L. J. F. (eds) (1980) *Roman Frontier Studies xii, 1979*, BAR, **71**(i).

Hanson, W. S. and Macinnes, L. (1980) 'Forests, forts and fields', *SAF*, **12**, 98–113.

Hanson, W. S. and Maxwell, G. S. (1983) *Rome's North West Frontier: the Antonine Wall.* Edinburgh Univ. Press.

Harden, D. B. (1956) *Dark-Age Britain.* London, including, by the editor, 'Glass vessels in Britain AD 400–1000', pp. 132–67. Methuen.

Harding, A. F. (1981) 'Excavations in the prehistoric ritual complex near Milfield, Northumberland', *PPS*, 47, 87–135.

Harding, A. and Young, R. (1979) 'Reconstruction of the hafting methods and function of stone implements', in Clough and Cummins (1979), p. 102.

Harding, D. W. (1970) 'County Durham in the prehistoric period', *Trans. Arch. and Arch. Soc. of Durham and Northumb.*, NS 2, 27–30.

Harding, D. W. (1971) 'Holme House villa', *Brit.* 2, 251–2.

Harding, D. W. (ed.) (1976) *Hillforts: Later Prehistoric Earthworks in Britain and Ireland.* Academic Press.

Harding, D. W. (1979) 'Air survey in the Tyne–Tees region, 1969–1979', in Higham (ed.) (1979), pp. 21–30.

Harding, D. W. (ed.) (1982) *Later Prehistoric Settlement in South-East Scotland.* Univ. of Edinburgh, Occ. Pap. 8.

Harper, R. P. (1968) 'Excavations at Piercebridge', *Trans. Arch. and Arch. Soc. of Durham and Northumb.*, NS 1, 27–44.

Harris, E. and Harris, J. R. (1965) *The Oriental Cults in Roman Britain.* Brill.

Hart, C. R. (1975) *The Early Charters of Northern England and the North Midlands.* Leicester Univ. Press.

Hartley, B. R. (1972) 'The Roman occupation of Scotland: the evidence of Samian ware', *Brit.*, 3, 1–55.

Hartley, B. R. (1980) 'The Brigantes and the Roman army', in Branigan (ed.) (1980), pp. 2–7.

Harwood Long, W. (1979) 'The low yields of corn in medieval England', *Ec.H.R.*, 30, 11.

Haselgrove, C. (1981) 'Indigenous settlement patterns in the Tyne–Tees lowlands', in Clack and Haselgrove (eds) (1981), pp. 57–104.

Haselgrove, C. C. and Allon, V. L. (1982) 'An Iron Age settlement at Westhouse, Coxhoe, Co. Durham', *AA5*, 10, 25.

Hassall, M. W. C. (1976) *Britain in the Notitia*, in BAR, Supplementary Series, 15, pp. 103–18.

Hatcher, J. (1977) *Plague, Population and the English Economy.* Macmillan.

Hawkes, C. F. C. and Smith, M. A. (1957) 'On some buckets and cauldrons of the Bronze and Early Iron Age', *Ant.J.*, 37, 131–98.

Henshall, A. S. (1963–72) *The Chambered Tombs of Scotland*, 2 vols. Edinburgh Univ. Press.

Henshall, A. S. (1970) 'The long cairns of Eastern Scotland', *SAF*, 2, 29–46.

Henshall, A. (1978) 'Manx megaliths again: an attempt at structural analysis', in Davey (ed.) (1978), pp. 171–6.

Herodian, *History*, 2 vols, transl. Whittaker, C. R. Loeb, 1969.

Heslop, D. H. (1983) 'The excavation of an Iron Age settlement at Thorp Thewles', in *Recent Excavations in Cleveland*, Cleveland County Council, Archaeology Section, pp. 17–26.

Heywood, B. (1965) 'The vallum – its problems restated', in Jarrett and Dobson (eds) (1965), pp. 85–94.

Higham, N. J. (1977) 'Settlement and Land-use in North Cumbria in the First Millennium A.D.: A Type Case for the Highland Zone', unpubl. Ph.D. Thesis, Manchester.

Higham, N. J. (1978a) 'Early field survival in North Cumbria', in Bowen and Fowler (eds) (1978), pp. 119–25.

Higham, N. J. (1978b) 'Dyke systems in North Cumbria', *Bull. B.C. Stud.*, **28**, 142–55.

Higham, N. J. (1978c) 'Continuity studies in the 1st millennium AD in North Cumbria', *NH*, **14**, 1–18.

Higham, N. J. (ed.) (1979) *The Changing Past.* Manchester Univ. Dept. of Extra Mural Studies.

Higham, N. J. (1979a) 'An aerial survey of the Upper Lune Valley', in Higham (ed.) (1979), pp. 31–8.

Higham, N. J. (1979b) 'Continuity in North West England in the 1st millennium AD', in Higham (ed.) (1979), pp. 43–52.

Higham, N. J. (1980) 'Native settlements west of the Pennines', in Branigan (ed.) (1980), pp. 41–7.

Higham, N. J. (1981a) 'Two enclosures at Dobcross Hall, Dalston', *CW*, NS **81**, 1–6.

Higham, N. J. (1981b) 'The Roman impact upon rural settlement in Cumbria', in Clack and Haselgrove (eds) (1982), pp. 105–22.

Higham, N. J. (1982a) 'Native settlements on the north slopes of the Lake District', *CW*, NS **82**, 29–33.

Higham, N. J. (1982b) 'Excavations at Tatton D.M.V. 1982: a preliminary report', in *Cheshire Arch. Bulletin*, **8**, 64–5.

Higham, N. J. (1983) 'A Romano-British field system at Yanwath Woodhouse', *CW*, NS **83**, 49–58.

Higham, N. J. (1984) *Tatton Village: Excavations 1978–83'*. Interim excavation report.

Higham, N. J. (1985) 'The Scandinavians in North Cumbria', in *Scandinavian Settlement in Cumbria*, ed. Whyte, I. The Scottish Society for Northern Studies, 37–52.

Higham, N. J. and Jones, G. D. B. (1975) 'Frontiers, forts and farmers, Cumbrian aerial survey, 1974–75', *Arch.J.*, **132**, 16–53.

Higham, N. J. and Jones, G. D. B. (1983) 'The excavations of two Romano-British farm sites in North Cumbria', *Brit.*, **14**, 45–72.

Higham, N. J. and Jones, G. D. B. (1985) *The Carvetii*. Gloucester, Suttons.

Hildyard, E. J. W. (1955) *The Archaeology of Weardale*. Pickering (privately publ.).

Hildyard, E. J. W. and Gillam, J. (1951) 'Renewed excavation at Low Borrow Bridge', *CW*, NS **51**, 40–66.

Hill, P. H. (1978) *Broxmouth Hillfort: Excavations 1977–8, An Interim Report.* Univ. of Edinburgh, Dept. of Archaeology.

Hill, P. H. (1982a) 'Towards a new classification of prehistoric houses', *Scot. Arch. Rev.*, **1**(1), 24–31.

Hill, P. H. (1982b) 'Settlement and chronology', in Harding (ed.) (1982), pp. 4–43.

Hill, P. H. (1982c) 'Broxmouth hill-fort excavations 1977–8', in Harding (ed.) (1982), pp. 141–88.

Hind, J. G. F. (1980) 'The Romano-British name for Corbridge', *Brit.*, **11**, 165.

Hind, J. G. F. (1983) 'Who betrayed Britain to the barbarians in AD. 367 ?', *NH*, **19**, 1–70.

Hinnells, J. R. (ed.) (1971) *Mithraic Studies*. Manchester Univ. Press.

Hodgson, G. W. I. (1968) 'A comparative account of the animal remains from *Corstopitum* and the Iron Age site of Catcote, near Hartlepool, Co. Durham', *AA4*, **46**, 127–62.

Hodgson, G. W. I. (1971) 'Report on the animal remains recovered from the site of the Roman fort at South Shields, Co. Durham', *AA4*, **49**, 135–8.

Hodgson, G. W. (1977) *The Animal Remains from Excavations at Vindolanda, 1970–75*. Vindolanda Trust, Reports 2.

Hodgson, K. S. (1935) 'Notes on stone circles at Broomrigg, Grey Yauds etc.', *CW*, NS **35**, 77–9.

Hodgson, K. S. (1940) 'Some excavations in the Bewcastle district', *CW*, NS **40**, 154.

Hodgson, K. S. (1954) 'Four querns from the Brampton area', *CW*, NS **53**, 209.

Hodgson, T. H. (1904) 'An ancient palisade on Bowness Common', *CW*, NS **4**, 211.

Hogg, A. H. A. (1943a) 'The native settlement at Gunnar Peak', *AA4*, **20**, 155–73.

Hogg, A. H. A. (1943b) 'Excavations in a native settlement at Ingram Hill, Northumberland', *AA4*, **20**.

Hogg, A. H. A. (1946) 'Llwyfenydd', *Ant.*, **20**, 210–11.

Hogg, A. H. A. (1951) 'The Votadini', in Grimes (1951), pp. 200–20.

Hogg, A. H. A. (1956) 'Further excavations at Ingram Hill', *AA4*, **34**, 150.

Hogg, A. H. A. (1975) *Hillforts of Britain*. Hart-Davies.

Hogg, A. H. A. and Hogg, N. (1956) 'Doddington and Horton Moors', *AA4*, **34**, 142–9.

Hogg, R. (1949) 'A Roman cemetery site at Beckfoot, Cumberland, *CW*, NS **49**, 32–7.

Hogg, R. (1965) 'Excavation of the Roman auxiliary tilery, Brampton', *CW*, NS **65**, 133–68.

Holder, P. A. (1982) *The Roman Army in Britain*. Batsford.

Hollingworth, S. E. (1929) 'The evolution of the Eden drainage in the south and west', *Proc. Geol. Assoc.*, **40**, 115–38.

Hollingworth, S. E. (1931) 'The glaciation of western Edenside and adjoining areas and the drumlins of the Edenside and Solway Basin', *Quart. J. Geol. Soc.*, **87**, 281–359.

Hollingworth, S. E. (1951) 'The influence of glaciation in the Lake District', *J. Inst. Wat. Engrs.*, **5**, 486–96.

Holmes, McQ. N. M. (1979) 'Excavations at Cramond, Edinburgh 1975–78', in Breeze (ed.) (1979), pp. 11–14.

Hope Dodds, M. (1940) *A History of Northumberland*. The Committee, Newcastle upon Tyne. A. Reid.

Hope-Taylor, B. (1966) 'Doonhill, Dungar, East Lothian', *Med. Arch.*, **10**, 175–6.

Hope-Taylor, B. (1977) *Yeavering: An Anglo-British Centre of Early Northumbria*. HMSO.

Horsley, J. (1732) *Brittania Romana: or the Roman antiquities of Britain*. Osborn.

Houlder, C. H. (1979) 'The Langdale and Scafell Pike axe factory sites: a field survey', in Clough and Cummins (1979), pp. 87–9.

Hughes, McKenny, T. (1912) 'On an ancient enclosure and interment on Heaves Fell', *CW*, NS **12**, pp. 397–402.

Iversen, J. (1956) 'Forest clearance in the Stone Age', *Scient. Am.*, **194**, 36–41.

Jackson, K. H. (1955) 'The Britons in southern Scotland', *Ant.*, **29**, 77–88.

Jackson, K. H. (1956) *Language and History in Early Britain*. Edinburgh Univ. Press.

Jackson, K. H. (1958) 'Sources for the Life of St. Kentigern', in Chadwick (ed.) (1958), p. 273.

Jackson, K. H. (1959) 'Edinburgh and the Anglian occupation of Lothian', in Clemoes (1959), pp. 35–42.

Jackson, K. H. (1963a) 'On the northern British section in Nennius', in Chadwick (ed.) (1963), p. 57.

Jackson, K. H. (1963b) 'Angles and Britons in Northumbria and Cumbria', in Lewis (ed.) (1963), pp. 60–84.

Jackson, K. H. (ed.) (1969) *The Gododdin: The Oldest Scottish Poem.* Edinburgh Univ. Press.

Jackson, K. H. (1970) 'Romano-British Names in the Antonine itinerary', *Brit.*, **1**, 68–82.

Jackson, K. H. (1982) 'Brigomaglos and St. Briog', *AA5*, **10**, 61–8.

Jacobi, R. M. (1973) 'Aspects of the mesolithic age in Gt Britain', in *The Mesolithic in Europe*, ed. Kozlowski, S. K. Warsaw Univ. Press, pp. 237–65.

Jacobi, R. M. (1975) 'Population and landscape in mesolithic lowland Britain', in Evans *et al.* (eds) (1975), p. 75.

Jacobi, R. M. (1976) 'Britain inside and outside mesolithic Europe', *PPS*, **42**, 67–84.

Jacobi, R. M. (1978) 'Northern England in the 8th millennium BC: an essay', in Mellars (ed.) (1978), *The Early Post-glacial Settlement of Northern Europe.* Duckworth.

Jacobi, R. M., Tallis, J. H. and Mellars, P. A. (1976) 'The southern Pennine mesolithic and the ecological record', *J. of Arch. Sc.*, **3**, 307–20.

Jarman, M. R. *et al.* (1968) 'Animal remains', a contribution to 'An Iron Age hill-fort at Grimthorpe, Yorkshire', Stead, I. M., *PPS*, **34**, 182–9.

Jarrett, M. G. (1954) 'A Christian monogram from Roman Maryport', *CW*, NS **54**, 268–70.

Jarrett, M. G. (1958) 'Excavations at Maiden Castle, Durham in 1956', *Trans. Arch. and Arch. Soc. of Durham and Northumb.*, **11**, 124–7.

Jarrett, M. G. (1976) *Maryport, Cumbria: A Roman Fort and its Garrison.* Kendal, Wilson.

Jarrett, M. G. and Dobson, B. (eds) (1965) *Britain and Rome.* Kendal, Wilson.

Jensen, G. F. (1973) 'Place-name research and northern history', *NH*, **8**, 1–23.

Jensen, G. F. (1978) *Scandinavian Settlement Names in the East Midlands.* Copenhagen, Kommission hos Akademisk forlag, Naunestudier udgivet af Institut for Nauneforskning, Nr 16.

Jobey, G. (1959) 'Excavations at the native settlement at Huckhoe, Northumb.', *AA4*, **37**, 217–79.

Jobey, G. (1960) 'Some rectilinear settlements of the Roman period in Northumberland, Part 1', *AA4*, **38**, 1–38.

Jobey, G. (1962) 'An Iron Age homestead at West Brandon, Durham', *AA4*, **40**, 1–34.

Jobey, G. (1963) 'Excavation of a native settlement at Marden, Tynemouth', *AA4*, **41**, 19–36.

Jobey, G. (1964) 'Enclosed stone built settlements in north Northumberland', *AA4*, **42**, 41–64.

Jobey, G. (1965a) 'Stott's House "Tumulus" and the Military Way, Walker', *AA4*, **43**, 77–86.

Jobey, G. (1965b) 'Hill-forts and settlements in Northumberland', *AA 4*, **43**, 21–64.

Jobey, G. (1966a) 'Homesteads and settlements of the Frontier Area', in *Rural Settlements in Roman Britain*, ed. Thomas C., pp. 1–13.

Jobey, G. (1966b) 'A field survey in Northumberland', in Rivet (1966), p. 89.

Jobey, G. (1967) 'Excavations at Tynemouth Priory and Castle', *AA4*, **45**, 33.

Jobey, G. (1968a) 'Excavations of cairns at Chatton Sandyford, Northumberland', *AA4*, **46**, 5–50.

Jobey, G. (1968b) 'An R.C. date for the palisaded settlement at Huckhoe', *AA4*, **46**, 293

Jobey, G. (1970a) 'An Iron Age settlement and homestead at Burradon, Northumberland', *AA4*, **47**, 51–96.

Jobey, G. (1970b) 'Birrenswark', in *Discovery and Excav. in Scotland*, p. 21.

Jobey, G. (1970c) 'Early settlement and topography in the border counties', *SAF*, **2**, 73–85.

Jobey, G. (1973a) 'A Romano-British settlement at Tower Knowe, Wellhaugh, Northumberland', *AA5*, **1**, 55–79.

Jobey, G. (1973b) 'A native settlement at Hartburn and, the Devil's Causeway, Northumberland', *AA5*, **1**, 11–54.

Jobey, G. (1974a) 'Excavations at Boonies, Westerkirk, and the nature of Romano-British settlements in eastern Dumfriesshire', *PSAS*, **105**, 119–40.

Jobey, G. (1974b) 'Notes on some population problems in the area between the two Roman walls', *AA5*, **2**, 17–26.

Jobey, G. (1975) 'A souterrain at Milfield Hill, Northumberland', *AA5*, **3**, 215–17.

Jobey, G. (1976) 'Traprain Law: a summary', in Harding (ed.) (1976), pp. 192–204.

Jobey, G. (1977) 'Iron Age and later farmsteads on Belling Law, Northumberland', *AA5*, **5**, 1–38.

Jobey, G. (1977–78) 'Burnswark Hill', *Dumfr. and Gall. N.H. and A.S. Trans.*, **53**, 57–104.

Jobey, G. (1978a) 'Iron Age and Romano-British settlements on Kennel Hall Knowe, North Tynedale, Northumberland', *AA5*, **6**, 1–28.

Jobey, G. (1978b) 'Unenclosed platforms and settlements of the 2nd millennium BC in northern Britain', *SAF*, **10**, 12.

Jobey, G. (1979a) 'Green Knowe unenclosed platform settlement and Harehope cairn, Peeblesshire', *PSAS*, **110**, 72–113.

Jobey, G. (1979b) 'Palisaded enclosures, a Roman temporary camp and Roman gravel quarries on Bishop Rigg, Corbridge', *AA5*, **7**, 100.

Jobey, G. (1980) 'Settlement potential in northern Britain in the later 2nd millennium B.C.', *BAR*, 83(2), pp. 371–6.

Jobey, G. (1981a) 'Groups of small cairns and the excavation of a cairnfield on Millstone Hill', *AA5*, **9**, 23–43.

Jobey, G. (1981b) 'Between Tyne and Forth: some problems', in Clack and Haselgrove (eds) (1981), pp. 7–20.

Jobey, G. (1982) 'The settlement at Doubstead and Romano-British settlement on the coastal plain between Tyne and Forth', *AA5*, **10**, 1–23.

Jobey, G. (1983a) 'Excavation of an unenclosed settlement on Standrop Rigg, Northumberland, and some problems related to similar settlements between Tyne and Forth', *AA5*, **12**, 1–21.

Jobey, G. (1983b) 'A note on some northern palisaded sites', in *From the Stone Age to the Forty Five*, eds O'Connor, A. and Clarke, D. V. Edinburgh, Donald, pp. 197–205.

Jobey, G. and Newman, T. G. (1975) 'A collared urn cremation on Howick Heugh, Northumberland', *AA5*, **3**, 1–16.

Jobey, G., Smith, D. J. and Tait, J. (1965) 'An early Bronze Age burial on Reaverhill Farm, Barrasford, Northumberland', *AA4*, **43**, 65–76.

Jobey, G. and Tait, J. (1966) 'Excavations on palisaded settlements and cairnfields at Alnham, Northumberland', *AA4*, **44**, 5–48.

Jobey, I. (1976) 'Excavations at Middle Gunnar Peak, Barrasford, Northumberland', *AA5*, **9**, 51.

Jobey, I. (1979) 'Housesteads warc – a Frisian tradition on Hadrian's Wall', *AA5*, **7**, 127–43.

Jobey, I. (1981) 'Excavation on the Romano-British settlement at Middle Gunnar Peak, Barrasford, Northumberland', *AA5*, **9**, 51–74.

John, E. (1966) *Orbis Britannia*. Leicester Univ. Press.

Johnson, G. A. L. and Dunham, K. C. (1962) *The Geology of Moor House*, Nature Conservancy, 2. HMSO.

Johnson, S. (1980) *Later Roman Britain*. Routledge and Kegan Paul.

Jolliffe, E. A. (1926) 'Northumbrian institutions', *EHR*, **41**, 1–42.

Jones, G. (1968) *A History of the Vikings*. O.U.P.

Jones, G. D. B. (1968) 'The Romans in the North-West', *NH*, **3**, 1–26.

Jones, G. D. B. (1975) 'The northwestern interface', in *Recent Work in Rural Archaeology*, ed. Fowler, P. J. Bradford-on-Avon, Flaydemouse, pp. 93–106.

Jones, G. D. B. (1976) 'The western extension of Hadrian's Wall', *Brit.*, **7**, 236–43.

Jones, G. D. B. (1979) 'Aerial photography in the north', in Higham (ed.) (1979), p. 75.

Jones, G. D. B. (1980) 'Archaeology and coastal change in the northwest', in *Coastal Archaeology*, eds Thompson, F. and Collins, R. London, Soc. of Antiquaries, Occasional Paper, New Series 1.

Jones, G. D. B. (1982) 'The Solway frontier', *Brit.*, **13**, 282–97.

Jones, G. D. B. and Walker, J. (1983) 'Towards a minimalist view of Romano-British agricultural settlement in the North West', in Chapman and Mytum (1983), pp. 185–204.

Jones, G. R. J. (1961) 'Basic patterns of settlement distribution in northern England', *Advancement of Science*, **18**, 192–200.

Jones, G. J. R. (1976) 'Multiple estates and early settlement', in Sawyer (ed.) (1976), pp. 15–40.

Jones, M. E. (1979) 'Climate nutrition and disease: an hypothesis of Romano-British population', in Casey (ed.) (1979), pp. 231–51.

Jones, M. J. (1977) 'Archaeological work at Brough-under-Stainmore, 1971–72, 1', *CW*, NS **77**, 17–48.

Jones, R. F. J. (1981) 'Cremation and inhumations, change in the 3rd century', in King and Henig (eds) (1981), pp. 15–20.

Kapelle, W. E. (1979) *The Norman Conquest of the North*. Croom Helm.

Keen, L. and Radley, J. (1971) 'Report on the petrological identification of stone axes from Yorkshire', *PPS*, **37**, 16–37.

Keiller, A., Piggott, S. and Wallis, F. S. (1941) 'First report of the sub-committee of the South-Western Group of Museums and Art Galleries on the petrological identification of stone axes', *PPS*, **7**, 50–72.

Kent, J. P. C. (1979) 'The end of Roman Britain: the literary and numismatic evidence reviewed', in Casey (ed.) (1979), pp. 15–28.

Kilbride-Jones, H. E. (1938) 'The excavation of a native settlement at Milking Gap, High Shield, Northumberland', *AA4*, **15**, 303–50.

King, A. and Henig, M. (1981) *The Roman West in the Third Century: Contributions in Archaeology and History*, BAR, Supplementary Series 109.

King, A. (1978) 'Gauber high pasture, Ribblehead – an interim report', in Hall (1978), pp. 21–5.

King, C. A. M. (1976) *Northern England*. Methuen.

Kinnes, I. (1975) 'Monumental functions in British Neolithic Practices', *World Arch.*, **7** (1), June.

Kirby, D. P. (1962) 'Strathclyde and Cumbria: a survey of historical development to 1092', *CW*, NS **62**, 77–94.

Kirby, D. P. (1974) *St. Wilfrid at Hexham*. Oriel Press.

Knowles, D. and St Joseph, J. (1952) *Monastic Sites from the Air*. C.U.P.

Laet, de S. J. (ed.) (1976) *Acculturation and Continuity in Atlantic Europe*. Brugge, De Tempel.

Laing, L. (ed.) (1977) *Celtic Survival*, BAR, 37.

Lamb, H. H. (1972–77) *Climate, Present, Past and Future*. Methuen.

Leech, R. H. (1983) 'Settlements and groups of small cairns on Birkby and Birker Fells, Eskdale, Cumbria. Survey undertaken in 1982', *CW*, NS **83**, 15–24.

Lewis, H. (ed.) (1963) *Angles and Britons*. The O'Donnell Lectures. University of Wales Press, Cardiff.

Limbrey, S. (1978) 'Changes in quality and distribution of the soils of lowland Britain', in Limbrey and Evans (eds) (1978), p. 21.

Limbrey, S. and Evans, J. G. (eds) (1978) *The Effect of Man on the Landscape: The Lowland Zone*, CBA Res. Rep. 21.

Lloyd-Morgan, G. (1977) 'Two Roman mirrors from Corbridge', *Brit.*, **8**, 335–8.

Longworth, I. H. (1961) 'Origins and development of the collared urn tradition in England and Wales', *PPS*, **27**, 263.

Longworth, I. H. (1967–70) 'Five sherds from Ford, Northumberland, and their relative date', *YAJ*, **42**, 258–61.

Lowndes, R. A. C. (1963) ' "Celtic" fields, farms and burial mounds in the Lune Valley', *CW*, NS **63**, 77–95.

Lowndes, R. A. C. (1964) 'Excavations of a Romano-British farmstead at Eller Beck', *CW*, NS **64**, 6–13.

Lund, N. (1976) 'Thorp names', in Sawyer (ed.) (1976), pp. 223–5.

Luttwak, E. N. (1976) *The Grand Strategy of the Roman Empire*. Baltimore and London, Johns Hopkins Univ. Press.

Lynch, F. and Ritchie, J. N. G. (1975) 'Small cairns in Argyll: some recent work', *PSAS*, **106**, 15–38.

Macinnes, L. (1982a) 'Classification and interpretation: some further problems of prehistoric houses', *Scot. Arch. Rev.*, **1** (1), 32–5.

Macinnes, L. (1982b) 'Pattern and purpose: the settlement evidence', in Harding (ed.) (1982), pp. 57–74.

Mackereth, F. J. H. (1966) 'Some chemical observations on post-glacial lake sediments', *Phil. Trans. R. Soc. Lond.*, B, **250**, 165–213.

Mackie, E. W. (1979) 'Excavations at Leckie, Stirlingshire, 1970–78', in Breeze (ed.) (1979), pp. 52–5.

Macmullen, R. (1960) 'Inscriptions on armour and the supply of arms in the Roman Empire', *Am. Journal of Arch.*, **64**, 23–40.

Macmullen, R. (1963) *Soldier and Civilian in the Later Roman Empire*. Cambridge, Mass., Harvard Univ. Press.

McCarthy, M. R. (1982) *Thomas Chadwick and Post-Roman Carlisle*, BAR, 102, 241–56.

McCarthy, M. R., Padley, T. G. and Henig, M. (1982) 'Excavations and finds from The Lanes, Carlisle', *Brit.*, **13**, 79.

McCord, N. and Jobey, J. (1971) 'Notes on air reconnaissance in Northumberland and Durham', *AA4*, **49**, 119–30.

McGrail, S. (1978) *Logboats of England and Wales*, BAR, 51 (2 vols).

McInnes, I. J. (1969a) 'Settlements in Later Neolithic Britain', in Simpson (ed.) (1969), p. 113.

McInnes, I. J. (1969b) 'A Scottish Neolithic pottery sequence', *SAF*, **1**, 19–30.

McIntire, W. T. (1939) 'The fords of the Solway', *CW*, NS **39**, 152–70.

Main, L. (1979) 'Excavations at the Fairy Knowe, Buchlyvie, Stirlingshire', in Breeze (ed.) (1979), pp. 47–51.

Manby, T. G. (1963) 'Excavation of the Willerby Wold Long Barrow', *PPS*, **29**, 173–205.

Manby, T. G. (1965) 'The distribution of rough-out "Cumbrian" and related axes of Lake District origin in northern England', *CW*, NS **65**, 1–37.

Manby, T. G. (1970) 'Long barrows of northern England: structural and dating evidence', *SAF*, **2**, 1–28.

Manby, T. G. (1973) 'Neolithic pottery from Hastings Hill, Co. Durham', *AA5*, **1**, 219–22.

Manby, T. G. (ed.) (1974) *Grooved Ware Sites in Yorkshire and the North of England*, BAR, 9.

Manby, T. G. (1975) 'Neolithic occupation sites on the Yorkshire Wolds', *YAJ*, **47**, 23–59.

Manby, T. G. (1976) 'The excavation of the Kilham long barrow', *PPS*, **42**, 111–60.

Manby, T. G. (1979) 'Typology, materials and the distribution of flint and stone axes in Yorkshire', in Clough and Cummins (eds) (1979), pp. 65–80.

Manley, G. (1959) 'The late glacial climate of North-West England', *Lpool. Manch. Geol. J.*, **2**, 188–215.

Mann, J. C. (1974) 'The northern frontier after AD 369', *Glasg. A. J.*, **3**, 34–42.

Mann, J. C. (1979) 'Hadrian's Wall: the last phases', in Casey (ed.) (1979), pp. 144–51.

Manning, W. H. (1966) 'A hoard of Romano-British ironwork from Brampton, Cumberland', *CW*, NS **66**, 1–36.

Manning, W. H. (1972) 'Ironwork hoards in Iron Age and Roman Britain', *Brit.*, **3**, 224–50.

Manning, W. H. (1975) 'Economic influence on land use in the military areas of the Highland Zone', in Evans, Limbrey and Cleere (eds) (1975), pp. 112–16.

Masters, L. (1973) 'The Lockhill long cairn', *Ant.*, **48**, 96.

Mawer, Sir A. (1920) *The Place-Names of Northumberland and Durham*. C.U.P.

Mawer, Sir A. (1921) *Early Northumbrian History in the Light of Place-Names*. Kendal, Wilson.

Maxwell, G. S. (1975) '*Casus belli:* native pressures and Roman policy', *SAF*, 7, 13–50.

Maxwell, G. S. (1980) 'The native background to the Roman occupation of Scotland', in Hanson and Keppie (eds) (1980), pp. 1–13.

Maxwell, G. S. (1983) ' "Roman" settlement in Scotland', in Chapman and Mytum (eds) (1983), p. 253.

Megaw, B. R. S. and Hardy, E. M. (1938) 'British decorated axes and their diffusion during the earlier part of the Bronze Age', *PPS*, 4, pp. 272–307.

Megaw, J. V. S. and Simpson, D. D. A. (1981) *Introduction to British Prehistory*. Leicester Univ. Press.

Mellars, P. A. (1969) 'Radio carbon dates for a new Cresswellian site', *Ant.*, 43, 308–10.

Mellars, P. A. (1970) 'An antler harpoon-head of "Obanian" affinities from Whitburn, Co. Durham', *AA4*, 48, 337–46.

Mellars, P. A. (1976a) 'Settlement patterns and industrial variability in the British mesolithic', in *Problems in Economic and Social Archaeology*, ed. Sieveking, Duckworth, pp. 375–400.

Mellars, P. A. (1976b) 'Fire ecology, animal populations and man: a study of some ecological relationships in prehistory', *PPS*, 42, 15–45.

Mellars, P. A. and Payne, S. (1971) 'Excavations of 2 mesolithic shell middens on the island of Oronsay (Inner Hebrides)', *Nature*, 231, 397–8.

Mellars, P. A. and Wilkinson, M. R. (1980) 'Fish otoliths as indicators of seasonality in prehistoric shell middens: the evidence from Oronsay (Inner Hebrides)', *PPS*, 46, 19–44.

Mercer, R. (1981) *Farming Practice in British Prehistory*. Edinburgh Univ. Press.

Miket, R. (1974) 'Excavation at Kirkhill, West Hepple, 1972', *AA5*, 2, 153.

Miket, R. (1976) *The Evidence for Neolithic Activity in the Milfield Basin, Northumberland*, in Burgess and Miket (eds) (1976), 133–42.

Miket, R. (1980) 'A re-statement of evidence for Bernician Anglo-Saxon Burials', in Rahtz, Dickinson and Watts (eds) (1980), pp. 289–306.

Miket, R. (1981) 'Pit alignments in the Milfield basin and the excavation of Ewart 1', *PPS*, 47, 137.

Miket, R. (1982) 'An Anglo-Saxon small long brooch from Hylton', *AA5*, 10, 209.

Miket, R. and Burgess, C. (eds) (1984) *Between and Beyond the Walls: Essays on the Prehistory and History of North Britain in Honour of G. Jobey*. Edinburgh, Donald.

Miket, R. and Maxfield, V. (1972) 'The excavation of turret 33B (Coesike)', *AA4*, 50, 145–78.

Miles, D. (ed.) (1982) *The Romano-British Countryside*, BAR, 103(i).

Miller, M. (1975a) 'Stilicho's Pictish War', *Brit.*, 6, 141–50.

Miller, M. (1975b) 'Bede's use of Gildas', *EHR*, 90, 241–61.

Miller, M. (1975c) 'Historicity and the pedigrees of the north countrymen' *Bull. B.C. Stud.*, 26(3), 255–80.

Miller, M. (1975d) 'The commanders at Arthuret', *CW*, NS 75, 96–118.

Mitchell, G. F. (ed.) (1977) 'Changing environmental conditions in Great Britain and Ireland during the Devensian Last Cold Stage', *Phil. Trans. R. Soc.*, B, 280, 103–374.

Moore, C. N. (1979) 'Stone axes from the East Midlands', in Clough and Cummins (eds) (1979), 82–6.

Moore, C. N. and Cummins, W. A. (1974) 'Petrological identification of stone implements from Derbyshire and Leicestershire', *PPS*, **40**, 59–78.

Moore, D. (ed.) (1970) *The Irish Sea Province in Archaeology and History*, Cardiff, Cambrian Archaeological Asscn.

Morris, C. D. (1977) 'Northumbria and the Viking settlement: the evidence for land-holding', *AA5*, **5**, 81–104.

Morris, J. R. (1968) 'The literary evidence', in Barley and Hanson (eds.) (1968) pp. 55–73.

Morris, J. R. (1973) *The Age of Arthur: A History of the British Isles from 350 to 650.* Phillimore.

Morris, J. R. (ed.) (1980) *Nennius and the Welsh Annals*, Chichester, Phillimore.

Morris-Jones, Sir J. (1918) 'Taliesin', *Y Cymmrodr*, **28**, 156.

Morrison, A. (1980) *Early Man in Britain and Ireland: An Introduction to Palaeolithic and Mesolithic cultures.* Croom Helm.

Mulholland, H. (1970) 'The microlithic industries of the Tweed Valley', *Dumfr. and Gall. N.H. and A.S. Trans.*, **47**, 81.

Needham, S. (1982) *The Ambleside Hoard*, British Museum Occ. Pap. 39.

Nennius, *Historia Brittonum*, ed. Wade Evans, A. W. as *Nennius's 'History of the Britons'.* Church Historical Soc., 1938.

Newbiggin, N. (1935) 'Neolithic 'A' pottery from Ford, Northumberland', *AA4*, **12**, 148–57.

Newbiggin, N. (1936) 'Excavations of a long and round cairn on Bellshiel Law, Redesdale', *AA4*, **13**, 293–310.

Newbiggin, N. (1941) 'A collection of prehistoric materials from Hebburn Moor, Northumberland', *AA4*, **19**, 104–16.

Newman, T. G. (1976) 'A crop-mark site at Hasting Hill, Tyne and Wear', *AA5*, **4**, 183.

Newman, T. G. (1977) 'Two Early Bronze Age cist burials in Northumberland', *AA5*, **5**, 39–46.

Newman, T. G. and Miket, R. (1973) 'A dagger grave at Allerwash, Newborough, Northumberland', *AA5*, **1**, 87–96.

Nickson, D. and McDonald, J. H. (1956) 'A preliminary report on a microlithic site at Drigg, Cumberland', *CW*, NS 55, 17.

Nicholaisen, W. F. H. (1976) *Scottish Place Names.* Batsford.

Noe-Hygaard, N. (1975) '2 shoulder blades with healed lesions from Star Carr', *PPS*, **41**, 10.

North, O. H. (1934) 'Finds from the Roman station at Watercrook', *CW*, NS **34**, 35–40.

North, O. H. (1936) 'Roman finds at Voreda', *CW*, NS **36**, 132–41.

Okasha, E. (1971) *Hand-list of Anglo-Saxon Non-Runic Inscriptions.* Cambridge Univ. Press.

Oldfield, F. (1960) 'Studies in the post-glacial history of British vegetation: Lowland Lonsdale', *New Phytol.*, **59**, 192–217.

Oldfield, F. (1963) 'Pollen analysis and man's role in the ecological history of the south-east Lake District', *Geog. Annlrs.*, **45**, 23–40.

Oldfield, F. and Statham, D. C. (1963) 'Pollen analytical data from Urswick Tarn and Ellerside Moss, North Lancashire', *New Phytol.*, **62**, 53–66.

O'Sullivan, D. M. (1980) 'A Re-assessment of the Early Christian Archaeology of Cumbria', unpubl. M.Phil. Thesis, Durham Univ.

Pagan, H. E. (1974) 'Anglo-Saxon coins found at Hexham', in Kirby (ed.) (1974), p. 168.

Pählsson, C. (1975/76) 'Rothbury, a note on a Northumberland place-name', *JEPNS*, 8, 9–11.

Patrick, St 'The confession and the letter to Coroticus', collected among *St. Patrick's Writings*, transl. Marsh A., Dundalk, Dundalgan Press, 1961.

Pausanias, *Description of Greece*, 6 vols, transl. Jones W. H. S. Loeb, 1918.

Peacock, D. P. S. (1969) 'Neolithic pottery production in Cornwall', *Ant.*, 43, 145–9.

Pearsall, W. H. and Pennington, W. (1947) 'Ecological history of the English Lake District', *J. Ecol.* 34, 137.

Pearsall, W. H. and Pennington, W. (1973) *The Lake District*. Collins.

Pearson, K., Roesdalh, E., Graham-Campbell, J. and Connor, P. (eds) (1981) *The Vikings in England*. The Anglo-Danish Viking Project.

Pearson, M. C. (1960) 'Muckle Moss, Northumberland', *Hist. J. Ecol.*, 48, 647–66.

Penney, S. H. (1983) 'Romano-British iron extraction in north Lancashire', *CW, NS* 83, 59–62.

Pennington, W. (1970) 'Vegetational history in the north-west of England – a regional study', in *Studies in the Vegetational History of the British Isles*, ed. Walker, D. and West, R. C.U.P., pp. 41–80.

Pennington, W. (1975) 'The effect of neolithic man on the environment in north-west England: the use of absolute pollen diagrams', in Evans, Limbrey, and Cleere (eds.) (1975), pp. 74–86.

Pennington, W. (1977) 'Late Devensian flora', in Mitchell (ed.) (1977), p. 247.

Petersen, F. (1972) 'Traditions of multiple burial in later Neolithic and early Bronze Age England', *Arch. J.*, 129, 22–55.

Phillips, E. J. (1976) 'A workshop of Roman sculptors at Carlisle', *Brit.*, 7, 101.

Phillips, E. J. (1979) 'A statue of a genius from Burgh-by-Sands' *Brit.*, 10, 179–82.

Phillips, P. (1979) 'Stone axes in ethnographic situations: some examples from New Guinea and the Soloman Islands', in Clough and Cummins (eds.) (1979), pp. 108–12.

Phillips, P. (1980) *The Prehistory of Europe*. Penguin.

Piggott, C. M. (1947–48) 'The excavations at Hownam Rings, Roxburghshire, 1948', *PSAS*, 82, 193–225.

Piggott, S. (1947–48) 'The excavations at Cairnpapple Hill, West Lothian, 1947–8', *PSAS*, 82, 68–123.

Piggott, S. (1952–53) 'Three metal-work hoards of the Roman period from southern Scotland', *PSAS*, 87, 1–50.

Piggott, S. (1954) *The Neolithic Cultures of the British Isles*. C.U.P.

Piggott, S. (1958) 'Native economies and the Roman occupation of N. Britain', in Richmond (ed.) (1958) pp. 1–27.

Piggott, S. (1972) 'Excavation of the Dalladies long barrow, Fettercairn, Kincardineshire', *PSAS*, 104, 23–47.

Piggott, S. (1981) *The Agrarian History of England and Wales* Vol. 1., Part 1. *Prehistory*, C.U.P.

Plint, R. G. (1962) 'Stone axe factory sites in the Cumbrian fells', *CW, NS* 62, 1–26.

Plint, R. G. (1978) 'More stone axe factory sites in the Cumbrian fells', *CW*, NS 78, 1–4.

Plummer, C. (ed.) (1896) *Historia Abbatum auctore Anonymo*. Clarendon Press, Oxf.

Pococke, M. and Miket, R. (1976) 'An Anglo-Saxon cemetery at Greenbank, Darlington', *Med. Arch.*, 20, 62–74.

Potter, T. W. (1975) 'Excavations at Bowness-on-Solway', *CW*, NS 75, 29–57.

Potter, T. W. (1979) *Romans in North-West England*. Kendal.

Potter, T. W. (1980) 'The Roman frontier in Cumbria', in Hanson and Keppie (eds.) (1980) pp. 195–200.

Potts, W. T. A. (1976) 'History and blood groups in the British Isles', in Sawyer (ed.) (1976), p. 236.

Poulter, A. (1982) 'Old Penrith: excavations 1977 and 1979', *CW*, NS 82, 51–66.

Powell, T. G. E. *et al.* (1963) 'Excavations at Skelmore Heads near Ulverston 1957 and 1959', *CW* NS 63, 1–30.

Powell, T. G. E. (1969) 'The neolithic in the west of Europe and megalithic sepulture: some points and problems', in *Megalithic Enquiries in the West of Britain*, ed. Powell T. G. E. *et al.* Leicester Univ. Press. pp. 247–72.

Powell, T. G. E. (1972) 'The tumulus at Skelmore Heads near Ulverston', *CW*, NS 72, 53–6.

Powell, T. G. E., Oldfield, F. and Corcoran, J. X. W. P. (1971) 'Excavations in Zone VII peat at Storrs Moss, Lancashire, England', *PPS*, 37, 112–37.

Preston, H. (1931–34) 'Microlithic and other industries of the Wear', *Proc. Soc. Ant. N.uponT.*, 4th ser., 5–6, 109–16.

Prosper Tiro, 'Chronicon Gratiani' in *Epitoma Chonicon*, publ. in *Chronica Minora*, Saec iv, v, vi, vii, pp. 314–500, ed. Mommsen, T., *Monumenta Germaniae Historica Autorum Antiquissimorum*, ix. Weidmann, 1892.

Ptolemy, *Geographia*, introd. by Skelton, R. A. Amsterdam, Theatrum Orbis Terrarum, 1969.

Radford, C. A. R. (1952) '*Locus Maponi*', *Dumfries and Gall. N.H. and A. S. Trans.*, 31, 35.

Radford, C. A. R. (1953) *The MOW Guide to Whithorn and Kirkmadrine*, HMSO.

Radley, J. and Marshall, G. (1963–66) 'Maglemosian sites in the Pennines', *YAJ*, 41, 394.

Radley, J. and Mellars, P. A. (1964) 'A mesolithic structure at Deepcar, Yorkshire, England, and the affinities of its associated flint industries' *PPS*, NS 30, 1–24.

Rahtz, P. A., Dickinson T. and Watts, L. (eds) (1980) *Anglo-Saxon Cemeteries*, BAR, 82.

Raistrick, A. (1931) 'Bronze Age settlements of the north of England', *AA4*, 8, 149–65.

Raistrick, A. (1933) 'Excavations of a cave at Bishop Middleham, Durham', *AA4*, 10, 111–22.

Raistrick, A. (1932–34) 'The distribution of mesolithic sites in the north of England', *YAJ*, 31, 141–56.

Raistrick, A. and Blackburn, K. B. (1932) 'The late glacial and post-glacial periods in the north Pennines', *Trans. N.N.U.*, I, 79–103.

Ramm, H. G., McDowall, R. W. and Mercer, E. (1970) *Sheilings and Bastles*. RCAHM.

Razi, J. (1980) *Life, Marriage and Death in a Medieval Parish*. Cambridge Univ. Press.

Reece, R. (1980a) 'Town and country: the end of Roman Britain', *World Arch.*, **12**, 77–92.

Reece, R. (1980b) 'Coins and frontiers: the Falkirk hoard reconsidered', in Hanson and Keppie (eds), (1980) pp. 119–29.

Rees, S. E. (1979) *Agricultural Implements in Prehistoric and Roman Britain*, BAR, 69, 1 and 2.

Rees, S. E. (1981) 'Agricultural tools: function and use', in Mercer (1981) pp. 66–84.

Renfrew, C. (ed.) (1974) *British Prehistory*. Duckworth.

Renfrew, C. (1976) 'Megaliths, territories and populations', in de Laet (1976) pp. 198–220.

Renfrew, J. M. (1973) *Palaeoethnobotany*. Methuen.

Reynolds, D. M. (1982) 'Aspects of later prehistoric timber construction in south-east Scotland', in Harding (ed.) (1982) pp. 44–56.

Reynolds, N. (1980) 'Dark Age timber halls and the background to excavation at Balbridie', *SAF*, **10**, 41–60.

Reynolds, P. (1981) 'Deadstock and livestock', in Mercer (1981), pp. 97–122.

Richardson, A. (1982) 'Evidence of cultivation in the Inglewood Forest', *CW*, NS 82, 67–72.

Richardson, C. (1982) 'Excavations at Birrel Sike near Low Prior Scales, Calder Valley, Cumbria', *CW*, NS 82, 7–27.

Richardson, G. H. (1962) 'Recent Roman discoveries at Piercebridge', *Trans. Arch. and Arch. Soc. of Durham and Northumb.*, **11**, 164–75.

Richardson, G. G. S. (1977) 'Romano-British farmstead at Fingland', *CW*, NS 77, 53–60.

Richmond, I. A. (1936a) 'Roman lead sealings from Brough-under-Stainmore,' *CW*, NS 36, 104.

Richmond, I. A. (1936b) 'Excavations at High Rochester and Risingham, 1935', *AA4*, 13, 184–98.

Richmond, I. A. (1951) 'A Roman arterial signalling system in the Stainmore Pass', in *Aspects of Archaeology in Britain and Beyond*, ed. Grimes W. F. London, Edwards. pp. 293–303.

Richmond, I. A. (ed.) (1958). *Roman and Native in North Britain*, Edinburgh and London, Nelson, including, by the editor, 'Roman and native in the 4th century AD and after', pp. 112–30, and 'Ancient geographical sources for Britain north of the Cheviots', pp. 131–56.

Richmond, I. A. and Crawford, O. G. S. (1949) 'The British section of the Ravenna cosmography', *Arch.*, 93, 1.

Richmond, I. A. and Gillam, J. P. (1951) 'The temple of Mithras at Carrawburgh', *AA4*, 22, 1–92.

Richmond, I. A., Hodgson, K. S. and St Joseph, K. (1938) 'The Roman fort at Bewcastle', *CW*, NS 38, 195–239.

Richmond, I. A. and McIntyre, J. (1934) 'The Roman camps at Reycross and Crackenthorpe', *CW*, 34, 50–61.

Richmond, I. A., Romans, T. and Wright, R. P. (1944) 'A civilian bath-house of the Roman period at Old Durham', *AA4*, 22, 1–21.

Ritchie, A. (1970) 'Palisaded sites in north Britain: their context and affinities', *SAF*, **2**, 48–67.

Ritchie, G. and Ritchie, A. (1981) *Scotland – Archaeology and Early History*. Thames and Hudson.

Ritchie, P. R. (1968) 'The stone implement trade in 3rd millennium Scotland', in *Studies in Ancient Europe*, eds Coles, J. M. and Simpson, D. D. A., essays presented to S. Piggott. Leicester Univ. Press.

Rivet, A. L. F. (ed.) (1966) *The Iron Age in Northern Britain*. Edinburgh Univ. Press.

Rivet, A. L. F. and Smith, C. (1979). *The Place Names of Roman Britain*. London, Batsford.

Roberts, B. K. (1977) *The Green Villages of Co. Durham*. Durham Univ. Press.

Roberts, B. K., Turner, J. and Ward, P. F. (1972) 'Recent forest history and land-use in Weardale, northern England', in *Quaternary Plant Ecology*, eds Birks, U. H. J. B. and West, R. G., Oxford, Blackwell.

Robertson, A. S. (1960–61) 'Roman coins found in Scotland, 1951–60', *PSAS*, **44**, 133–83.

Robertson, A. S. (1975) *Birrens Blatobulgium*. Edinburgh, Dumfr. and Gall.

Roe, F. E. S. (1979). 'Typology of stone implements with shaft holes', in Clough and Cummins (1979).

Roger of Wendover *Liber qui dicitur flores historiarum ab MCLIV* (ed.) Hewlett, H. G. London, 1884. Rolls Series, 84, Longman/Dent.

Rollinson, W. (1967) *A History of Man in the Lake District*. London, Dent.

Romans, J. C. C. and Robertson, C. (1983) 'The environment of North Britain: soils', in Chapman and Mytum (eds), (1983), pp. 55–80.

Roper, M. (1974a) 'Wilfrid's landholdings in Northumbria', in Kirby (ed.) (1974), pp. 61–79.

Roper, M. (1974b) 'The donation of Hexham', in Kirby (ed.) (1974), pp. 169–71.

Ross, A. (1961) 'The horned god of the Brigantes', *AA4*, 39, 63.

Rostovtseff, M. (1923) 'Commodus-Hercules in Britain', *JRS*, **13**, 91–109.

Rowley-Conwy, P. (1981) 'Slash and burn in the temperate European neolithic', in Mercer (ed.) (1981) pp. 85–96.

Royal Commission on the Ancient Monuments and Constructions of England (Royal Commission on Ancient and Historical Monuments) (1936) *An inventory of the Historical Monuments of Westmorland*. H.M.S.O.

Rubin, S. (1975) 'St. Cuthbert of Lindisfarne: a medical reconstruction', *Trans. Arch. and Arch. Soc. of Durham and Northumb.*, NS 4, 101–4.

Salway, P. (1965) *The Frontier People of Roman Britain*. Cambridge.

Salway, P. (1980) 'The *Vici*: urbanisation in the North', in Branigan (ed.) (1980) pp. 8–17.

Salway, P. (1981) *Roman Britain*. O.U.P.

Savory, H. N. (1958) 'The late Bronze Age in Wales: some new discoveries and interpretations', *Arch. Camb.*, **107**, 3–63.

Sawyer, P. H. (1971) *The Age of the Vikings*. Edward Arnold.

Sawyer, P. H. (ed.) (1976) *Medieval Settlement*. Edward Arnold.

Sawyer, P. H. (ed.) (1978) *Names, Words and Graves: Early Medieval Settlement*. Leeds University, School of History.

Scott, J. G. (1976) 'The Roman occupation of South West Scotland from the recall of Agricola to the withdrawal under Trajan', *Glasg. Arch. J.* 4, 29–44.

Scott, P. R. (1972) 'Excavations at Holme House (West), Piercebridge, 1971 – summary report', *Durham Arch. News Bulletin*, **61**.

Scott, P. R. (1978) 'Excavations at Piercebridge, Co. Durham, 1976–7. summary report', *Arch. R. for 1977*, Univ. of Durham, pp. 16–21.

Scott, P. R. (1982) 'The bridges at Piercebridge, Co. Durham: a reassessment', *Trans. Arch. and Arch. Soc. of Durham and Northumb.*, NS 6, 77–82.

Scott, P. R. and Large, S. (1980) 'Excavations at Piercebridge 1978–79', *Arch. Rep. for 1979*, Univ. of Durham, pp. 11–12.

Scriptores Historiae Augustae, 3 vols., transl. Magie, D. Loeb, 1922.

Sekulla, M. F. (1982) 'The Roman coins from Traprain Law', *PSAS*, **112**, 285–94.

Selkirk, R. (1983) *The Piercebridge Formula* Cambridge, Stephens.

Shepherd, I. A. G. and Tuckwell, A. N. (1976–77) 'Traces of beaker-period cultivation at Rosinish, Benbecula', *PSAS*, **108**, 108.

Shotter, D. C. A. (1973) '*Numeri Barcariorum*: a note on RIB 601', *Brit.*, **4**, 206–9.

Shotter, D. C. A. (1978a) 'Roman coins from Kirkby Thore', *CW*, NS 78, 17–22.

Shotter, D. C. A. (1978b) 'A hoard of Roman coins in Kendal Museum', *CW*, NS 78, 29–36.

Shotter, D. C. A. (1979) 'The evidence of coin-loss and the Roman occupation of N-W. England', in Higham (1979a), pp. 1–13.

Shotton, F. W. (1959) 'New petrological groups based on axes from the West Midlands', *PPS*, **25**, 135–43.

Sieveking, G. de G. (ed.) (1971) *Prehistoric and Roman Studies*, British Museum.

Simmons, I. G. (1969) 'Evidence for vegetation changes associated with mesolithic man in Britain', in *The Domestication and Exploitation of Plants and Animals*, eds. Ucko, P. J. and Dimbleby, G. W. Duckworth, p. 113.

Simmons, I. G. (1975a) 'The ecological setting of mesolithic man in the Highland Zone' in Evans, Limbrey and Cleere (eds) (1975), pp. 57–63.

Simmons, I. G. (1975b) 'Late mesolithic societies and the environment of the uplands of England and Wales', *J. of Arch. Sc.*, **2**, 1–15.

Simmons, I. G., Dimbleby, G. W. and Grigson, C. (1981) 'The Mesolithic' in Simmons and Tooley (eds) (1981), pp. 82–124.

Simmons, I. G. and Tooley, M. J. (eds) (1981) *The Environment in British Prehistory*, Duckworth.

Simpson, D. D. A. (ed.) (1971) *Economy and Settlement in Neolithic and Early Bronze Age Britain and Europe*, including, by the editor, 'Beaker houses and settlements in Britain', pp. 131–52. Leicester Univ. Press.

Simpson, F. G. (1976) *Watermills and Military lvvvmoooWorks on Hadrian's Wall.* Kendal, Wilson.

Simpson, F. G. and Hodgson, K. S. (1948) The coastal mile-fortlet at Cardurnock', *CW*, NS 48, 78–127.

Simpson, F. G. and Richmond, I. A. (1934) Report of the Cumberland Excavation Committee for 1933. 1. Birdoswald', *CW*, NS 34, 120–30.

Simpson, F. G. and Richmond, I. A. (1936) 'The Roman fort on the Stanegate, and other remains at Old Church, Brampton', *CW*, NS 36, 172.

Simpson, F. G. and Richmond, I. A. (1941) 'The Roman fort on Hadrian's Wall at Benwell', *AA4*, 19, 1–43.

Simpson, G. (1974) 'Haltwhistle Burn, Corstopitum and the Antonine Wall', *Brit.*, **5**, 317–39.

Simpson, G. and Brassington, M. (1980) '*Concordia* and *Discipulina* on the North British frontier', in Hanson and Keppie (eds.) (1980), 141–50.

Smith, A. G. (1959) 'The mires of south-western Westmorland', *New Phytol*, .58, 105.

Smith, A. G. (1965) 'Problems of inertia and threshold related to post-glacial habitat changes', *PRS*, B, **161**, 331–42.

Smith, A. G. (1970) 'The influence of mesolithic and neolithic man on British vegetation: a discussion' in Walker and West (eds), (1970), pp. 81–96.

Smith, A. H. (1961) *The Place-names of the West Riding of Yorkshire*, Vovl. 6. EPNS. C.U.P.

Smith, A. H. (1967) *The Place-names of Westmorland*, 2 vols. EPNS.

Smith, C. (1979) *Romano-British Place-names in Bede*, BAR, 72, pp. 1–20.

Smith, D. J. (1959) 'A Palmyrene sculptor from South Shields', *AA4*, 37, 203–10.

Smith, G. H. (1978) 'Excavations near Hadrian's Wall at Tarraby Lane, 1976', *Brit.*, 9, 19–56.

Smith, I. F. (1974) 'The Neolithic' in Renfrew (1974), p. 100.

Smith, I. F. (1979) The chronology of British stone implemneents', in Clough and Cummins (eds) (1979), pp. 13–22.

Smyth, A. P. (1975) *Scandinavian York and Dublin*. Dublin, Temple Kieran Press.

Soden Smith, R. H. (1870) 'Notice of circles of stones in the Parish of Crosby Ravensworth, Westmorland, *Arch. J.*, 27, 200–3.

Sorensen, J. K. (1978) 'Place-names and settlement history', in Sawyer (ed.) (1978), pp. 1–33.

Spence, J. E. (1933) 'Preliminary report on the Petteril Green Camp', CW, NS 33, 227–32.

Spence, J. E. (1937a) 'A tumulus in Mecklin Park, Santon Bridge', CW NS 37, 104.

Spence, J. E. (1937b) 'Bolton Wood enclosure', CW NS 37, 43–8.

Spratt, D. A. (1979) *The Archaeology of Cleveland*, Middlesbrough.

Statius *Silvae*, transl. Mozley J. H. Loeb, 1928.

Steer, K. A. (1958) 'Roman and native in North Britain: the Severan reorganisation' in Richmond (1958), 91–111.

Stenton, D. (1970) *Preparatory to Anglo-Saxon England*. Oxford.

Stenton, F. M. (1936) 'Pre-conquest Westmorland', in Stenton D. (1970), p. 214, 1st publ. RCAHM.

Stenton, F. M. (1943) *Anglo-Saxon England*. O.U.P.

Stephen Briggs, C. (1976) 'Notes on the distribution of some raw materials in later prehistoric Britain', in Burgess and Miket (eds), (1976), pp. 267–82.

Stevens, C. E. (1934) 'A Roman inscription from Beltingham' *AA4*, 11, 138.

Stevens, C. E. (1951) 'A Roman author in northwest Britain', CW, NS, 50, 70.

Stevens, C. E. (1966) 'The social and economic aspects of rural settlement', in Thomas (ed.) (1966), pp. 108–28.

Stevenson, R. B. K. (1954–56) 'Native bangles and roman glass', *PSAS*, 88, 208.

Stevenson, R. B. K. (1976) 'Romano-British glass bangles', *Glasg. Arch. J.*, 4, 45–54.

Stone, J. F. S. and Wallis, F. S. (1951) 'Third report of the sub-committee of the South-Western Group of Museums and Art Galleries on the petrological identification of stone axes', *PPS*, 17, 99–158.

Stout, H. B. (1961) 'Gretigate stone circles, Sides, Gosforth', CW, **61**, 1.

Strabo *Geography*, 8 vols., transl. Jones, H. L. Loeb, 1917.

Stukeley, W. *Itinerarium curiosum; or an account of the antiquities and remarkable curiosities in nature or art, observed in travels through Great Britain*, 2 parts, 2nd edn. Bateman, 1776.

Sturdy, D. (1972) 'A ring-cairn in Levens Park, Westmorland', *SAF*, 4, 52–60.

Symeon of Durham *Symeonis monachi opera ovmnia*, ed. Arnold, T. Rolls Series 75. Longmans, 1882.

Synge, F. M. (1977) 'Records of sea levels during the late Devensian', in Mitchell (ed.) (1977) p. 211.

Tacitus, C. *De Vita Agricolae* ed. Ogilvie, R. M. and Richmond, Sir I. O.U.P., 1967.

Tacitus, C. *Annales*, 5 vols., transl. Jackson, J. Loeb, 1970.

Tacitus, C. *Historiae*, 2 vols., ed. Capps, E. *et al.* Loeb, 1925.

Tainter, J. A. (1975) 'Social inference and mortuary practices: an experiment in numerical classification', *World Arch.*, 7, 1–15.

Tait, J. (1965) *Beakers from Northumberland*. Oriel Press, Newcastle-upon-Tyne.

Tait, J. (1968) 'Neolithic pottery from Northumberland', *AA4*, 46, 275–81.

Tait, J. and Jobey, G. (1971) 'Romano-British burials at Beadnell, Northumberland', *AA4*, 49, 53–70.

Taylor, J. and Taylor, H. (1963) 'Pre-Norman churches of the Border', in Chadwick (ed.) (1963), pp. 210–57.

Taylor, J. A. (1975) The role of climatic factors in environmental and cultural changes in prehistoric times', in Evans, Limbrey and Cleere (eds.) (1975), p. 6.

Taylor, B. J., Burgess, I. C., Land, D. H., Mills, A. C., Smith, D. B. and Warren, P. T. (1971) *Northern England*, British Regional Geol. HMSO.

Thomas, A. C. (1961) 'The animal art of the Scottish Iron Age and its origins', *Arch. J.*, 118, 14–64.

Thomas, A. C. (ed.) (1966) *Rural Settlement in Roman Britain*. CBA

Thomas, A. C. (1968) 'The evidence from north Britain' in Barley and Hanson (eds) (1968), pp. 93–122.

Thomas, A. C. (1971) *The Early Christian Archaeology of North Britain*. O.U.P.

Thomas, A. C. (1979) 'St Patrick and 5th century Britain', in Casey (1979) p. 81.

Thomas, A. C. (1981) *Christianity in Roman Britain*. Batsford.

Thompson, E. A. (1977) 'Britain AD 406–410', *Brit.*, 8, 303–18.

Tinsley, H. M. (1981) 'The Bronze Age', in Simmons and Tooley (1981), pp. 210–49.

Todd, M. (1977) '*Famosa VVvmvPestis* and Britain in the fifth century', *Brit.*, 8, 319–25.

Tomlin, R. S. O. (1974) 'The date of the "Barbarian Conspiracy"', *Brit.*, 5, 303–9.

Tooley, M. J. (1975) 'A prehistoric skeleton from Hartlepool', *Bulletin, Durham County Conservation Trust*, pp. 29–31.

Tooley, M. J. (1978a) *Sea-level changes in North-West England during the Flandrian Period*. Oxford. Clarendon Press.

Tooley, M. J. (1978b) 'The history of Hartlepool Bay', *Int. J. Naut. Arch. and Underwater Expl.*, 7(1), 71–5.

Toynbee, J. M. C. and Wilkins, A. (1982) 'The Vindolanda horse', *Brit.*, 13, 245–52.

Trechmann, C. T. (1914) 'Prehistoric burials in the County of Durham', *AA3*, 11, 125–56.

Trechmann, C. T. (1936) 'Mesolithic flints from the submerged forest at West Hartlepool', *PPS*, 2, 161–8.

Trechmann, C. T. (1942–46) 'Late Roman Pottery along the Durham coast', *Proc. Soc. Ant. N.uponT.*, 4(10), 341.

Trechmann, C. T. (1947–49) 'The submerged forest beds of the Durham coast', *Yorksh. Geol. Soc.*, 27, 23.

Triscott, J. (1982) 'Excavations at Dryburn Bridge, East Lothian', in Harding (ed.) (1982), pp. 117–24.

Trotter, F. M. (1929a) 'The Tertiary uplift and resultant drainage of the Alston block and adjacent areas', *Yorksh. Geol Soc.*, 21, 161–80.

Trotter, F. M. (1929b) 'The glaciation of eastern Edenside, the Alston block and the Carlisle plain', *Quart. J. Geol. Soc.*, 85, 549–612.

Turner, J. (1965) 'A contribution to the history of forest clearance' *PRS*, B, **161**, 343–54.

Turner, J. (1970) 'Post-neolithic disturbance in British vegetation', in Walker and West (eds.) (1970), pp. 97–116.

Turner, J. (1975) 'The evidence for land-use by prehistoric farming communities: the use of three-dimensional pollen diagrams', in Evans, Limbrey and Cleere (eds.) (1975), p. 86.

Turner, J. (1978) 'History of vegetation and flora', in *Upper Teesdale; the Area and its Natural History*, ed. Clapham, A. R. Collins, pp. 88–101.

Turner, J. (1981) 'The Iron Age' in Simmons and Tooley (eds) (1981) p. 250.

Turner, J. (1983) 'Some pollen evidence for the environment of north Britain 1000 BC to AD 1000', in Chapman and Mytum (eds) (1983), pp. 3–28.

Turner, J., Hewetson, V. P., Hibbert, F. A., Lowry, K. H. and Chambers, C. (1973) 'The History of the vegetation and flora of Widdybank Fell and Cow Green Reservoir basin, Upper Teesdale', *Phil. Trans. R. Soc. Lond.*, B, **870**, 327–408.

Turner, J. and Hodgson, J. (1983) 'The composition of the mid-Flandrian forests of the northern Pennines', *J. Ecol.*, 71, 95–118.

Turner, J. and Kershaw, A. P. (1973) 'A late- and post-glacial pollen diagram from Cranberry, Bog, near Beamish, Co. Durham', *New Phytol.*, 72(2), 915–28.

Veen, van der M. and Haselgrove, C. C. (1983) 'Evidence for pre-Roman crops from Coxhoe, Co. Durham', *AA5*, 11, 23–5.

Vita Hadriani: Historia Augusta, ed. Birley, A. R. Penguin, 1976.

Wade Evans, A. W. (ed.) (1938) *Nenniu's 'History of the Britons'*, Church Historical Society.

Wainwright, F. T. (1975) *Scandinavian England*. Phillimore.

Wainwright, G. and Longworth, I. (1970) 'The excavation of a group of round barrows on Ampleforth Moor, Yorkshire', *YAJ*, **42**, 283–294.

Walker, D. (1955) 'Studies in the post-glacial history of British vegetation XIV; Skelsmergh Tarn and Kentmere, Westmorland', *New Phytol*, 54, 209.

Walker, D. (1965a) 'Excavations at Barnscar', *CW*, NS 65, 53–65.

Walker, D. (1965b) 'The post-glacial period in the Langdale Fells, English Lake District', *New Phytol*, **64**, 488.

Walker, D. (1966) 'The late Quaternary history of the Cumberland lowlands', *Phil. Trans. R. Soc.*, B, **251**, 1–210.

Walker, D. and West, R. (eds) (1970) *Vegetational History of the British Isles*. Cambridge.

Wall, J. (1965) 'Christian evidences in the Roman Period', *AA4*, 43, 201–25, and 1966, *AA4*, 44, 147–64.

Walthew, C. V. (1975) 'The town house and the villa house', *Brit.*, 6, 189–205.

Ward, J. E. (1974) 'Wooden objects uncovered at Branthwaite, Workington in 1956 and 1971', *CW NS 74*, 18–28.

Ward, J. E. (1977) 'Cairns on Corney Fell', *CW* NS 77, 1–5.

Watkin, W. T. W. (1883) *Roman Lancashire*. Liverpool.

Watson, E. (1977) 'The periglacial environment', in Mitchell (ed.) (1977), pp. 183–98.

Watson, G. R. (1968) 'Christianity in the Roman Army in Britain', in Barley and Hanson (eds) (1968), pp. 51–4.

Watts, V. E. (1970) 'Place-names', in Dewdney (ed.) (1970), pp. 251–65.

Watts, V. E. (1976) 'The evidence of place-names II', in Sawyer (ed.) (1976), 212–22.

Watts, V. E. (1978) 'The earliest Anglian names in Durham', *Nomina*, 2.

Watts, V. E. and Prince, E. F. M. (1982) 'Old English *Walh* in English place-names: an addendum', *JEPNS*; 14 32–6.

Webster, P. V. (1972) 'Severn Valley ware on Hadrian's Wall', *AA4*, 50, 191–203.

Webster, P. V. (1977) Severn Valley ware on the Antonine frontier', in Dore and Greene (eds) (1977), pp. 163–76.

Webster, R. A. (1969) *The Romano-British Settlement in Westmorland – A Study in Cultural Ecology*, unpubl. Ph.D. Thesis, Reading University.

Webster, R. A. (1971) 'A morphological study of Romano-British settlements in Westmorland', *CW*, NS 71, 64–71.

Webster, R. A. (1972) 'The excavation of a Romano-British settlement at Waitby', *CW*, NS 72, 66–73.

Welsby, D. D. (1980) 'Roman building inscriptions recording buildings collapsed through age or destroyed by the enemy', *AA5*, 8, 89–94.

Welsby, D. A. (1982) *The Roman Military Defence of the British Provinces in its Later Phases*, BAR, 101.

Weyman, J. (1980) 'A flint-chipping site at Low Shilford, Riding Mill, Northumberland', *AA5*, 8, 159.

Wheeler, R. E. M. (1954) *The Stanwick Fortifications*. O.U.P., for the Society of Antiquities of London.

Whimster, R. (1981) *Burial Practices in Iron Age Britain*, BAR. 90.

Whitelock, D. (ed.) (1955) *English Historical Documents I. c. 500–1042*. Eyre and Spottiswoode.

Whitelock, D. (1959) 'The dealings of the kings of England with Northumbria in the 10th and 11th centuries', in Clemoes (ed.) (1959), pp. 70–88.

Whittle, A. W. R. (1977) *The Earlier Neolithic of Southern England and its Continental Background*, BAR, Supplementary Series, 35.

Wild, J. P. (1977) *The Textiles from Vindolanda, 1973–75*. Vindolanda Trust Report No. 3.

Wilkes, J. (1961) 'Excavations in Housesteads', *AA4*, 39, 279–300.

Wilkes, J. (1966) 'Early 4th century rebuilding in Hadrian's Wall forts', in Jarrett and Dobson (eds) (1966), pp. 114–38.

Williams, D. (1983) 'The vallum's original intentions: a multi-purpose work of frontier support', *CW*, NS 83, 33–40.

Williams, Sir I. (1951) 'Wales and the North', *CW*, NS 51, 73–88.

Williams, Sir I. (ed.) (1968) *The Poems of Taliesin*. Dublin, Institute for Advanced Studies.

Wilson, D. M. (ed.) (1976) *The Archaeology of Anglo-Saxon England*. Methuen.

Wilson, D. M. (1978) 'The art and archaeology of Bedan Northumberland', in Farrell (1978) pp. 1–31.

Wilson, P. A. (1966) 'On the use of the terms "Strathclyde" and "Cumbria"', *CW*, NS 66, 57–92.

Wilson, P. A. (1978) 'Eaglesfield: the place, the name, the burials', *CW*, NS 78, 47–54.

Winterbottom, M. (ed.) (1978) *Gildas, The Ruin of Britain and Other Works*. Chichester, Phillimore.

Wood, R. H., Ashmead, F. and Mellars, P. A. (1970) 'First report on the archaeological excavations at Kirkhead Cavern', *North West Speleology*, 1, 19–24.

Woodman, P. C. (1973–74) 'Settlement patterns of the Irish mesolithic', *Ulster J. of Arch.*, 36–7, 1–16.

Woodman, P. C. (1976) 'The Irish Mesolithic/Neolithic transition', in de Laet (ed.) (1976), p. 296.

Woodman, P. C. (1978) 'A re-appraisal of the Manx Mesolithic', in Davey (ed.) (1978), pp. 119–40.

Woolacott, D. (1905) 'The superficial deposits and pre-glacial valleys of the Northumberland and Durham coalfield', *Quart. J. Geol. Soc.*, 61, 64–96.

Wormald, P. (1978) 'Bede, *Beowulf*' and the conversion of the Anglo-Saxon aristocracy', in Farrell (ed.) (1978), 32–95.

Wright, R. P. (1963) 'Roman Britain in 1962: inscriptions', *JRS*, 53, 160.

Wright, R. P. (1965a) 'A Hadrianic building-inscription from Hardknott, Cumberland', *CW*, NS 65, 169–75.

Wright, R. P. (1965b) 'Roman Britain in 1965. ii Inscriptions', *JRS*, 55, 222.

Wright, R. P. and Gillam, J. P. (1951) 'Second report on Roman buildings at Old Durham', *AA4*, 29, 203.

Wright, R. P. and Gillam, J. P. (1953) 'Third report on Roman buildings at Old Durham', *AA4*, 31, 116.

Wright, R. P. and Philips, E. J. (1975) *Roman Inscribed and Sculptured Stones in Carlisle Museum*. Carlisle.

Wrigley, E. A. and Schofield, R. S. (1981) *The Population History of England, 1541–1871*. Edward Arnold.

Wymer, J. J. (1977) *A Mesolithic Gazetteer*. CBA.

Young, C. J. (1977) 'Oxford ware and the Roman Army', in Dore and Greene (eds.) (1977) pp. 289–300.

Young, R. (1980) 'An inventory of Barrows in Co. Durham', *Trans. Arch. and Arch. Soc. of Durham and Northumb.*, NS 5.

Index

377